THE PHYSICAL NATURE OF CONSCIOUSNESS

ADVANCES IN CONSCIOUSNESS RESEARCH

ADVANCES IN CONSCIOUSNESS RESEARCH provides a forum for scholars from different scientific disciplines and fields of knowledge who study consciousness in its multifaceted aspects. Thus the Series will include (but not be limited to) the various areas of cognitive science, including cognitive psychology, linguistics, brain science and philosophy. The orientation of the Series is toward developing new interdisciplinary and integrative approaches for the investigation, description and theory of consciousness, as well as the practical consequences of this research for the individual and society.

Series A: Theory and method. Contributions on the development of theory and method in the study of consciousness.

Volume 29

Philip Van Loocke (ed.)

The Physical Nature of Consciousness

THE PHYSICAL NATURE OF CONSCIOUSNESS

Edited by

PHILIP VAN LOOCKE
University of Ghent

JOHN BENJAMINS PUBLISHING COMPANY
AMSTERDAM/PHILADELPHIA

The paper used in this publication meets the minimum requirements of the American National Standard for Information Sciences – Permanence of Paper for Printed Library Materials, ANSI z39.48-1984.

Library of Congress Cataloging-in-Publication Data

The Physical Nature of Consciousness / Edited by Philip Van Loocke.
p. cm. (Advances in Consciousness Research, ISSN 1381-589X ; v. 29)
Includes bibliographical references and index.
1. Consciousness. 2. Quantum theory. I. Loocke, Philip R. Van, 1963-. II. Series.
QP411.P474 2000
612.8'2--dc21 00-045560
ISBN 978 90 272 5149 7 (Pb ; alk. paper)
ISBN 978 90 272 9985 7 (Eb)

John Benjamins Publishing Co. · P.O. Box 36224 · 1020 ME Amsterdam · The Netherlands
John Benjamins North America · P.O. Box 27519 · Philadelphia PA 19118-0519 · USA

Table of contents

Preface

Ever since they appeared on this world, philosophers saw themselves confronted with deep problems. Several of these have remained with us. For example, there is the problem of realism. How can one be sure that there is a reality beyond our phenomenal experiences? There is the problem of solipsism. How can one know for sure that other persons exist, and that they are actually conscious instead of behaving as if? These questions did not receive a philosophical answer — or at least not an answer that is universally accepted.

But this never lead to practical dilemmas in the past. Suppose that — in twenty, fifty or hundred years — artificial intelligence technology, or a quantum version of this technology, would reach the stage in which humans can effectively be simulated. Then, our behavior towards robots and computers would depend strongly on our intuitions about the presence or absence of consciousness in these systems. Further, some might like to replace humans partially or entirely by hardware (or artificial wetware) constructions, since they would be more durable, or more easy to repair. Obviously, if we would not really be sure if the artificial versions of our wetware generate the same consciousness, the ones who would consider to put themselves into artificial material would take a serious risk.

History of thought takes an ironical course in these matters. The deep philosophical problems have never been solved, but in the past few centuries, their presence — at least in academic contexts — has been partially masked by scientific achievements, and, especially in the twentieth century, by technological realizations. Many philosophers, especially in the positivist tradition, reduced the task of the philosopher to applauding for the insights acquired by science, and tried to make forget the public that deep mysteries remained with us as plain as before. But exactly the advance of science confronts us again with some of the deep philosophical problems. And this time, the problems not only appear on a theoretical level, but our provisory answers to them may have to direct future actions of unprecedented importance.

The chapters of this book address the fundamental problems of consciousness. They all touch on the problem of the relation between physics — especially quantum physics — and consciousness. The first three chapters present quantum mechanical approaches to consciousness (S. Hameroff, E. Walker and F. Beck). Then, two chapters deal with quantum holographical approaches and their philosophical ramifications (K. Pribram, P. Marcer and E. Mitchell). Subsequently, quantum mechanical views on consciousness are related to postmodernism and phenomenology (G. Globus and C. Clarke). Two chapters take a fundamental reformulation of physics as their point of departure (I. Prigogine and M. Pitkanen). D. Bierman assesses anamalous phenomena, and finally Van Loocke relates the selection concept with connectionism and generative art.

For entire decades in the twentieth century, it took large amounts of intellectual courage to address (instead of to ignore) the deep problems of consciousness in the academic world. Some of the most important authors in this respect have written a chapter for this book — along with other original thinkers on the nature of consciousness. The editor wishes to thank them all for their very kind cooperation.

Biological feasibility of quantum approaches to consciousness

The Penrose-Hameroff 'Orch OR' model

Stuart Hameroff

Abstract

Quantum approaches have enormous explanatory power for understanding enigmatic features of consciousness. The Penrose-Hameroff 'Orch OR' model involves quantum superposition/computation in microtubules within the brain's neurons. As technological quantum processes require extreme cold and isolation to avoid thermal decoherence, conventional wisdom holds against biological quantum processes in the apparently "warm, wet and noisy" brain. Methods which biological systems may have evolved to avoid decoherence are discussed.

1. Conventional approaches to consciousness — Why they fail

How does brain activity produce conscious experience? Why do we *feel* love, *hear* a flute, *see* the redness of a rose? Philosophers call the raw components which comprise conscious experience 'qualia' (e.g. Chalmers 1996). It is not at all obvious why we need qualia from an evolutionary standpoint — complex, adaptive behavior of unfeeling zombie-like creatures might well have enabled them to flourish. However it seems unlikely that, for example, a zombie could have painted the Mona Lisa. How and why do we differ from unfeeling zombies, or computer-based robots? Enigmatic features of consciousness include:

- The nature of subjective experience, or 'qualia' — our 'inner life' (Chalmers' "hard problem");
- Subjective binding of spatially distributed brain activities into unitary objects in vision, and a coherent sense of self, or 'oneness';

- Transition from pre-conscious processes to consciousness itself;
- Non-computability, or the notion that consciousness involves a factor which is neither random, nor algorithmic, and that consciousness cannot be simulated (Penrose 1989, 1994, 1997);
- Free will;
- Subjective time flow; apparent time anomalies (e.g. Libet et al. 1979; Zeki & Bartels 1998)

1.1 *Emergent computation*

How does science approach these enigmatic features? Conventional explanations most commonly portray consciousness as an emergent property of classical computer-like activities in the brain's neural networks. The current leading candidate for brain activities most directly related to consciousness involves neuronal circuits oscillating synchronously in thalamus and cerebral cortex. Since the pioneering work of Herbert Jasper in the 1960's (e.g. Jasper & Komaya 1968), sensory input has been recognized to pass through thalamus where it is "broadcast" to cortex (e.g. the lateral geniculate nucleus in thalamus transmitting visual information to visual cortex). Some thalamo-cortical projections carry specific sensory modalities whereas others (including the "reticular activating system") are non-specific, but necessary for arousal and consciousness.

In recent decades numerous studies have also revealed extensive downward projections from cortex to thalamus, and a consensus view holds that reverberatory feedback ("recurrent loops") between thalamus and pyramidal cell neurons in cortex provides the "neural correlate of consciousness" (e.g. "global workspace", Baars 1988). Electrophysiological recordings further reveal coherent firing of these thalamo-cortical loops with frequencies varying from slow EEG frequencies (2–12 Hz) to rapid gamma oscillations in the 40 Hz range and upward. Coherent gamma frequency thalamo-cortical oscillations (collectively known as "coherent 40 Hz") are suggested to mediate temporal binding of conscious experience (e.g. Singer et al. 1990; Crick & Koch 1990; Joliot et al. 1994; Gray 1998). The 40 Hz coherence has recently been shown to be driven by networks of inhibitory inter-neurons linked by gap junctions (Galarreta & Hestrin 1999; Gibson et al. 1999; Tamas et al 2000). "Thalamo-cortical 40 Hz" activity stands as a prevalent view of the neural-level substrate for consciousness (although basal forebrain cholinergic projections to cortex have also been implicated — e.g. Woolf 1997).

But how do thalamo-cortical neuronal oscillations produce qualia of conscious experience, account for a pre-conscious to conscious threshold or explain other enigmatic features? For these problems the phenomenon of emergence is often suggested.

Emergence implies that a specific novel property occurs ("emerges") at some level in a hierarchical system dependent on activities at both lower and higher levels of organization (Table 1). The brain is viewed as a hierarchical system, comprised of layers of organization with bottom-up, as well as top-down feedback. In this view consciousness emerges as a novel property at an upper level of the hierarchy from nonlinear interactions among layers. Because novel properties can indeed emerge from complex interactions among simple components in a variety of systems (e.g. wetness from water, music or hurricanes from vibrations of air molecules), the inference is that conscious experience emerges as a novel property of complex interactions among relatively simple neurons.

The bottom level in most hierarchical schemes is comprised of synaptic events and neuronal firings as fundamental units ("bits"). This view suggests computer-like activities in neural networks, broad analogies between the workings of the brain, mind and modern computer, and claims that consciousness will emerge from silicon-based computation (e.g. Moravec 1987).

However there are significant problems with this brain/mind/computer analogy and emergence conjecture. To begin, no testable predictions are suggested — no critical level, or threshold of neuronal complexity is identified for the emergence of consciousness. And in fitting the brain to a computer analogy, potentially important biological details are eliminated. For example the lower cutoff of most hierarchical schemes at the level of neurons or membrane proteins is arbitrary, customized to fit the standard dogma of neurons or synapses as fundamental bits (Hameroff 1999).

1.2 *Brain features overlooked in emergent computation*

Emergent computation overlooks certain properties of brain function which don't easily fit the brain/mind/computer analogy. These include:

- Widespread apparent randomness at all levels of neural processes;
- Glial cells (which account for some 80% of brain);
- Cytoplasmic/cytoskeletal activities;
- Dendritic-dendritic processing;
- Electrotonic gap junctions;
- Cognition in single cells; and
- Living state (the brain is alive!).

Let's examine each of these.

1.2.1 *Apparent randomness*

In the standard brain/mind/computer emergence approach, axonal firings resulting in neurotransmitter release are the basic currency of information. However only a fraction of axonal firings (~15%) results in neurotransmitter release which seems random (although local cytoskeletal factors could be influential). Beck and Eccles (1992) suggested that quantum indeterminacy is governing the process through an organelle at the very end of the axon which docks and releases vesicles ("pre-synaptic vesicular grid"). But apparent randomness is rampant throughout the brain. Much of what we know about the brain's neuronal activity has been derived from electrophysiological recordings which typically include a great deal of background drift, or "noise". Electrophysiologists commonly eliminate the noise by taking the average of many recordings. But what exactly is the background drift being discarded?

Aviram Grinvald and colleagues (Arieli et al. 1996) recorded "background noise" (terming it "ongoing activity") simultaneously in various areas of mammalian brain and found that the ongoing activity correlates (is synchronous) across brain regions! Could the apparent noise represent some heretofore unrecognized nonlocal signaling or information (Ferster 1996)?

1.2.2 *Glial cells*

Approximately 80 per cent of the brain is glia, assumed in the conventional model to be primarily insulation. However glia have excitable membranes, ion channels, receptors, cytoskeletal microtubules, and are connected to neurons and other glia by gap junctions. How do we know glia are not involved in consciousness?

1.2.3 *Cytoplasmic/cytoskeletal activities*

Conventional approaches consider synapses and membrane proteins as the bottom rung in the hierarchical arrangement leading to cognition and consciousness. These structures are actually short-lived, and turn over on a scale of hours to days. They are maintained by a system of axoplasmic transport, in which materials necessary for synaptic functions are synthesized in the neuronal cell body and supplied to the synapse some distance away by microtubule-dependent transport (aided by feedback signals from synapse to cell body). There is some debate as to whether the transport utilizes microtubules in purely a passive manner (the 'rails' on which vesicles and other materials move via motor proteins) or actively direct the materials. Evidence suggests cooperative interactions among motor proteins attached at some distance away on a given microtubule (Muto et al. 1999). In any case microtubules and other cytoskeletal structures also establish neuronal form, new synapses, and up-regulate and down-regulate existing synaptic efficacy. So sensitivity of synapses — the cornerstone of learning and cognitive function — depends on cytoskeletal microtubules. Microtubules within neurons may also communicate among dendrites, and propagate "error" signals (as in neural network "back-propagation") to facilitate learning (Dayhoff et al. 1994).

Conventional approaches assume intra-neuronal information processing occurs strictly by diffusion of soluble biomolecules (second messengers, ionic flux etc). But microtubules have been shown to transmit information from membrane proteins through to the cell nucleus (Maniotis et al. 1997a, 1997b), they perform numerous types of signaling in a variety of simple organisms (Margulis et al. 1998), and their structure is well suited as a solid-state information system.

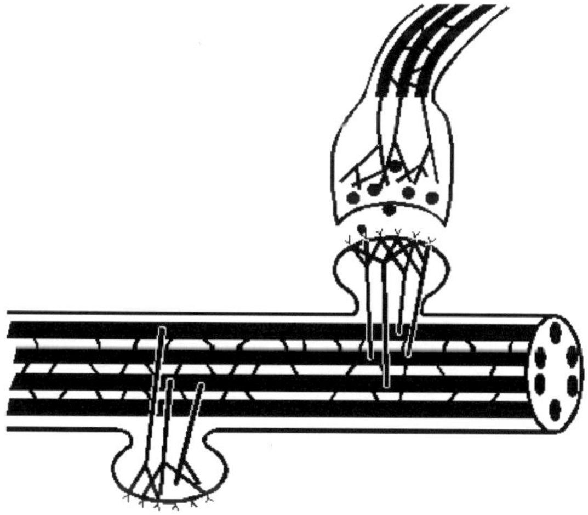

Figure 1. *Schematic of neural synapse showing cytoskeletal structures within two neurons. Top: Pre-synaptic axon terminal releases neurotransmitter vesicles (black spheres) into synaptic cleft. Thick, black rod-like structures at top indicate microtubules; thinner filaments (e.g. synapsin) facilitate vesicle release. Bottom: Dendrite on post-synaptic neuron with two dendritic spines. Microtubules in main dendrite are interconnected by microtubule-associated proteins. Other cytoskeletal structures (fodrin, actin filaments, etc.) connect membrane receptors to microtubules. Based on Hirokawa (1991).*

1.2.4 *Dendritic-dendritic processing*

Dendrites are highly complex, branching structures in which "the real work of the nervous system takes place" (Stuart et al. 1999). The dendrites of neurons receive thousands of synaptic inputs from other neurons, as well as from

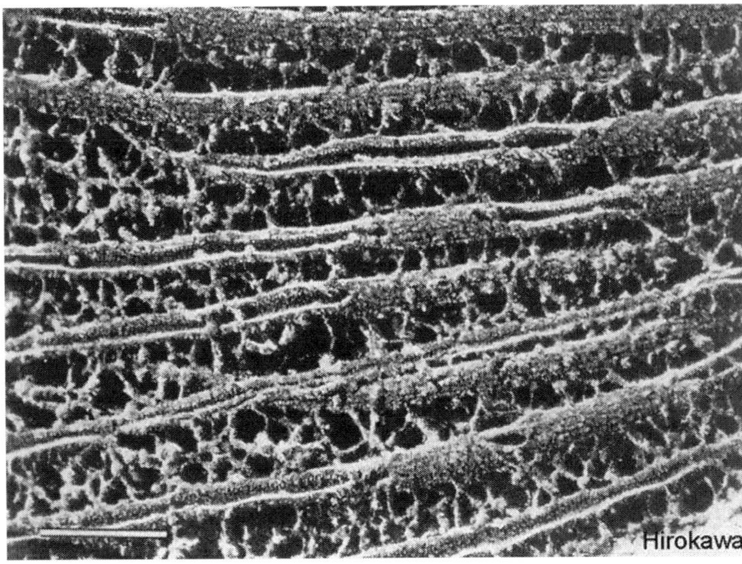

Figure 2. *The neuronal cytoskeleton. Immunoelectron micrograph of dendritic microtubules interconnected by dendrite-specific MAPs. Some microtubules have been sheared, revealing internal hollow core. The granular "corn-cob" surface of microtubules is barely evident to close inspection. Scale bar, lower left: 1·00 nanometers. With permission from Hirokawa (1991).*

dendrites on the same and other neurons. Dendrites not only collect and funnel inputs to the neuronal soma and axon, they shape and integrate the inputs in complex ways. How do they do so? One likely way is via the dendritic cytoskeleton. Microtubules in dendrites are quite different from those in axons. Axonal microtubules are all of the same polarity and continuous; dendritic microtubules are short and interrupted, of mixed polarity, and interconnected by MAP2, the dendrite-specific microtubule-associated protein (Figure 3). MAP2 is dephosphorylated with each synaptic event, and couples the dendritic cytoskeleton to synaptic membrane activities. Dendritic microtubule-MAP2 circuits may be ideal information processing networks whereas continous unipolar axonal MTs are ideal for information transfer (Tuszynski et al. 1995).

The prevalent view is that neuronal network circuits involved in consciousness occur through one particular type of neural-neural interaction: axonal-to-dendritic chemical synaptic transmission. However there are other possibilities. Both Sir John Eccles (1992) and Karl Pribram (1991) have advocated dendritic-

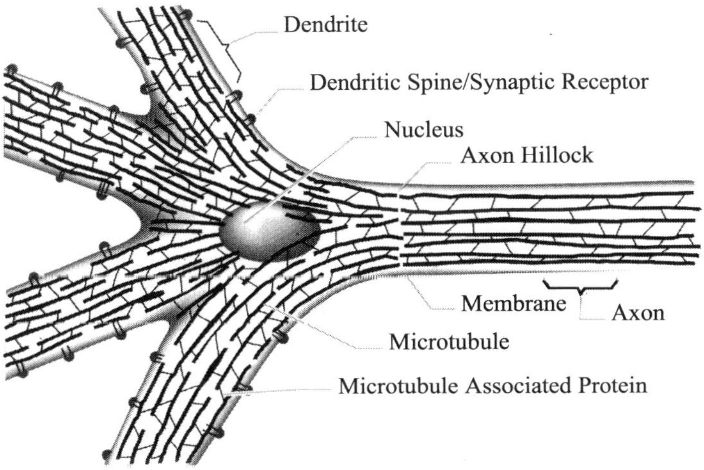

Figure 3. *Schematic of central region of neuron (distal axon and dendrites not shown) showing parallel arrayed microtubules interconnected by MAPs. Microtubules in axons are lengthy and continuous, whereas in dendrites they are interrupted and of mixed polarity. Linking proteins connect microtubules to membrane proteins including receptors on dendritic spines.*

dendritic processing, including interactions among dendrites on the same neuron. Eccles in particular pointed at dendritic arborizations of pyramidal cells in cerebral cortex as the loci of conscious processes.

1.2.5 *Gap junctions*

In addition to chemical synaptic connections, neurons (and glia) are interconnected by electrotonic gap junctions. These are window-like portholes between adjacent neural processes (axon-dendrite, dendrite-dendrite, dendrite-glial cell) through which cytoplasm flows. Gap junctions separate adjacent processes by only 4 nanometers. Neurons connected by gap junctions are electrically coupled and fire synchronously, prompting Eric Kandel to remark that neurons connected by gap junctions behave like "one giant neuron".

Gap junctions are generally considered to be more primitive connections than chemical synapses, essential for embryological development but fading into the background in mature brains. However brain gap junctions remain active throughout adult life, and are being appreciated as more and more prevalent (though still sparser than chemical synapses — a rough estimate is that gap junctions comprise 15% of all inter-neuron brain connections). Recent identification of gap junction-connected neuronal networks mediating coherent 40 Hz hints at relevance to consciousness (Galarreta & Hestrin 1999; Gibson et al. 1999; Tamas et al. 2000). As will be discussed later, gap junctions could be important for macroscopic spread of quantum states among neurons and glia. Biological electron tunneling can occur up to a separation of 5 nanometers, so the 4 nanometer separation afforded by gap junctions may enable tunneling through the gaps, spreading a quantum state among neurons. In the past few years specific intracellular organelles have been discovered in dendrites, immediately adjacent to dendritic-dendritic gap junctions. These are layers of membrane covering a mitochondrion, and are called "dendritic lamellar bodies — DLBs" (de Zeeuw 1995). The DLBs are tethered to small cytoskeletal proteins anchored to microtubules. Perhaps mitochondria provide free electrons for tunneling, and DLBs form a sort of tunneling diode pair or Josephson junction between cells, permitting spread of cytoplasmic quantum states throughout widespread brain regions (Figure 4).

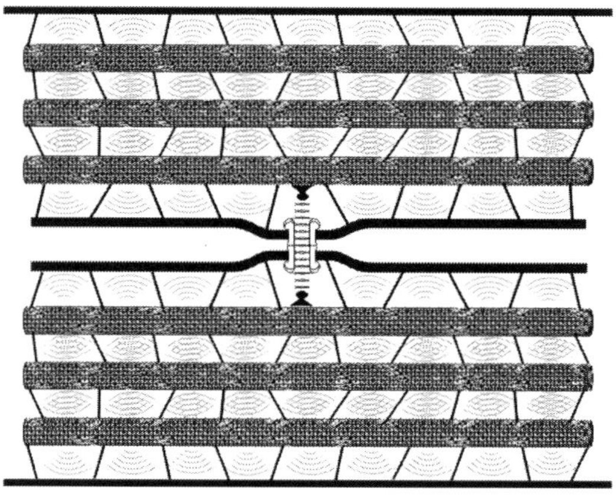

Figure 4. *Schematic representation of a gap junction connecting two dendrites in which microtubules are in quantum superposition/quantum computation "tuned" by interconnecting MAP proteins as suggested in the Penrose-Hameroff Orch OR model. On either side of the gap junction, dendritic lamellar bodies (DLBs) containing mitochondria may act as tunneling diodes to convey the quantum state between the dendrites.*

1.2.6 *Cognition in single cell organisms*

Single cell organisms such as paramecium swim, avoid obstacles, find food and mates, have sex and learn, escaping from capillary tubes more quickly with subsequent trials. As single cells they have no synapses — they utilize membrane and especially cytoskeletal microtubules as their nervous system. If a single cell paramecium can swim around and find food and companionship, isn't a single cell neuron more capable than a simple on-off switch? Processing within the neuron, for example in the cytoskeleton might well be relevant to consciousness.

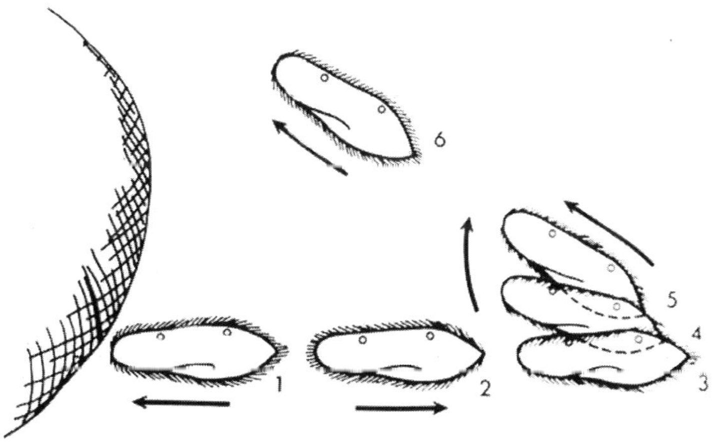

Figure 5. *Single cell paramecium can swim and avoid obstacles using its cytoskeleton.*

1.2.7 *Living state*

Conventional approaches don't distingush neurons from non-living entities. Could life, or a property of living systems be essential to consciousness? What is life?

Life is a process generally described in terms of its properties and functions including self-organization, metabolism (energy utilization), adaptive behavior, reproduction, and evolution. Whether or not this functional description is complete is a matter of contention. Historically two broad types of approaches have attempted to characterize the essential nature of the living state: (1) functionalism and (2) vitalism. Functionalism (much like the conventional approach to consciousness) implies that life is independent of its material substrate. For example, certain types of self-organizing computer programs exhibit life-like functions, and “artificial life” proponents view such systems as “alive”. Functional approaches dominate present day molecular biology, demystified by genetic engineering. “Life” is ascribed to an emergent property of biochemical processes and functional activities.

Nonetheless, a commonly held contrary viewpoint is that functional descriptions fail to explain an essential “unitary oneness” or other property present in living systems. To nineteenth-century biologists this quality was ascribed to a (presumably electromagnetic) “life force”, “elan vital”, or “life energy”. However as molecular and cell biology began to reveal the biochemical and physical processes involved in cellular activities, the apparent need for a life force waned, and “vitalists” (or “animists”) were vilified. Electromagnetic fields associated with cells and tissues were seen as effects, rather than causes of biological activity. However recently quantum interactions have been suggested as a unifying factor in biomolecular systems, paving the way for a possible “quantum vitalism”.

1.3 *If not emergent computation, then what?*

But if consciousness is not an emergent property of complex ‘computer-like’ neuronal activities, what is it? The current brain/mind/computer analogy is due in part to historical comparison to the most advanced form of technological information processing. In ancient Greece memory was compared to a ‘seal ring in wax’, in the 19th century the mind was compared to a telegraph switching circuit, in the 20th century a hologram, and presently to the most deeply developed and successful metaphor — the classical computer. On the horizon for information processing technology is quantum computation.

If quantum computers become technological reality and supersede classical computers as our most advanced form of information technology, the brain/mind will be expected to be at least equally advanced, and hence utilize some type of quantum computation. Even if quantum computers do not become successful technology, their mere theoretical existence has profound implications for fundamental physics, and consciousness.

2. The quantum approach to consciousness

Quantum states are unitary, in that perturbation of any component affects the entire system. Application of such unity to the problem of “binding” has been one motivation for quantum brain theorists. It turns out that quantum approaches have explanatory power for all enigmatic features of consciousness, including the problem of 'qualia', or conscious experience.

2.1 *'Qualia' and fundamental reality*

If conscious experience is not purely an emergent property, an alternative possibility is that qualia are primitive, fundamental aspects of reality, irreducible to anything else, something like spin, or charge. Philosophical renditions along these lines have included panpsychism (e.g. Spinoza, 1677), panexperientialism (e.g. Whitehead 1920) and most recently pan-protopsychism (Chalmers 1996). In panpsychism all matter has some consciousness, whereas in panexperientialism and pan-protopsychism there exists a fundamental proto-conscious entity convertible to consciousness by some action of the brain. Perhaps most compatible with modern physics is Whitehead's panexperientialism which portrays consciousness as a sequence of discrete events ("occasions of experience") occurring in a wider, proto-conscious field. (Abner Shimony in 1993 pointed out that Whitehead's discrete events were consistent with quantum state reductions.)

Could Whitehead's proto-conscious field be the basic level of physical reality? Perhaps qualia exist as fundamental features of the universe, somehow accessed by brain processes to adorn neuronal activities with conscious experience? What physical features of the universe could relate to qualia? Can qualia be given a physical correlate, say in modern descriptions of the fundamental nature of the universe?

What *is* the fundamental nature of the universe? Whether or not fundamental reality — empty space — is a true void or has some underlying structure is a question which dates to the Greeks. Democritus saw a true void, while Aristotle saw a background pattern or "plenum" with 3 dimensions. In the 19th century Maxwell postulated a "luminiferous ether" as a background pattern to explain the propagation of electromagnetic waves in a vacuum, but the Michelson-Morley experiment seemed to rule out a background medium. Einstein's special relativity appeared to confirm the view of a true void with its lack of preferred reference frames, (although it did introduce the concept of a four dimensional universe, unifying space and time).

However Einstein's general relativity stated that a massive object such as the sun curves spacetime around itself, much as a bowling ball would form a depression in a rubber sheet. Smaller objects such as the earth and other planets move around the object like marbles would roll down the depression in the rubber sheet. Therefore gravity was not a mysterious force but curvatures in reality itself, what Einstein called the spacetime metric.

Einstein's general relativity with its curvatures and spacetime metric swung the prevalent scientific view back to an underlying pattern. But what exactly is the spacetime metric? And what is happening at the smallest scales? We know that at the level of the Planck scale (10^{-33} cm, 10^{-43} sec) spacetime is no longer smooth, but quantized. Descriptions of fundamental reality, whether string theory, "M" theory, or spin networks offer potential sites for 'funda-mental' proto-conscious qualia. How could brain processes access this fundamental level of reality?

2.2 *Quantum mechanics and 'collapse' of the wave function*

Quantum mechanics explains how particles and energy behave at small scales. Surprisingly, quantum particles act as both particles and waves, and can exist in quantum "superposition" of two or more states or locations simultaneously! Despite the illogical nature of the situation, experiments have repeatedly shown that an atom, ion and even a molecule as large as 60 carbon fullerenes may exist in quantum superposition, separated "from itself" by 80 nanometers or so.

Another odd feature of quantum particle/waves is quantum entanglement. If two quantum partices are coupled but then go separate ways, they remain somehow connected over space and time. Measurement of one will affect the state of the other. Also, particles can condense into one collective quantum object in which all components are governed by the same wave function (e.g. Bose-Einstein condensate).

But let us return to quantum superposition. How can an object, no matter how microscopic, be in two or more states or locations simultaneously, and why don't we see this quantum weirdness in our macroscopic world?

(The following paragraphs from Hameroff and Penrose 1996a were written by Roger Penrose):

> The boundary between the microscopic, quantum world and the macroscopic, classical world remains enigmatic. Behavior of wave-like, quantum-level objects can be satisfactorily described in terms of a deterministic, unitarily evolving process (e.g. state vector evolving according to the Schrödinger equation) denoted by U (Table 1). Large-scale (classical) systems seem to obey (different) computable deterministic laws. The transition when system effects are magnified from the small, quantum scale to the large, classical scale (measurement process) chooses a particular "eigenstate" (one state of many possible states). According to the conventional Copenhagen interpretation of quantum theory, the "choice" of eigenstate is purely random. The non-computable R

Table 1. *Descriptions of wave function collapse*

Context	*Cause of Collapse (Reduction)*	*Description*	*Acronym*
Quantum coherent superposition	No collapse	Evolution of the wave function (Schrödinger equation)	*U*
Conventional quantum theory (Copenhagen interpretation)	Environmental entanglement, measurement, conscious observation	Reduction; subjective reduction	*R* *SR*
New physics (Penrose 1994)	Self-collapse — quantum gravity induced (Penrose, Diósi, etc)	Objective reduction	*OR*
Consciousness (present paper)	Self-collapse, quantum gravity threshold in microtubules orchestrated by MAPs etc.	Orchestrated objective reduction	*Orch OR*

process is known in various contexts as collapse of the wave function, quantum jump, Heisenberg event and/or state reduction.

Von Neumann, Schrödinger and other early quantum theorists supposed that quantum collapse, or R effectively occurred when a quantum system interacted with its environment, was otherwise "measured" or consciously observed. Exactly why and how collapse occurs, and how eigenstates are determined, are unknown and indicate a gap in physics knowledge: R is not taken to be an objectively real, independent phenomenon in the standard Copenhagen interpretation. A number of physicists have argued in support of specific models (or of general schemes) in which the rules of standard U-quantum mechanics are modified by the inclusion of some additional procedure according to which R does become an objectively real process. The relevant procedure of any such specific scheme is here denoted by OR (objective reduction). In Shadows of the Mind, Penrose (1994) describes OR in which quantum superposition persists until it reaches a critical threshold related to quantum gravity, and then abruptly self-collapses. Other schemes for OR include those due to Pearle (1989), and to Ghirardi et al. (1986), and those which are based on gravitational effects, such as Károlházy et al. (1986), Diósi (1989), Ghirardi et al. (1990), and also Penrose (1989). Pearle and Squires (1994) lend some considerable support, on general and observational grounds, for a

> gravitational OR scheme. There are also strong arguments from other directions (Penrose 1987, 1989) supporting a belief that the appropriate union of general relativity with quantum mechanics will lead to a significant change in the latter theory (as well as in the former — which is generally accepted). There is also some tentative, but direct, evidence in favor of this union being a non-computable theory (e.g. Geroch & Hartle 1986; Deutsch unpublished; cf. Penrose 1994) and as argued by Penrose (1989, 1994), non-computability is an essential feature of human consciousness which distinguishes us from purely algorithmic systems like classical computers."

To understand the rationale for Penrose's non-computable OR, we must attempt to come to grips with the basic question of superposition — how can an object be in two or more states or locations simultaneously? To do so requires a merger of quantum mechanics with general relativity, and suggests a link to fundamental spacetime geometry in which proto-conscious qualia may be embedded.

(The following paragrahs from Hameroff and Penrose 1996b were written by Roger Penrose).

> According to modern accepted physical pictures, reality is rooted in 3-dimensional space and a 1-dimensional time, combined together into a 4-dimensional space–time. This space–time is slightly curved, in accordance with Einstein's general theory of relativity, in a way which encodes the gravitational fields of all distributions of mass density. Each mass density effects a space–time curvature, albeit tiny.
>
> This is the standard picture according to classical physics. On the other hand, when quantum systems have been considered by physicists, this mass-induced tiny curvature in the structure of space–time has been almost invariably ignored, gravitational effects having been assumed to be totally insignificant for normal problems in which quantum theory is important. Surprising as it may seem, however, such tiny differences in space–time structure can have large effects, for they entail subtle but fundamental influences on the very rules of quantum mechanics.
>
> Superposed quantum states for which the respective mass distributions differ significantly from one another will have space–time geometries which correspondingly differ. Thus, according to standard quantum theory, the superposed state would have to involve a quantum superposition of these differing space–times. In the absence of a coherent theory of quantum gravity there is no accepted way of handling such a superposition. Indeed the basic principles of Einstein's general relativity begin to come into profound conflict with those of quantum mechanics (cf. Penrose 1996).

Figures 6–8 (adapted from Penrose 1994: 338) schematically illustrate the way in which space–time structure can be affected when two macroscopically different

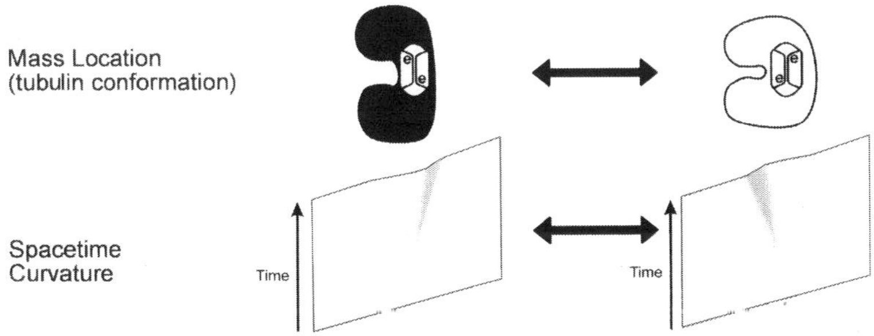

Figure 6. *According to Einstein's general relativity, mass is equivalent to curvature in spacetime geometry. Penrose applies this equivalence to the fundamental Planck scale. The motion of an object between two conformational states of a protein such as tubulin (top) is equivalent to two curvatures in spacetime geometry as represented as a two-dimensional spacetime sheet (bottom).*

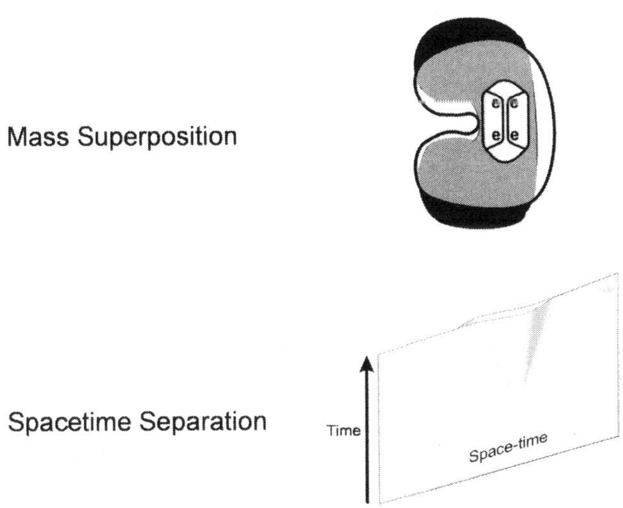

Figure 7. *Mass superposition, e.g. a protein occupying two different conformational states simultaneously (top) is equivalent, according to Penrose, to simultaneous spacetime curvature in opposite directions — a separation, or bubble ("blister") in fundamental spacetime geometry.*

mass distributions take part in a quantum superposition. Each mass distribution (e.g. conformational state of a tubulin protein, as depicted in Figure 6) gives rise to a separate space–time, the two differing slightly in their curvatures. So long as the two distributions remain in quantum superposition (of *both* conformations: Figure 7), we must consider that the two space–times remain in superposition. Since, according to the principles of general relativity, there is no natural way to identify the points of one space–time with corresponding points of the other, we have to consider the two as separated from one another in some sense, resulting in a kind of "blister" where the space–time bifurcates Figures 7 and 8).

A bifurcating space–time is depicted in the lowest of the three diagrams in Figure 8, this being the union ("glued together version") of the two alternative space–time histories that are depicted at the top of Figure 8. The initial part of each space–time is at the lower end of each individual space–time diagram. The bottom space–time diagram (the bifurcating one) illustrates two alternative mass distributions actually in quantum superposition, whereas the top two illustrate the two individual alternatives which take part in the superposition. The combined space–time describes a superposition in which the alternative locations of a mass move gradually away from each other as we proceed in the upward direction in the diagram. Quantum-mechanically (so long as OR has not taken place), we must think of the "physical reality" of this situation as being illustrated as an actual superposition of these two slightly differing space–time manifolds, as

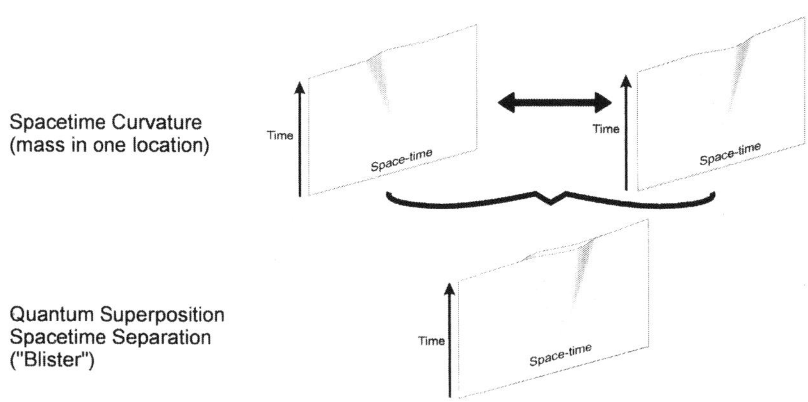

Figure 8. *Spacetime superposition/separation bubble (bottom) will reduce, or collapse to one or the other spacetime curvatures (top).*

indicated in the bottom diagram. As soon as reduction/collapse has occurred, one of the two individual space–times takes over, as depicted as one of the two sheets of the bifurcation. For clarity only, the bifurcating parts of these two sheets are illustrated as being one convex and the other concave. Of course there is additional artistic license involved in drawing the space–time sheets as 2-dimensional, whereas the actual space–time constituents are 4-dimensional. Moreover, there is no significance to be attached to the imagined "3-dimensional space" within which the space–time sheets seem to be residing. There is no "actual" higher dimensional space there, the "intrinsic geometry" of the bifurcating space–time being all that has physical significance.

When the "separation" of the two space–time sheets reaches a critical amount, one of the two sheets "dies" — in accordance with the OR criterion — the other being the one that persists in physical reality. The quantum state thus reduces (OR), by choosing between either the "concave" or "convex" space–time of Figure 8.

It should be made clear that this measure of separation is only very schematically illustrated as the "distance" between the two sheets in the lower diagram in Figure 8. As remarked above, there is no physically existing "ambient higher dimensional space" inside which the two sheets reside. The degree of separation between the space–time sheets is a more abstract mathematical thing; it would be more appropriately described in terms of a symplectic measure on the space of 4-dimensional metrics (cf. Penrose 1993) — but the details (and difficulties) of this will not be important for us here. It may be noted, however, that this separation is a space–time separation, not just a spatial one. Thus the time of separation contributes as well as the spatial displacement. Roughly speaking, it is the product of the temporal separation T with the spatial separation S that measures the overall degree of separation, and OR takes place when this overall separation reaches the critical amount. [This critical amount would be of the order of unity, in absolute units, for which the Planck-Dirac constant $\hbar$ (Planck's constant over 2π), the gravitational constant G, and the velocity of light c, all take the value unity, cf. Penrose 1994: 337–339.] Thus for small S, the lifetime T of the superposed state will be large; on the other hand, if S is large, then T will be small. To calculate S, we compute (in the Newtonian limit of weak gravitational fields) the gravitational self-energy E of the difference between the mass distributions of the two superposed states. (That is, one mass distribution counts positively and the other, negatively; see Penrose 1994, 1995.) The quantity S is then given by:

$$S = E$$

Thus

$$E = \hbar / T$$

Schematically, since S represents three dimensions of displacement rather than the one dimension involved in T, we can imagine that this displacement is shared equally between each of these three dimensions of space — and this is what has been depicted in Figure 8. However, it should be emphasized that this is for pictorial purposes only, the appropriate rule being the one given above. These 2 equations relate the mass distribution, time of coherence, and space–time separation for a given OR event. If, as some philosophers contend, proto-conscious experience is contained in space–time, OR events are self-organizing processes in that proto-conscious medium, and a candidate for consciousness.
Could OR events occur in the brain? The critical spacetime separation precipitating Penrose's OR is given by the uncertainty principle $E=\hbar/T$. E is the energy of the superposed mass, $\hbar$ is Planck's constant over 2π, and T is the coherence time until reduction. The size (and energy) of a superposed system (degree of spacetime separation) is inversely related to the time T until self-collapse. If isolated, a large system will undergo OR very quickly (e.g. Schrödinger's mythical one kilogram cat would self-collapse in only 10^{-37} seconds). A small system such as a single isolated superposed atom would undergo OR only after 10^7 years. OR brain events would be linked to neural processes with T in the range of tens to hundreds of milliseconds (e.g. 25 msec intervals in coherent 40 Hz). For $T=25$ msec (40 Hz) OR events, E corresponds to roughly 3 nanograms (3×10^{-9} gram) of superposed brain mass.

But where in the brain, and how, could coherent superposition and OR occur, and what structures could utilize it purposefully? A number of sites and various types of quantum interactions have been proposed. We strongly favor microtubules as an important ingredient, however various organelles and biomolecular structures including clathrins, myelin (glial cells), pre-synaptic vesicular grids (Beck & Eccles 1992) and neural membrane proteins (Marshall 1989) might also participate.

OR and non-computability in microtubules relevant to consciousness was first considered in somewhat general terms in Penrose's *Shadows of the Mind*, and elaborated as the "Orch OR" model in a series of papers (Penrose & Hameroff 1995; Hameroff & Penrose 1996a, 1996b; Hameroff 1998a–d) in which emergence of quantum coherence U and subsequent OR are "guided" and "tuned" ("orchestrated") by microtubule-associated proteins ("MAPs") interconnecting microtubules.

How could OR and Orch OR be relevant, or useful in understanding brain function and consciousness? It turns out quantum superposition and subsequent reduction is indeed relevant to a new form of technological computing — quantum computing.

2.3 *Quantum computation*

Described theoretically in the 1980's (e.g. by Benioff, Feynman, Deutsch), "quantum computing" is suggested to utilize quantum superposition, in which a particle can exist in two or more states, or locations simultaneously. Whereas current computers represent information as "bits" of either 1 or 0, quantum computers are proposed to utilize quantum bits — "qubits" — of both 1 AND 0.

Potential advantages in quantum computing stem from qubits in superposition interacting nonlocally by quantum coherence or entanglement, implementing near-infinite quantum parallelism. These interactions perform computations and, at some point, the qubits collapse, or reduce to a single set of classical bits — the "solution". Significant technological and commercial advantages are offered by quantum computers if they are ever able to be constructed (prototypes now exist, and research activity is intense). Although technological quantum computers are envisioned to reduce to classical output "solutions" by environmental interactions (R, or SR rather than OR), the Orch OR model proposes reduction of the quantum computation to a solution by OR self-collapse. OR introduces non-computability, an essential feature of consciousness, and the self-organizing reduction occurs at the level of fundamental spacetime geometry in which proto-conscious qualia may be embedded. OR can also account for the pre-conscious to conscious transition. By this standard, technological quantum computers which reduce by R, or SR would not be conscious.

Can quantum states suitable for quantum computation or other quantum features potentially useful in consciousness occur in the brain?

2.4 *Quantum claims*

Let's look at the types of claims or suggestions for quantum states in biological systems relevant to consciousness. They are presented here roughly in order of increasingly "strong" claims.

- Quantum effects mediate bonds, inter-atomic forces in biomolecules. This is generally agreed upon; there are no implications for macroscopic effects or coherence, nor for consciousness or the living state.
- Quantum superposition originating in electrons and/or protons mediate functional activities in biomolecules, e.g. protein conformation (e.g. Conrad 1994, evidence from protein chemistry, protein folding problem) This does not necessarily imply cell-wide, or tissue-wide macroscopic effects or coherence but raises the scale of the quantum state to that capable of regulating a single protein.

- Quantum influence on protein assemblies (e.g. pre-synaptic vesicular grid) releasing neurotransmitters into synaptic cleft (Beck & Eccles 1992). This does not necessarily imply macroscopic or coherent effects, in fact Beck and Eccles saw the quantum influence as a purely random, probabilistic effect. But it suggests quantum states/influence on the scale of an organelle, or assembly of proteins.
- Sites where anesthetics bind by quantum mechanical London forces suggests a distributed array of entangled quantum loci as the microsite of consciousness
- Quantum influence on locations of ions, e.g. calcium ions, which influence neural function (e.g. Stapp 1993). Macroscopic coherence implied through unity of quantum wave function
- Quantum tunneling across synapses and among intra-neuronal biomolecules constitute a substrate for consciousness (Walker 2000)
- Bose-Einstein condensate among distributed neural proteins, e.g. using Fröhlich mechanism to drive coherent excitations/phonons (Marshall 1989). The macroscopic condensate manifests unitary consciousness. Marshall's distributed neural proteins may be the array of hydrophobic pockets which mediate anesthesia.
- Macroscopic quantum state arise from ordered water effects, spontaneous symmetry breaking, super-radiance, generation of evanescent photons with 50 micron coherence length (Jibu et al. 1994) serving the unity of consciousness
- Macroscopic quantum states in protein assemblies, in particular microtubules. The crystal-like lattice periodicity in microtubule structure facilitates tunneling/entanglement/condensation among quantum states in the arrayed subunit proteins (tubulin), with coherent pumping due to a Fröhlich type mechanism, stochastic quantum resonance, or Conrad funneling.
- The microtubule based quantum state spreads among different neuronal dendrites via tunneling through gap junctions, enabling brain-wide quantum states.
- Quantum states of individual tubulins in microtubules function as 'qubits', and microtubules perform quantum compution. Quantum superposition/ quantum computation phase is sustained long enough (10–500 msec) to reach threshold for self-collapse by Penrose's quantum gravity 'objective reduction'. Such objective reductions constitute conscious moments (the Orch OR model).

3. The brain's biology

The conventional wisdom in academic science holds decidedly against the relevance of quantum mechanisms in consciousness (or living processes in general) above the level of inter-atomic, intra-molecular and inter-molecular forces which mediate chemical interactions. Above this level, the wisdom holds, quantum effects are washed out by thermal decoherence, or environmental interaction in the brain's "warm, wet and noisy" milieu. Let's examine that milieu.

3.1 *Is the brain "warm"?*

Yes, clearly the brain operates at 37.6 degrees centigrade, and deviations in brain temperature in either direction are not well tolerated for consciousness. This temperature is indeed quite warm compared to the extreme cold needed for some quantum technological devices in which the extreme cold serves to prevent thermal excitations which could disrupt (decohere) the quantum state. However proposals for biological quantum states suggest that biological heat is funneled (Conrad) or used to pump coherent excitations (Fröhlich phonons, Fermi-Pasta-Ulam resonance, or Davydov solitons). In other words biomolecular systems may have evolved to utilize thermal energy to drive coherence.

A related question is whether consciousness is dissipative. Clearly biological processes are dissipative in general, but there's some suggestion that consciousness is not dissipative. Evidence from brain imaging shows a discrepancy between increased blood flow and oxygen uptake in areas actively involved in cognitive processing (and presumably neural correlates of consciousness). Large increases in blood flow are accompanied by little or no increase in oxygen uptake. This has prompted some brain imagers (e.g. Peter Fox at San Antonio) to suggest that consciousness is anaerobic — does not require oxygen. As everyone knows, the brain cannot function or survive without oxygen for more than seconds or minutes, and so at first glance the suggestion seems preposterous. However as Fox points out, the energy cost of a phone system is largely in setting up and maintaining lines of communication; communication itself (talking on the phone) is very cheap energetically. Aerobic processes may be necessary to set the stage for consciousness which, in and of itself may be anaerobic and non-dissipative. (Quantum computation must be reversible, and hence non-dissipative). How could this be?

One possibility is that processes related to consciousness are phasic, with cycles of 1) aerobic, dissipative classical processes alternating with 2) anaerobic, non-dissipative quantum processes (consciousness may be the transition from 2 to 1).

Phase 2 would be the pre-conscious quantum phase isolated from environment by actin gelation (see later section). Quantum computation would thus be well suited to an anaerobic, non-dissipative phase. Input/output environmental interactions would be well suited to an aerobic, dissipative classical phase.

In summary, the brain is indeed warm. The assumption/prediction by quantum advocates is that biological systems have evolved techniques to funnel thermal energy to coherent vibrations conducive to quantum coherence, and/or insulate quantum states through gelation, ordered water or plasma phase screens.

3.2 *Is the brain "wet"?*

The interiors of neurons and all of our cells exist in alternating phases of "sol" (solution, liquid) and "gel" (solid, gelatinous). The sol-gel transition is a very primitive biological phenomenon, related to movement of single cells like amoeba, growing axons and dendrites, and immune cells like lymphocytes. In these cases actin polymerizes in one direction, and liquefies behind it, causing a directional flow of cytoplasm. (Actin also polymerizes in response to light). In the 19th century Claude Bernard studied this phenomenon, which he called cytoplasmic streaming, and discovered it was inhibited by exposure to the anesthetic gas chloroform. In more complex, asymmetrical cells like neurons, transport and motion utilize polymerization of microtubules, in conjunction with actin gelation.

The particular character of actin gel depends on actin cross-linking. Of the various cross-linker related types of gels, some are viscoelastic, but others (e.g. those induced by the actin cross-linker avidin) are solid and can be deformed by an applied force without any response (Wacchstock et al. 1994). Such shock-absorbance could be useful in quantum isolation. Cycles of actin gelation/solution can be quite rapid, occurring for example at 40 Hz. In neurons Miyamoto (1995) and Muallem et al. (1995) have shown that cycles of actin gelation/solution correlate with release of neurotransmitter vesicles from pre-synaptic axon terminals. In dendritic spines, whose synaptic efficacy mediates learning, rapid actin gelation and motility mediate synaptic function, and are sensitive to anesthetics (Kaech et al. 1997; Fischer et al. 1998; Kaech et al. 1999).

Even in the "sol", or liquid phase of cytoplasm, water within cells is not truly liquid and random. Water molecules form all kinds of transient forms (Linus Pauling termed them "clathrates"). Pioneering work by Clegg (1984) and others have shown that water within cells is to a large extent "ordered", and plays the role of an active component rather than inert background solvent. Cytoskeleton including actin gel binds water, and neutron diffraction studies

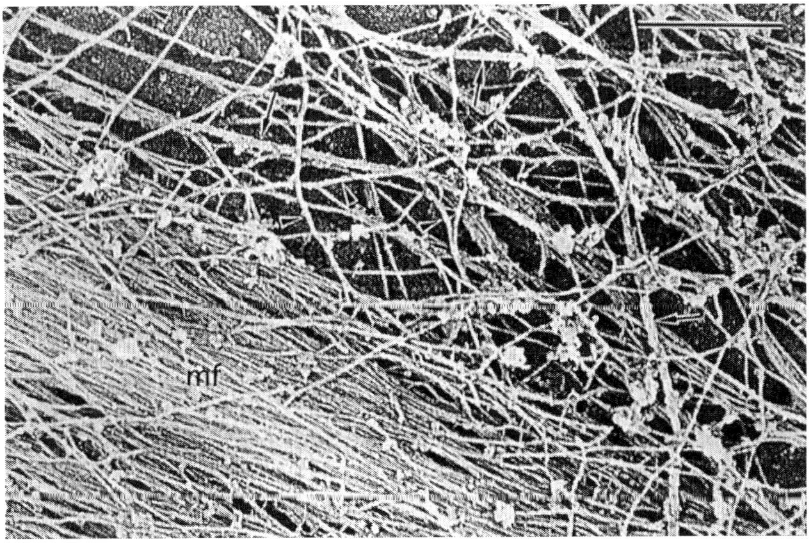

Figure 9. *Actin gel. Immunoelectron micrograph of cytoplasm showing microtubules (arrows), intermediate filaments (arrowheads) and actin microfilaments (mf). Dense gel of actin (lower left) completely obscures (?isolates) microtubules. Actin sol-gel transitions can occur at 40 Hz or faster. Scale bar (upper right): 500 nanometers. With permission from Svitkina et al. (1995).*

indicate several layers of ordered water on such surfaces with several additional layers of partially ordered water.

Protein-water binding/ordering is well studied, and linked to events in hydrophobic pockets on the protein interior. Wulf and Featherstone (1967) showed that anesthetic binding in a hydrophobic pocket altered the number of water molecules bound at the protein surface. Water molecules bound to actin and other cytoskeletal surfaces are ordered and coupled to the actin/cytoskeletal dynamics. Watterson (1981, 1996) observes that in living cytoplasmic gels, water doesn't flow — even though the gel is over 75% water. NMR studies have shown that actin assembly results in reduced water mobility (ordering), and that distribution of ordered water through the cell is a heterogeneous and dynamic process. Pauser et al. (1995) demonstrated that 55% of water of the vegetal pole region of frog oocytes is bound water, with less bound (~25%) near the animal pole cytoplasm, and ~10% bound in the nucleus. Ordered water distribution changes in time also. For example cell cycle (mitosis) changes correlate with actin polymerization, gelation, and reduced cytoplasmic water motion (Cameron et al. 1987).

Quantum field theorists have historically proposed that ordering of cytoplasmic water leads to biological quantum states through spontaneous symmetry breaking and generation of bosons (e.g. Stuart, Ricciardi, Umezawa, Takahashi, del Giudice, Vitiello and more recently Jibu, Yasue and Hagan). In one aspect of this approach, Jibu, Yasue, Hagan and others (Jibu et al. 1995) have proposed that water in the hollow microtubule core is ordered by microtubule dynamics leading to spontaneous symmetry breaking and generation of evanescent photons, "super-radiance" and "self-induced transparency" of photons in microtubule cores. Quantum coherent regions of 50 microns are predicted.

Charged surfaces (cytoskeleton, membranes) also attract soluble ions of the opposite charge, leading to plasma-like layers (Debye layer) which can have quantum properties, and/or quantum isolation properties. Such plasma-like regions have been proposed adjacent to membranes (Green and Triffet 1985), and surrounding microtubules. Sackett has shown that at precisely physiological pH there exists a plasma sleeve around microtubules which could serve to isolate MT quantum processes from thermal decoherence (Sackett 1995).

3.3 *Is the brain "noisy?"*

Let's consider two types of noise: a) intracellular noise, presumably from thermal energy of water, and b) electrical noise as manifest in electrophysiological recordings. Several proposals have been put forth suggesting that thermal energy in biological systems is transformed into coherent excitations in biomolecules. Michael Conrad describes "funneling" of thermal energy, and quantized couplings of energy and conformation (Davydov soliton) has been suggested and discussed for many years.

Herbert Fröhlich, an early contributor to the understanding of superconductivity, predicted quantum coherence in living cells (based on earlier work by Oliver Penrose and Lars Onsager (1956). Fröhlich (1968, 1970, 1975) theorized that sets of protein dipoles (centered in hydrophobic pockets) in a common electromagnetic field (e.g. proteins within a polarized membrane, subunits within an electret polymer like microtubules) undergo coherent conformational excitations if thermal energy is supplied. Fröhlich postulated that biochemical and thermal energy from the surrounding "heat bath" provides such energy.

Coherent excitation frequencies on the order of 10^9 to 10^{11} Hz (the time domain for functional protein conformational changes, and in the microwave or gigaHz spectral region) were deduced by Fröhlich who termed them acoustoconformational transitions, or coherent (pumped) phonons, or optical phonons. Such coherent states are termed Bose-Einstein condensates in quantum physics and have been suggested by Marshall (1989) to provide macroscopic quantum states which support the unitary binding feature in consciousness. Experimental searches for Fröhlich coherence have been confusing, and to some extent disappointing. However biological mechanisms developed to isolate and protect quantum coherence mechanisms could also make their detection quite difficult. Nevertheless experimental evidence for Fröhlich-like coherent excitations in biological systems includes observation of gigaHz-range phonons in proteins (Genberg et al. 1991) sharp-resonant non-thermal effects of microwave irradiation on living cells (Grundler & Keilman 1983; Genzel et al. 1983), gigaHz induced activation of microtubule pinocytosis in rat brain (Neubauer et al. 1990), and laser Raman spectroscopy detection of Fröhlich frequency energy (Vos et al. 1993).

The second type of noise commonly assumed is electrical. As previously described, electrophysiological recordings of single cell events detect fluctuations in baseline voltage over various time scales, but eliminate them by signal averaging. The assumption is that background fluctuations are meaningless noise. However Grinvald's group in Israel have shown this background to correlate over wide regions of brain. Perhaps it isn't noise (Arielei et al. 1996; Ferster 1996).

In summary, the brain may not be as inhospitable to quantum states as generally believed. Next we consider the mechanism of the primary currency of biological information and efficacy: protein conformational dynamics.

3.4 *Protein conformational dynamics*

Real-time dynamical regulation of cellular activity depends on conformational states of proteins including ion channels opening or closing, cytoplasm flowing by actin protein self-assembly (gelation), receptors changing shape upon binding of neurotransmitter, enzymes catalyzing a reaction, "second messengers" or cytoskeletal protein changing shape to signal or facilitate movement or transport. How are protein conformational states regulated?

Individual proteins are synthesized as linear chains of amino acids which "fold" into 3 dimensional conformation. The precise folding depends on attractive and repellent forces among various amino acid side groups, and a current view is that many possible intermediate conformations precede the final one (Baldwin 1994). Predicting final 3-dimensional folded shape using computer simulation has proven difficult if not impossible. This conundrum is known as the "protein folding problem" and so far appears to be "NP complete": the answer can be calculated in theory, but the space and time required of any classical computer is prohibitive. Perhaps protein folding is a quantum computation?

The main driving force in protein folding occurs as uncharged non-polar amino acid groups join together, repelled by solvent water. These "hydrophobic" groups attract each other by dipole couplings known as van der Waals forces and bury themselves within the protein interior. Intra-protein "hydrophobic pockets" result, composed of side groups of non-polar (but polarizable) amino acids such as leucine, isoleucine, phenylalanine, tryptophan, tyrosine and valine. Volumes of the hydrophobic pockets (~400 cubic angstroms, or 0.4 cubic nanometers) are roughly 1/30 to 1/250 the total volume of a single protein, and their physical solvent characteristics most closely resemble olive oil, or octanol (e.g. Franks & Lieb 1985). Van der Waals forces in hydrophobic pockets establish protein shape during folding, and also regulate dynamic conformational changes.

Proteins in a living state are dynamical, with transitions occurring at many scales, however conformational transitions in which proteins move globally and upon which protein function generally depends occur in the nanosecond (10^{-9} sec) to 10 picosecond (10^{-11} sec) time scale (Karplus & McCammon 1983). Proteins are also only marginally stable. A protein of 100 amino acids is stable against denaturation by only ~40 kiloJoules per mole (kJ mol^{-1}) whereas thousands of kJ mol^{-1} are available in a protein from side group interactions including van der Waals forces. Consequently protein conformation is a "delicate balance among powerful countervailing forces" (Voet & Voet 1995).

The types of forces operating among amino acid side groups within a protein include charged interactions such as ionic forces and hydrogen bonds, as well as interactions between dipoles — separated charges in electrically neutral groups. Dipole-dipole interactions are known as van der Waals forces and include three types:

1. Permanent dipole – permanent dipole
2. Permanent dipole – induced dipole
3. Induced dipole – induced dipole

Type 3 induced dipole – induced dipole interactions are the weakest but most purely non-polar. They are known as London dispersion forces, and although quite delicate (40 times weaker than hydrogen bonds) are numerous and influential. The London force attraction between any two atoms is usually less than a few kiloJoules, however thousands occur in each protein. As other forces cancel out, London forces in hydrophobic pockets can govern protein conformational states.

London forces ensue from the fact that atoms and molecules which are electrically neutral and spherically symmetrical nevertheless have instantaneous

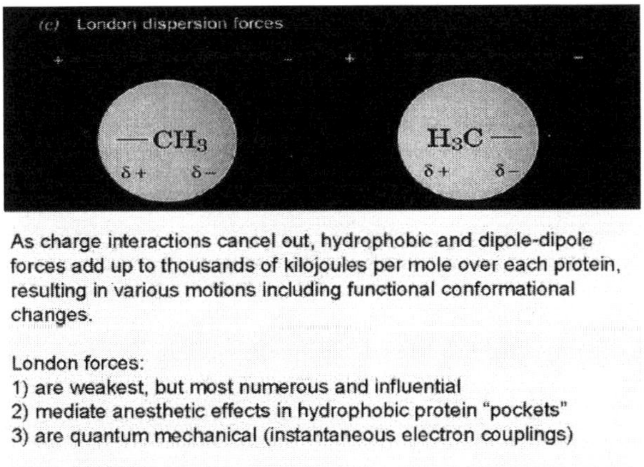

Figure 10. *London forces are instantaneous couplings of electron clouds in adjacent atoms or groups within a protein. Although weak, the quantum mechanical London forces are numerous, and collectively able to influence protein conformation (from Voet & Voet 1995).*

electric dipoles due to asymmetry in their electron distribution. The electric field from each fluctuating dipole couples to others in electron clouds of adjacent non-polar amino acid side groups. Due to inherent uncertainty in electron localization, London forces are quantum effects which may couple to "zero point fluctuations" of the quantum vacuum (London 1937; Milloni 1994).

Quantum dipole oscillations within hydrophobic pockets were first proposed by Fröhlich (1968) to regulate protein conformation and engage in macroscopic coherence, and Conrad (1994) suggested quantum superposition of various possible protein conformations occur before one is selected. Roitberg et al. (1995) showed functional protein vibrations which depend on quantum effects centered in two hydrophobic phenylalanine residues, and Tejada et al. (1996) have evidence to suggest quantum coherent states exist in the protein ferritin.

Evidence for a pivotal role for quantum effects in protein conformational regulation (and consciousness) comes from studying the opposite of consciousness — anesthesia.

3.5 *Anesthesia and consciousness*

Another clue to consciousness is the molecular mechanism of anesthesia. At just the right anesthetic dose, consciousness is erased while other brain activities continue.

A variety of compounds are anesthetic, particularly a group of gases which have been known for over 100 years to share one common feature — solubility in a particular type of environment.

In 1897 Meyer in Germany and in 1899 Overton in England independently came to the same conclusion: over many orders of magnitude, potency of various anesthetic gases was directly proportional to their solubility in a particular lipid-like environment, most closely identified with olive oil or octanol.

It turns out the brain is loaded with such environment, both in lipid membranes and "hydrophobic" lipid-like pockets within certain brain proteins. For many years it was assumed that anesthetics acted in lipid regions of membranes, however Nicholas Franks and William Lieb at Imperial College in London showed in a series of experiments during the 1980's that anesthetics inhibit individual protein function even when there is no membrane in the picture. They concluded that anesthetics exert their effect by entering hydrophobic pockets, binding there by very weak van der Waals (London) forces. The hydrophobic pockets are typically less than 1/30 of the total protein volume, but seem to somehow act as the "brain" of the protein. Somehow weak (quantum) interactions in these tiny regions have profound effects on the function of particular proteins, and consciousness.

Which brain proteins mediate anesthetic effect? Franks and Lieb (1998) conclude that the particular proteins most sensitive to inhalation anesthetics are post-synaptic receptors for $GABA_A$, glycine, serotonin $5HT_3$, and nicotinic acetylcholine as well as some potassium channels. Franks and Lieb add that other slightly less sensitive proteins (e.g. voltage-sensitive channels, gap junctions, G-proteins, cytoskeletal actin and microtubules) which are more abundant and/or directly involved in activities relevant to consciousness may also mediate anesthetic effects. Normal function of glycine receptors (Delon & Legendre 1995) and of $GABA_A$, receptors (Whatley et al. 1994) depend on integrity of cytoskeletal microtubules, so it seems likely that a variety of receptors, channels, second messenger and cytoskeletal proteins engage in collective (?quantum) dynamics necessary for consciousness (and inhibition by anesthetics). This can explain why disruption of either excitatory (e.g. acetylcholine) or inhibitory (e.g. $GABA_A$) receptor function contribute to anesthesia. The essential feature common to molecular sites of anesthetic action is the hydrophobic pocket.

Franks and Lieb (1994) had concluded that anesthetic action was due to their mere presence in hydrophobic pockets preventing conformational switching. However a variety of molecules which follow the Meyer-Overton correlation and occupy the same hydrophobic pockets are nonanesthetic, or even convulsant

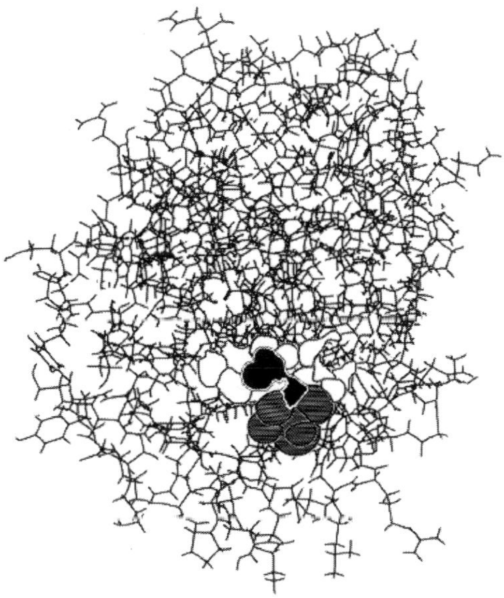

Figure 11. *Computer simulation of the anesthetic-sensitive enzyme papain with halothane "docked" by energy minimization into its major hydrophobic pocket. Scale bar: 1 nanometer. (From Louria & Hameroff 1996 with permission).*

(Fang et al. 1996). The mere presence of molecules in hydrophobic pockets is insufficient to explain anesthesia.

Given that normally occurring van der Waals London forces mediate protein conformational dynamics in hydrophobic pockets, and that anesthetics form London forces in hydrophobic pockets, a logical conclusion is that anesthetics somehow disrupt van der Waals London force interactions normally occurring in hydrophobic pockets in proteins critical to consciousness. London force superposition (theoretically implicated in consciousness) requires electron mobility — electron pairs must be relatively free to roam among allowed orbitals. Evidence shows that anesthetics retard electron mobility — the movement of free electrons in a corona discharge is inhibited by anesthetics (Hameroff & Watt 1983). By forming their own London force attractions in hydrophobic pockets, anesthetics may retard electron mobility required for protein dynamics, quantum superposition and consciousness.

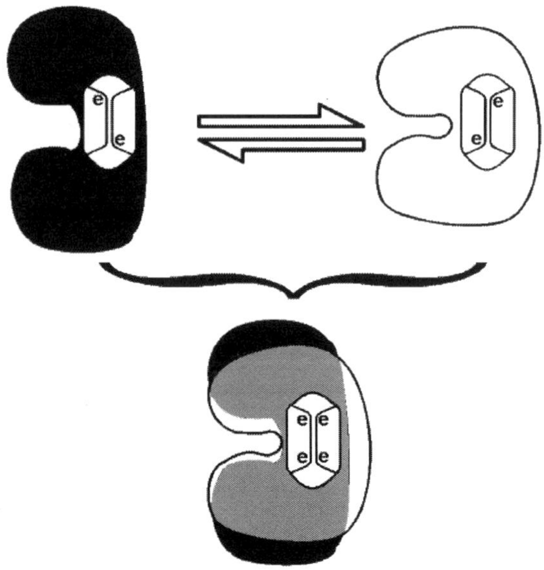

Figure 12. *Schematized protein capable of switching between two conformational states governed by van der Waals interactions in a hydrophobic pocket. Proteins may actually have several smaller collectively governing hydrophobic pockets. Top: Protein switching between 2 conformational states coupled to localization of paired electrons (London force) within a hydrophobic pocket. Bottom: quantum superposition (simultaneous existence in two distinct states) of the electron pair and protein conformation.*

Can we learn about consciousness from drugs which have opposite effects from anesthetics? In the 1970's pharmacologists studied a series of drugs with psychedelic, or hallucinogenic properties looking for physical correlates of the drugs' hallucinogenic potency. They found that potency correlated with the degree of electron resonance energy donation from drug molecule to receptor. The more electron energy able to be transferred, the greater the hallucinogenic potency. Such electron energy donation/mobility would enhance likelihood of quantum superposition states in receptor proteins (the exact opposite of anesthetics). Altered, expanded ("psychedelic") states may involve enhanced quantum superpositions, equivalent to expanded access to normally non-conscious quantum information.

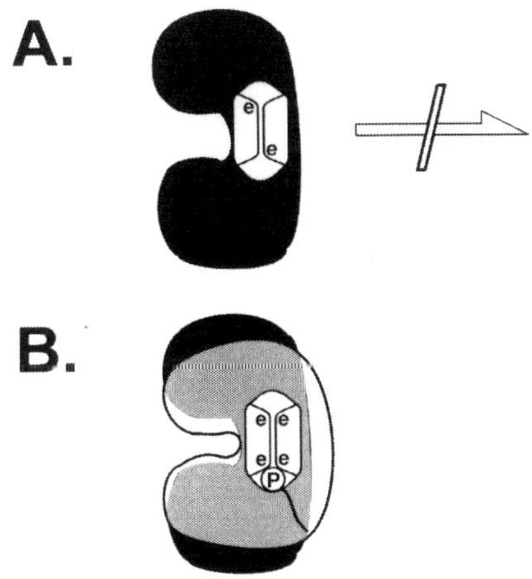

Figure 13. *A. An anesthetic gas molecule (A) in a hydrophobic pocket of critical brain protein (receptors, channels, tubulin etc.) prevents normally occurring London forces, preventing protein conformational dynamics and superposition necessary for consciousness. B. A psychedelic hallucinogen (P) acts in hydrophobic pocket in critical brain protein to promote and sustain superposition, 'expanding' consciousness.*

4. The Penrose-Hameroff 'Orch OR' model

4.1 *Microtubules*

Interiors of living cells are functionally organized by webs of protein polymers — the cytoskeleton whose major components are microtubules, self-assembling hollow crystalline cylinders whose walls are hexagonal lattices of subunit proteins known as tubulin. Microtubules ("MT") are essential for a variety of biological functions including cell movement, cell division (mitosis) and establishment and maintenance of cell form and function. In neurons, microtubules self-assemble to extend axons and dendrites and form synaptic connections; microtubules then help maintain and regulate synaptic strengths responsible for learning and cognitive functions. (For a more complete description of the role of microtubules and other cytoskeletal structures in cognitive functions see Dayhoff et al. 1994; Hameroff & Penrose 1996a; Hameroff 1994). While microtubules have traditionally been considered as purely structural components, recent evidence has demonstrated mechanical signaling and communication functions (Glanz 1997; Maniotis et al. 1997a, 1997b; Vernon & Wooley 1995). Microtubules

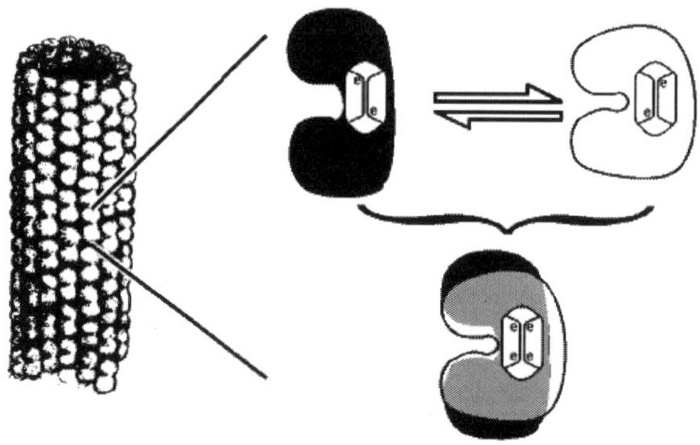

Figure 14. *Left: Microtubule (MT) structure: a hollow tube of 25 nanometers diameter, consisting of 13 columns of tubulin dimers arranged in a skewed hexagonal lattice (Penrose 1994). Right (top): Each tubulin molecule may switch between two (or more) conformations, coupled to London forces in a hydrophobic pocket. Right (bottom): Each tubulin can also exist in quantum superposition of both conformational states.*

interact with membrane structures and activities by linking proteins (e.g. fodrin, ankyrin) and "second messenger" chemical signals.

4.2 *Microtubule information processing*

How could microtubules implement information processing? Theoretical models propose that microtubule subunit tubulins undergo coherent excitations, for example, in the gigaHz range by a mechanism suggested by Fröhlich ("pumped phonons" — Fröhlich 1968, 1970, 1975; cf. O. Penrose & L. Onsager 1956). Fröhlich excitations of tubulin subunits within microtubules have been suggested to support computation and information processing (e.g. Hameroff & Watt 1982; Rasmussen et al. 1990) by "clocking" computational transitions occurring among neighboring tubulins acting as "cells" as in molecular scale "cellular automata". Dipole coupling among neighboring tubulins in the microtubule lattice act as "transition rules" for simulated microtubule automata exhibiting information processing, transmission and learning (Figure 15).

Classical microtubule automata switching in the nanosecond scale offer a potentially huge increase in the brain's computational capacity. Conventional approaches focus on synaptic switching (roughly 10^{11} brain neurons, 10^3

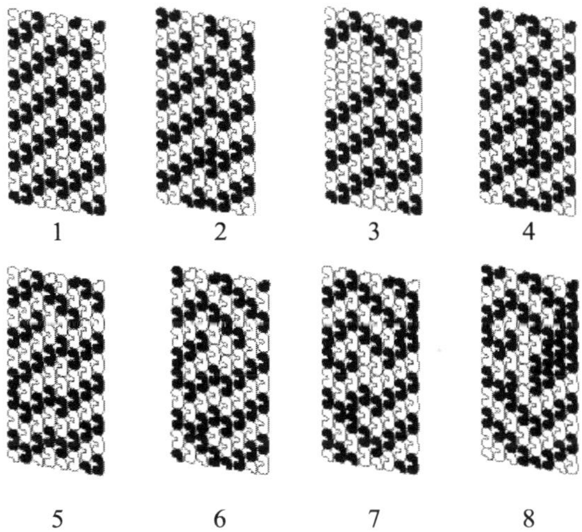

Figure 15. *Microtubule automaton simulation (from Rasmussen et al. 1990). Black and white tubulins correspond to black and white states shown in Figures 1a and 3. Eight nanosecond time steps of a segment of one microtubule are shown in "classical computing" mode in which conformational states of tubulins are determined by dipole-dipole coupling between each tubulin and its six (asymmetrical) lattice neighbors calculated by* $f_{net} = (e^2/4\pi\varepsilon)\Sigma_{i=1}^{6}\ y_i/r_i^3$ *where* y_i *and* r_i *are inter-tubulin distances, e is the electron charge, and* ε *is the average protein permittivity. Conformational states form patterns which move, evolve, interact and lead to emergence of new patterns.*

synapses/neuron, switching in the millisecond range of 10^3 operations per second) and predict about 10^{17} bit states per second for a human brain (e.g. Moravec 1985). However as biological cells typically each contain approximately 10^7 tubulins (Yu & Bass 1994), nanosecond switching in microtubule automata predicts roughly 10^{16} operations per second, per neuron. This capacity could account for the adaptive behaviors of single cell organisms like paramecium, for example, who elegantly swim, avoid obstacles, and find food and mates without benefit of a nervous system or synapses. As the human brain contains about 10^{11} neurons, nanosecond microtubule automata offer about 10^{27} brain operations per second.

However even a vast increase in computational complexity won't by itself address the difficult issues related to consciousness. Quantum coherent, or entangled states and quantum computation with objective reduction (Orch OR) could possibly do so.

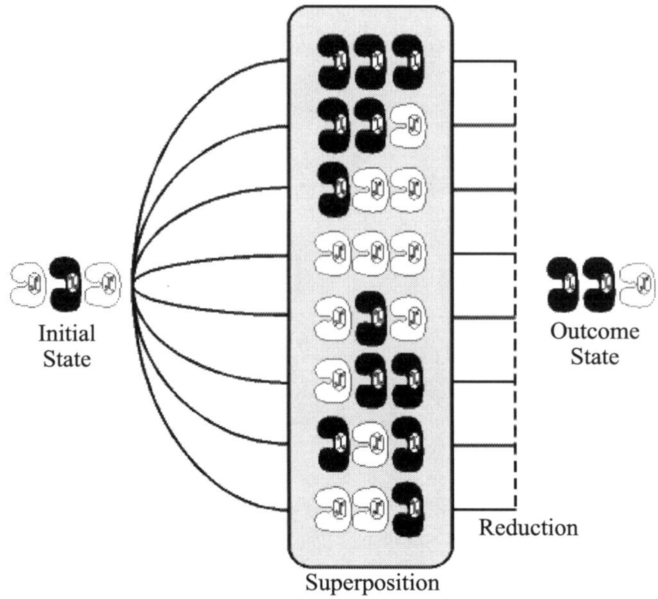

Figure 16. *Schematic of quantum computation of three tubulins which begin (left) in initial classical states, then enter isolated quantum superposition in which all possible states coexist. After reduction, one particular classical outcome state is chosen (right).*

4.3 *Quantum computation in microtubules—The Penrose-Hameroff Orch OR model*

Full rationale and details of the Orch OR model are given in Penrose and Hameroff (1995) and Hameroff and Penrose (1996a, 1996b). Key points are listed here:

1. Conformational states of individual tubulin proteins in brain microtubules are sensitive to internal quantum events (e.g. London forces in hydrophobic pockets) and able to cooperatively interact with other tubulins in both classical and quantum computation (Figures 16–18). Classical phase computation (microtubule automata) regulates chemical synapses and other neural membrane activities.
2. Quantum coherent superposition supporting quantum computation emerges among London forces in hydrophobic pockets of microtubule subunit tubulins (e.g. in a manner described by Fröhlich 1968, 1975). In this phase, quantum computation among tubulins evolves linearly according to the Schrodinger equation (quantum microtubule automata). Actin gelation and a condensed charge phase surrounds, isolates and insulates microtubules during the quantum phase (Figure 18).

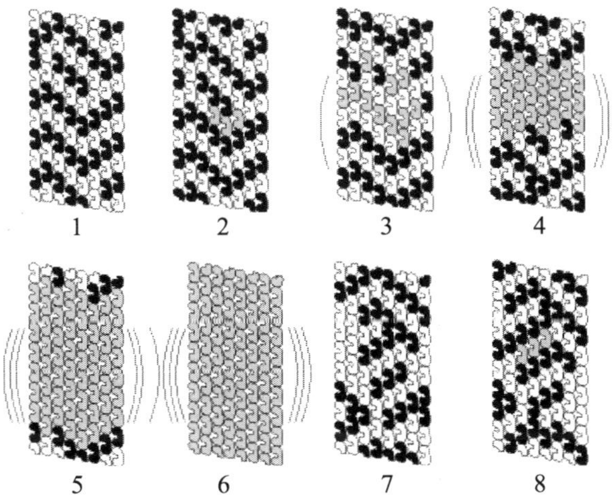

Figure 17. *Microtubule automata entering quantum superposition/computation mode (gray) and meeting objective reduction threshold (between steps 6 and 7) for self-collapse to non-computably chosen outcome states. The self-collapse is an Orch OR conscious moment.*

3. The proposed quantum superposition/computation phase in neural microtubules corresponds to pre-conscious (implicit) processing, which continues until the threshold for Penrose's objective reduction is reached. Objective reduction (OR) — a discrete event then occurs, and post-OR tubulin states (chosen non-computably) proceed by classical microtubule automata to regulate synapses and other neural membrane activities (Figure 19). The events are proposed to be conscious (to have qualia, experience) for reasons that relate to a merger of modern physics and philosophical pan-experientialism. A sequence of such events gives rise to a stream of consciousness (Figure 20).

4. Microtubule quantum states link to those in other neurons and glia by tunneling through gap junctions (or quantum coherent photons traversing membranes — Jibu & Yasue 1995; Jibu et al. 1994, 1996). This spread enables macroscopic quantum states in networks of gap junction-connected cells (neurons and glia) throughout large brain volumes (Figure 4).

5. Probabilities and possibilities for pre-conscious quantum superpositions are influenced by biological feedback including attachments of microtubule-associated proteins ("MAPs"), which tune and "orchestrate" quantum oscillations (Figure 4). We thus term the self-tuning OR process in microtubules "orchestrated" objective reduction Orch OR.

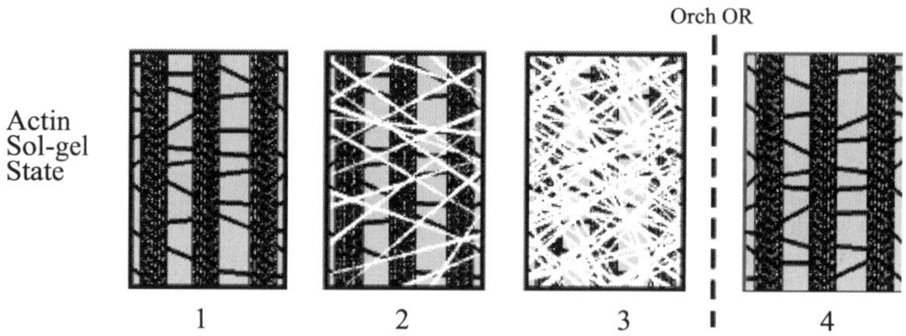

Figure 18. *Schematic sequence of phases of actin gelation/quantum isolation (1–3) alternating with phases of solution/environmental communication (4) surrounding microtubules. Cycles may occur rapidly, e.g. 25 msec intervals (40 Hz).*

6. Orch OR events may be of variable intensity and duration of pre-conscious processing. Calculating from $E = \hbar/T$, for a pre-conscious processing time of e.g. $T = 25$ msec (thalamo-cortical 40 Hz), E is roughly the superposition/separation of 2×10^{10} tubulins. For $T = 100$ msec (alpha EEG) E would involve 5×10^9 tubulins. For $T = 500$ msec (e.g. shown by Libet et al. 1979, as a typical pre-conscious processing time for low intensity stimuli), E is equivalent to 10^9 tubulins. Thus 2×10^{10} tubulins maintained in isolated quantum coherent superposition for 25 msec (or 5×10^9 tubulins for 100 msec, or 10^9 tubulins for 500 msec, etc.) will self-collapse (Orch OR) and elicit a conscious event.

7. Each brain neuron is estimated to contain about 10^7 tubulins (Yu & Bass 1994). If, say, 10 percent of each neuron's tubulins became coherent, then Orch OR of tubulins within roughly 20,000 (gap-junction connected) neurons would be required for a 25 msec conscious event, 5,000 neurons for a 100 msec event, or 1,000 neurons for a 500 msec event, etc.

8. Each instantaneous Orch OR event binds superposed information encoded in microtubules whose net displacement reaches threshold at a particular moment: a variety of different modes of information is thus bound into a "now" event. As quantum state reductions are irreversible in time, cascades of Orch OR events present a forward flow of time and "stream of consciousness". As events in fundamental spacetime geometry, Orch OR events access and select particular configurations of qualia.

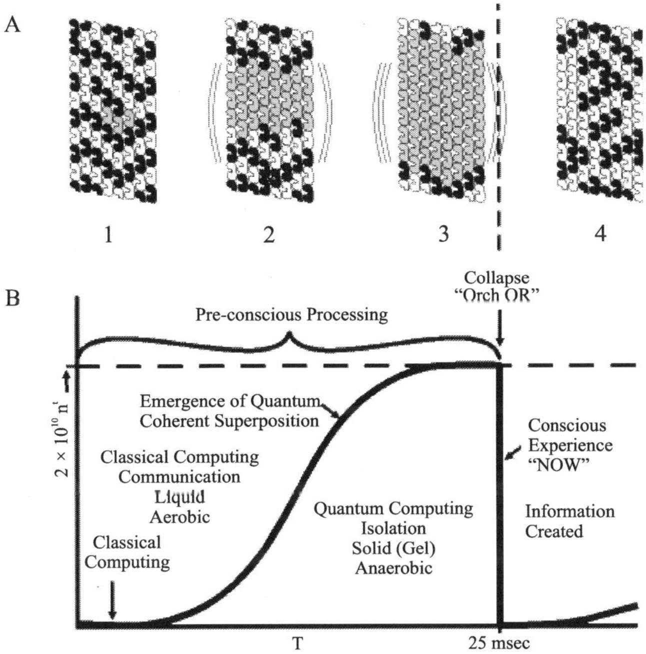

Figure 19. *An Orch OR event.*
(a) Microtubule simulation in which classical computing (step 1) leads to emergence of quantum coherent superposition (and quantum computing (steps 2–3) in certain (gray) tubulins. Step 3 (in coherence with other microtubule tublins) meets critical threshold related to quantum gravity for self-collapse (Orch OR). A conscious event (Orch OR) occurs in the step 3 to 4 transition (equivalent to the 6 to 7 transition in Figure 17). Tubulin states in step 4 are non-computably chosen in the collapse, and evolve by classical computing to regulate neural function.
(b) Schematic graph of proposed quantum coherence (number of tubulins) emerging versus time in microtubules. Area under curve connects superposed mass energy E with collapse time T in accordance with $E = \hbar/T$. E may be expressed as N_t, the number of tubulins whose mass separation (and separation of underlying space time) for time T will self-collapse. For $T = 25$ msec (e.g. 40 Hz oscillations), $N_t = 2 \times 10^{10}$ tubulins.

4.4 *Orch OR and enigmatic features of consciousness*

Six enigmatic features of consciousness were described in Section I: (1) the nature of subjective experience, (2) “binding” in vision and sense of “self”, (3) transition from pre-conscious processing to consciousness, (4) non-computability and (5) free will, (6) subjective time flow/time anomalies. Can Orch OR address these issues?

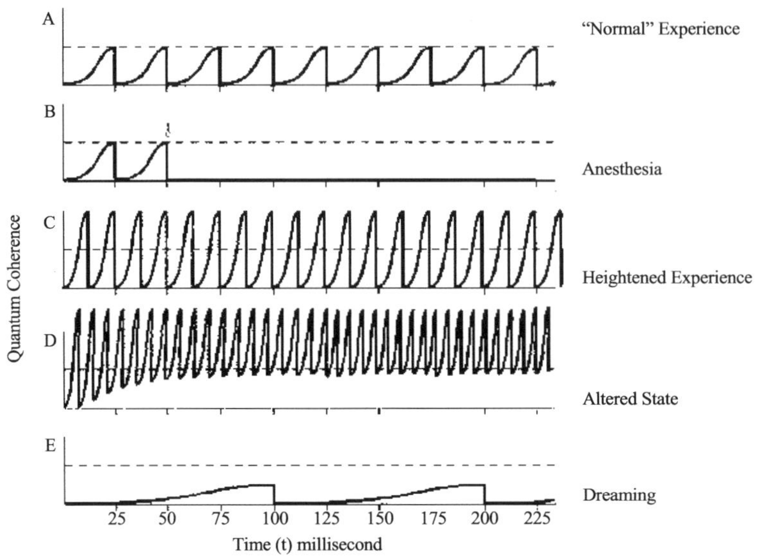

Figure 20. *Quantum superposition/entanglement in microtubules for 5 states related to consciousness. Area under each curve equivalent in all cases. A. Normal 40 Hz experience: as in Figure 19. B. Anesthesia: anesthetics bind in hydrophobic pockets and prevent quantum delocalizability and coherent superposition. C. Heightened Experience: increased sensory experience input (for example) increases rate of emergence of quantum superposition. Orch OR threshold is reached faster, and Orch OR frequency increases. D. Altered State: even greater rate of emergence of quantum superposition due to sensory input and other factors promoting quantum state (e.g. meditation, psychedelic drug etc.). Predisposition to quantum state results in baseline shift and collapse so that conscious experience merges with normally sub-conscious quantum computing mode. E. Dreaming: prolonged sub-threshold quantum superposition time.*

As described earlier, Feature (1) subjective experience is the most difficult, but is approachable through a pan-protopsychist philosophy in which qualia (and Platonic values) are embedded at the fundamental level of spacetime geometry. Being a reconfiguration of fundamental spacetime geometry, OR (and Orch OR) is a process which can access and select particular configurations of experience.

The second difficult issue related to consciousness is (2) binding and is potentially resolved by the unitary nature of quantum states (e.g. Penrose 1987). Marshall (1989) suggested that binding was a feature of Bose-Einstein condensates among certain of the brain's neural proteins. In the Orch OR model, an

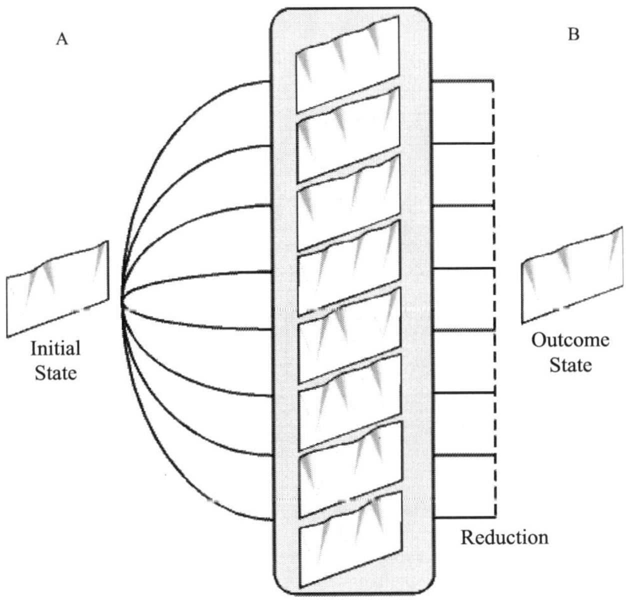

Figure 21. *Schematic quantum computation in spacetime curvature for three mass distributions (e.g. tubulin conformations in Figure 16) which begin (A) in initial classical states, then enter isolated quantum superposition in which all possible states coexist. After reduction, one particular classical outcome state is chosen (B). If proto-conscious qualia exist in fundamental spacetime geometry, such a process would be accessing and selecting particular qualia.*

instantaneous event binds superposed information whose net mass/spacetime displacement reaches threshold at a particular moment: different modes and time scales of information are bound into a unitary "now" event.

Feature (3) is the transition from pre-conscious processing to consciousness itself. In Orch OR pre-conscious processing is equivalent to the quantum superposition phase of quantum computation. Potential possibilities interact and then abruptly self-collapse, a slight quake in spacetime geometry. As quantum state reductions are irreversible, cascades of Orch OR events present a forward flow of subjective time and "stream of consciousness". As intervals between reductions are "atemporal", the "backwards time referral" suggested by Libet (1979) and binding of temporally asynchronous visual percepts (Zeki & Bartels 1998; Zeki & Moutassis 1997) may be explained.

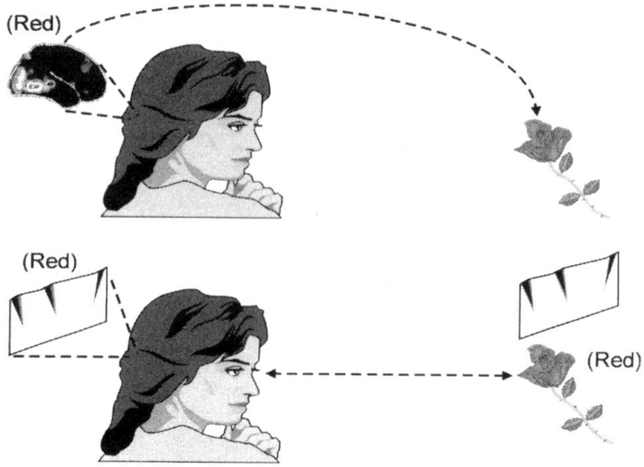

Figure 22. *Is the redness of a rose a pattern of neural activity, or a pattern expressed in fundamental spacetime geometry?*

Quantum computation with objective reduction is potentially applicable to cognitive activities. Functions like face recognition and volitional choice may require a series of conscious events arriving at intermediate solutions. For the purpose of illustration consider single Orch OR events in these two types of cognitive activities.

Imagine you briefly see a familiar woman's face. Is she Amy, Betty, or Carol? Possibilities may superpose in a quantum computation. For example during 25 milliseconds of pre-conscious processing, quantum computation occurs with information (Amy, Betty, Carol) in the form of "qubits" — superposed states of microtubule tubulin subunits within groups of neurons. As threshold for objective reduction is reached, an instantaneous conscious event occurs. The superposed tubulin qubits reduce to definite states, becoming bits. Now, you recognize that she is Carol! (an immense number of possibilities could be superposed in a human brain's 10^{19} tubulins).

In a volitional act possible choices may be superposed. Suppose for example you are selecting dinner from a menu. During pre-conscious processing, shrimp, sushi and pasta are superposed in a quantum computation. As threshold for objective reduction is reached, the quantum state reduces to a single classical state. A choice is made. You'll have sushi (Figure 23)!

How does the choice actually occur? Can the selection criteria be described by a deterministic algorithm? These questions relate to features (4) non-computability and (5) free will.

The problem in understanding free will is that our actions seem neither totally deterministic nor random (probabilistic). What else is there in nature? As previously described, in OR (and Orch OR) the reduction outcomes are neither deterministic nor probabilistic, but “non-computable”. The microtubule quantum superposition evolves linearly (analogous to a quantum computer) but is influenced at the instant of collapse by hidden non-local variables (quantum-mathematical logic inherent in fundamental spacetime geometry?). The possible outcomes are limited, or probabilities set (“orchestrated”), by neurobiological feedback (in particular microtubule associated proteins-MAPs, Figure 4). The precise outcome — our free will actions — are chosen by effects of the hidden logic on the quantum system poised at the edge of objective reduction.

Consider a sailboat analogy for free will. A sailor sets the sail in a certain way; the direction the boat sails is determined by the action of the wind on the sail. Let’s pretend the sailor is a non-conscious robot zombie run by a quantum computer which is trained and programmed to sail. Setting and adjusting of the sail, sensing the wind and position and so forth are algorithmic and deterministic, and may be analogous to the pre-conscious, quantum computing phase of Orch OR. The direction and intensity of the wind (seemingly capricious, or unpredictable) may be analogous to Planck scale hidden non-local variables (e.g. non-computable “Platonic” quantum-mathematical logic inherent in space–time geometry). The choice, or outcome (the direction the boat sails, the point on shore it lands) depends on the deterministic sail settings acted on repeatedly by the apparently unpredictable wind. Our “free will” actions could be the net result of deterministic processes acted on by hidden quantum logic at each Orch OR event. This can explain why we generally do things in an orderly, deterministic fashion, but occasionally our actions or thoughts are surprising, even to ourselves.

In summary, in relation to consciousness Orch OR and other quantum models have enormous explanatory power.

4.5 *Are microtubules quantum computers?*

What similarities may be found between microtubules and technological proposals for quantum computation. A “potentially realizable” quantum computer has been described by Lloyd (1993) as “... arrays of weakly coupled quantum systems. Computation is effected by ... a sequence of electromagnetic pulses that induce transitions between locally defined quantum states ... in a crystal lattice.”

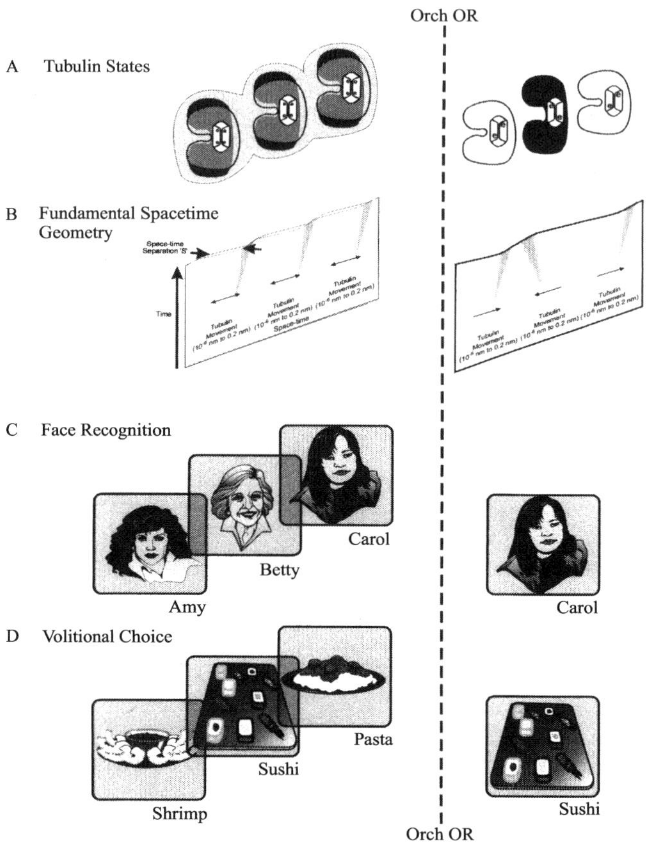

Figure 23. *An Orch OR event (a) (left) Three tubulins in quantum superposition prior to 25 msec Orch OR After reduction (right), particular classical states are selected. (b) Fundamental spacetime geometry view. Prior to Orch OR (left), spacetime corresponding with three superposed tubulins is separated as Planck scale bubbles: curvatures in opposite directions. The Planck-scale spacetime separations S are very tiny in ordinary terms, but relatively large mass movements (e.g., hundreds of tubulin conformations, each moving from* 10^{-16} *to 0.2 nm) indeed have precisely such very tiny effects on the space-time curvature. A critical degree of separation causes Orch OR and an abrupt selection of single curvatures (and a particular geometry of experience). (c) Cognitive facial recognition. A familiar face induces superposition (left) of three possible solutions (Amy, Betty, Carol) which "collapse" to the correct answer Carol (right). (d) Cognitive volition. Three possible dinner selections (shrimp, sushi, pasta) are considered in superposition (left), and collapse via Orch OR to choice of sushi (right).*

In the Orch OR model, the microtubule assembly corresponds to Lloyd's crystal lattice. Rather than trapped ions or nuclear spins, quantum superposition is proposed to occur at the level of conformational states of tubulins, and the role of pulsed transitions played by coherent Fröhlich excitations.

The Orch OR proposal may be compared to technological schemes in terms of a "Figure of Merit M" (Table 3; Barenco 1996; DiVincenzo 1995). M is the time $T_{decohere}$ until decoherence divided by the time t_{elem} of each elementary operation, and gives the number of operations allowable per computational unit before decoherence. With t_{elem} of 10^{-9} secs (Fröhlich frequency) and $T_{decohere}$ of e.g. 100 msec (EEG alpha), the Orch OR model yields a respectable M of 10^8 operations per tubulin before a conscious event occurs.
According to the proposals put forth in the Orch OR model, microtubules seem to be well designed (perhaps ideally designed) quantum computers. If so, technological efforts can possibly mimic some of nature's design principles such as cylindrical lattice automata and alternating phases of isolation and communication. The massive parallelism and specific microtubule lattice geometry (e.g. helical patterns following the Fibonacci series) may also facilitate quantum error correction. However technology will be hard-pressed to emulate objective reduction which, it is argued, is required for consciousness. Presently envisioned technological quantum computers will implement superposition of ions, electrons, nuclei or other small entities. To achieve objective reduction in a reasonable and useful time scale, a fairly large superposed mass (i.e. nanograms) will be required. While such a task seems formidable, it is possible. Quantum computation with objective reduction may hold the only promise for future conscious computers.

4.6 *Quantum skeptics*

A number of skeptics have published papers criticizing the biological feasibility of quantum mechanisms in consciousness. Here three skeptical reviews are presented with my rebuttal.

4.6.1 *Max Tegmark*

In an attempt to refute quantum models of consciousness, physicist Max Tegmark at the University of Pennsylvania has attempted to refute the quantum microtubule approach (Tegmark 2000; cf. Seife 2000) Tegmark's main point may be summarized:

> The make or break issue for all these quantum models is whether the relevant degrees of freedom of the brain can be sufficiently isolated to retain their quantum coherence, and opinions are divided. For instance Stapp has argued

Table 2. *Figure of Merit M for different proposed quantum computing technologies and microtubules. (Modified from Barenco 1996 and from DiVincenzo 1995)*

Technology	t_{elem} (seconds)	$T_{decohere}$ (in seconds)	M (pre-decoherence (operations/qubit)
Mossbauer nucleus	10^{-19}	10^{-10}	10^{9}
Electrons GaAs	10^{-13}	10^{-10}	10^{3}
Electrons Au	10^{-14}	10^{-8}	10^{6}
Trapped ions	10^{-14}	10^{-1}	10^{13}
Optical cavities	10^{-14}	10^{-5}	10^{9}
Electron spin	10^{-7}	10^{-3}	10^{4}
Electron quantum dot	10^{-6}	10^{-3}	10^{3}
Nuclear spin	10^{-3}	10^{4}	10^{7}
Superconductor islands	10^{-9}	10^{3}	10^{6}
Microtubule tubulins	10^{-9}	10^{-1}	10^{8}

> that interaction with the environment is probably small enough to be unimportant for neural processes whereas Hawking and Scott have conjectured that environment-induced coherence will rapidly destroy macrosuperpositions in the brain. It is therefore timely to try and settle the issue with detailed calculations of the relevant decoherence rates. This is the purpose of the present work.

But what are the relevant degrees of freedom and decoherence rates, and how are the decoherence rates calculated (see Hagan et al. 2000, 2001)? Tegmark gives two treatments of quantum proposals: (1) superpositions of neurons firing and not firing, (2) superpositions of the location of a soliton on a microtubule. He calculates decoherence times due to interaction with environmental ions as 10^{-20} sec for superpositions of neurons firing/not firing, and 10^{-13} seconds for superpositions of solitons on microtubules.

I agree with his assessment that superpositions of neurons firing and not firing is unlikely. However regarding microtubules, Tegmark considers a model of classical kinks/solitons traveling along microtubules published by Sataric et al (1992; based on our classical microtubule automaton model). Though he targets Penrose, Tegmark ignores the specifics of the Penrose-Hameroff Orch OR proposal. Incorrectly attributing the idea to Penrose, Tegmark considers a kink/soliton in superposition of two different locations along the microtubule and then calculates interactions between the soliton displacement and calcium ions associated with the microtubule. So the degrees of freedom he is using in "refuting Penrose" are from a quantum model he himself has invented! Interestingly, Tegmark ignores interactions between proposed quantum states and surrounding water, taking the suggestion that surrounding water is "ordered" (though he attributes this notion to Mavromatos and Nanopoulos 1998 who got the idea from Penrose-Hameroff). As far as ions inducing decoherence, this is a bit puzzling if Tegmark is assuming the water is ordered. Because if the water is ordered then the ions in the water (depending on their size relative to water) are also ordered. Ions whose radius is smaller than the H_20 radius (1.38 Ångstrom) do not disturb the ordering (Ergin 1983; Uedaira and Osaka 1989; Jibu et al. 1995). Sodium ions (radius 0.98 Ångstrom), calcium ions (1.0 Ångstrom) and magnesium ions (0.72 Ångstrom) can all embed in ordered water without disturbance. Ions whose radius is close to that of water (e.g. potassium 1.38 Ångstroms) can replace water molecules without disturbance, whereas larger ions will disturb ordering. Chloride (1.81 Ångstrom) is in the latter category and should disrupt water ordering. Chloride intra-cellular concentration is extremely low except for terminal phase of an action potential.

In any case Tegmark calculates a decoherence time for his superpositioned kink/solitons of 10^{-13} seconds based on an equation with the following characteristics (eqs 19 and 22 in his paper). The decoherence lifetime is related to an expression which has in it's numerator (square root of) temperature. Thus according to Tegmark as temperature increases the decoherence lifetime lengthens and as the temperature decreases the decoherence lifetime diminishes toward zero. This is precisely the opposite of what is commonly observed! Therefore Tegmark's whole approach and calculations are highly suspect.

The denominator in Tegmark's equation includes the separation distance between superpositioned kink/solitons which he takes to be several tubulin lengths, or roughly 24 nanometers. However in the Orch OR model the separation of tubulin proteins from themselves only requires the diameter of one atomic nucleus, or fermi length ($\sim 10^{-6}$ nanometers). Thus using Tegmark's (flawed) calculation with the proper superposition separation stipulated in the Orch OR model lengthens the decoherence lifetime by a factor of 2×10^7.

Furthermore, Tegmark ignores the shielding/isolation mechanisms proposed in the Orch OR model (see Section 3). But the critical issue is the decoherence time compared to the relevant timescale for either the quantum objects (microtubules) or the ionic environment. While the Orch OR model has aimed for avoidance of decoherence long enough for electrophysiological events (e.g. 25 msec for 40 Hz, 100 msec for alpha EEG, 500 msec for Libet's sensory threshold) the decoherence time need not necessarily be that long. By correcting Tegmark's calculated decoherence time by 2×10^7 due to the superposition separation factor described above, his decoherence time becomes (rather than 10^{-13} seconds) 2×10^{-6} seconds, ignoring shielding/isolation which would further lengthen the time. This is already longer than Tegmark's estimate for his kink-like soliton traversing the a microtubule at 5×10^{-7} sec, and longer than the dynamical timescale of the environment assuming a Frohlich-type mechanism (10^{-9} to 10^{-11} sec). In the latter case the ionic environment would be "refreshed", or re-cohere before decoherence of the microtubule quantum state would occur. And (as suggested in a personal communication from physicist Paola Zizzi) Orch OR events may be faster than electrophysiological events (e.g. 10^{-6} sec) with sequences of many such events leading to electrophysiological activities in the millisecond range or longer. For a complete critique of Tegmark's attack, see Hagan et al. (2000, 2001).

4.6.2 *Jack Tuszynski and colleagues*

A special issue of the Philosophical Transactions of the Royal Society is devoted to quantum computation. It includes a pair of articles about the possibility of quantum computation in microtubules — one positive (by me), and one skeptical by Jack Tuszynski et al. Here are Jack's criticisms (*in italics*) followed by my responses.

Gravitational effects should be entirely overshadowed by the remaining processes

The energy from an Orch OR event is indeed very small compared to thermal noise (kT) and would seemingly drown in an aqueous medium. Isolation/insulation mechanisms are thus required to shield microtubules from thermal noise or any type of environmental decoherence. The Orch OR model suggests that quantum coherent superposition occurs in microtubules which are immediately surrounded by an insulating charge condensation and encased (cyclically) in actin gelation. Cyclical isolation allows for alternating phases of communication (input/output) and isolated quantum computation.

In addition to isolation, microtubule subunits (tubulins) must also be sensitive to quantum influences from other superposed tubulins and non-computable influences in Planck scale geometry. In questioning the robustness of proposed quantum effects, Tuszynski et al. ascribe the gravitational energy for a tubulin protein in Orch OR to be the attraction between two masses given by the standard Gm^2/r, where G is the gravitational constant, m is the mass of tubulin, and r is the distance between the two masses which Tuszynski and Brown take to be the radius of tubulin. This would accurately describe the gravitational attraction between two adjacent tubulins (or tubulin monomers), and yields an appropriately small energy of 10^{-27} eV. However the relevant energy in Orch OR is the gravitational self-energy E of a superposed mass m separated from itself by distance a, given (for complete separation) by $E = Gm^2/a$. In Hameroff and Penrose (1996) we calculated this energy for three cases: 1) partial separation of the entire protein by one tenth its radius, and 2) complete separation at the level of each protein's atomic nuclei (a = 2.5 fermi lengths), and 3) complete separation at the level of each protein's nucleons (a = 0.5 fermi). Of these, highest energies were for separation at the level of atomic nuclei, roughly 10^{-21} eV per tubulin (although separation at the level of, say, atoms or amino acids may yield higher energy). As roughly 2×10^{10} tubulins are involved in each proposed Orch OR event (e.g. for superpositions lasting 25 msec) the energy is on the order of roughly 10^{-10} eV, or 10^{-28} joules, still extremely tiny (kT is about 10^{-4} eV). However the 10^{-28} joule energy emerges abruptly, e.g. within one Planck time of 10^{-43} seconds. So the power is quite high. This may be equivalent to an instantaneous karate chop of 10^{13} watts (joules/sec), roughly 1 kilowatt per tubulin per conscious event.

The size of the tubulin protein is probably too large to make quantum effects easily sustainable
Nanometer size proteins such as tubulin (8 nm × 4 nm × 4 nm) may be optimal scale for a quantum/macroscopic interface (Watterson 1991; Conrad 1994). Smaller biomolecules lack causal efficacy of structural protein conformational changes responsible for a host of biological functions. Larger molecules would be insufficiently sensitive to quantum effects.

Conformational effects are expected to involve distances of 10 angstroms (1 nanometer), larger than those called for in the Orch OR model
The superposition separation distance (e.g. 1 atomic nucleus, 10^{-6} nanometer in the case cited) is indeed much smaller than conformational changes which may approach 1 nanometer. As described earlier proteins are relatively unstable and their conformation regulated through nonlinear "quakes" mediated through quantum-level London forces. That is, superpositioned states (separation 2.5 fermi) each lead to a specific conformation (~1 nanometer difference).

Physiological temperature requirements make it extremely difficult to defend the use of the quantum regime due to the persistence of thermal noise
A biological quantum state must be isolated/insulated from thermal noise, or funnel it into coherence, features nature may have evolved in cytoplasmic actin gelation and condensed charged layers. Some evidence supports biological quantum states (e.g. Tejada et al. 1996; Walleczek 1995). According to the Fröhlich mechanism, thermal energy in biological systems may condense to a coherent mode.

... microtubules are extremely sensitive to their environment ... we doubt that microtubules can be shielded

As described earlier, nature may have solved the problem of both isolation and communication by alternating cytoplasmic phases of solution ("sol", liquid, sensitive to environment, classical) and gelation ("gel", solid, shielded/insulated, quantum). Thus microtubules can be both sensitive to their environment ("sol" phase) and isolated/shielded ("gel" phase).

... two (or possibly more) conformational states of tubulin are separated by a sizable potential barrier which again requires an external stimulus (such as GTP hydrolysis) to overcome it.
Tubulin has numerous possible conformations which can interchange without GTP hydrolysis. The two state tubulin model is a simplification. The structure of tubulin has recently been clarified (Nogales et al. 1998) so molecular simulations will soon be available.

... the 500 msec preconscious processing time may be directly related to the action potential travel time along the axon plus the refractory lag time in synaptic transmission rather than to the quantum collapse time.
In the Orch OR model the "quantum collapse time" T is chosen to match known neurophysiological time intervals related to pre-conscious processes; the gravitational self-energy E and related mass may then be calculated. For example we have used 25 msec (e.g. in coherent 40 Hz oscillations), 100 msec (e.g. EEG alpha rhythm), and 500 msec (e.g. Libet's pre-conscious threshold for low intensity sensory stimuli). If quantum superposition correlates with pre-conscious processing, then dendritic activities (more than axonal firings) are likely to be relevant to consciousness (e.g. Pribram 1991). Microtubules in dendrites are of mixed polarity (unlike those in axons), an arrangement conducive to cooperative computation.

Tuszynski and Brown raise valid objections; quantum states in a biological milieu appear at first glance to be unlikely. However nature may have evolved specific conditions for isolation, thermal screening and amplification. Life itself may be a macroscopic quantum state.

4.6.3 *Alwyn Scott*

In an article in the *Journal of Consciousness Studies*, Alwyn Scott makes the following points (italics):

Brain activities relevant to consciousness are nonlinear, and quantum theory is linear (implying classical nonlinear dynamics is more fertile ground).
While the Schrödinger equation and the evolution of the quantum wave function may be linear, the collapse of the wave function — particularly in the Penrose 'objective reduction' formulation — is decidedly nonlinear.

The Born-Oppenheimer approximation indicates that quantum effects are insignificant in molecular dynamics.
The Born-Oppenheimer approximation concerns the relative influences of an atomic nucleus and its surrounding electrons, and treats them something like the earth and a soccer ball, respectively. That is, the nucleus may be considered stationary, able to influence the electron whereas the electron moves but is unable to influence the nucleus. Michael Conrad (1994) points out that although the mass of nucleus is far greater than that of the electrons, net charge is equal. Electrons which delocalize — that is travel among resonance orbitals of several atoms such as an aromatic ring in a hydrophobic amino acid such as tryptophan — can indeed influence nuclei, and hence protein conformation.

Due to the mass of tubulin, quantum delocalization would only extend a fraction of an atomic diameter.
In Orch OR we claim superposition-separation of each tubulin by one atomic nucleus radius, roughly 1/4000 of an atomic diameter. So a fraction of an atomic diameter is more than adequate.

Hodgkin-Huxley equations. Scott describes how the purely classical H-H equations accurately describe the nonlinear propagation of an action potential along an axon without need to resort to quantum effects.
No problem. Axonal action potentials (as opposed to dendritic and cytoskeletal processes) may not be directly involved in consciousness. There are many brain activities which are classical and have nothing to do with consciousness.

"Schrodinger's cat" illustrate the inappropriateness of applying quantum effects to biology.
We know the story — a cat is in a box which has a poison vial. A microscopic quantum event, e.g. passage of a photon through a half silvered mirror is coupled to the poison. According to (the Copenhagen interpretation of) quantum theory, the photon both passes through, and does not pass through the mirror (and both triggers and doesn't trigger the poison). Therefore until the box is opened and consciously observed the cat is both dead and alive.

Despite the ridiculousness of the scenario, the answer is still somewhat puzzling. Scott offers his objections, one of which I'll comment upon. He states that "a conservative estimate suggests that a time very much longer than the age of the universe would be required for the cat's wave function to rotate from being dead to being alive. For all practical purposes this implies that a quantum mechanical cat would be either dead or alive".

On the contrary, in Penrose objective reduction an isolated superposition will self-collapse by $E=\hbar/T$, where T is the time until collapse, $\hbar$ is Planck's constant over 2π, and E is the degree of superposition. Small masses in superposition will self-collapse only after a very long time (for an an isolated superposed electron, 10 million years). An isolated superposed cat of roughly 1 kilogram would self-collapse in 10^{-37} seconds. For all practical purposes this implies that a quantum mechanical cat would be either dead or alive.

5. Conclusion

Conventional approaches to the problem of consciousness fail to (1) address the difficult issues, (2) accurately represent details of brain activity, (3) generate testable predictions. As quantum computers become technological reality, comparisons between brain, mind and quantum computer will be inevitable. Quantum approaches (e.g. the Penrose-Hameroff Orch OR model) along the lines of quantum computation offer a great deal of explanatory power for consciousness. At first glance the feasibility of macroscopic quantum brain states seems unlikely, however closer examination suggests the brain has evolved specific mechanisms to isolate and support macroscopic quantum states, and avoid decoherence.

The Orch OR model connects quantum computation in brain microtubules with rearrangements of fundamental spacetime geometry in which (according to certain philosophical principles) proto-conscious qualia may be embedded. Orch OR is thus potentially able to explain the problem of conscious experience, as well as other enigmatic features of consciousness.

The proposals described in Orch OR and other models are testable, if not presently then in the foreseeable future. Attempts to dismiss quantum proposals out-of-hand or by incorrect assumptions should be resisted. Time will tell.

Testable predictions of Orch OR are found in Appendix 1.

Acknowledgments

Thanks to Roger Penrose for collaboration, Dave Cantrell for illustrations, Carol Ebbecke and Patti Bergin for expert assistance, and Denise Hameroff for inspiration. Support from the Fetzer Institute and Starlab are greatly appreciated.

Appendix 1. Testable predictions of the Orch OR model

Here major assumptions (italics) and corresponding testable predictions (numbered) of the Orch OR model are listed:

Neuronal microtubules are directly necessary for consciousness

1. Synaptic sensitivity and plasticity correlate with cytoskeletal architecture/activities in both pre-synaptic and post-synaptic neuronal cytoplasm.
2. Actions of psychoactive drugs including antidepressants involve neuronal microtubules.
3. Neuronal microtubule-stabilizing/protecting drugs may prove useful in Alzheimer's disease, ischemia, and other conditions.

Microtubules communicate by cooperative dynamics of tubulin subunits

4. Laser spectroscopy (e.g. Vos et al. 1993) will demonstrate coherent gigaHz Fröhlich excitations in microtubules.
5. Dynamic vibrational states in microtubule networks correlate with cellular activity.
6. Stable patterns of microtubule-cytoskeletal networks (including neurofilaments) and intra-microtubule diversity of tubulin states correlate with memory and neural behavior.
7. Cortical dendrites contain largely "A-lattice" microtubules (compared to "B-lattice" microtubule, A-lattice microtubules are preferable for information processing (Tuszynski et al. 1995).

Quantum coherence occurs in microtubules

8. Studies similar to the famous "Aspect experiment" in physics (which verified non-local quantum correlations — Aspect et al. 1982) will demonstrate quantum correlations between spatially separated microtubule subunit states a) on the same microtubule, b) on different microtubules in the same neuron, c) on microtubules in different neurons connected by gap junctions.
9. Experiments with SQUIDs (Superconducting Quantum Interference Device) such as those suggested by Leggett (1984) will detect phases of quantum coherence in microtubules.
10. Coherent photons will be detected from microtubules.
11. Brain regions involved in conscious processes will be more transparent to applied photons than non-conscious regions.

Microtubule quantum coherence requires isolation by cycles of surrounding actin-gelation

12. Neuronal microtubules in cortical dendrites and other brain areas are intermittently surrounded by tightly cross-linked actin gels.
13. Cycles of gelation and dissolution in neuronal cytoplasm occur concomitantly with membrane electrical activity (e.g. synchronized 40 Hz activities in dendrites).
14. The sol-gel cycles surrounding microtubules are regulated by calcium ions released and reabsorbed by calmodulin associated with microtubules.

Macroscopic quantum coherence occurs among MT in hundreds/thousands of distributed neurons and glia linked by gap junctions

15. Electrotonic gap junctions link synchronously firing networks of cortical neurons, and thalamo-cortical networks

16. Quantum tunneling occurs across gap junctions.

18. Quantum correlation occurs between microtubule subunit states in different neurons connected by gap junctions (the microtubule "Aspect experiment" in different neurons)

The amount of neural tissue involved in a conscious event is inversely proportional to the event time by $E = \hbar/T$

19. The amount of neural mass involved in a particular cognitive task or conscious event (as measurable by near-future advances in brain imaging techniques) is inversely proportional to the preconscious time (e.g. visual perception, reaction times).

An isolated, unperturbed quantum system self-collapses according to $E = \hbar/T$.

20. Isolated technological quantum superpositions will self-collapse according to $E = \hbar/T$. (Experiments involving superposition of crystals have begun in Anton Zeilinger's lab in Vienna.)

Microtubule-based cilia/centriole structures are quantum optical devices

21. Microtubule-based cilia in rods and cones directly detect visual photons and connect with retinal glial cell microtubule via gap junctions.

A critical degree of cytoskeletal assembly (coinciding with the onset of rudimentary consciousness) had significant impact on the rate of evolution

22. Fossil records and comparison with present-day biology will show that organisms which emerged during the early Cambrian period with onset roughly 540 million years ago had critical degrees of microtubule-cytoskeletal size, complexity and capability for quantum isolation (e.g. tight actin gels, gap junctions; see Hameroff 1998b).

References

Andreu, J. M. (1986) Hydrophobic interaction of tubulin. Ann. *NY Acad. Sci.* 466: 626–630.

Arieli, A., Sterkin, A., Grinvald, A., Aertsen, A. (1996) Dynamics of ongoing activity: Explanation of the large variability in evoked cortical responses. *Science* 273: 1868–1874.

Aspect, A., Grangier, P., and Roger, G. (1982) Experimental realization of Einstein-Podolsky-Rosen-Bohm Gedankenexperiment: a new violation of Bell's inequalities. *Phys. Rev. Lett.* 48: 91–94.

Baars, B. (1988) *A cognitive theory of consciousness.* Cambridge, U. K. Cambridge Press.

Baldwin, R. L. (1994) Matching speed and stability. *Nature* 369: 183–84.

Barenco, A. (1996) Quantum physics and computers. *Contemporary Physics* 37(5): 375–389.

Beck, F., Eccles, J. C. (1992) Quantum aspects of brain activity and the role of consciousness. *Proc. Natl. Acad. Sci. USA* 89(23): 11357–11361.

Benioff, P. (1982) Quantum mechanical Hamiltonian models of Turing Machines. *J. Stat. Phys.* 29: 515–546.

Bennett CH (1995) Quantum information and computation. *Physics Today*, October: 24–30.

Bohm, D. and Hiley B. J. (1993) *The Undivided Universe.* Routledge, New York.

Cameron, I. L., Cook, K. R., Edwards, D., Fullerton, G. D., Schaten, G., Zimmerman, A. M., Zimmerman, S. (1987) Cell cycle changes in water properties in sea urchin eggs. *J. Cell Physiol.* 133(1): 14–24.

Chalmers, D. J. (1996) *The conscious mind — In search of a fundamental theory.* Oxford University Press, New York.

Churchland, P. S. (1986) *Neurophilosophy: Toward a Unified Science of the Mind-Brain.* Cambridge, MA, MIT Press.

Churchland, P. S., and Sejnowski, T. J. (1992) *The Computational Brain.* Cambridge, MA, MIT Press.

Cianci, C., Graff, D., Gao, B., and Weisenberg, R. C. (1986) ATP-dependent gelation-contraction of microtubules in vitro. *Ann. NY Acad. Sci.* 466: 656–659.

Clegg J. S. (1984) Properties and metabolism of the aqueous cytoplasm. *Am J Physiol.* 246: R133–R151.

Conrad, M. (1994) Amplification of superpositional effects through electronic-conformational interactions. *Chaos, Solitons and Fractals* 4: 423–438.

Crick, F., and Koch, C. (1990) Towards a neurobiological theory of consciousness. *Seminars in the Neurosciences* 2: 263–275.

Crowell, L. (1996) Personal communication.

Cruzeiro-Hansson, L. (1996) Dynamics of a mixed quantum-classical system of finite temperature. *Europhysics Letters* 33(9): 655–659.

Cruzerio-Hansson, L., Takeno, S. (1997) Davydov model: The quantum, mixed quantum-classical and full classical systems. *Physical Review* E 56 (1): 894–906.

Dayhoff, J., Hameroff, S., Lahoz-Beltra, R., and Swenberg, C. E. (1994) Cytoskeletal involvement in neuronal learning: a review. *European Biophysics Journal* 23: 79–83.

Delon J., Legendre P. (1995) Effects of nocodazole and taxol on glycine evoked currents in rat spinal-cord neurons in culture. *Neuroreport* 6: 1932–1936.

Dennett, D. (1991) *Consciousness explained.* Boston, Little, Brown.

Dermietzel, R., and Spray, D. C. (1993) Gap junctions in the brain: where, what type, how many and why? *Trends in Neurosciences* 16(5): 186–192.

Deutsch, D. (1985) Quantum theory, the Church-Turing principle and the universal quantum computer. *Proc. Royal Soc.* (London) A400: 97–117.

Deutsch, D., and Josza, R. (1992) Rapid solution of problems by quantum computation. *Proc. Royal Soc.* (London) A439: 553–556.

Devlin, T. M. (1992) *Textbook of Biochemistry with Clinical Correlations,* Third Edition. Wiley-Liss, New York, pp. 74–75.

Diosi, L. (1989) Models for universal reduction of macroscopic quantum fluctuations. *Phys. Rev. A.* 40: 1165–1174.

DiVincenzo, D. (1995) Physical Review A 50: 1015.

Eccles, J. (1992) Evolution of consciousness. *Proceedings of the National Academy of Science of the USA,* 89: 7320–7324.

Eger E. I., Koblin D. D., Harris R. A., Kendig J. J., Pohorille A., Halsy M. J. and Trudell J. R. (1996) Hypothesis: Inhaled anesthetics produce immobility and amnesia by different mechanisms at different sites. *Anesth. Analg.* 84: 915–918.

Engelborghs, Y. (1992) Dynamic aspects of the conformational states of tubulin and microtubules. *Nanobiology* 1: 97–105.

Ergin, V. (1983) *Magintnye svoistva I struktura rastvorov elektritov.* Moscow, Nauta (in Russian).

Fang, Z. X., Sonner, J., Laster, M. J. et al. (1996) Anesthetic and convulsant properties of aromatic compounds and cycloalkanes: Implications for mechanisms of narcosis. *Anesthesia and Analgesia* 83(5): 1097–1104.

Ferster, D. (1996) Is neural noise just a nuisance? Science 272: 1812.

Feynman, R. P. (1986) Quantum mechanical computers. *Foundations of Physics* 16(6): 507–531.

Fischer, M., Kaech, S., Knutti, D., Matus, A. (1998) Rapid actin-based plasticity in dendritic spines. *Neuron* 20: 847–854.

Franks N. P. and Lieb W. R. (1982) Molecular mechanisms of general anaesthesia. *Nature* 300: 487–493.

Franks N. P. and Lieb W. R. (1984) Do general anesthetics act by competitive binding to specific receptors? *Nature* 310: 599–601.

Franks N. P. and Lieb W. R. (1985) Mapping of general anaesthetic target sites provides a molecular basis for cut-off effects. *Nature* 316: 349–351.

Franks N. P. and Lieb W. R. (1994) Molecular and cellular mechanisms of general anaesthesia. *Nature* 367: 607–614.

Franks N. P. and Lieb W. R. (1998) The molecular basis of general anesthesia: Current ideas. In *Toward a Science of Consciousness II — The Second Tucson Discussions and Debates.* Eds: S. Hameroff, A. Kaszniak, A. C. Scott. Cambridge MA, MIT Press, pp 443–457.

Fröhlich, H. (1968) Long-range coherence and energy storage in biological systems. Int. J. *Quantum Chem.* 2: 641–9.

Fröhlich, H. (1970) Long range coherence and the actions of enzymes. *Nature* 228: 1093.

Fröhlich, H. (1975) The extraordinary dielectric properties of biological materials and the action of enzymes. *Proc. Natl. Acad. Sci.*, U. S. A. 72: 4211–4215.

Galarreta, M., Hestrin, S. (1999) A network of fast-spiking cells in the neocortex connected by electrical synapses. *Nature* 402: 72–75.

Genberg, L., Richard, L., McLendon, G. and Dwayne-Miller, R. J. (1991) Direct observation of global protein motion in hemoglobin and myoglobin on picosecond time scales. *Science,* 251: 1051–1054.

Genzel, L., Kremer, F., Poglitsch, A., and Bechtold, G. (1983) Relaxation processes on a picosecond time scale in hemoglobin and poly-l-alanine observed by millimeter-wave spectroscopy. *Biopolymers* 22: 1715–1729.

Geroch, R., and Hartle, J. B. (1986) Computability and physical theories. *Foundations of Physics* 16: 533.

Ghirardi, G. C., Grassi, R., and Rimini, A. (1990) Continuous-spontaneous reduction model involving gravity. *Phys. Rev. A.* 42: 1057–1064.

Ghirardi, G. C., Rimini, A., and Weber, T. (1986) Unified dynamics for microscopic and macroscopic systems. *Phys. Rev. D.* 34: 470.

Gibson, J. R., Belerlein, M., Connors, B. W. (1999) Two networks of electrically coupled inhibitory neurons in neocortex. *Nature* 402: 75–79.

Glanz, J. (1997) Force-carrying web pervades living cell. *Science* 276: 678–679.

Gray, J. A. (1998) Creeping up on the hard question of consciousness. In: *Toward a Science of Consciousness II – The Second Tucson Discussions and Debates.* Eds. S. Hameroff, A. Kaszniak, A. Scott. MIT Press, Cambridge MA, pp 279–291.

Green, H. S., Triffet, T. (1985) Extracellular fields within the cortex. *Journal of Theoretical Biology* 115(1): 43–64.

Grundler, W., and Keilmann, F. (1983) Sharp resonances in yeast growth prove non-thermal sensitivity to microwaves. *Phys. Rev. Lett.* 51: 1214–1216.

Hagan, S., Hameroff, S. R., Tuszynski J. A. (2001) Quantum computations in brain microtubules? Decoherence and feasibility issues. *Phys. Rev. E.* (in press).

Hagan, S., Hameroff, S. R., Tuszynski J. A. (2000) Quantum computations in brain microtubules? Decoherence and feasibility issues. http://xxx/laul.gov/abs/quant-ph0005025.

Halsey, M. J. (1989) Molecular mechanisms of anesthesia. In: *General Anaesthesia,* Fifth Edition. J. F. Nunn, J.E Utting and B. R. Brown, Jr. (Eds.) Butterworths, London, pp. 19–29.

Hameroff, S. R. (1994) Quantum coherence in microtubules: A neural basis for emergent consciousness. *Journal of Consciousness Studies* 1(1): 91–118.

Hameroff S. R. (1998a) Funda-mentality: is the conscious mind subtly linked to a basic level of the universe? *Trends in Cognitive Science* 2(4): 119–127.

Hameroff, S. R. (1998d) Fundamental geometry: The Penrose-Hameroff 'Orch OR' model of consciousness. *The geometric universe - Science, geometry, and the work of Roger Penrose.* Eds. S. A. Huggett, L. V. Mason, K. P. Tod, S. T. Tsov and N. M. J. Woodhouse. Oxford, Oxford University Press.

Hameroff, S. (1998b) Did consciousness cause the Cambrian evolutionary explosion? In: *Toward a Science of Consciousness II — The Second Tucson Discussions and Debates.* Eds. S. Hameroff, A. Kaszniak, A. Scott. MIT Press, Cambridge, MA, pp 421–437.

Hameroff, S. R. (1998c) "More neural than thou": Reply to Churchland's "Brainshy" in: *Toward a Science of Consciousness II — The Second Tucson Discussions and Debates.* Eds. S. Hameroff, A. Kaszniak, A. Scott. MIT Press, Cambridge, MA, pp 197–213.

Hameroff, S. R., and Penrose, R. (1996a) Orchestrated reduction of quantum coherence in brain microtubules: A model for consciousness. In: *Toward a Science of Consciousness — The First Tucson Discussions and Debates.* Hameroff, S. R., Kaszniak, A. and Scott, A. C. (eds.), MIT Press, Cambridge, MA. pp 507–540. (also published in) *Mathematics and Computers in Simulation* (1996) 40: 453–480. http://www.consciousness.arizona.edu/hameroff/or.html.

Hameroff, S. R., and Penrose, R. (1996b) Conscious events as orchestrated spacetime selections. *Journal of Consciousness Studies* 3(1): 36–53 http://www.consciousness.arizona.edu/hameroff/hardfina.html.

Hameroff, S. R. (1999) The neurondoctrine is an insult to neurons. *Behavioural and Brain Sciences* 22(5): 838–839.

Hameroff, S. R. (1998) Quantum computation in brain microtubes? The Penrose-Hameroff 'Orch OR' model of consciousness. *Phil. Trans. Royal Society* 356(1743): 1869–1896. http://www.consciousness.arizona.edu/hameroff/royal2.html.

Hameroff S. R., and Watt R. C. (1982) Information processing in microtubules. *Journal of Theoretical Biology* 98: 549–561.

Hameroff S. R. and Watt R. C. (1983) Do anesthetics act by altering electron mobility? *Anesth. Analg.* 62: 936–940.

Haroche, S., Raimond, J.-M. (1996) Quantum computing: Dream or nightmare? *Physics Today* (August) 51–52.

Hirokawa, N. (1991) Molecular architecture and dynamics of the neuronal cytoskeleton. In *The neuronal cytoskeleton,* Ed. R. Burgoyne. New York, Wiley-Liss, pp. 5–74.

Hunt, C., Stebbings, H. (1994) Role of MAPs and motors in the bundling and shimmering of native microtubules from insect ovarioles. *Cell Motility and the Cytoskeleton* 27: 69–78.

Jasper, H. and Komaya, I. (1968) Amino acids released from the cortical surface in cats following stimulation of the mesial thalamus and midbrain reticular formation. *Electroencephalography and Clinical Neurophysiology* 24(3): 292.

Jibu, M. (1990) On a heuristic model of the coherent mechanism of the global reaction process of a group of cells. *Bussei Kenkyuu* (Material Physics Research) 53 (4): 431–436 (in Japanese).

Jibu, M., Hagan, S., Hameroff, S. R., Pribram, K. H., and Yasue, K. (1994) Quantum optical coherence in cytoskeletal microtubules: implications for brain function. *BioSystems* 32: 195–209.

Jibu, M. and Yasue, K. (1995) *Quantum brain dynamics: An introduction.* John Benjamins, Amsterdam.

Jibu, M., Pribram, K. H., Yasue, K. (1996) From conscious experience to memory storage and retrieval: The role of quantum brain dynamics and Boson condensation of evanescent photons. *Int J Modern Physics* B10(13, 14): 1735–1754.

Joliot, M., Ribary, U., Llinas, R. (1994) Human oscillatory brain activity near 40 Hz coexists with cognitive temporal binding. *Proc. Natl. Acad. Sci.* USA 91(24): 11748–11751.

Kaech, S., Brinkhaus, H., Matus, A. (1999) Volatile anesthetics block actin-based motility in dendritic spines. *Proc. Natl. Acad. Sci.* USA 96: 10433–10437.

Kaech, S., Fischer, M., Doli, T., Matus, A. (1997) Isoform specificity in the relationship of actin to dendritic spines. *The Journal of Neuroscience* 17(24): 9565–9572.

Kandel ER, Siegelbaum SA, Schwartz JH (1991) Synaptic transmission. In *Principles of Neural Science* (Third Edition) Eds: ER Kandel, JH Schwartz, TM Jessell. Elsevier NY, pp. 121–134.

Kang, S., Green, J. P. (1970) Steric and electronic relationships among some hallucinogenic compounds *Proc. Natl. Acad. Sci.* USA 67(1): 62–67.

Karolhazy, F., Frenkel, A., and Lukacs, B. (1986) On the possible role of gravity on the reduction of the wave function. In *Quantum Concepts in Space and Time,* R. Penrose and C. J. Isham (eds.), Oxford University Press.

Karplus, M., and McCammon, J. A. (1983) Protein ion channels, gates, receptors. In Dynamics of Proteins: Elements and Function. *Ann. Rev. Biochem.*, J. King (ed.), Benjamin/Cummings, Menlo Park, pp. 263–300.

Koenig SH (1995) Classes of hydration sites at protein-water interfaces: the source of contrast in magnetic resonance imaging. *Biophysical Journal* 69(2): 593–603.

Leggett, A. J. (1984) Schrödinger's cat and her laboratory cousins. Contemp. *Phys.* 25(6): 582.

Leibniz, G. W. (1768) *Opera Omnia.* 6 volumes, Louis Dutens, ed., Geneva.

Libet, B., Wright, E. W. Jr., Feinstein, B., and Pearl, D. K. (1979) Subjective referral of the timing for a conscious sensory experience. *Brain* 102: 193–224.

Lloyd, S. (1993) A potentially realizable quantum computer. *Science* 261: 1569–1571.

London, F. (1937) *Transactions of the Faraday Society* 33: 8.

Louria, D. and Hameroff, S. R. (1996) Computer simulation of anesthetic action. In: *Toward a Science of Consciousness — The First Tucson Discussions and Debates,* S. R. Hameroff, A. Kaszniak and A. C. Scott (eds.), MIT Press, Cambridge, MA. pp. 425–434.

Maniotis A. J., Bojanowski, K., Ingber, D. E. (1997a) Mechanical continuity and reversible chromosome disassembly within intact genomes removed from living cells. *Journal of Cellular Biochemistry* 65: 114–130.

Maniotis A. J., Chen C. S., Ingber D. I. (1997b) Demonstration of mechanical connections between integrins, cytoskeletal filaments, and nucleoplasm that stabilize nuclear structure. *Proc. Natl. Acad. Sci.* USA 94: 849–854.

Margulis L., Schwartz K. V., Gould S. V. (1998) *Five Kingdoms; An illustrated guide to the phyla of life on earth.* W. H. Freeman.

Marshall, I. N. (1989) Consciousness and Bose-Einstein condensates. *New Ideas in Psychology* 7: 73–83.

Mavromatos, N., Nanopoulos, D. (1998) Quantum mechanics in cell microtubules: wild imagination or realistic possiblity, LANL Archives quant-ph/9802063.

Melki, R., Carlier, M. F., Pantaloni, D., and Timasheff, S. N. (1989) Cold depolymerization of microtubules to double rings: geometric stabilization of assemblies. *Biochemistry* 28: 9143–9152.

Meyer, H. (1899) Theorie der Alkoholnarcose. Arch. Exp. Pathol. *Pharmokol.*, 42: 109–118.

Micevych, P. E., Abelson, L. (1991) Distribution of mRNAs coding for liver and heart gap junction protein in the rat central nervous system. *Journal of Comparative Neurology* 305: 96–118.

Milloni (1994) The Quantum Vacuum: an introduction to quantum electrodynamics.

Miyamoto, S. (1995) Changes in mobility of synaptic vesicles with assembly and disassembly of actin network. *Biochimica et Biophysica Acta* 1244: 85–91.

Moravec H. P. (1987) *Mind Children.* University Press, San Francisco.

Muallem, S., Kwiatkowska, K., Xu, X., Yin, H. L. (1995) Actin filament disassembly is a sufficient final trigger for exocytosis in nonexcitable cells. *J. Cell Biol.* 128: 589–598.

Nagel, T. (1974) What is it like to be a bat? *Philosophical Review* 83: 435–450.

Neubauer, C., Phelan, A. M., Keus, H. and Lange, D. G. (1990) Microwave irradiation of rats at 2.45 GHz activates pinocytotic-like uptake of tracer by capillary endothelial cells of cerebral cortex. *Bioelectromagnetics* 11: 261–268.

Nichols DE, Shulgin AT, Dyer DC (1977) Directional lipophilic characteristics of psychomimetic phenylethylamine derivatives. *Life Sciences* 21(4): 569–576.

Nichols DE (1986) Studies of the relationship between molecular structure and hallucinogenic activity. *Pharmacological Biochemistry and Behavior* 24: 335–340.

Nogales, E., Wolf, S. G., Downing, K. H. (1998) Structure of the tubulin dimer by electron crystallography. *Nature* 391: 199–203.

Overton, E. (1901) *Studien uber die Narcose und zugleich ein beitrag zur allgemeinen Pharmakologie.* Jena: Gustav Fischer.

Pauser, S., Zschunke, A., Khuen, A., Keller, K. (1995) Estimation of water content and water mobility in the nucleus and cytoplasm of Xenopus laevis oocytes by NMR microscopy. *Magnetic Resonance Imaging* 13(2): 269–276.

Pearle, P. (1989) Combining stochastic dynamical state-vector reduction with spontaneous localization. *Phys. Rev. D.* 13: 857–868.

Pearle, P., and Squires, E. (1994) Bound-state excitation, nucleon decay experiments and models of wave-function collapse. *Phys. Rev. Letts.* 73(1): 1–5.

Penrose, O., Onsager, L. (1956) Bose-Einstein condensation and liquid helium. *Phys. Rev.* 104: 576–584.

Penrose, R. (1971) in *Quantum Theory and Beyond.* Ed. E. A. Bastin. Cambridge University Press, Cambridge, U. K.

Penrose, R. (1987) Newton, quantum theory and reality. In *300 Years of Gravity,* Eds. S. W. Hawking and W. Israel, Cambridge, U. K., Cambridge Press.

Penrose, R. (1989) *The Emperor's New Mind.* Oxford Press, Oxford UK.

Penrose, R. (1994) *Shadows of the Mind.* Oxford Press, Oxford, UK.

Penrose, R. and Hameroff, S. R. (1995) What gaps? Reply to Grush and Churchland. *Journal of Consciousness Studies* 2(2): 98–112.

Penrose, R. (1996) On gravity's role in quantum state reduction. General relativity and gravitation. 28(5): 581–600.

Penrose, R. (1997) On understanding understanding. *International Studies in the Philosophy of Science* 11(1): 7–20.

Pribram, K. H. (1991) *Brain and Perception.* Lawrence Erlbaum, New Jersey.

Rasmussen, S., Karampurwala, H., Vaidyanath, R., Jensen, K. S., and Hameroff, S. (1990) Computational connectionism within neurons: A model of cytoskeletal automata subserving neural networks. *Physica* D 42: 428–449.

Roitberg A., Gerber R. B., Elber R. and Ratner M. A. (1995) Anharmonic wave functions of proteins: quantum self-consistent field calculations of BPTI. *Science* 268(5315): 1319–1322.

Rovelli, C., Smolin, L. (1995a) Discreteness of area and volume in quantum gravity. *Nuclear Physics* B 442: 593–619.

Rovelli, C., Smolin, L. (1995b) Spin networks in quantum gravity. *Physical Review* D 52(10): 5743–5759.

Sackett, D. (1995) Structure and function in the tubulin dimer and the role of acidic carboxyl terminus. Subcellular biochemistry-proteins: structure, function and engineering 24: 255–302.

Sataric, M. V., Zalula, R. B., Tuszynski, J. A. (1992) A model of the energy transfer mechanism in microtubules involving a single soliton, *Nanobiology* 1(4): 445–456.

Scott, A. (1994) *Stairway to the mind.* Springer Verlag, Berlin.

Seife, C. (2000) Cold numbers unmake the quantum mind. *Science* 287: 791.

Shimony, A. (1993) *Search for a Naturalistic World View — Volume II. Natural Science and Metaphysics.* Cambridge University Press, Cambridge, U. K.

Shor, P. W. (1994) Polynomial time algorithms for discrete logarithms and factoring on a quantum computer. In: *Algorithmic Number Theory.* First International Symposium, ANTS-1 Proceedings, Eds. L. M. Adleman and M. D. Huang, Springer-Verlag, Berlin.

Singer, W., Gray, C., Engel, A., Konig, P., Artola, A., Brocher, S. (1990) Formation of cortical cell assemblies. *Cold Spring Harbor Symposia on Quantitative Biology* 55: 939–952.

Smolin, L. (1997) *Life of the Cosmos.* Oxford Press, N. Y.

Snyder SH, Merrill CR (1965) A relationship between the hallucinogenic activity of drugs and their electronic configuration. *Proc. Natl. Acad. Sci.* USA 54: 258–266.

Spinoza, B. (1677) *Ethica in Opera quotque reperta sunt.* 3rd edition, eds. J. van Vloten and J. P. N. Land. Netherlands: Den Haag.

Stapp, H. P. (1993) *Mind, matter and quantum mechanics.* Berlin, Springer-Verlag.

Stebbings, H., Hunt, C. (1982) The nature of the clear zone around microtubules. *Cell Tissue Res.* 227: 609–617.

Stuart, G., Spruston, N., Hausser, M. (1999) *Dendrites.* Oxford University Press, Oxford, UK.

Tamás, G., Buhl E. H., Lorincz, A., Somogyi, P. (2000) Proximally targeted GABAergic synapses and gap junctions synchronize cortical interneurons. *Nature Neuroscience* 3(4); 366–371.

Tegmark, M. (1999) *The quantum brain.* Los Alamos Archive quant-ph/99070095, july 1999.

Tegmark M. (2000) The importance of quantum decoherence in brain processes. *Phys. Rev.* E 61: 4194–4208.

Tejada J., Garg A., Gider S., Awschalom D. D., DiVincenzo D. P. and Loss D. (1996) Does macroscopic quantum coherence occur in ferritin? *Science* 272, 424–426.

Tuszynski, J., Hameroff, S., Sataric, M.V., Trpisova, B., and Nip, M.L.A. (1995) Ferroelectric behavior in microtubule dipole lattices; implications for information processing, signaling and assembly/disassembly. *J. Theor. Biol.* 174: 371–380.

Tuszynski J.A., Brown, J.A., P. Hawrylak (1998) Dielectric polarization, electrical conduction, information processing and quantum computation in microtubules, are they plausible? *Phil. Trans. Royal Society* A 356(1743): 1897–1926.

Uedaira, H., Osaka, A. (1989) *Water in biological systems.* Tokyo, Kodansha Scientific (in Japanese).

Vos, M.H., Rappaport, J., Lambry, J.Ch., Breton, J., Martin, J.L. (1993) Visualization of coherent nuclear motion in a membrane protein by femtosecond laser spectroscopy. *Nature* 363: 320–325.

Vernon, G.G., Woolley, D.M. (1995) The propagation of a zone of activation along groups of flagellar doublet microtubules. *Experimental Cell Research* 220(2): 482–494.

Voet, D., Voet, J.G. (1995) *Biochemistry,* 2nd edition. Wiley, New York.

Vos, M.H., Rappaport, J., Lambry, J.Ch., Breton, J., Martin, J.L. (1992) Visualization of coherent nuclear motion in a membrane protein by femtosecond laser spectroscopy. *Nature* 363: 320–325.

Wachsstock D.H., Schwarz W.H., Pollard T.D. (1994) Cross-linker dynamics determine the mechanical properties of actin gels. *Biophysical Journal* 66(3 Pt 1): 801–809.

Walker, E. (2000) *The physics of consciousness — The quantum mind and the meaning of life.* Perseus books.

Wallace, R. (1996) Quantum computation in the neural membrane. In: *Toward a Science of Consciousness — The First Tucson Discussions and Debates,* S.R. Hameroff, A. Kaszniak and A.C. Scott (eds.), MIT Press, Cambridge, MA. pp. 419–424.

Walleczek, J. (1995) Magnetokinetic effects on radical pairs: a possible paradigm for understanding sub-kT magnetic field interactions with biological systems. *In Electromagnetic Fields: Biological Interactions and Mechanisms.* M Blank (ed) Advances in Chemistry No 250 American Chemical Society Books Washington DC.

Watterson JG (1981) *Biophysics of Water.* Wiley, NY.

Watterson, J.G. (1991) The interaction of water and proteins in cellular function. *Prog. Molec. Subcell. Biol.* 12: 113–134.

Watterson JG (1996) Water clusters: Pixels of life. In: *Toward a Science of Consciousness — The First Tucson Discussions and Debates,* S.R. Hameroff, A. Kaszniak and A.C. Scott (eds.), MIT Press, Cambridge, MA. pp 397–405.

Whatley V.J., Mihic S.J., Allan A.M., McQuilkin S.J. and Harris R.A. (1994) Gamma-aminobutyric $acid_A$ receptor function is inhibited by microtubule depolymerization. *J. Biol. Chem.* 269: 19546–19552.

Wheeler, J.A. (1990) Information, physics, quantum: The search for links. In W. Zurek, (Ed.) *Complexity, Entropy, and the Physics of Information.* Addison-Wesley.

Whitehead, A.N. (1929) *Process and Reality.* Macmillan, N.Y.

Woolf, N.J. (1997) A possible role for cholinergic neurons of the basal forebrain and pontomesencephalon in consciousness. *Consciousness and Cognition* 6: 574–596.

Wulf, R. J., Featherstone, R. M. (1957) A correlation of van der Waal's constants with anesthetic potency. *Anesthesiology* 18: 97–105.

Yagi, T., Kamimura, S., Kamiya, R. (1994) Nanometer scale vibration in mutant axonemes of Chlamydonas Cell Motility and the Cytoskeleton 29: 177–185.

Yu, W., and Baas, P. W. (1994) Changes in microtubule number and length during axon differentiation. J. *Neuroscience* 14(5): 2818–2829.

Zeki, S., Bartels, A. (1998) The autonomy of the visual systems and the modularity of conscious vision. *Phil. Trans. R. Society* London B 353: 1911–1914.

Zeki, S., Moutassis, K. (1997) Temporal hierarchy of the visual perceptive systems in the Mondrian world. *Proc. Roy. Soc.* London B 264: 1415–1419.

The natural philosophy and physics of consciousness

Evan Harris Walker

Abstract

Consciousness comes out of quantum mechanics — from the presence of tunneling in the brain, and from state vector collapse brought on by the brain's comparison loops. This fact is tied to the machinery of the MSE — the modified Schrödinger equation. This understanding of consciousness also lets us resolve problems in neurophysiology and even in physics — the resolution of the disparity that has long beset general relativity *vis a vis* quantum theory. We use this understanding of consciousness as a quantum process to resolve the measurement problem in quantum mechanics and to obtain quantities that allow us to test experimentally the viability of this theory.

1. The philosophy

Isaac Newton in a letter to the Reverend Dr. Richard Bentley stated in regard to the hypothesis presuming "action at a distance" (Cohen 1978: 302–303):

> That Gravity should be innate, inherent, and essential to Matter, so that one Body may act upon another at a Distance thro' a *Vacuum*, without the Mediation of any thing else, by and through which their Action and Force may be conveyed from one to another, is to me so great an Absurdity, that I believe no Man who has in philosophical Matters a competent Faculty of thinking, can ever fall into it.

And yet Newton's theory of gravitation has come down to us as an action at a distance through empty space. Moreover, we know now that all forces act through empty space. We now know that there were things about reality that could not have been comprehended at the time that Bentley and Newton lived. We now have a far more complete understanding of nature that has come with the development of mathematical physics. We have the theory of general relativity in which it is the geometry of that empty space itself that is the cause of gravity. What seemed to be absurd at first has come to be the abiding basis for our knowledge.

And so it will be for the understanding of the nature of consciousness.

2. Monism? Dualism?

Clearly, consciousness is something that cannot be made public. It was the central theme of Wittgenstein's philosophy that this consciousness that cannot be made public should be removed from our discourse — removed so as to solve the problem of the nature of consciousness as being merely something that arises from the misuse of the language. Wittgenstein presaged Rile's "ghost in the machine" gambit. Ryle (1949: 20) argued that the existence of consciousness was a category mistake — no more an objective reality than a Wednesday.

The problem about the nature of consciousness comes from different causes, and leads us to different answers — answers that we could not have begun to understand until quite recently because the relevant physics did not exist, nor did we possess the needed understanding of the brain's structure.

The problem of the nature of consciousness comes right out of the monism — duality conundrum. We know that consciousness exists — as much as we know that anything exists. The question is the nature of its existence. We know that it is not like the rocks of physical reality, so it seems to be something that is not physical. So we tend to feel that there must be a duality. A duality with Gods and souls and all the embellishments of a thousand years of imaginings.

Consciousness exists, but since it is not objective like physical objects, it seems there must be a duality. But we are conscious of the things of the physical world — so this consciousness must be a part of that physical world, or we could not know of its existence. Thus we must have a monistic reality. Thus the "hard problem", as Churchland (1984) has called it.

3. Solving the problem

To get anywhere with the question of the nature of consciousness, we have to solve this hard problem first. It might be thought that the hard problem *is* the problem, but as we will see, it is just the beginning. Still, the whole approach to this problem, to the solution of the overall consciousness problem must come out of an initial understanding of this question about its fundamental nature — dual or mono.

And the solution to this problem is simple. It requires just a couple of statements, and some measure of perspective. The answer comes in just about five statements:

1. Consciousness is something real.
2. Physics defines what constitutes physicality.
3. Measurement is the cornerstone of physics; if something is not physically measurable, it is not a part of physical reality.
4. It is not possible to measure consciousness.
5. Thus, the fact that consciousness exists, but is not physically measurable, means the consciousness is real but nonphysical.

And thus reality is dualistic, and not monistic. Let us look at these points in more detail.

First: Consciousness is something real. It has quantitative characteristics that make it amenable to analysis in its own right. We will see this in much more detail later, but for now suffice it to say that the mere fact that consciousness can be localized to the brain's activities means that it has characteristics that are subject to scientific quantification and study. Later we will take a look at quite a few additional characteristics, some of them being quantitative characteristics that will allow us to analyze consciousness in some detail.

Second: Physics defines what constitutes physicality. Contrary to the practice in much of the history of philosophy, we have to turn to the science of physics in order to define the meaning of: "What is physical reality?" Physics has been far more successful in its determination of what this means than have the efforts of any armchair analysis.

Third: Measurement is the cornerstone of physics. If something is not physically measurable, it is not a part of physical reality. The history of twentieth century physics has amply demonstrated the fundamental nature of measurability. All of the great achievements in physics since the beginning of the twentieth century have been the result of the recognition of subtleties as to the nature of measurement. The constancy of the speed of light in relativity — special and general, the Heisenberg uncertainty principle in quantum mechanics, indistinguishability in thermodynamics, symmetries in particle physics — all have evolved out of the recognition that measurement determines the content and the bounds of what can be said to be physically real. If it is not in principle measurable by the means at the disposal of physics, then it is not physically real.

Fourth: It is not possible to measure consciousness. It is impossible to determine by means of physical measurements the answer to the simple, but meaningful question: "Does an ice cube feel pain when it melts?"

Fifth: The fact that consciousness exists, but is not physically measurable, means the consciousness is real but nonphysical. Since consciousness is not physically measurable, and so, not physically real, and yet it exists — having characteristics that make it amenable to study and analysis, it must be *real, but nonphysical*. This, by the way is the reason that consciousness in not definable — objectively definable, that is.

And so, reality must be dual.

4. The science of consciousness, the physics of duality

We said at the outset: "To get anywhere with the question of the nature of consciousness, we have to solve this hard problem [of dualism versus monism] first." We have done this, but we have not! There must be a duality. Reason and the facts learned in the development of the natural philosophy of physics have proved this to be the case. But we have not come to grips with the hard part of the realization. We know that there is a duality, but we now find ourselves in the same situation that Isaac Newton found himself. The answer is absurd — seemingly. The problem now is to understand how it is possible to have a duality — consciousness and rocks, if you will — things that are totally separate, so separate that we must have philosophic categories that separate them, and yet so intimately connected that consciousness has nothing, seemingly, as its subject matter but these rocks!

Often when I have addressed the question of the nature of consciousness, I have shown that we must have a dualism, and I have shown why that is important to the development of a viable and productive theory of consciousness — a theory that can give us quantitative tests to prove its correctness. But this, as vital as it is, is not necessarily the next question. The next question in the mind of the reader may be: "How is it possible to have a dualism?" And if this question is not addressed, the reader may justly slump into a comatose state for the rest of the chapter. But the answer to this question is a difficult subject. Since the definition of physical reality hinges on physics, any extension of our understanding of that reality will also have to make appeal to physics.

5. The measurement problem in quantum mechanics

The approach to solving this problem has been made slightly easier by the fact that the problem has already become a primary problem area in physics itself. The problem goes by the deceptive name, *the measurement problem.*

The Schrödinger equation, $H\Psi = i\hbar\partial\Psi/\partial t$, gives solutions in terms of the state vector Ψ. In general, the state vector contains component states, ψ_i that are each equally viable potentialities of the system under consideration — the quantities $\psi_i^* \psi_i$ giving the probabilities for the occurrence of the respective states. These solutions in terms of the state vector rather than simply a stochastically occurring single state can be demonstrated experimentally to be real in as much as the several terms are actually manifest in the structure of interference patterns that arise from the presence of the several terms simultaneously. Now, because the Schrödinger equation is linear in Ψ, the equation has no mathematical mechanism whereby these component states can change their probabilities. Thus, there is no means for one state, out of the selection of possible states, to become the actualized state — the way we see the world.

The Schrödinger equation provides an extraordinarily precise description of the physical world. However, the world that is supposed to be represented by the basic equation of physics is never seen; on measurement, what is seen is always one out of the collection of possible states. On measurement, observation, the system is always found to have collapsed into one of the possible component states. The state vector Ψ does transition from the collection of component states to a single, seemingly randomly occurring actual state. Moreover, there seems to be nothing physically that distinguishes *one* interaction that would according to the Schrödinger equation result in a further proliferation of component states from *another* interaction that *we* designate as a measurement that would lead to state vector collapse resulting in a single component state.

And that is the measurement problem. Well, not quite. I left out the most important aspect of the problem. There is one way to tell the measurement interaction from any other interaction. The measurement interaction is the one that we observe. Thus, there is the implication that the thing that brings about state vector collapse is the involvement of our consciousness as the observer.

The point is that within the discipline that is our cornerstone defining what constitutes physical reality, there already exists a duality — a duality that separates physical objects from consciousness. This is consciousness that is something not only outside of physical reality but is also something that has a ponderable effect on what happens in the physical world.

The measurement problem exists as a problem because the Schrödinger equation does not provide within its formalism any way for actual events to occur. Actual events are seen to arise from measurement — and measurement has to be defined outside the strict formalism of the mechanics.

The measurement problem perfectly parallels the duality problem of philosophy — and its presence points the way to the solution of the problem.

6. This way to state vector collapse

Both problems still exist. Philosophy still has the conundrum that dualism is a logical impossibility. Physics still has a fundamental equation that seems to describe everything — everything but the fact that things happen. Solving one of these problems means that we have solved the other. But how do we solve either problem?

The obvious answer to this question is to add a term to the Schrödinger equation so as to make the equation nonlinear. Physicists have tried this over and over. The difficulty is that the Schrödinger equation is just too good! The slightest change leads to changes in what the equation predicts. Any change that will bring about state vector collapse in a time short enough to be consistent with experimental results — experiments that have already been done — gives predicted experimental results that differ significantly from the results observed. Conversely, any change in the equation that keeps the accuracy of the predictions of experiments results in collapses that are too slow. This trade-off parallels the Heisenberg time-energy uncertainty relationship, and comes from the same characteristics of the Schrödinger equation that lead to that theorem.

Thus, it would seem, we are stuck. There is, however, a wonderful way out — a way that tells us a great deal about the structure of time, consciousness, and reality. It is an answer that involves three things: a re-evaluation of the Einstein-Podolsky-Rosen paradox, something called von Neumann's dispersion measure, and a curious quirk in the mathematics of information measures.

7. The Einstein-Podolsky-Rosen paradox

The measurement problem comes in many guises. The Einstein-Podolsky-Rosen paradox is one of these, and in many ways it was the father of the revolution in the measurement problem that gave birth to Bell's theorem and to the tests of the Bell's theorem that have proved, finally, that the measurement problem can no more be interpreted away than could philosophy succeed in interpreting away the consciousness/duality problem. The Einstein-Podolsky-Rosen paradox is rather easy to present. Orthodox quantum theory says that any system described by a solution to the Schrödinger equation having multiple states resides in all those mutually exclusive and mutually inconsistent states up to the time of measurement. That is to say, before measurement pins down the location or the momentum of an object, the object exists in all the allowed states simultaneously. Impossible, but there it is.

Einstein, Podolsky, and Rosen in a paper written in 1935 observed that if, as a result of some interaction between two particles, the two particles came away with correlated quantum states — such as they would have if initially they started with a total momentum of zero and started out from the same location — then it would be possible, using the conservation laws to make a measurement on one of the particles in order to determine exactly the corresponding quantity for the other particle. EPR observed that if without in any way disturbing a particle (here the particle on which no measurement was made) one can determine that particle's position or momentum, then the particle's position and momentum must have physical reality before the measurement — contrary to the teachings of quantum mechanics.

Bell's theorem is just a way to test to see if Einstein, Podolsky, and Rosen were correct or quantum theory had things right. Bell was able to derive a theorem to test which was correct by observing that if EPR were correct, then probabilities for the various possible states would add like classical probabilities — a linear sum for mutually exclusive states. Quantum mechanics calls for the probabilities to come from squaring the quantities representing the state *amplitudes*. When the experimental results came in, when Bell's theorem was tested, quantum theory proved to be correct. Things do not have an independent, albeit unknown, reality before measurement.

8. A new twist to Bell's Theorem

If we go back through the history of twentieth century physics, we find that whenever there was some subtle anomaly about the way measurements happen — like the constancy of the speed of light (despite the fact that the speed might be measured from different moving platforms) that led to relativity — physics has had to take a turn toward a new understanding of the nature of physical reality. Once again, we are confronted with new experimental results stemming from the experiments to test Bell's theorem. These tests have given results that are entirely inconsistent with all that we have imagined before to lie at the base of physical reality. They seem to be contradictory to all else in physics, and so we must carefully examine the experiment to discover where the new subtlety lies that hides nature's new truth.

If we look at the experiment that Einstein, Podolsky, and Rosen described once again, there is one small leap that they took in reaching their final conclusion that provides us with the key we need to unravel the mystery. Remember that EPR said that if one did the measurement on one of the two particles then one would know the value on the other. The experiments that tested Bell's theorem proved that such is not the case. That means EPR was wrong. They were wrong because they failed to finish their experiment. They failed to realize that one has to actually measure the other particle's position or momentum, or whatever, before one can conclude that one does in fact know the other particle's values.

If, now, one actually does this; if one carries out such a sequence of interactions and measurements on a pair of correlated/entangled particles, and writes out the result, one will discover something extraordinary. The outcome will contain the original state vector that described the first particle, but it will also be multiplied by a function describing the state of the second particle. One can separate out this combined factor; it is $\Psi_A\Psi_B$, where the subscripts A and B are labels for the two particles. Now, let us make a small hypothesis. We note that if Ψ_A is in, say, its 14-th state when measured, i.e., ψ_{A14}, then Ψ_B will turn out on measurement to be in state ψ_{B14} as well. That is to say, Ψ_A and Ψ_B, are merely the complements — the dual space conjugates — of one another (although described somewhat differently)! We make the hypothesis that $\Psi_B \equiv \Psi_A^\dagger$. That is to say, $\Psi_A\Psi_B$ is just $\Psi_A\Psi_A^\dagger$. What is marvelous about this is that the components of $\Psi_A\Psi_A^\dagger$ are real numbers. We have arrived at a condition for state vector collapse through the intervention of measurements on both parts of an interaction — something that tests on Bell's theorem say should be a prerequisite for state collapse — together with a comparison measurement that brings the two branches of the interaction back into contact.

This tells us of a distinctive interaction that can help bring about state vector collapse automatically (through the intervention of these special kinds of measurement loops), but now we need to make a change in the Schrödinger equation so as to be able to take advantage of this fact. To accomplish this, we need next to look at the question of von Neumann's dispersion measures.

9. Von Neumann and his dispersion measure

Before measurement, as the tests of Bell's theorem have taught us, the potentialities of any quantum system are "disperse". That is to say, any of the potentialities could turn out to be the measured reality. Von Neumann proposed a measure so as to quantify this characteristic of dispersion that systems have before — and after measurement. The von Neumann dispersion measure, σ_i, for the ith state is given by the equation: $\sigma_i = p_i - p_i^2$, where the quantities p_i are the probabilities for the individual quantum states. The total dispersion, s, is obtained by summing over all the states of the state vector. The meaning of the dispersion measure is that before state vector collapse, before the system goes into any single state on measurement, the dispersion measure will have some fractional value — more than zero, less than one. After observation, however, one state will be the one actualized on measurement taking on a probability of unity, while all the rest will have probabilities of zero. The resulting dispersion measures will all become zero — no dispersion.

The dispersion measure provides a quantitative characterization of one of the central characteristics of quantum mechanics and of the state vector. Interestingly, there is another, much more unique formula, that also can be used to characterize the dispersion of the states. This is the information measure $-p_i \log p_i$. This measure, too, has a fractional value when the states are just potentialities, but becomes zero when one of the states becomes the actualized state.

But with this new dispersion measure, there is something more. As an information measure, it can be tied to the thing that appears to be at the cause of the state vector collapse — the change in the information content resulting from the measurement itself. And because of this, it will also involve the observer, the conscious observer, which appears to be the unique thing that brings about state vector collapse.

This gives us the opportunity to add to the Schrödinger equation a new term — giving us a modified Schrödinger equation (MSE). This new term will be non-linear. Being non-linear, it will cause the new MSE to drive the individual states so that they can collapse into a single state. Moreover, this new term, on the completion of a measurement loop (as discussed above) will take on the form: $-p_i \log p_i$. Having taken that form, when the individual states go to values of one or zero, this added term will then immediately vanish. Thus, on the completion of a measurement loop, this modified Schrödinger equation will lose the added term, revert to the standard Schrödinger equation, and give us a divided dualistic reality. We will not be able to see by any measurement the presence of the added term because that term vanishes on completion of the measurement!

What is the form of this term that will give us $-p_i \log p_i$ on completion of the measurement loop? The form is $-\psi_i \log \psi_i$, expressed in terms of the component states of the state vector. Thus, the MSE has the form: $H\Psi = i\hbar(\partial\Psi/\partial t - \mu G\Psi\log\Psi^{\dagger})$. The symbol μ is just a constant. The symbol G stands for a very special kind of matrix — something not seen in our physics before, because it really is not there!

Let me explain. The state vector is really a vector in Hilbert space. As a vector, it has a direction in that space. (Because our basic equation is no longer linear, we have to talk about a non-linear Hilbert space, a space that becomes Hilbert-like on state vector collapse — that is, the components are Hilbert-like, but only realizable on collapse.) Because the MSE has imaginary terms, all the solutions are complex, and the complex world is not observable. Moreover, because the MSE is non-linear, it has no steady solutions — except those for which the added term vanishes. Thus, the direction of that vector can change. When it changes so as to align with one of the component states, and if that component is real (like the $\Psi_A\Psi_A^{\dagger}$ that we saw earlier come out of the closed measurement loop of interactions) then we will get state vector collapse automatically.

Because of the measurement problem's involvement with the observer, because of the consciousness problem that I have elsewhere (Walker 1970) shown to involve quantum mechanics (specifically this matter of the state vector establishment and collapse), this selection of what state the system goes into properly is to be identified with the consciousness of the system having the necessary properties to bring about state vector collapse. (Why this involves brain function specifically is something that will be discussed below.) Thus, there is something that causes the state selection, namely, consciousness. The MSE does not actually represent how it selects specific states. However, we introduce into the MSE this matrix, this G factor, to represent the outcome of the over-all interaction, including the action of the mind in selecting the state that occurs.

The G matrix is a simple diagonal square matrix having 0 off-diagonal terms, 1s for all but one of the diagonal terms, and for that term, the term corresponding to the state that happens on measurement, we have -1. Thus, $G = \mathrm{diag}(1\ 1\ 1\ \dots\ -1\ \dots\ 1)$, where the position of the -1 is random. The matrix G is not really in the MSE, but if we put it in, then the dynamics simulates the state selection of the collapse process.

10. Fixing the fix

There is one minor item that should be addressed. Preservation of the correct probabilities in this state selection process requires a further elaboration of the

MSE. Specifically, it is necessary to redefine how the state vector is set up. The state vector has to be defined in terms of component vectors that represent individual measurement events — something like this is encountered in the so-called *stochastic ensemble* interpretation of quantum theory. Thus, each component state of the state vector is itself a vector consisting of an infinite number of infinitesimal and orthogonal component vectors such that the original components of the original state vector retain their original ratios. This is a technical matter that need not concern us further here. It has been discussed in the literature previously (Walker 1988).

11. The modified Dirac Equation

We have introduced the MSE to solve not only the measurement problem, but to show how there can exist a meaningful duality — and in so doing resolve the central question of philosophy.

As for physics, this just whets the appetite. We now must generalize the MSE into a modified Dirac equation. In the paper, "Information Measures in Quantum Mechanics" (Walker 1988) there is the suggestion that at the heart of physical reality there exists only the observer — and as a consequence — that which is observed. But assuming a symmetry, and taking our cue from what we learned about the role of the dual space, we can see in the observed events the observer sees, a mirror reflecting an observer that looks back. Moreover, it must be that at the heart of things there has to be the observed events, and the existence of these events implies that there must be the observed choices as to what can be observed. All in all, we have that at the root of reality there must exist only the time derivative of the probabilities, expressed as state vectors, and the information operators. This might look something like: $\partial\Psi/\partial t = G\Psi\log\Psi^{\dagger}$.

But there is more that we can do to reduce this expression. The logarithm is the result of integration, and so should be expressed as such. There is something else that can be done as well — and it has to do with G.

As we pointed out previously, $G = \mathrm{diag}(1\ 1\ \ldots\ -1\ \ldots\ 1)$. Now the position of the columns in this matrix is entirely arbitrary. One can always rearrange the columns of a matrix equation. Thus we can rearrange the columns of the G matrix for each quantum event so that it can be expressed as: $G = \mathrm{diag}(1\ 1\ \ldots\ -1)$.

There is one more remarkable observation to be made about the matrix. Usually, if we wish to talk about probabilities, there is a minimum size that we should expect for the G matrix. We should expect that since a probability of an event having only one outcome is essentially a meaningless choice, the minimum is a selection between two outcomes. In such a case, G would have to be diag(1 −1), keeping in mind our rearrangement convention. That is the case in classical probability theory. That is also the case for the MSE. However, it is not the case if we wish to have a modified Dirac equation (MDE). Let us assume that we wish to express G in the form $G=\Gamma\Gamma^{\dagger}$, as would be necessary for a MDE. These Γ matrices, then, are the same gammas encountered in the Dirac equation. As a result, the minimum size for the G matrix changes. The minimum size is a 4 by 4 matrix having the form: $G=\mathrm{diag}(1\ 1\ 1\ {-1})$ (Jauch & Rohrlich 1959).

Now where have we seen that before? That is the form of the signature matrix for the x, y, z, ict for our four-dimensional space–time continuum! Thus, if we take the form $\partial\Psi/\partial t=G\Psi\log\Psi^{\dagger}$, write $\partial_t\Psi$ for $\partial\Psi/\partial t$, put the log in an integral form, and write Ψ as $\Psi=\Gamma\partial_{\mu}A^{\nu}=\partial A$, we will get

$$(\partial t - G\int\Psi^{\dagger-1}{}_{©}d\Psi^{\dagger}{}_{®})\Psi = 0$$

Where the subscripts represent: for t that the derivative is for the time development of the probabilities only, for © that the vector is a column vector and for ® that we have a row vector. This becomes; noting that Ψ is unitary — at least *post hoc* on collapse:

$$(\partial_t - G\int\Psi d\Psi^{\dagger})\Psi = 0$$

Since $G=\Gamma\Gamma^{\dagger}$ this becomes, substituting and rearranging terms:

$$(\partial - \int\Gamma^{\dagger}\Psi d\Psi^{\dagger})\Psi = 0$$

or, equivalently, $(\partial-\int\partial_{\mu}A^{\mu}\,d\Psi^{\dagger})\Psi=0$. The Γ's have been absorbed into the ∂ symbol, thus creating space–time out of the structure of Hilbert space in which before there were only the four probabilistic outcomes of temporal state selection. That is, *there is no such thing as space*!

Now note, if $\partial_{\mu}A^{\mu}=0$, we will have $\partial\partial A=0$, i.e., Maxwell's equations. We also can write, $(\partial-\int\Gamma^{\dagger}\Psi d\Psi^{\dagger})\Psi=0$, or in the more familiar form, simply the standard field free Dirac equation $(\partial+m)\Psi=0$. It should be noted, however, that m is no longer just the mass of the electron.

This handling of the problem has several consequences:

1. We have unified the two realms of quantum theory and of general relativity. There is no such thing as space. There is only time and the probabilistic structure of Hilbert space.
2. Letting Ψ take the form ∂A, in which A is a vector potential, we are able to insert Maxwell's equations into the Dirac field free equation.
3. Since $\Psi=\partial\mathrm{A}$, one can obtain expressions for the fields surrounding any particle described by $(\partial+\mathrm{m})\Psi=0$. Since the latter is easily solved, one can

compute the electric field surrounding the particle, and thus, the charge on the electron. This calculation has not yet been carried out, but is underway.

12. Unification — Relativity and the quantum world

The unification of general relativity with quantum theory has been central to physics for more than seventy years. The problem arises because of the Heisenberg relations. The concept of space–time that appears in quantum theory is fundamentally different from what general relativity presumes at the outset. In the above treatment, we have forged a new framework that makes possible the construction of a bridge between quantum theory and general relativity. This new conception involves a new understanding as to the nature of space–time. In this new understanding, space is not fundamental, but arises out of the stuff of Hilbert space. Space is basically a reflection of the probabilistic and dual nature of reality.

This leaves us with a new problem, however. In the treatment given above, the minimum ordered G matrix is simply: diag($1\ \ 1\ \ 1\ -1$). We have nothing of the structure found in general relativity. There are no off-diagonal terms and no functions for the diagonal terms, as we can have in the case of general relativity for its G matrix [i.e., the matrix ($g_{\mu\nu}$)]. A full integration of these two domains of physics should resolve this problem. It is a problem that is particularly perplexing in as much as it would seem that probabilities would have to wind up being either zero or one — never a function of the stress-energy distribution in space.

The answer to this difficulty seems to lie in an odd fact. General relativity has led us to the marvelous understanding of the Big Bang creation of the universe. There was an initial time, and indeed, one can show that this fact leads us to another fact: that contrary to what the differential form of the equations of general relativity say, once the equations are integrated so a to describe an entire space, the Robertson-Walker-Friedmann metric, there is an absolute reference frame for the measurement of velocities. This curiosity, however, is not the point. The big point is the fact that because of the Noether theorem, the loss of symmetry at the initial time point means that energy, momentum and probabilities concerning these quantities cannot be conserved. The temporal and spatial symmetries necessary for these conservation laws to hold do not exist. This means that the G matrix near the singularity cannot have the form given to it above. The G matrix must be modified to account for the probability non-conservation. The easy way to do this is to use the equations of general relativity to give the G matrix, keeping in mind in the handling of the problem that the spatial representation is merely a reference to the Hilbert space representation of states of the state vector. To do this, one need only solve the general relativity equation for ($g_{\mu\nu}$) and put this back into the MDE, dropping the stress energy tensor $T_{\mu\nu}$ term where it is redundant to the corresponding terms in the MDE.

13. The mind

In my previous presentations of the quantum mind, I have always presented the philosophical arguments for the need for a duality, and then jumped immediately into a presentation of the way consciousness arises in the brain. As I said in the beginning, this leaves one wondering how a dualism is possible. Here we have concentrated on the problem of that dualism, the measurement problem in quantum mechanics, generalized that, and finally made an excursion into general relativity — showing that consciousness lies at the base of everything in physics. But we have left to the end the important fact that when it is all done, consciousness is tied to the brain. How and why must be considered now.

One of the important facts about the existence of a duality lies in the fact that it provides the proper starting point for understanding the nature of consciousness in the brain. Were we to have determined that consciousness is merely monistic, a material property, then our investigation of consciousness in the brain would properly have centered on determining the neural pathways in the brain that give rise to the various aspects of consciousness that we experience. The fact that we have a dualism changes all this. The first step in understanding the mind-brain as a duality has to be to find the physical construct, that thing in the basic equations of physics, that provides the link between consciousness and brain. This was the approach given in my original work (Walker 1970), and it has been done in my book, *the Physics of Consciousness* (Walker 2000). At this point in the present chapter, it will come as no surprise that the result of that search is that consciousness is found to be linked to the brain by way of quantum processes in the brain.

14. The synapse

As it turns out, we find that there is only one way that it is possible for consciousness to enter into the dynamics of the brain, and have as a result the characteristics of the consciousness that we experience — namely, that we are conscious of the data handling that transpires in the brain. And that is that the consciousness must be tied to quantum processes that go on at the synapses of the neural network, which is where the brain's data switching operations are handled. We find that one can better understand the functioning of synapses in terms of the quantum mechanical tunneling of electrons from *postsynaptic* molecules (known as Grey's projections) to certain macromolecules on the *presynaptic* surface where they each carry 70 meV (altogether, some 7 to 9 electrons tunnel across to bring a total of from 0.49 to 0.63 meV needed to open a vesicle gate) available when the action potential arrives at the synapse, and thus provide the energy needed to fire the synapse by causing the release of chemicals present in vesicles at the synaptic cleft.

The electron tunneling at the synaptic cleft provides the key. A simple calculation shows that given the conditions and materials present at the synaptic cleft, electron tunneling will play its critical role if and only if the synaptic cleft is about 180 Å in thickness. This calculation takes into account the fact that the electron will be tied to a macromolecule in the postsynapse, moving to and fro toward the cleft many times during the 0.3 ms required for synaptic firing. As it turns out, the synaptic cleft (in chemical synapses) is indeed just that thick! (The rather rare electrical synapses, so called ephapses, have thinner clefts. Their functioning is also described by the electron tunneling mechanism as well. Gap synapses, synapses having no cleft at all, provide direct contact between neurons without the need for electron tunneling.) As spelled out in "Quantum Mechanical Tunneling in Synaptic and Ephaptic Transmission" (Walker 1977) all the many characteristics of the functioning of these neuronal structures can be understood quantitatively and in detail in terms of this quantum mechanism. Parenthetically it may be observed that the so-called calcium hypothesis does not work satisfactorily to account for the triggering of synaptic functioning. Experiments to demonstrate the fact that calcium ion injection into synapses can cause synaptic firing require a quantity of calcium ions sufficient to entirely depolarize the presynapse (Llinas 1982) — a quantity that would have fired the synapse regardless of the type of ion introduced — even if the ions had been uranium! In addition, computer modeling of the calcium mechanism to date does not provide a good match with experiments, even on introducing entirely arbitrarily adjustable coefficients into the computer simulations (Fogelson & Zucker 1985). Thus, electron tunneling is the mechanism behind synaptic functioning, and that is the mechanism that ties consciousness and quantum mechanics to the brain.

15. Inter-neuronal tunneling and the binding problem

To have discovered the quantum mechanism at work in the individual synapse provides a link to the presence of consciousness in the brain, but it does not solve the problem of how quantum mechanisms link up the entire brain. For this to happen, there must exist not just a tie-in of quantum tunneling at specific synapses, but this tunneling mechanism must also be able to link synapses throughout the brain — that is, indeed, the characteristic of consciousness as experienced. The only way that we can have tunneling cause synaptic firing at an individual synapse and allow for tunneling to cause the occasional firing of a remote synapse at some distance in the brain from the first synapse is to have the distant tunneling aided by a mechanism called hopping conduction. Thus, if we assume that, say, soluble RNA molecules in the brain serve as "stepping stone" molecules in the tunneling process, then it may be possible for the distant coupling between synapses to happen by quantum mechanical means.

This mechanism is clearly an unlikely possibility. For it to ever happen, quite a number of things have to come together at the same time. There must be a sufficient number of these RNA molecules available. The tunneling time from one RNA molecule to the next must be extremely short. There must be a sufficient number of activated synapses waiting to fire if an electron tunneling from the first synapse to the second is to cause synaptic firing. In fact, it is possible to write down a simple expression that specifies the condition under which such remote tunneling influences can bring about synaptic firing, and produce a state of sustained inter-synaptic firings so as to account for an ongoing state of consciousness in the brain by this means. The condition is: $nt^2Nf/M\tau \geq 1$, where n is the number of electrons available for tunneling (equal to the number of Grey projection molecules), about 200,000, t is the synaptic delay time, 0.3 ms, N is the number of synapses in the brain, 2.35×10^{13}, f is the synaptic activation frequency, having a nominal value of 0.018 s^{-1}(see below), M is the number of the soluble RNA molecules, 7.45×10^{20}, and τ is the tunneling time between these molecules, computed to be 8.4×10^{-12} s. These numbers are all readily available, and as shown in *The Physics of Consciousness* (Walker 2000), the numbers satisfy this condition. Thus, the so-called binding problem is solved by the fact that quantum mechanical tunneling serves to knit together the portion of the synaptic activity that is involved in our on-going stream of consciousness.

16. The consciousness data stream

The above expression for the occurrence of the conditions under which the synapses can "communicate" by means of quantum tunneling holds a further remarkable characteristic of consciousness. Consciousness is an on-set phenomenon. If the level of brain activity falls too low, we are no longer conscious. Indeed, even when we go to sleep (except for dreaming consciousness), consciousness is interrupted. This happens even though the level of synaptic and brain activity drops off only slightly, only by a factor of two. Remarkably, this fact is already a part of the condition we just gave. Solving for the firing rate of the synapses, we have for the minimum firing rate that just gives rise to consciousness: $f_{\min} = M\tau / nt^2N$. The data used above gives $f_{\min} = 0.018\ \mathrm{s}^{-1}$ as the theoretical value. The experimental values are: $f_{\mathrm{sleep}} = 0.009\ \mathrm{s}^{-1}$ and $f_{\mathrm{awake}} = 0.036\ \mathrm{s}^{-1}$. This is a very good result supporting the theory.

In addition, the consciousness data rate is easily obtained from the same expression. We can use the original expression for the occurrence of consciousness (that is $nt^2Nf/M\tau \geq 1$), to define a quantity Q, where we write $Q/n = nt^2Nf/M\tau$. In this case, Q is just the number of synapses that are linked at any one time by means of the electron tunneling. Dividing Q by the synaptic firing time t and multiplying by i, the information carried by each synaptic event, gives us an expression for the consciousness channel capacity of the quantum mind: $C = iQ/t$. The value of i can be calculated to be 0.0293 bit. This equation gives $C = 47.5$ Mbit/s, a value consistent with independent estimates that range from 50 to 200 Mbit/s, as discussed in *The Physics of Consciousness* (Walker 2000).

There are several other quantitative characteristics of consciousness that are also easily confirmed using this quantum tunneling theory of consciousness. Experiments by Libet have shown, for example, that direct stimulation of brain neurons requires something like a half second before the individual consciously perceives this stimulation. The number is easily calculated from the fact that most synapses are not usually participating in our perceived experience, and the half second is the nominal time delay before it is likely that a synapse on a particular neuron being stimulated will also be a part of the ongoing consciousness data stream.

Sleep is also understood in terms of this quantum mechanism of consciousness. As noted above, the equation for the minimum firing rate that just gives rise to consciousness, $f_{\min} = M\tau / nt^2N$, depends on the value of M, the number of available RNA molecules on which electrons can temporarily (or really, virtually) reside during the tunneling from one synapse. The problem is that most of the electrons involved in this tunneling never make the full journey. Most wind up on one of these molecules, putting the molecule out of service until sleep gives a reduced level of activity and giving the brain a chance to catch up. Now there are 200,000 virtual electrons that make the trip from each synapse, but actually 20,000 real electrons — the number of charges actually available on the inner surface of the presynapse. This number is just enough so that with 2.35×10^{13} synapses firing at the nominal rate, the 7.45×10^{20} supply of these propagator molecules will be used up during the day — steadily increasing the difficulty of maintaining the conditions needed for consciousness.

The characteristic "length" associated with consciousness — that consciousness spans the brain — is also already basically a part of the theory. The hopping conduction has to be able to couple synapses that are as far apart as the dimension of the brain. Thus, at 8.4×10^{-12} seconds for each jump, and about 100 Å for each jump, how far can the tunneling get in the time $t = 0.3$ ms? The number comes out to be 35 cm, adequate for the brain job.

There is also the "temporal length" characteristic of consciousness. This is discussed in my book, *The Physics of Consciousness* (Walker 2000), and there the value of about 40 ms is obtained. The reason — one of the reasons — that the experienced temporal span of consciousness is not just the 0.3 ms needed for the electron tunneling is the fact that this 40 ms is the time associated with the process, discussed below, that causes state vector collapse in the brain. Now the number of 40 ms together with the consciousness data stream gives just under 2 million bits of information that form the consciousness "screen" at each moment.

17. Pixel size

One further item may not be so easily recognized as a characteristic of consciousness that needs explaining. What gives the pixels of our consciousness their pixel size? That is to say, we have some 2 million bits of information that form our consciousness experience at any moment. Much of that goes into our visual experience. But what creates the sense of visual space? That is, why are the points not jammed together? To create both the information we experience in a visual field and the sense of the field itself requires two kinds of information structuring. Once again, the theory provides the answer. This sense of separation between the individual points of visual data, the pixel size itself, is caused by the fact that many synaptic and electron tunneling events are needed to give rise to one bit of information. The answer comes from the fact that the value given above for "*i*" was not unity, but 0.0293. That is to say, it requires some thirty odd synaptic firings that are a part of the consciousness data stream to form one pixel. This gives the pixel size.

18. Why the brain?

What is special about the brain that it causes state vector collapse? Note that we assumed that it is the conscious observer that causes state vector collapse of quantum systems. Then we showed that the consciousness arises from the presence of just such a quantum process in the brain. Isn't this just circular logic?

As we discussed above, state vector collapse is caused by measurement loops — comparisons of separate measurements on different parts of the same system. Bringing together again the results of separate measurements gives rise to the conditions needed for state vector collapse. The important thing here is that this is just what happens in the brain over and over, each time requiring some 40 ms of the brain's neural activity to carry out. It is something that should be somewhat rare in nature otherwise. This causes the consciousness we experience.

19. Conclusions

Consciousness comes out of quantum mechanics — from the presence of tunneling in the brain, and from state vector collapse brought on by the brain's comparison loops. This fact is tied to the machinery of the MSE — the modified Schrödinger equation. And it is this machinery with its vanishing term that causes state vector collapse that makes possible the duality of conscious existence, the great problem of philosophy. We have seen that this understanding of consciousness also lets us resolve problems in neurophysiology and even in physics — the resolution of the disparity that has long beset general relativity *vis a vis* quantum theory. We have been able to use this understanding of consciousness as a quantum process to resolve the measurement problem in quantum mechanics and to obtain quantities that allow us to test experimentally the viability of this new understanding. And this is just the beginning.

References

Churchland, P. M. (1984) *Matter and Consciousness, A Contemporary Introduction to the Philosophy of Mind.* Cambridge, MA: MIT press, 1984.

Cohen, B.I (1978) *Isaac Newton's Papers & Letters on Natural Philosophy.* Cambridge Massachusetts: Harvard University Press, 2nd edition, pp. 302–303.

Fogelson, A. L. and Zucker R. S. (1985) Presynaptic Calcium Diffusion from Various Arrays of Single Channels, *Biophys. J.* 48: 1003–1017.

Jauch J. M., Rohrlich, F. (1959) *The Theory of Electrons and Photons.* Reading MA: Addison-Wesley Publishing Company, 2nd edition, p. 427.

Llinas, R. L. (1982) Calcium in Synaptic Transmission, *Scientific American* October, pp. 56–65.

Ryle, G. (1949) *The Concept of Mind.* London: Hutchinson, p. 20.

Walker E. W. (1970) 'The Nature of Consciousness.' *Math. Biosciences* 7: 131–178, 1970.

Walker, E. W. (1977) Quantum Mechanical Tunneling in Synaptic and Ephaptic Transmission, *Int. J. of Quantum Chemistry* 11: 103–127.

Walker E. W. (1988) Information Measures in Quantum Mechanics, *Physica B* 151: 332–338.

Walker E. W. (2000) *The Physics of Consciousness.* Boston, Massachusetts: Perseus Books.

Quantum Brain Dynamics and Consciousness

Friedrich Beck

1. Introduction

The last decades of the 19th century have brought us tremendous progress in understanding complex biological structures. This has been achieved on one hand by refined microbiological experimental techniques, and on the other by an increased understanding of complexity on the basis of nonlinear dynamics. In brain research this has led to new insight into the brain's topological structure during specific activities like attention, volition, ideation, or neurochemical abnormalities (Posner et al. 1985; Corbetta et al. 1990; Ingvar 1990; Pardo et al. 1991). One of the most intensely studied areas is the visual cortex where pattern recognition techniques have revealed insight into the transformation of incoming nerve signals into coherent spatio-temporal patterns (Singer 1990). These empirical studies have been accompanied by modelings of the neural net as noisy and dissipative open system, leading to characteristic self-organization processes (Haken 1996; Freeman 1996). Following these lines it is tempting to regard brain activity solely as a complicated and highly involved input-output process, moderated by the brain's memorial history, and working on similar lines as complicated artificial intelligence programs. Many neuroscientists adopt this concept, as, e.g., expressed in the works of Crick & Koch (1990) and of Edelman (1989). In their opinion *consciousness*, the special qualia of human responsive behavior, finds here its natural physical explanation, avoiding the so-called *Cartesian dilemma*.

Despite this apparently convincing and scientifically satisfactory argumentation of these concepts of *identity theory* (Feigl 1967), the problem of consciousness is far from being settled, since not everybody is willing to accept such a materialistic viewpoint. Too strong was at all times the believe, based on personal experience, that *self-consciousness* governs our actions in the world, and that this requires the ability for free, not in any respect pre-determined, activities.

Natural scientists, however, were quite aware that such a non-materialist view would cause an unsurpassable conflict with the laws of the completely deterministic classical physics, as formulated in Newton's mechanics and Maxwell's electrodynamics, which established the complete description of the physical world by the end of the 19th century. Undoubtedly, biological objects, human bodies, including the brain, underly these laws of nature. The frustration could not be better expressed than in an address of the neurophysiologist and science philosopher Emil du Bois-Reymond in an address which he presented in 1872 at the German Natural Scientists and Physicians Society Meeting:

> There occurs at a certain point of evolution of life in the world, which we do not know and whose determination is of no importance in this connection, something new and hitherto incommensurable. Something which is, like the nature of matter and force and like the first motion, mysterious (...) This new mystery is consciousness. I shall now, as I believe in an unambiguous manner, outline that not only by our present knowledge consciousness can not be explained out of its material conditions, what apparently everybody would admit, but that by its own nature, it will be never explainable from these conditions. (Quoted from du Bois-Reymond 1916, transl. by author).

He ended his address with the apodictic prognosis *'ignorabimus'*.

The *'mystery'*, as stated by du Bois-Reymond, has survived up to within our days. It has been rationalized by the Austrian-British philosopher Karl Popper in his 'three-world-classification' comprising all existents and experiences that mankind has achieved (Popper 1972, Figure 1). There has been quite some misunderstanding of Popper's three worlds, insofar as they were regarded as *physically* separated, instead of *categorically* separated. This misunderstanding produced severe criticism of Popper's classification in tying him up with a primitive version of Cartesian dualism. Popper, however, was very well aware of the epistemological problems in mind-brain dualism, and shortly before his death he took the discussion up again (Popper et al. 1993; Lindahl & Århem 1994; Beck 1996a). A critical evaluation of the different positions, as presented in the contemporary debate on the nature of consciousness can be found in Eccles (1994).

An important qualitatively new aspect has been brought into the debate on the mind-brain problem when several authors realized that quantum physics frees physical processes from the strict determinism of the classical mechanistic picture, which has led du Bois-Reymond to his *'mystery'*. The quantum aspect, however, opened only rather late a new pathway to understand consciousness, pioneered by Wigner (1964), and later followed on by several authors (Margenau 1984; Squires 1988; Eccles 1990; Donald 1990; Stapp 1991). Most influential in broader public discussions were the two books of Penrose (1984, 1994).

World 1 *Physical Objects and States*	**World 2** States of Consciousness	**World 3** *Objective Knowledge*
1. Inorganic: *Matter, energy* 2. Biology: *Structure and actions of all living beings, human brains* 3. Artefacts: *Material substrates of human creativity, tools, books, works of art*	Subjective knowledge *Experience of* *perception* *thinking* *emotions* *intentions* *memories* *dreams* *creative acts*	Cultural heritage: *philosophical* *theological* *scientific* *historical* *literary* *artistic* *technological* Theoretical systems: *scientific problems* *critical arguments*

Figure 1. *Tabular representation of the three worlds of Karl Popper, comprising the real world and the world of our experiences.*

It should be emphasized, however, that the general discussion on quantum action in the brain has two facets. One resides on the epistemological level of quantum logic, which, in turn is related to the interpretation of quantum mechanics. The other attempt is the search for a better understanding of synaptic and neural actions, and their relation to microscopic and eventually large scale coherence formation on the basis of present-day theory of mesoscopic quantum systems embedded in noisy and dissipative surroundings. This is certainly open to experimental and theoretical research in contemporary brain physiology, and it is completely free from epistemological interpretations. Actually, very little of the cited work on quantum action in the brain devotes itself to the latter question.

In this contribution we present work which establishes a model for quantum brain dynamics, based on realistic and well established facts of neocortical activity. The model was originally introduced by Beck & Eccles (1992), and later on extended in Beck (1996b) and Beck & Eccles (1998). Section 2 gives an outline of quantum logic in relation to the question of determinacy and consciousness (the epistemological question). Section 3 contains a brief introduction to the structure of the neocortex and the role of synaptic action. In Section 4 we present the synaptic quantum trigger model and its possible biophysical realization, while Section 5 discusses the problems of binding and large scale coherence. Section 6 gives our conclusions.

2. The quantum world

Quantum mechanics is the general framework for all microscopic processes, from the atomic and molecular level to solid state and nuclear physics, the structure of elementary particles, the dynamics in the early universe, and the creation of matter in supernovae. Up to now, it has never failed, even in the modern sophisticated optical attempts to discover unexpected results in the Einstein-Podolsky-Rosen (EPR) experiment or with entangled photons (Zurek 1991). Despite of this success there has been a continuing discussion on its interpretation, from the early days up to know. The struggle is connected with the Schroedinger's cat paradox, or vice versa the role of the observer in the measuring process (Wheeler & Zurek 1983). Without entering here into the debate or presenting the different arguing, it suffices to say that we take the standpoint that quantum mechanics is valid throughout the whole universe, and that it is a theory for the single event, and not an ensemble theory.

The essence of quantum mechanics can be demonstrated in the very simple Young interference experiment (Figure 2). A beam of particles (e.g. electrons), described according to de Broglie's hypothesis by an incoming plane wave, hits a screen with two slits, which produces (Huygens' principle) two interfering waves with complex amplitudes A_1 and A_2. On the screen S they generate an interference pattern which results from the absolute square of the added amplitudes, $|A_1 + A_2|^2$. This is depicted by the piles behind the screen which indicate the number of particles registered by detectors at different positions. So far this experiment is completely analogous to a corresponding experiment with light, where the outcome is the well known result of wave diffraction. Quantum mechanics, however, is a theory for the single event. What happens if one reduces the intensity of the particle beam, so that finally only one particle hits the screen S at a time? Now the occurrence of the particle at the screen is *completely undetermined*! This is the *non causal nature of quantum mechanics* for the outcome of a single event. It is the consequence of the *von Neumann reduction of the wave function*, or state collapse which reduces the whole interference pattern to a single registration in one of the detectors (von Neumann 1955).[1] It comprises the *indeterminacy* of the future in the microscopic world. Quantum mechanics does this by subsequent interactions with the neighborhood,[2] and there is no need for an obscure 'orchestrated reduction' by background gravitational fields (Penrose 1994).

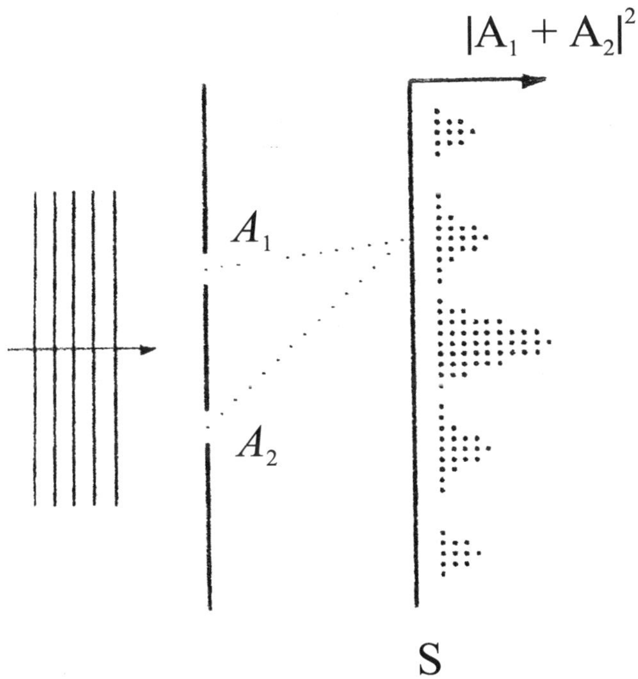

Figure 2. *A particle wave incident on a wall with two openings. Behind the openings secondary waves are propagating with complex amplitudes A_1 and A_2. At the screen detectors measure for ensembles of many particles the intensity $|A_1+A_2|^2$ which is schematically sketched. For a single event the outcome is undetermined. (The distance of the openings is of the same order as the de Broglie wavelength of the particles, after Fliessbach 1991)*

The basic difference between classical and quantum dynamics can be made clear on a somewhat more abstract basis in a simple diagram without entering into the formal subtleties of the theory. The generation of a physical process consists of preparing an *input* (the initial condition) followed by a more or less complicated *process*, leading to an *output* (the result) depending on initial conditions and the dynamics of the process. The output can be observed by measurement. For simplicity, we restrict the distinguishable components of the output to only two states (Figure 3). In classical dynamics the output is *unique* (strict determinism), which means the result is *either* state I *or* state II: *excluding* states (Figure 3A). The very *essence* of a quantum process is, contrary to this, that the output is *not unique* (no strict determinism), we have *neither* state I *nor* state II but a coherent superposition of both states: *interfering* states (Figure 3B).

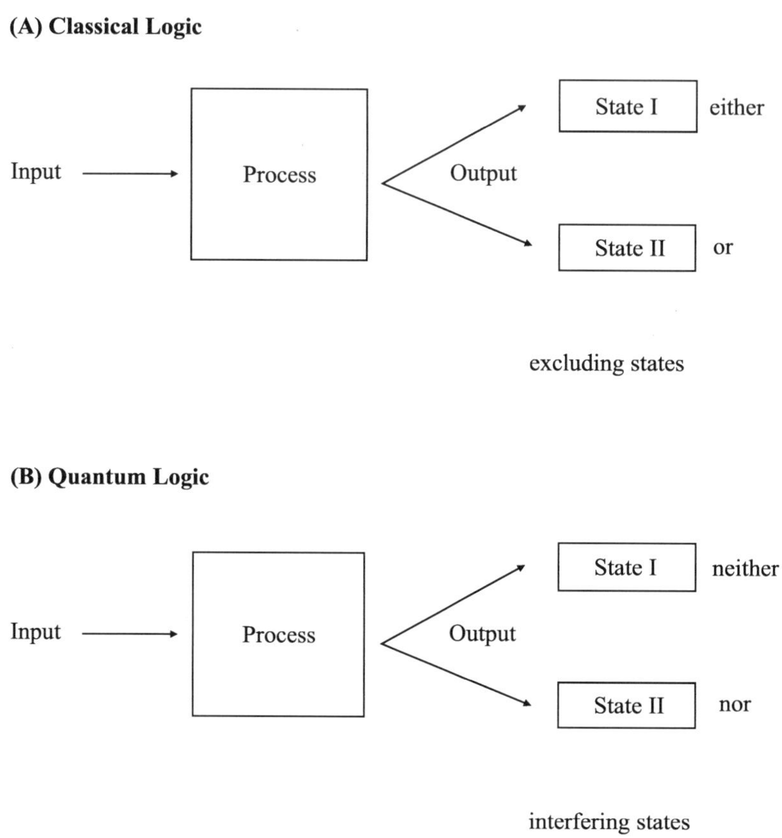

Figure 3. *Schematic diagram of classical and quantum evolutions. (A) excluding states (classical determinism), (B) interfering states (quantum indeterminism).*

In both cases the time evolution of the system is given by hyperbolic differential equations of first order in the time variable (Newton's or Maxwell's equations in the classical case, Schroedinger's equation in the quantum case) which describe the dynamics in a strictly *causal* way: the initial conditions determine *uniquely* the output. The *non-causal* element in the quantum case enters through the already mentioned *von Neumann state collapse* which occurs if one tries to realize the output state, either by a measurement, or by letting the output state undergo a successive process. Then the coherent superposition

$$\alpha \cdot |state\ I> + \beta \cdot |state\ II>$$

collapses into

either	$\|state\ I>$	with probability $\|\alpha\|^2$
or	$\|state\ II>$	with probability $\|\beta\|^2$
and	$\|\alpha\|^2 + \|\beta\|^2 = 1$	

For the *single event* — and we once more emphasize that quantum mechanics is a theory for the single event, and not an ensemble theory — the outcome is *completely unpredictable* (provided that not all but one of the amplitudes are zero, which would imply the one state left occurs with certainty). This constitutes the *non-predictable* character of quantum events. It is evident that the deterministic logic underlying Cartesian dualism, which runs so heavily into conflict with the material world of classical physics, no longer applies if elementary quantum processes play a decisive role in brain dynamics.

It is worthwhile to notice here an important difference in applying quantum dynamics either to simple or to complex microscopic systems. The probabilities given by the absolute squares of the amplitudes can be measured only in ensemble averages of many identical systems with the same initial conditions (like the electron beam of Figure 2 producing the interference pattern). Such ensembles are, however, never realized in complex objects such as the brain, where each new event finds itself borne in a new initial state. For these the non-predictability for the single event prevails.

3. Neocortical activity

Evolution has generated the neocortical structure in the brain which distinguishes all mammalian brains from its evolutionary predecessors, e.g. reptiles and birds. This cerebral cortex consists of the cellular layer covering the whole cortex, and it contains the most diverse motor and sensory transmitting areas of the cortex (cf. Figure 4). The cerebral cortex is created by densely packed nerve cells with their associated nerve fibers, about $4 \times 10^4\,\text{mm}^{-2}$, which results in a total of about 1×10^{10} for the whole cortex. Figure 5 presents a Golgi preparation of the rat visual cortex. Of special importance are pyramidal cells (2–6), each with its apical dendrite ascending upwards through different laminae (IV–II) towards the surface, and its axon descending to leave the cortex. The bundles and clusters are not well recognized in Figure 5 because only a fraction of the pyramidal cells is stained by the Golgi method. From these studies Szentàgothai derived a schematic representation of the universally accepted six laminae of the neocortex (Szentàgothai 1978). Figure 6A shows his three-dimensional construct with two large pyramidal cells in lamina V, three in Lamina III, and two in lamina II. The pyramidal apical dendrites finish in a tuft-like branching in lamina I (Figure 7A). There is agreement by Fleischhauer, Peters and their associates (Schmolke & Fleischhauer 1984; Peters & Kara 1987) that the apical bundles, diagrammatically shown in Figure 7B, are the basic anatomical units of the neocortex. They are observed in all areas of the cortex that have been investigated in all mammals, including humans. It has been proposed that these bundles are the cortical units for reception (Eccles 1990), which would give them a preeminent role. Since they are composed essentially of dendrites, the name *dendron* was adopted.

Figure 6B illustrates a typical spine synapse that makes an intimate contact with an apical dendrite of a pyramidal cell. The ultrastructure of such a synapse has been intensively studied by Akert and his associates (Pfenninger et al. 1969; Akert et al. 1975). The inner surface of a bouton confronting the synaptic cleft (d in Figure 6B, the active zone in Figure 8) forms the presynaptic vesicular grid (PVG) (VAS in Figure 8). The spherical synaptic vesicles, 50–60 Å in diameter, with their content of transmitter molecules, can be seen in the idealized drawing of the PVG (SV in Figure 8). They arrange themselves in a hexagonal array on the presynaptic vesicular grid (VAS) (Pfenninger et al. 1969; Akert et al. 1975).

A nerve impulse propagating into a bouton causes a process called exocytosis, the discharge of transmitter substance docked in vesicles into the synaptic cleft as shown in Figure 9. In many cases, and especially at the neocortical spine synapses, a nerve impulse evokes at most one single exocytosis from a PVG. Exocytosis is the basic unitary activity of the cerebral cortex. Each all-or-nothing exocytosis of synaptic transmitter results in a brief excitatory postsynaptic depolarization (EPSP). Summation by electrotonic transmission of many hundreds of these milli-EPSPs is required for an EPSP large enough (10–20 mV) to generate the discharge of an impulse by a pyramidal cell (Figure 11). This impulse will travel along its axon to make effective excitation at its many synapses. This is the conventional macro-operation of a pyramidal cell of the neocortex, and it can be satisfactorily described by conventional neuroscience, even in the most complex design of neural network theory and neuronal group selection (Szentàgothai 1978; Mountcastle 1978; Edelman 1989).

Exocytosis has been intensively studied in the mammalian central nervous

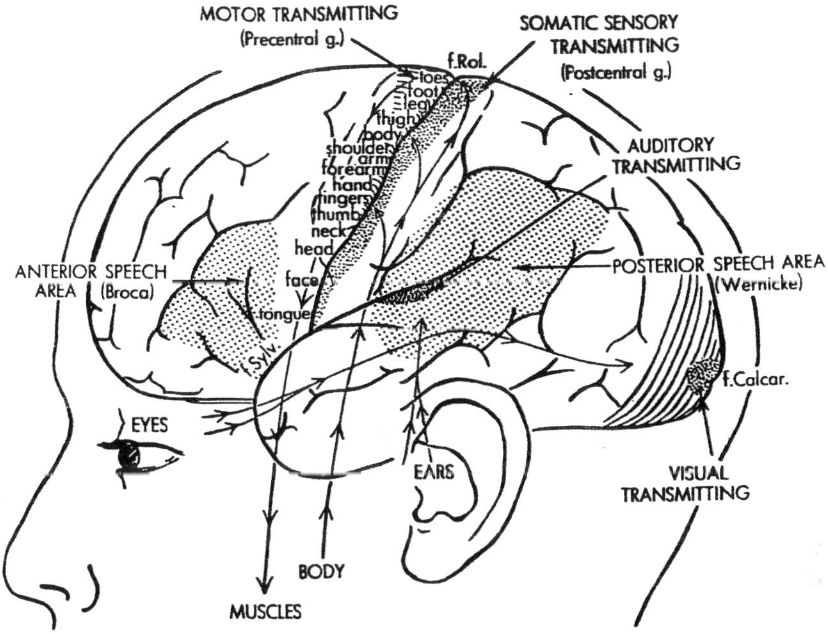

Figure 4. *The motor and sensory transmitting areas of the cerebral cortex. The motor transmitting areas are shown in the precentral gyrus, while the somatic sensory transmitting areas lie in the postcentral gyrus. (f.Rol.: the fissure of Roland, or central fissure; f.Sylv.: the fissure of Sylvus; f.Calcar.: the calcarine fissure). (Eccles 1989)*

system, where it is meanwhile possible to refine the study by utilizing a single excitatory impulse to generate EPSPs in single neurons that are being studied by intracellular recordings, see Figure 10. The initial studies were on the monosynaptic action on motoneurons by single impulses in the large Ia afferent fibers from muscle (Jack et al. 1981). More recently it was found (Walmsley et al. 1987) that the signal-to-noise ratio was much better for the neurons projecting up the dorso-spino-cerebellar tract (DSCT) to the cerebellum. The quantal EPSPs had a mean probability of 0.76.

This successful quantal resolution for DSCT neurons and motoneurons gives confidence in the much more difficult analysis of neurons of the cerebral cortex, which provide the key structures of neural events which relate to consciousness. The signal-to-noise ratio was so low in the studies of CA1 neurons of the

(a)

(b)

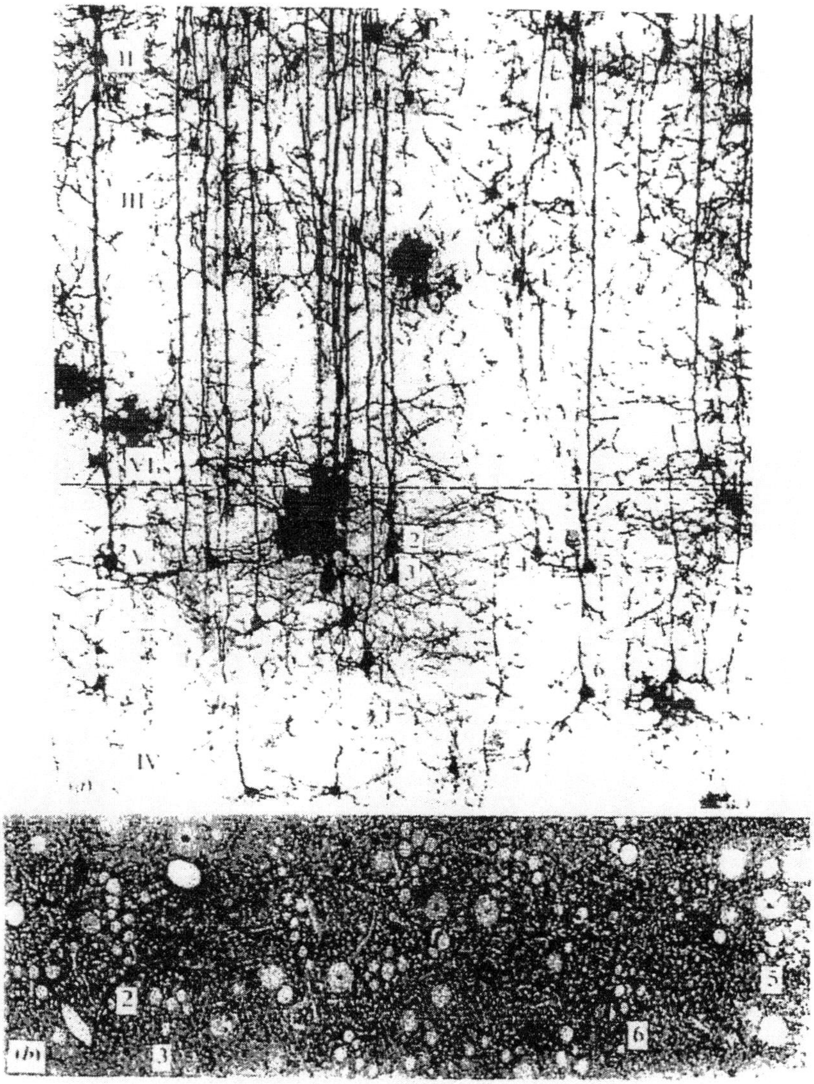

Figure 5. (a) *Golgi preparation of the rat visual cortex in a vertical section, showing apical dendrites of pyramidal cells projecting upward.* (b) *A tangential section at the level indicated by the broken line in (a). It shows the arrangement of apical dendrites in clusters. (Peters & Kara 1987)*

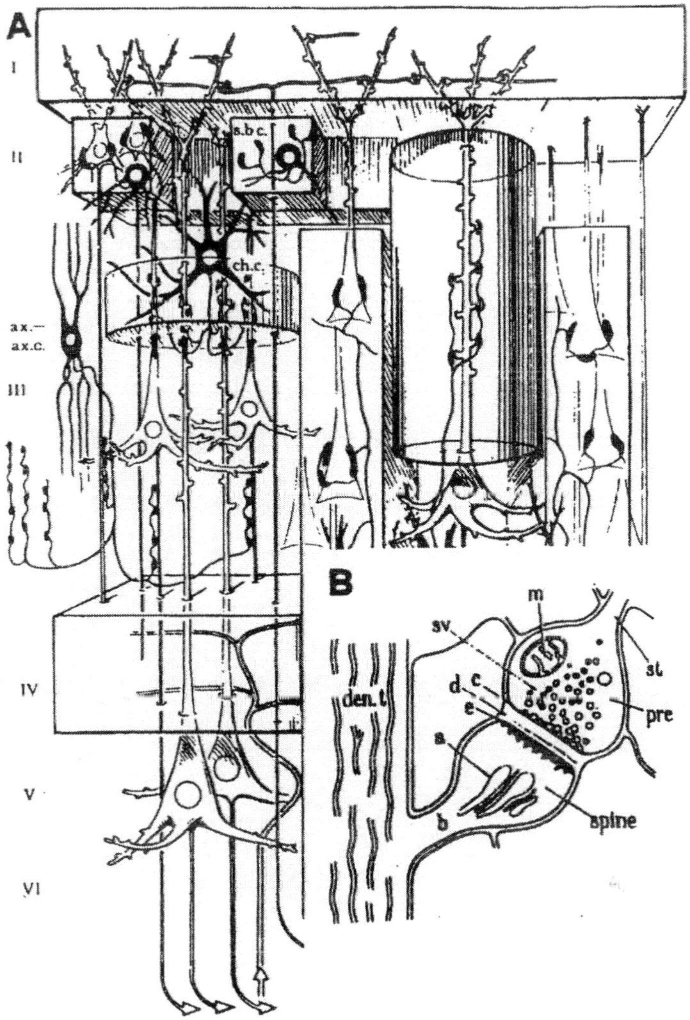

Figure 6. *(A) Three-dimensional construct by Szentàgothai (1978) showing cortical neurons of various types. There are two pyramidal cells in lamina V and three in lamina III, one being shown in detail in a column to the right, and two in lamina II. (B) detailed structure of a spine synapse on a dendrite (den.t); st, axon terminating in synaptic bouton or presynaptic terminal (pre); sv, synaptic vesicles; c, presynaptic vesicular grid (PVG in text); d, synaptic cleft; e, postsynaptic membrane; a, spine apparatus; b, spine stalk; m, mitochondrion. (Gray 1982)*

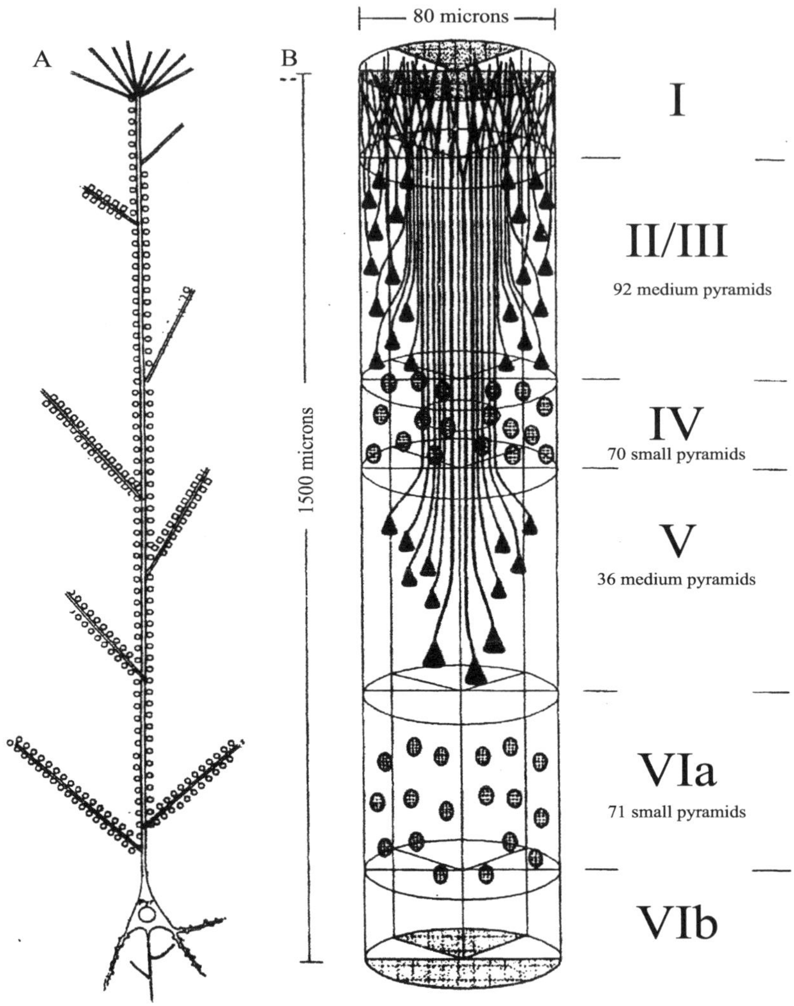

Figure 7. *(A) Drawing of a lamina V pyramidal cell with its apical dendrite showing the side branches and the terminal tuft, all studded with spine synapses (not all shown). The soma with its basal dendrites has an axon with axon collateral before leaving the cortex. (B) Drawing of the six laminae of the cerebral cortex with the apical dendrites of pyramidal cells of laminae II, III and V, showing the manner in which they bunch in ascending to lamina I, where they end in tufts. (Beck & Eccles 1992)*

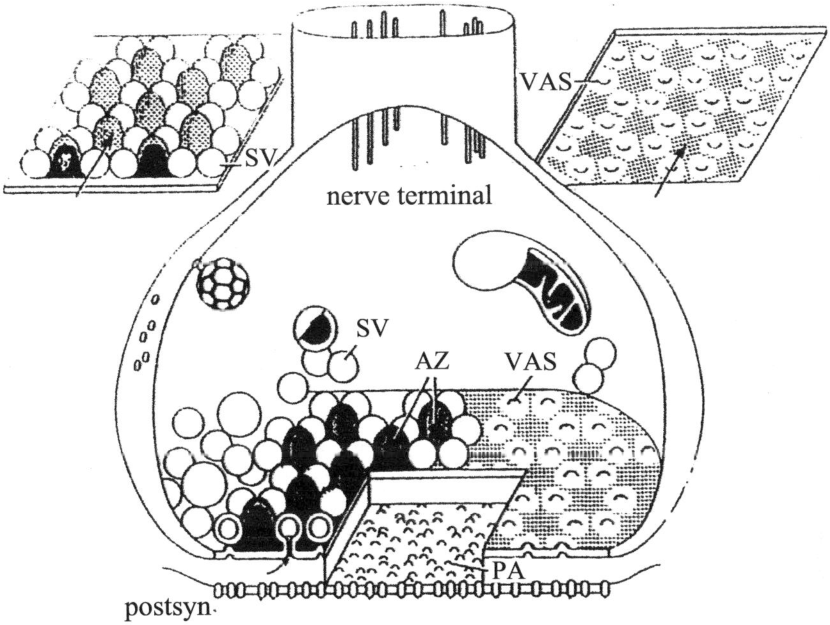

Figure 8. *Scheme of a nerve terminal, or bouton, of a mammalian central synapse showing the active zone (AZ), the presynaptic vesicular grid with vesicles (SV) in hexagonal array. One vesicle is shown in the process of exocytosis, indicated by an arrow in the synaptic cleft. The cut-out shows the postsynaptic membrane (PA). The inset to the left shows the presynaptic vesicular grid, the inset on the right shows the vesicle attachment sites (VAS). (Akert et al. 1975, modified in Eccles 1994)*

hippocampus that so far only three quantal analyses have been reliable in the complex deconvolution procedure by fluctuation analysis. In the most reliable case, a single axon of a CA3 hippocampal pyramidal cell set up an EPSP of quantal size 278 μV (mean value) in a single CA1 hippocampal pyramidal cell with approximately equal probabilities of release at each active site ($n=5$) of 0.27 (Sayer et al. 1990). In the alternative procedure the single CA3 impulse projecting to a CA1 pyramidal cell was directly stimulated in the stratum radiatum. The EPSPs delivered by the deconvolution analysis of the two CA1 pyramidal cells were of quantal sizes 224 μV and 193 μV with probabilities ($n=3$) of 0.24 and ($n=6$) of 0.16, respectively (Sayer et al. 1989). For a systematic review, see Redman 1990.

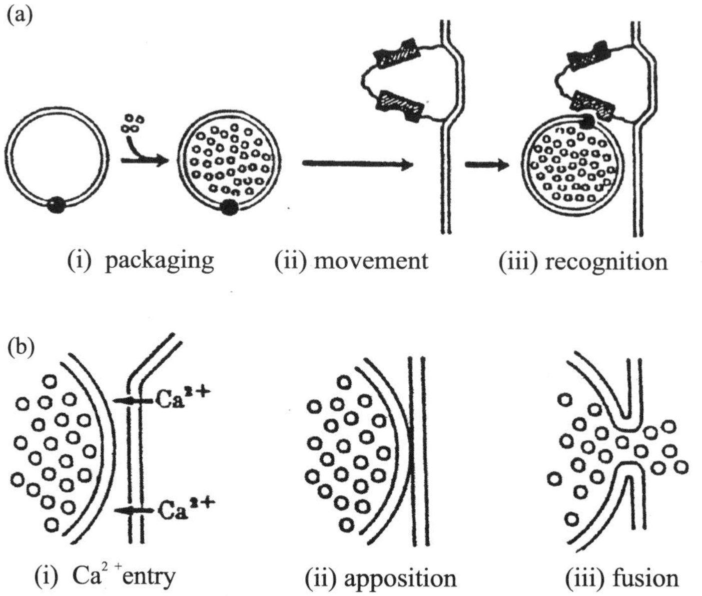

Figure 9. *Different stages of synaptic vesicle propagation: (a) filling, movement towards the presynaptic membrane, docking. (b) stages of exocytosis. Note the essential role of Ca^{2+} after depolarization by a nerve impulse (Kelly et al. 1979).*

The key results of these observations on the presynaptic functioning of a single Ia fiber on a motoneuron are:

1. There is a wide range of probabilities for exocytosis, usually $\ll 1$, but more than one discharge per incoming nerve impulse is generally not observed at the same bouton.
2. Usually a Ia fiber connects 3–5 boutons to a motoneuron (Figure 10b), but the range can extend to 1–10.

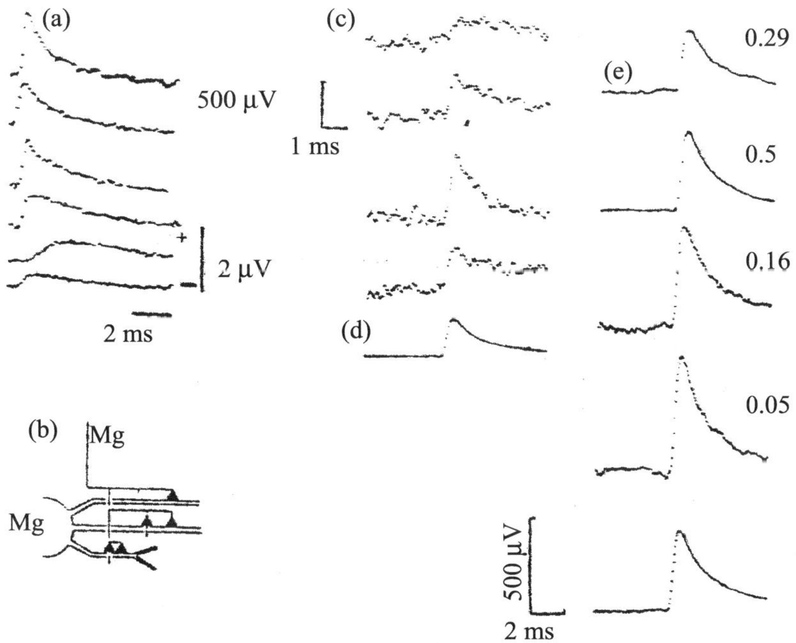

Figure 10. *Experimental setup and typical results for measuring monosynaptic action on motoneurons. (a) Averaged recordings of EPSPs produced by impulses in the same Ia fiber terminating on six different motoneurons (Mendell & Henneman 1971). (b) Schematic diagram showing the location of Ia synapses from a single medial gastrocnemius (Mg) Ia fiber on to a medial gastrocnemius motoneuron at five sites on three different dendrites (Brown 1981). (c) Four different EPSPs selected from a population of 800 responses whose average is shown in (d). (e)-(h) The components 1 to 4 of the EPSP derived from fluctuation analysis. The probabilities of occurrence of these components are indicated to the right of each, ranging from 0.05 to 0.5. The sizes of the quantal EPSPs are 302, 406, 505, and 607 μV, respectively. (i) The reconstructed EPSP obtained by adding the weighted sum of components 1 to 4. This gives an accurate reconstruction of the EPSP produced by a single fiber, identical with figure 2(d) when rescaled for the different voltage scales. It can be concluded that the four derived EPSPs (e ... h) are produced by single synapses at various distances from the some, as in (b) (Jack et al. 1981).*

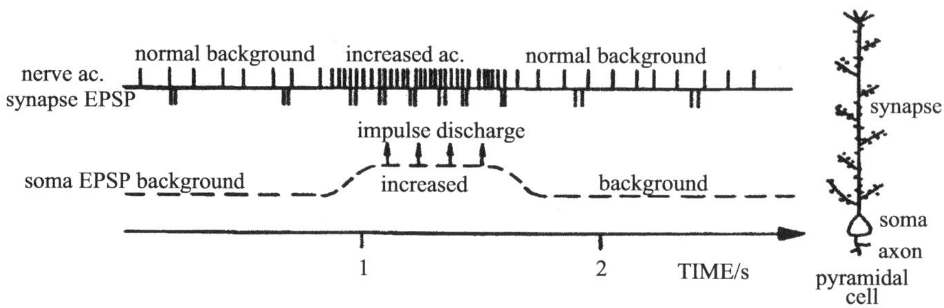

Figure 11. *Impulse processing in a pyramidal cell (shown to the right). Upper trace. normal background and increased nerve activity. By filtering via synaptic exocytosis it produces reduced EPSPs, shown in the lower trace. The summed EPSP at the soma (excitation curve in the lower part) is not strong enough in normal background activity to produce an impulse discharge. This happens only with increased activity. (Beck & Eccles 1992, sketch due to Helena Eccles)*

4. The synaptic quantum trigger model

Quantum versus classical brain dynamics

In the brain there exists an interplay between micro- and macrostructures. The latter consist of pyramidal cells, dendrites and their bundles (dendrons), electrochemical transitions, while microstructures involve synaptic membranes and microtubules. Nerve impulses, propagating along nerve cells are, independent of external stimuli or internal brain activity, always present and constitute a stochastic background in the brain. Recent investigations suggest that the neural net stays close to instability, and in this way can be switched by minute action between different states (Freeman 1996). In order to control such a system, a stable regulator has to be present which generates a coherent pattern in the active cortical unit. According to the cortical ultrastructure, as outlined in the previous section, synaptic action contributes certainly in a dominant form to this regulation. This has been demonstrated in various biochemical studies of the influence of drugs and anesthesia on the ion channel properties of the synaptic membrane (Flohr 1996), and by the role which synaptic dysfunction plays in mental diseases like schizophrenia, or Alsheimer's disease. We argue in the following that because of the stochastic thermal background quantum action could only be effective in brain dynamics if it establishes itself as a 'quantum switch' within the microstructures.

Micro- and macrostructures in the brain are clearly separated by time, or correspondingly, energy scales. The macrostructure is typically characterized by the fact that the brain lives in hot and wet surroundings of $T \approx 300$ K. This raises immediately the question of quantum coherence vs. thermal fluctuations. We have to deal with a quantum system embedded into a fluctuating and dissipative medium. The situation is analogous to the recently widely studied so-called *'mesoscopic systems'* where the all-important question is how long a quantum state can live before it looses its coherence.

As is well known, as soon as thermal energies surpass quantal energies classical thermal statistics prevails.[3] To quantify this situation, two characteristic energies can be defined:

i. the thermal energy per degree of freedom

$$E_{th} = \frac{1}{2} k_b T \tag{1}$$

with k_b: Boltzmann's constant.

ii. the quantal energy, defined as zero point energy of a quasiparticle of effective mass m_{eff} which is localized over a distance Δq. From Heisenberg's uncertainty relation $\Delta p \times \Delta q \geq 2\pi\hbar$ it follows (using the equal sign)

$$E_{qu} = \frac{(\Delta p)^2}{2\, m_{eff}} \cong \left(\frac{2\,\pi\hbar}{\Delta q} \right)^2 \frac{1}{2\, m_{eff}} \tag{2}$$

These relations define *two energy regimes*

$E_{qu} \ll E_c = E_{th}$: *the thermal regime*
$E_{qu} \gg E_c$: *the quantal regime*

with the breaking point E_c, separating both regimes which at physiological temperature of $T \approx 300$ K amounts to an Energy $E_c \sim 1.3 \times 10^{-2}$ eV.

An estimate with physiologically meaningful numbers, $T = 300$ K and localization distances in biological microsites of a few nm (some tens of Å), and quasiparticle masses of a few eV leads to the result shown in Figure 12A. Here the logarithm of the quantal energy, E_{qu}, is plotted in its dependence on localization distance, Δq, and effective mass, m_{eff}. Also shown is the plane of the constant breaking point energy, E_c. The diagram shows that for moderate Δq of about 2–4 nm and effective masses below 10 m_e the quantal energy is well above the thermal regime extending below E_c. This would certainly not be the case if mass and localization would grow up into the molecular dimensions. The relation between effective mass and localization dimension can be shown more directly by a cut of the 3D-diagram at fixed energy, chosen as the break point energy E_c. This is presented in Figure 12B. It shows that increasing effective masses need unphysically small localizations.

From these numbers we can also derive a *critical frequency* $\hbar\omega_c = E_c$ which

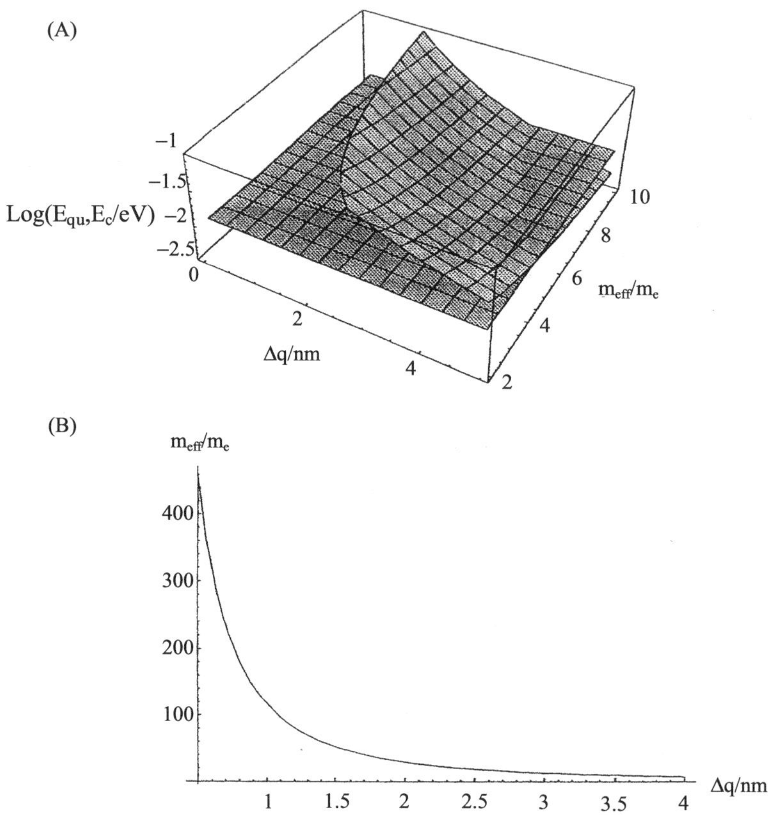

Figure 12. *(A) Three-dimensional plot of the logarithm of the quantal energy E_{qu} in its dependence on the localization dimension) Δq and on the effective mass m_{eff} in units of the electron mass m_e. Also shown is the plain of the break point E_c = const. between the quantal and the thermal regimes. (B) The effective mass m_{eff} in units of the electron mass me as function of the localization length) q.*

in turn defines a *signal time* $\tau_c = 2\pi\omega_c$ which characterizes the upper limit of the quantal time scale. With $E_c = 1.3 \times 10^{-2}$ eV one obtains

$$\omega_c = 2 \times 10^{13}\ \mathrm{s}^{-1} ; \tau_c = 0.3\ \mathrm{ps}\ . \tag{3}$$

These relations show that quantum processes at physiological temperatures involve frequencies smaller than the picosecond scale. They correspond to electronic transitions like electron transfer or changes in molecular bonds (breaking of a hydrogene bridge, etc.). In comparison, cellular dynamics is characterized by time scales $\tau_{cell} > 0.4$ ns (following from $E_{cell} \sim 10^{-5}$ eV, Tuszynski et al. 1998).

Our analysis leads to the consequence that in brain dynamics two well separated regions with different time scales exist:

i. The *macroscopic*, or cellular, dynamics with time scales in the milli-, and down to the nanosecond range.
ii. The *microscopic*, or quantal, dynamics with time scales in the pico- and down to the femtosecond range.

The large difference in time scales makes it possible to deal with quantum processes in the individual microsites, and decoupled from the neural net. On the other hand, it explains why the usual biochemical and biophysical studies do not show the need for introducing quantum considerations. To uncover them one has to employ ultra-short time spectroscopy (Vos et al. 1993).

Quantum triggering of exocytosis

The all important regulatory function of spine synapses results from the fact that exocytosis, the release of transmitter molecules across the presynaptic membrane, occurs only with probabilities much smaller than one upon each incoming nerve impulse (Redman 1990). We therefore regard exocytosis as a candidate for quantum processes to enter the network, and thus regulating its performance (Beck & Eccles 1992).

The remarkably low transition probabilities observed in synaptic exocytosis (Jack et al. 1981; Redman 1990; see also Figure 10) imply that there exists an activation barrier against opening of an ion channel in the PVG. Barrier transitions can either occur purely stochastically by thermal fluctuations, or by stimulation of a trigger process. Here we propose a two-state quantum trigger which is realized by quasi-particle tunneling. This is motivated by the predominant role of exocytosis as the synaptic regulator of cortical activity, and the fine-tuning possible by adjusting the activation energy below the barrier. On the other hand, primary electron transfer processes play a decisive role in membrane transport phenomena (Vos et al. 1993). Exocytosis as a whole certainly involves macromolecular dynamics (Figure 9). We propose, however, that it is initiated by a quantum trigger mechanism: An incoming nerve impulse excites some electronic configuration to a metastable level, separated energetically by a potential barrier $V(q)$ from the state which leads in a unidirectional process to exocytosis. Here, q denotes a collective coordinate representing the path along the coupled electronic and molecular motions between two states. The motion along this path is described by a quasiparticle of mass m_{eff} which is able to tunnel through the barrier quantum-mechanically. As has been shown in the previous section, m_{eff} can be at most of the order of a few eV to decouple from thermal fluctuations. This implies that ion channel dynamics as a whole does not qualify for significant quantum processes in the brain.

The quasiparticle assumption allows the treatment of the complicated molecular transition as an effective one-body problem whose solution follows from the time dependent Schroedinger equation

$$i\hbar\frac{\partial}{\partial t}\Psi(q;t)=-\frac{\hbar^2}{2m_{eff}}\frac{\partial^2}{\partial q^2}\Psi(q;t)+V(q)\times\Psi(q;t). \qquad (4)$$

Figure 13 shows schematically the initial state at $t=0$ (after activation by the incoming impulse), and at the end of the activation period, $t=t_1$. Here it is assumed that the activated state of the presynaptic cell lasts for a finite time t_1 only before it recombines. t_1, however, is of the macroscopic time scale (micro- to nanosecond), as discussed in the previous paragraph. At $t=t_1$ the state has evolved into a part still sitting to the left of the barrier in region (I), while the part in region (III) has tunneled through the barrier. We can now separate the total wave function at time t_1 into two components, representing left and right parts:

$$\Psi(q;t_1)=\Psi_{left}(q;t_1)+\Psi_{right}(q;t_1), \qquad (5)$$

and this constitutes the two interfering amplitudes for the alternative results of the same process as discussed in the 2nd section: either exocytosis *has happened* (Ψ_{right}), or exocytosis *has not happened* (Ψ_{left}, inhibition).

State collapse transforms this into the separate components Ψ_{left}, Ψ_{right}, respectively, from which follow the probabilities

$$\begin{aligned} &\textit{exocytosis}: \quad \text{probability} \quad p_{ex}(t_1)=\int\left|\Psi_{right}\right|^2 dq \\ &\textit{inhibition}: \quad \text{probabiliy} \quad p_{in}(t_1)=\int\left|\Psi_{left}\right|^2 dq \end{aligned} \qquad (6)$$

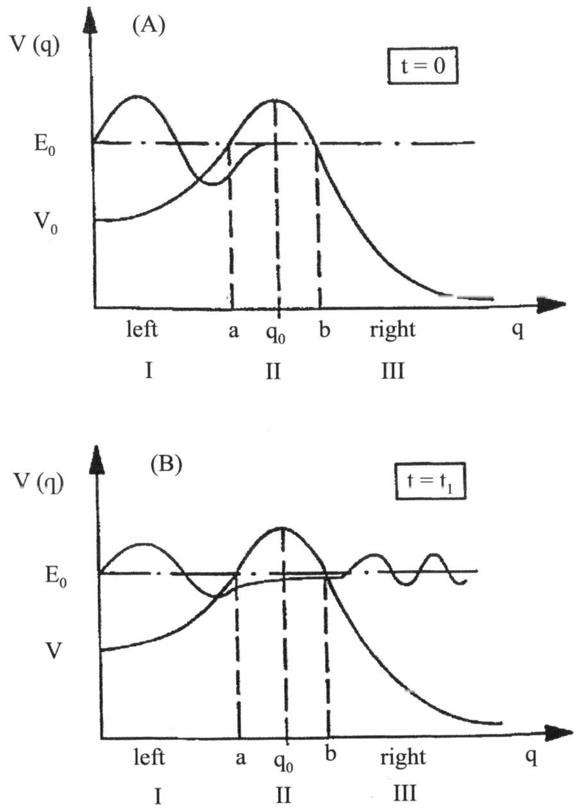

Figure 13. *(A) The initial state (t=0) of the quasiparticle in the potential V(q). The wave function is located to the left of the barrier.* E_0 *is the energy of the activated state which starts to tunnel through the barrier. (B) After time* t_1 *the wave function has components on both sides of the barrier. a, b: classical turning points of the motion inside and outside the barrier (Beck & Eccles 1992).*

To once more estimating numbers using physically meaningful parameters we can evaluate the tunneling process using the Wentzel-Kramers-Brillouin (WKB) approximation (Messiah 1961). This results for the barrier transmission coefficient T in

$$T = \exp\left\{-2\int_a^b \frac{\sqrt{2m_{eff}\left[V(q)-E_0\right]}}{\hbar}\right\}dq \tag{7}$$

with E_0, the energy of the activated initial state. The result is presented in Figure 14A for a range of values of the barrier width, $w = b - a$, and the effective barrier height V, defined as

$$\sqrt{V} = \frac{1}{b-a} \int_a^b \sqrt{V(q) - E_0}\, dq \tag{8}$$

For barrier widths slightly above 1 nm and effective barrier heights of 0.05 to 0.1 eV (which lies still above the energy of thermal fluctuations, cf. Section 4) one obtains transmission coefficients in the range 10^{-1} to 10^{-10}.

For a rough estimate of the exocytosis probability, $p_{ex}(t_1)$ (equation 6) one can use the Gamow-approximation of multiplying the frequency of hitting the barrier per unit time with the activation time t_1,

$$p_{ex}(t_1) = t_1 \varpi_0 T. \tag{9}$$

Using an intermediate value of $T = 10^{-7}$, Figure 14B presents the results for $p_{ex}(t_1)$ in dependence on the activation time t_1 which lies in the (macroscopic) ns time scale, and the excitation energy E_0 (the energy of the activated quantum state before tunneling starts). Reasonable values for these two parameters cover the range between 0 and 0.7 for the probability of exocytosis, in agreement with the measured values (Jack et al. 1981).

Electron transfer in biomolecules

As a possible realization of our quantum trigger model for exocytosis we can consider electron transfer (ET) between biomolecules (Beck 1996b). In biological reaction centers such processes lead to charge transfer across biological membranes (Vos et al. 1993). The quasiparticle describes the electron coupled to nuclear motion according to the Franck-Condon principle. The theory has been worked out by Marcus (1956), and was later put into a quantum mechanical version by Jortner (1976). The initializing step of ET is excitation of donor D, usually a dye molecule, with subsequent transport of an electron to acceptor A, producing the polar system D^+A^-. This is accompanied by rearrangement of the molecular coordinates leading to unidirectional charge separation and, over several further electronic transitions with increasing time constants, to the creation of an action potential across the membrane. The energetics is shown in Figure 15. Figure 15A shows the potential energy curves separately for electrons and nuclear conformations, while Figure 15B gives the combined potential in the

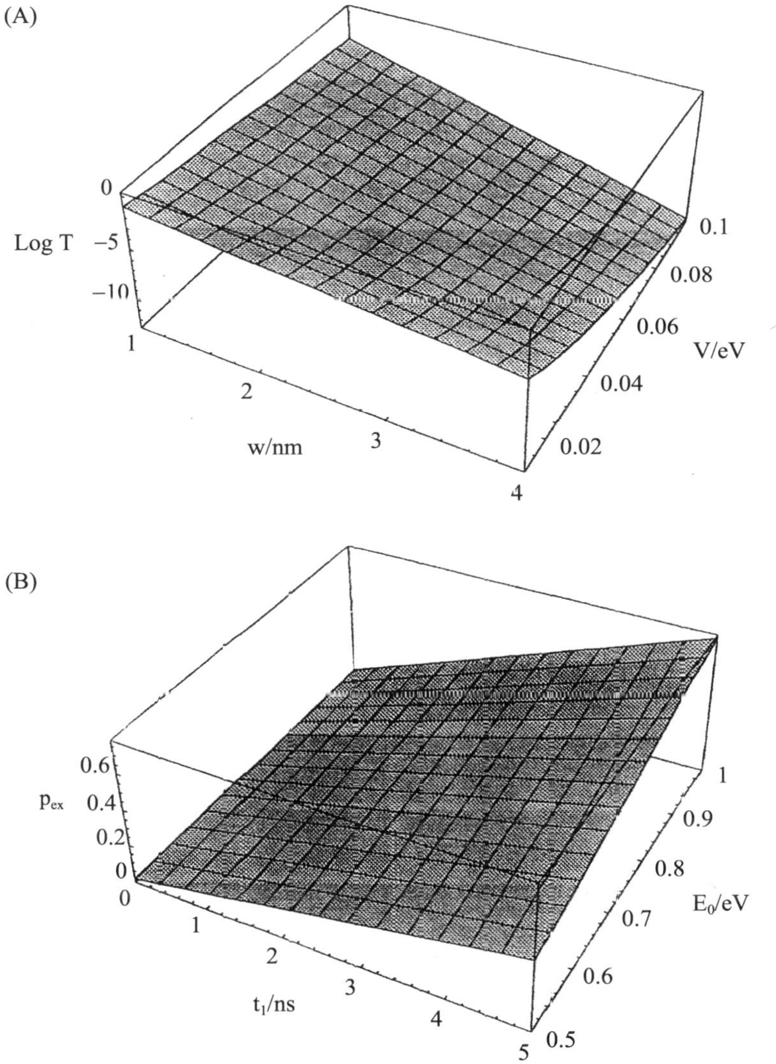

Figure 14. *(A) 3D-plot of the logarithm of the transmission coefficient T in its dependence on the width w of the tunneling barrier, and on the effective barrier height V. (B) Exocytosis probability* $p_{ex}(t_1)$ *(equation 6) calculated with fixed transmission coefficient* $T=10^{-7}$ *and depending on the (macroscopic) activation time* t_1 *and on the excitation energy* E_0 *of the activated trigger state before tunneling.*

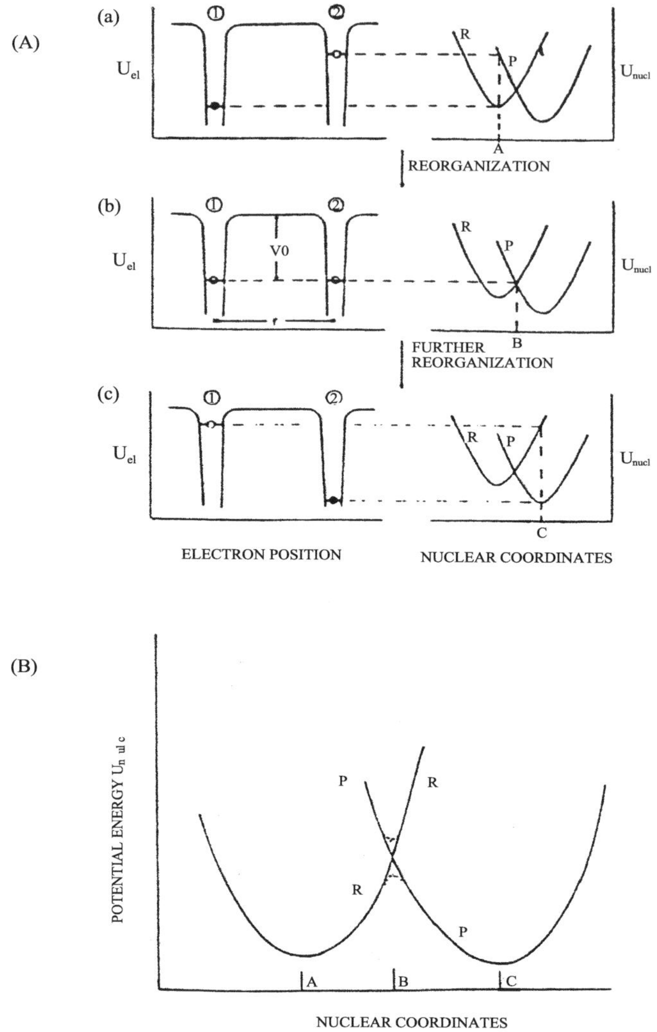

Figure 15. *(A) Electron transfer coupled to nuclear motion. Left: electronic potential energy curves, right: corresponding nuclear potential curves. (a), (b), (c): electronic energies in the two wells for the nuclear positions A, B, C. The transition proceeds from (a) over the barrier (b) to the final state (c). (B) The same situation in the quasiparticle picture. The potential energy surfaces of donor (R) and acceptor (P) are shown. The positions correspond to (A), (B), (C) in (A). The dotted lines indicate splitting due to electron interactions between donor and acceptor. (Marcus & Sutin 1985)*

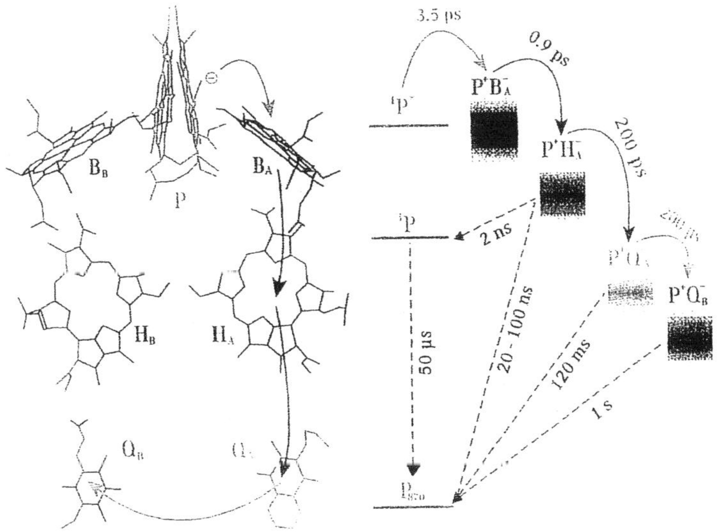

Figure 16. *Energetics and time constants of the photo reaction center in Rb. sphaeroides. After excitation of the dimer P by photon absorption electron transfer from the donor P to the acceptor B_A leads to the excited system $P^+B_A^-$, and from there to further complexes with increasing transfer and comparibly slower recombination rates. This leads to unidirectional electron transport to the final state. (After Ogrodnik et al. 1994)*

quasiparticle picture (Marcus & Sutin 1985). This latter form resembles closely the effective potential assumed in our quantum trigger model presented earlier in this section.

In the electron transfer picture (Jortner 1976) the transition process is described via product states in the electronic coordinates coupled to the nuclear motion:

$$\Psi_i\,(r_e)\otimes\chi_i\,(q)\rightarrow\Psi_f\,(r_e)\otimes\chi_f\,(q) \tag{10}$$

with Ψ, χ: electronic and nuclear states, respectively. The transition rate $i\rightarrow f$ is given by *Fermi's Golden Rule*

$$w_{fi}=\frac{2\pi}{\hbar}\left|H_{fi}\right|^2\times FC, \tag{11}$$

with H_{fi}, the transition matrix element, and FC the Franck-Condon factor which is defined as overlap integral between initial an final wave functions.

High frequency (femtosecond) spectroscopy has not yet been applied to synaptic neural structures. There exists, however, an extensive study with a biological reaction center in photobacteria by Vos et al. (1993) and Ogrodnik et al. (1994). For the photobacteria *Rhodopseudomonas sphaeroides* these authors succeeded in a complete energetic analysis of the transfer steps after photonic excitation of the reaction center. Figure 16 shows their result for the cascade from the first step which is the electron transfer from the excited dimer state ${}^1P^*$ to the donor-acceptor complex $P^+B_A^-$ to a final state with long lifetime, producing an electrochemical potential for subsequent biochemical processes. The cascade with increasing reaction times shows clearly the transfer from the fast primary step to the macroscopic times characteristic for biochemical reactions. Since this photoreaction is a very typical process for creating charge transfer across a biomembrane one could very well speculate that a similar mechanism is responsible for the initiation of exocytosis through the presynaptic membrane (cf. Figure 9) after stimulation of the presynaptic system by an incoming nerve impulse, as is proposed in our model.

5. Neural coherence

The *'hard problem'* in brain research is the binding problem, characterized by coherent action of specific areas in the brain (Posner et al. 1985; Singer 1990; Corbetta et al. 1990; Eccles 1994). Activated brain areas are characterized by an increase in regional cerebral blood flow, as demonstrated in radio-Xenon technology (Roland 1981), or more recently by positron emission tomography (PET, Pardo et al. 1991). Activation generates most complex spatio-temporal patterns which characterize the specific perception (visual, audible, taste or touch) or intention (silent thinking, moves). These patterns are intimately related to memory and the learned inventory of pyramidal cells (Kandel & Schwartz 1982). In the neural bundles ('dendrons', cf. Figure 7), which comprise the active area, there are thousands of modifiable synapses which have to act cooperatively to generate the increased action potential needed to bring out the observed activity (Figure 11). Since the synapses can only modify (increase or decrease) their exocytosis probability upon incoming nerve impulses, there has to be a constant background activity which will be modulated coherently by a large number of synapses.

This poses the quest for spatio-temporal patterns in the neuronal net, and their regulation by synaptic action and possibly diffusive couplings between nerve cells. Several authors concerned with quantum brain dynamics attribute long range coherence in the neuronal net to *macroscopic quantum states*. The most serious of these approaches has been presented by Hameroff & Penrose (1996). None of these papers, however, gives an explicit dynamical framework of how such states could preserve their coherent structure against thermal fluctuations at room temperature.

From empirical evidence (Freeman 1996; Spitzer & Neumann 1996), and from successful modeling (Haken 1996), we would rather attribute long range cooperative action in the active zones of the brain to nonlinear dynamics of a driven open system. Such a system is far from thermal equilibrium and close to instability, and it can organize itself by external stimuli in a variety of synchronous activity patterns (Gray et al. 1989). Synaptic exocytosis in such a system serves as regulator, and the cooperation of the many synapses in the dendrons (active area) produce the spatio-temporal patterns above noise. Quantum action and subsequent state reduction in the individual synapse produce the non-algorithmic binding in cortical units. Figure 17 presents a schematic sketch of three bundles of pyramidal cells (dendrons) surrounded by their spatial pattern which are produced temporarily by cooperation within the individual cells. Since these patterns are activated by perception and intention, as well as in ideation (Ingvar 1990) they represent the basic units of consciousness. To give them a name which expresses their outstanding importance, Eccles (1990) coined them *'psychons'*. The physiological mechanisms of pattern formation and signal transduction in the brain are not yet fully understood. Recent rapid progress in uncovering many facets of nonlinear dynamics in biological systems (cf., e.g., Goldbeter 1996) gives, nevertheless, hope to proceed substantially in understanding large scale brain dynamics in the near future.

A most promising approach to combine noisy structures with the enhancement of regular signals is presented by the observation of *stochastic resonance* (Gammaitoni et al. 1998). A recent study of stochastic resonance in a neuronal net (Jung & Mayer-Kress 1995) is presented in Figure 18. It shows for increasing noise level the time development (left to right) of spiral waves in the excitable medium generated by an initially firing column of elements. The reuslts show clearly the constructive influence of noise on coherent pattern formation (*'stochastic resonance'*). The combination of quantum tunneling states with a noisy surroundings has recently also been studied by Grifoni & Haenggi (1996).

The important role of quantum events does, however, not depend on the exact nature of this large scale structures, but it relies on the concept of state superposition in microscopic molecular transitions. Finally, a word concerning the *qualia* of consciousness may be added. Science can not, by its very nature, present any answer to the philosophical, ethical or religious questions related to

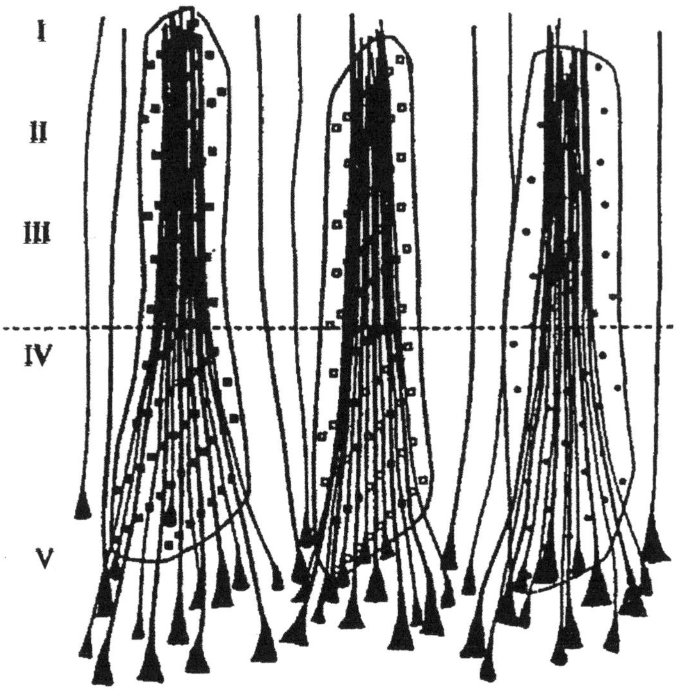

Figure 17. *Coherent couplings of bundles of dendritic pyramidal cells (dendrons) to form spatio-temporal patterns. (Eccles 1990)*

the mind. It can, however, and it does by the quantum logic of microprocesses, provide the openness which is essential to make discussions beyond the limitations of science possible. In this way, the *'ignorabimus'* of du Bois-Reymond (cf. Section 1) has been turned into a hopeful *'non ignorabimus'* through the events of quantum and non-linear physics!

6. Conclusions

Quantum state collapse is the decisive process which distinguishes quantum mechanics from classical physics. In a single event it is non-predictable. By this it qualifies for the indecisive and non-computable nature of brain functioning. It is emphasized that this introduces a new logical concept, different from classical

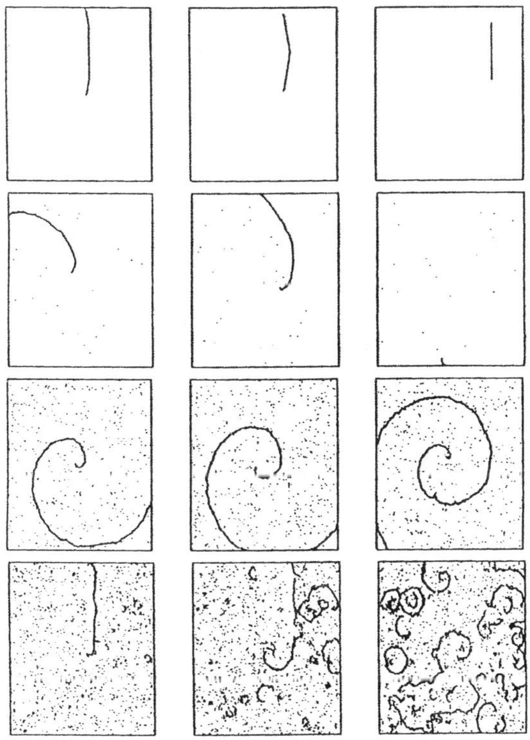

a

b

c

d

Figure 18. *Spatio-temporal pattern formation in a two-dimensional excitable neuronal net model by stochastic resonance. Shown is the formation of spiral waves out of an initially firing column of elements. From left to right: snapshots of firing patterns of elemnts in position (i,j) with i,j = 1,...,400 as time evolves. (a) noise turned off, (b)-(d): increasing noise level (Jung & Mayer-Kress 1995).*

determinism which underlies the struggle between dualism, identity theory, and the call for 'free will'. The interpretation of quantum mechanics as a succession of single events produces in a natural way the fundamental difference between past and future, in so far as the *past is known* (by events having manifestly occurred) while *the future is not known* (by the unpredictability of state reduction). One could, however, object against this interpretation by arguing that the Schroedinger equation is causal, and consequently describes the time evolution of the probability amplitudes unambiguously. Thus, the *probabilities* for future events are completely determined. This, however, relates to ensemble averages of a large number of identical systems under identical initial conditions. Such ensembles can be realized in the material world of microscopic atomic systems but they are never realized in the world of complex objects such as the brain. Each new event finds itself borne in a new initial state. For these the non-predictability for single events prevails.

In view of these new and important concepts for elevating consciousness finally up to a scientific basis, we present evidence for a realistic implementation of quantum events into brain dynamics. It is based on our present knowledge of cortical structure and the synaptic regulation of neural impulses. Basic assumptions and results are:

- Quantum processes in the wet and hot surroundings of the brain are only possible at the microscopic level of (electron) transitions in the pico- to femtosecond time scale.
- Spine synapses are important regulators in brain activity, filtering the ever present firings of nerve impulses.
- Exocytosis, the release of transmitter substance across the presynaptic membrane, is an all-or-nothing event which occurs with probabilities much smaller than one.
- A model, based on electron transfer, relates exocytosis with a two-state quantum trigger, leading by quantum tunneling to the superposition of these two states, followed by state reduction (collapse into one definite final state).
- The coherent coupling of synapses via microtubular connections is still an open problem. Quantum coherence ('macroscopic quantum state') is not needed to couple microsites, which exhibit quantum transitions with their definite phase relations, to produce spatio-temporal patterns. The quantum trigger can however initialize transitions between different macroscopic modes (stochastic limit cycles, Grifoni & Haenggi 1996).
- The quantum trigger opens a doorway for a better understanding of the relations between brain dynamics and consciousness.

Acknowledgments

My interest in brain dynamics was evoked in a vivid discussion with the late Sir John Eccles on quantum mechanics and brain. With his intimate knowledge of brain physiology he gave me a masterful introduction into the relevant functioning of neocortical actions which allowed us to present our first paper on quantum brain dynamics only one year after our intense collaboration. I am deeply obliged to John Eccles, one of the great heroes of neuroscience in the 20th century, for opening me a fascinating field of interdisciplinary research.

Notes

1. In his book von Neumann describes the difference between the ensemble result and the single event rather drastically: *'The everything leveling of the law of large numbers obscures completely the real nature of the single process'*.
2. One may argue that in this scenario the result depends on the place where the cut is made (e.g. in the above example at the screen or, alternatively, including the whole dynamics of the detectors). This is, however, not the case since cutting the dynamics at a later stage requires tracing over the non observed variables which makes the result independent of the cut.
3. This was realized as early as 1907 when Einstein explained the deviation of the specific heat from the Dulong-Petit law by freezing of the quantal oscillators.

References

Akert, K., Peper, K. and Sandri, C. 1975. Structural organization of motor end plate and central synapses, in: *Cholinergic Mechanisms*, ed. P. G. Waser. Raven, New York, 43–57.

Beck, F. and Eccles, J. C. 1992. Quantum aspects of brain activity and the role of consciousness. *Proc. Natl. Acad. Sci USA* 89: 11357–11361.

Beck, F. 1996a. Mind-brain interaction: comments on an article by B. I. B. Lindahl and P. Århem. *J. theor. Biol.* 180: 87–89.

Beck, F. 1996b. Can quantum processes control synaptic emission?. *Int. J. Neural Systems* 7: 343–353.

Beck, F. and Eccles, J. C. 1998. Quantum processes in the brain: a scientific basis of consciousness. *Cognitive Studies* 5(2): 95–109.

Brown, A. G. 1981. *Organization in the Spinal Cord: The Anatomy and Physiology of Identified Neurons*. Springer, Berlin, Heidelberg.

Corbetta, M., Miezin, F. M., Dobmeyer, S., Shulman, G. L. and Petersen, S. E. 1990. Attentional modulation of neural processing of shape, color and velocity in humans. *Science* 248: 1356–1359.

Crick, F. and Koch, C. 1990. Towards a Neurobiological Theory of Consciousness. *Seminars in the Neurosciences* 2: 263–275.

Donald, M. J. 1990. Quantum theory and the brain. *Proc. R. Soc. London* A427: 43–93.

du Bois-Reymond, E. 1916. *Über die Grenzen des Naturerkennens*. Veit and Co., Leipzig.

Eccles, J. C. 1989. *Evolution of the Brain: Creation of the Self*. Routledge, London, New York.

Eccles, J. C. 1990. A unitary hypothesis of mind-brain interaction in the cerebral cortex. *Proc. R. Soc. London* B240: 433–451.

Eccles, J. C. 1994. *How the Self Controls Its Brain*. Springer, Berlin, Heidelberg, New York.

Edelman, G. M. 1989. *The Remembered Present. A Biological Theory of Consciousness*. Basic Books, New York.

Feigl, H. 1967. *The Mental and the Physical*. University of Minnesota Press, Minneapolis.

Fliessbach, T. 1991. *Quantenmechanik.* BI-Wiss.-Verl., Mannheim, Wien, Zürich.

Flohr, H. 1995. An information processing theory of anesthesia. *Neuropsychologia* 33: 1169–1180.

Freeman, W. J. 1996. Random activity at the microscopic neural level in cortex ("noise") sustains and is regulated by low-dimensional dynamics of macroscopic cortical activity ("chaos"). *Int. Journal of Neural Systems* 7: 473–480.

Gammaitoni, L., Haenggi, P., Jung, P. and Marchesoni, F. 1998. Stochastic resonance. *Rev. Mod. Physics* 70: 223–287.

Gray, E. G. 1982. Rehabilitating the dendric spine. *Trends Neurosci.* 5: 5–6.

Gray, C. M., König, P., Engel, A. K. and Singer, W. 1989. Oscillatory response in cat visual cortex exhibit inter-columnar synchronization which reflects global stimulus properties. *Nature* 338: 334–337.

Grifoni, M. and Haenggi, P. 1996. Coherent and incoherent quantum stochastic resonance. *Phys. Rev. Letters* 76: 1611–1614.

Goldbeter, A. 1996. *Biochemical Oscillations and Cellular Rhythmics.* Cambridge University Press, Cambridge U. K.

Haken, H. 1996. Noise in the brain: A physical network model. *Internatl. J. Neural Systems* 7: 551–557.

Hameroff, S. R. and Penrose, R. 1996. Conscious events as orchestrated space–time selections. *Journal of Consciousness Studies* 3(1): 36–53.

Ingvar, D. H. 1990. On ideation and 'ideography', in: *The Principles of Design and Operation of the Brain*, eds. J. C. Eccles and O. Creutzfeld. Experimental Brain Research 21, Springer-Verlag, Berlin, Heidelberg.

Jack, J. J. B., Redman, S. J. and Wong, K. 1981. The components of synaptic potentials evoked in cat spinal motoneurons by impulses in single group Ia afferents. *J. Physiol. London* 321: 65–96.

Jortner, J. 1976. Temperature dependent activation energy for electron transfer beween biological molecules. *J. Chem. Phys.* 64: 4860–4867.

Jung, P. and Mayer-Kress, G. 1995. Spatiotemporal stochastic resonance in excitable media. *Phys. Rev. Letters* 74: 2130–2133.

Kandel, E. K. and Schwartz, J. H. 1982. Molecular biology of learning: modulation of transmitter release. *Science* 218: 433–443.

Kelly, R. B., Deutsch, J. W., Carlson, S. S. and Wagner, J. A. 1979. Biochemistry of neurotransmitter release. *Ann. Rev. Neurosci.* 2: 399–446.

Lindahl, B. I. B. and Århem, P. 1994. Mind as a force field: comments on a new interactionistic hypothesis. *J. theor. Biol.* 171: 111–122.

Marcus, R. A. 1956. On the theory of oxydation-reduction reactions involving electron transfer. *J. Chem. Phys.* 24: 966–978.

Marcus, R. A. and Sutin, N. 1985. Electron transfer in chemistry and biology. *Biochim. Biophys. Acta* 811: 265–322.

Margenau, H. 1984. *The Miracle of Existence.* Ox Bow, Woodbridge, CT.

Mendell, L. M. and Henneman, E. 1971. Terminals of single Ia fibers: location, density and distribution within a pool of 300 homogenous motoneurons. *J. Neurophysiol.* 34: 171–187.

Messiah, A. 1961. *Quantum Mechanics I.* North Holland, Amsterdam, 231–242.

Mountcastle, V. B. 1978. An organizing principle for cerebral function: the unit module and the distributed system, in: *The Mindful Brain*, ed. F. C. Schmitt. MIT Press, Cambridge MA, 7–50.

Ogrodnik, A., Keupp, W., Volk, M., Aumeier, G. and Michel-Beyerle, M. E. 1994. Inhomogeneity of radial pair energies in photosynthetic reaction centers revealed by differences in recombination dynamics of $P^{+}H_{A}^{-}$ when detected in delayed emission and in absorption. *J. Phys. Chem.* 98: 3432–3439.

Pardo, J. V., Fox, P. T. and Raichle, M. E. 1991. Localization of a human system for sustained attention by positron emission tomography. *Nature* 349: 61–64.

Penrose, R. 1984. *The Emperor's New Mind: Concerning Computers, Minds and the Laws of Physics*. Oxford Univ. Press, Oxford.

Penrose, R. 1994. *Shadows of the Mind: An Approach to the Missing Science of Consciousness.* Oxford Univ. Press, Oxford.

Peters, A. and Kara, D. A. 1987. The neuronal composition of area 17 of rat visual cortex. IV. The organization of pyramidal cells. *J. Comp. Neurol.* 260: 573–590.

Pfenninger, K., Sandri, C., Akert, K. and Eugster, C. H. 1969. Contribution to the problem of structural organization of the presynaptic area. *Brain Res.* 12: 10–18.

Popper, K. R. 1972. *Objective Knowledge: An Evolutionary Approach.* Clarendon, Oxford.

Popper, K. R., Lindahl, B. I. B. and Århem, P. 1993. A discussion of the mind-brain problem. *Theor. Med.* 14: 167–180.

Posner, M. I., Petersen, S. E., Fox, P. T. and Raichle, M. E. 1985. Localization of cognitive operations in the human brain. *Science* 240: 1627–1631.

Redman, S. J. 1990. Quantal analysis of synaptic potentials in neurons of the central nervous system. *Physiol. Rev.* 70: 165–198.

Roland, P. E., Larsen, B., Lassen, N. A. and Skinhøj, E. 1980. Supplemental motor area and other cortical areas in organization of voluntary movements in man. *J. Neurophysiol.* 43: 118–136.

Sayer, R. J., Redman, S. J. and Andersen, P. 1989. Amplitude fluctuations in small EPSPs recorded from CA1 pyramidal cells in the guinea pig hippocampal slice. *J. Neurosci.* 9: 845–850.

Sayer, R. J., Friedlaender, M. J. and Redman, S. J. 1990. The time-course and amplitude of EPSPs evoked at synapses between pairs of CA3/CA1 neurons in the hippocampal slice. *J. Neurosci.* 10: 626–636.

Schmolke, C. and Fleischhauer, K. 1984. Morphological characteristics of neocortical laminae when studied in tangential semi-thin sections through the visual cortex in the rabbit. *Anat. Embryol.* 169: 125–132.

Singer, W. 1990. Search for coherence: a basic principle of cortical self-organization. *Concepts Neurosci.* 1: 1–26.

Spitzer, M. and Neumann, M. 1996. Noise in models of neurological and psychiatric disorders. *Internatl. J. Neural Systems* 7: 355–361.

Squires, E. J. 1988. The unique world of the Everett version of quantum theory. *Found. Physics Lett.* 1: 13–20.

Stapp, H. P. 1991. Brain-mind connection. *Found. Physics* 21: 1451–1477.

Szentàgothai, J. 1978. The neuron network of the cerebral cortex: a functional interpretation. *Proc. R. Soc. London* B201: 219–248.

Tuszynski, J. A., Brown, J. A. and Hawrylak, P. 1998. Dielectric polarization, electrical conduction, information processing and quantum computation in microtubules. Are they plausible? *Phil. Trans. R. Soc. London* A356: 1897–1926.

von Neumann, J. 1955. *Mathematical Foundations of Quantum Mechanics*. Princeton University Press, Princeton NJ, Chap.IV.

Vos, M. H., Rappaport, F., Lambry, J. C., Beton, J. and Martin, J.-L. 1993. Visualization of coherent nuclear motion in a membrane protein by femtosecond spectroscopy. *Nature* 363: 320–325.

Walmsley, B., Edwards, F. R. and Tracey, D. J. 1987. The probabilistic nature of synaptic transmission at a mammalian excitatory central synapse. *J. Neurosci.* 7: 1037–1046.

Wheeler, J. A. and Zurek, W. H. (eds.) 1983. *Quantum Theory and Measurements.* Princeton University Press, Princeton, NJ.

Wigner, E. P. 1964. Two kinds of reality. *Monist* 48: 248–264.

Zurek, W. H. 1991. Decoherence and the transition from quantum to classical. *Physics Today* 44(10): 36–44.

Neuropsychological Investigations

Karl H. Pribram

Abstract

It is conjectured that each organism, like a Leibnizian monad, re-presents the universe, and the universe reflects, in some manner, the organism that observes it. The perceptions of an organism cannot be understood without an understanding of the nature of the physical universe and the nature of the physical universe cannot be understood without an understanding of the perceptual process. The Leibnizian position gets significantly reinforced by quantum theory, but remarkably in a way in which the space–time and spectral perspectives get reconciled and appear to be no more divisive than the two faces of the same coin. This occurs via Planck's constant h, which opens up a bridge between space–time locatable concepts such as mass and undulatory concepts such as energy measured as frequency, wavelength, amplitude and phase. On the basis of such reasoning, the brain is seen to be the medium for transformations into and out of a potential distributed energetic and an experienced spacetime order.

1. Introduction

Words: Conscious experience, global consciousness, free will, conscience, embodied emotions; these are some of the key labels that characterize discourse in current cognitive neuroscience. A half century ago these words were taboo in the annals of neurobehavioral inquiry. I have been surprised by the overwhelming power of scientific fashion. Science appears to be no more immune to trendiness than the clothing industry. One might expect philosophical inquiry to maintain a steadier course; but alas, 'tis not so.

By contrast, clinical observations and experimental results have, from time to time, made it necessary for me to depart from the prevailing fashion, and so, over the years I have written a number of books and theoretical essays covering the topics to which these names refer, making me appear a traitor to my colleagues. For reasons that I hope will become apparent, I will, therefore, write the current observations in the spirit, if not in the form, of Wittgenstein's Investigations.

I began my research into the mind-brain interface at a time when vitalism had been successfully banished from biology. My aim was to help eradicate psychologism from brain science. Behaviorism was made to order, and I studied and actively participated in its various forms. Had eliminative materialism been around, I am sure to have been a devotee.

Behaviorism served me well, especially in the laboratory. Technical behaviorism has provided a major advance in data acquisition and in understanding the brain-behavior relationship, much as did positivism in clarifying issues in philosophy. However, just as Wittgenstein found a world beyond the *Tractatus*, I found issues that were intractable within the behaviorist frame.

One such issue centered on serial processing. How am I able to produce this typescript? What brain processes allow me to place the *p* before the *l* before the *a* before the *c* before the final *e*? During the late 1950s it became plausible to suggest that serial ordering was controlled by the brain in a fashion similar to the way it was controlled by a computer program. The cognitive revolution in psychology was born (Pribram 1960a).

Another issue: how is it that a rat with a lesion in the region of the ventromedial nucleus of the hypothalamus will overeat when food is available *ad libitum*, but will undereat when it has to work for that food? In the language of stimulus-response behaviorism, the rat simultaneously displays both an increased and a decreased "drive". The construct "effort" seems more appropriate but, of course, is a cognitive term (Pribram 1967).

In short, psychology was not to be got rid of so readily. So far there was nothing like the synthesis of urea from inorganic molecules which had taken place in biochemistry. But why not define "effort" in hard science terms? It can be done via information measurement theory as the amount of work involved in reducing equivocation (redundancy plus noise). Effort turned out to be a useful indicator, not only of hypothalamic, but of hippocampal function in my work with non-human primates (Pribram & McGuinness 1975).

I have put my faith in being able to provide rigorous definitions for terms commonly used in folk psychology. This has got me in trouble with behaviorists and eliminatists. And I often sympathize with them: the going is hard, not because of the way folk use psychological terms, but because cognitive neuroscientists and philosophers either fail to provide definitions or play loose by not agreeing on common definitions. Anatomists have meetings once a decade to decide on nomenclature. I suggested this to a colleague in psychology: his response was "how undemocratic".

2. A subjective behaviorism

Perhaps the language of folk psychology is too ambiguous and the answers to the mind-brain relationship lie in mathematical language. Recourse to mathematical concepts has rewarded me with exciting new insights. More on this anon. But in obtaining data from observations and experiments in studying the brain-mind relationship, one cannot abandon the language of folk psychology for several reasons: For one, natural language systems enfold an age-old wisdom that we can ill afford to neglect. For another, patients with brain malfunctions cannot communicate in any other way. And such patients are a rich source of data for those of us who want to know about brain processes.

In my own development, a patient who had received a bilateral amygdalectomy made it necessary to pay heed to natural language. This patient was seen to stuff herself and had gained a great deal of weight since the surgery. I asked her whether this was due to hunger or some special appetites. The answer was always "no". But one day, after again denying any increased feeling of hunger, I opened the door of the examining room onto the common room where luncheon was being served. The patient dashed to the table, pushed others aside, and began to grab food and stuff it into her mouth. I brought the patient back to the examining room, asked her what the immediately foregoing behavior was all about, whether perhaps she was hungry after all. All I received from the patient was denial. She simply did not know why she behaved the way she did. The lesson for me: Observations of behavior are not enough; we need to attend human subjectivity as accessed through verbal report (Pribram 1962). In *Plans and the Structure of Behavior* (Miller, Galanter & Pribram 1960) we called ourselves subjective behaviorists.

3. Of conscious experience and consciousness

Once we admit subjectivity to scientific investigation, we come up against the hard problems of how to cope with each others' conscious experience and how the brain is involved in organizing such experiences. Immediately, one is distracted by a definition of consciousness held by many philosophers and lay people: a definition that can best be expressed as cosmic consciousness. Thus, many efforts have been made to raise our consciousness to encompass the damage our civilization is wreaking on our planet, to become conscious of the consciousness of other beings and even rocks, etc.

If we simply substitute other terms for the word consciousness, the issue might be simply resolved, albeit much less interesting. Instead of raising consciousness we can draw attention to the way in which we are trashing the earth. Instead of insisting that rocks have some form of attenuated consciousness, we can note that all matter is organized and that organization *per se*, its patterning, has common elements no matter where we find it.

Having, for the moment, rid ourselves of these distractions, we can concentrate on conscious (subjective) experience, consciousness as experienced by humans and expressed in verbal and nonverbal communication. Each of us experiences these experiences, and we attempt to share them through communication. We also try to understand the experiences by manipulating them, analyzing their components. We find that people with brain injuries communicate to us that their conscious experiences are no longer what they were prior to the injury, nor are they like our own ordinary experiences. Brain apparently has a role in organizing our conscious experience.

We can leave it at that and simply say that conscious experience is a product of our brain, an emergent property (a patterned organization) of brain processes. We might add that the contents of conscious experience are partly determined by inherited properties of the body, including the brain, and partly learned from our cultural heritage. Pushing a little further, we might add that these contents of consciousness are composed of patterns that actually exist in the cosmos, that our perceptions not only resonate to (in some way match) our social and cultural milieu but to patterns that occur in the universe. If so, the distracting cosmic consciousness ceases to be a distraction.

The above paragraph needs considerable unpacking. The statements assume that there is a reality and that our experience matches or resonates to that reality. For the scale of ordinary experience this assumption fits the theoretical formulations of evolution — if our experience were not in some way consonant with reality, we should not survive. When we look at some other scale, say that of the quantum physicist or that of the cosmologist, the evolutionary argument does not hold. Instead we have the observation that mathematicians invent or discover formulations which then prove to be immensely useful to the quantum physicist and cosmologist in organizing their observations. A most likely explanation is that the human brain, being part of the cosmos, formulates patterns that are consonant with the cosmos. There is a good deal of circularity, of tautology, in these arguments — thus their axiomatic nature.

Another opacity in the above paragraph concerns the terms match and resonance. Matching need not entail a picture-like template matching procedure. Rather a set of transfer functions, preferably invertable, can be involved. These transfer functions may utilize statistical procedures, vector matrices, and when performed in the spectral domain, resonances. Many of these types of procedures are different ways to formulate the same processes (such as the Schroedinger equations and the Heisenberg matrices).

4. The hermeneutics of dualism

When we have to rely on language to gauge one another's subjective experience (and even in our own thought processes), an historical and ontological analysis sheds light on the hold dualistic formulations have had on the mind/brain relationship. In linguistic communication the elementary structures, holophrases, quickly develop into propositional utterances. In large part this is due to the human tendency to reify and name, a useful tendency that brings with it the possibility of richness due to a prodigious capacity for memory but with the danger of loss of flexibility. Thus, Yahveh, "being", becomes "A Being". To restore some flexibility "The Being" needs to do something, perhaps to someone. Yahveh gives Moses the tablets containing the ten commandments: subject, verb, object. Subject becomes the object of our prayers. Dualism is born. The subjective mind finds an objective brain as its "cause". The subject, "brain process" gives rise to a reified object "The Mind".

Aspects of mind come to distinguish self from other. The intentional, agency aspects of self arise as a consequence. The power of nominalization (reification) can be gleaned not only from its use in science but from such observations as those of Helen Keller, whose world came to life (and her ethical sense awakened) once she could name, objectify, items previously experienced only as processes (Pribram 1985a: 701–702):

> I knew then that w-a-t-e-r meant that wonderful cool something that was flowing over my hand. That living word awakened my soul, gave it light, hope, joy, set it free! There were barriers still it is true, but barriers that could in time, be swept away. I left the well-house eager to learn. Everything had a name, and each name gave birth to a new thought. As we returned to the house, every object which I touched seemed to quiver with life. That was because I saw everything with a strange new sight that had come to me. On entering the door, I remembered the doll I had broken. I felt my way to the hearth and picked up the pieces. I tried vainly to put them together. Then my

> eyes filled with tears for I realized what I had done [she had earlier destroyed the doll in a fit of temper], and for the first time I felt repentance and sorrow. (Helen Keller 1903/1954)

> Here ... in a small space and a short time something extremely important and mysterious had happened. Seven year old Helen made her breakthrough from the good responding animal which behaviorists study so successfully to the strange name-giving and sentence-uttering creature which is Homo Sapiens.
>
> ... [Seven-year-old Helen] did not make the mistake of the radical behaviorists — subject as well as object were attended. Note also that in doing so, propositions were formed, remembrances, repentances, and sorrows could be entertained. Subject could be responsible for object, cause could lead to effect.

Irrespective of whether process descriptions in terms of verbs preceded or arose coterminally with nominalization and whether nominalization preceded or arose coterminally with "propositional utterances", the entire set of linguistic operations described above did occur in human prehistory and do occur in the development of every human being. Thus the mind-brain issue is joined at the very inception of what makes us human — our ability to make propositions, i.e., to conceptualize processes [in terms of duals such as] subjects acting on objects [mind acting on brain, or vice-versa]. In order to nominalize a process into a proposition made up of a subject, verb, and object, we must first categorize and then hierarchically arrange categories into logical relationships. We thus become *logical* animals — the word *logical* being derived from the word *logos*, Greek for "word".

We have been presented here with the origin of *linguistic* duality. Its relation to the mind/brain duality is obvious whether we view mind as being organized by brain or vice versa. The mind/brain duality becomes even more intriguing when we speak of spirituality. For example, an aspect of "mind", "soul", is often treated as a "thing" in the English language.

This is not surprising since the German word for social science, *Seelenwissenschaft* (as opposed to *Naturwissenschaft*, the natural science) translates as "science of the soul". The French term *conscience* means both conscious and con*science* (another English noun standing for a process, the capacity to determine right from wrong).

No one today denies that minding exists. Minding is attending, the process that integrates conscious states with conscious contents. But are we being misled by our universal tendency to reify — which doesn't always work? I hold that reifying minding into a *thing*, a material mind which has mass and therefore extension in time and space, is leading us astray. There is another way to understand "mind" as process, as attending, minding.

In closing this section, a warning needs to be noted: confusing a reductionist position such as materialism as monistic is an error. Eliminatist materialism is a covert dualism. Just as there is no down without an up, there cannot be a materialist position without an implicit acknowledgment of the existence of a mentalism. And vice-versa.

5. Experiences that locate an "objective me"

Philosophers alert us to the issues involved in scientific exploration and discovery. But the explorations must be accomplished by bench scientists who grapple with the problems posed by philosophers. For the mind-brain issue, clinical observations and experiments performed by neuropsychologists have provided a wealth of data relevant to relating conscious experience (minding) to brain and brain to conscious experience. The situation can be compared to that obtained in evolutionary theory: the apparent gap between early homonids and homo sapiens is continually being filled with new finds that clarify, step by step, the relationships that connect early with later species.

Take as an example blindsight. Blindsight occurs as a result of an occipital lesion, almost always limited to one hemisphere and presumably to the primary sensory receiving area of that hemisphere. Subjects with blindsight respond correctly by guessing the location and configuration of a pattern presented visually, but they cannot "see" such a pattern when it is located in the "blind" hemifield.

Blindsight is not unique in such dissociations between patients' verbal reports of introspection and their behavior. Another such dissociation occurs after parietal lobe lesions and provides a somewhat clearer view of what patients experience when a still appropriately functioning limb contralateral to the lesion is excluded from awareness. Here is a case history presented by a student in my class who is experiencing such "neglect".

> From Mrs. C.:
> I was doing laundry about mid-morning when I had a migraine. I felt a sharp pain in my left temple and my left arm felt funny. I finished my laundry towards mid-afternoon and called my neurologist. He told me to go to the emergency room. I packed a few things and drove about 85 miles to the hospital where he is on staff (the nearest was 15 minutes away). In the E. R. the same thing happened again. And again, the next morning after I was hospitalized, only it was worse. The diagnosis of a stroke came as a complete surprise to me because I felt fine, and I didn't notice anything different about myself. I remember having no emotional response to the news. I felt annoyed and more concerned about getting home, because I was in the process of moving.

> Not until several days later while I was in rehabilitation did I notice strange things happening to me. I was not frightened, angry or annoyed. I didn't feel anything — nothing at all. Fourteen days after I was admitted to the hospital, I became extremely dizzy, and I felt I was falling out of my wheelchair. The floor was tilting to my left and the wheelchair was sliding off the floor. Any stimulus on my left side or repetitive movement with my left arm caused a disturbance in my relationship with my environment. For instance, the room would tilt down to the left, and I felt my wheelchair sliding downhill of the floor, and I was falling out of my chair. I would become disoriented, could hardly speak, and my whole being seemed to enter a new dimension. When my left side was placed next to a wall or away from any stimuli, this disturbance would gradually disappear. During this period, the left hand would contract, and the arm would draw up next to my body. It didn't feel or look like it belonged to me.
>
> I call that arm Alice (Alice doesn't live here anymore) — the arm I don't like. It doesn't look like my arm and doesn't feel like my arm. I think it's ugly, and I wish it would go away. Whenever things go wrong, I'll slap it and say, "Bad Alice" or "It's Alice's fault." I never know what it's doing or where it is in space unless I am looking at it. I can use it, but I never do so consciously because I'm unaware of having a left arm. I don't neglect my left side, just Alice. Whatever it does, it does on its own, and most of the time, I don't know it's doing it. I'll be doing homework and then I'll take a sip of coffee. The cup will be empty. I was drinking coffee with that hand and didn't know it. Yet I take classical guitar lessons. I don't feel the strings or frets. I don't know where my fingers are nor what they are doing, but still I play.
>
> How do I live with an illness I'm not aware of having? How do I function when I'm not aware that I have deficits? How do I stay safe when I'm not aware of being in danger?

Ms. C. is obviously intelligent, attending lecture material, asking interesting questions. She is a widowed lady in her mid-fifties, enrolled in adult education, majoring in clinical psychology. She gets around splendidly despite Alice and despite a history of a temporary left hemi-paresis. The diagnosis was damage of the right temporal-parietal cortex confirmed by an abnormal EEG recorded from that location. The damage was not sufficiently extensive to show in a PET scan.

Placed in juxtaposition with blindsight, a simple conclusion can be reached: In humans, there are separate brain systems that organize allocentric (such as occulocentric) and egocentric (body centered) awareness. Damage to these systems "deletes" awareness but minimally impairs instrumental behavior. When, however, additional brain damage occurs and "denial" of the impairment in awareness is added, then behavior can become severely maladaptive: A driver of an automobile will run into a telephone pole because he/she is unaware of his/her hemianopic loss of awareness; a patient will inadvertently mutilate his/her neglected limb because he/she is unaware of the neglect. Denial ordinarily occurs when the brain lesion is more anterior and medial to that which produces simple blindsight and neglect.

5.1 *The relation between allocentric and egocentric experience*

Given a separate allocentric and egocentric awareness, how do these relate to each other? I once had a patient who, after an auto accident, experienced the onset of sudden dizzy spells during which his visual world would rotate and end upside down. After 10–15 minutes he would have another spell and his world was right side up once more. During the spells, he would brace himself against a wall or hold onto something solid. While his visual world was upside down he could navigate, but cautiously. The spells were becoming fewer, and his main complaint was his annoyance that when he saw girls walking upside down, their skirts remained up/down.

I had no chance to examine this patient while his visual world had turned. But recently two undergraduate students undertook to experiment with ocular prisms that inverted the visual world. Following the work of Stratton (1896) and Ivo Köhler (1964) we expected it would take a week or so for the visual world to appear right side up once more after continuous wearing of the prisms. One of the two students became the guide for the one wearing the prisms. As expected, in about eight days, the visual world was "right side up" for both the students even though the prisms inverted the ocular image for one of them.

What I wanted to know is where did the prism wearer's feet appear to him: within his occulocentric, allocentric space or within his egocentric experience? The answer was forthright: in his egocentric body space. The same with his hands. I then inserted my hand to match his within his egocentric awareness. No problem. But when I held my hand in exactly the same way beyond the reach of his arm, it was now upside-down from how it had been for him when "inside" his egocentric frame. At the border of his reach, things became confused and he simply "couldn't tell".

Mountcastle et. al (1975) have shown in monkeys that cells in the parietal lobe will become active (fire) when a piece of food is displayed within the reach of the monkey even when he is prevented from reaching. When the food is presented beyond reach, no activation is recorded.

To summarize: separate brain systems organize an occulocentric, that is, allocentric "space" and another, a body centered, egocentric "space". These two "spaces" meet at the boundary of the person's reach. Injury to these systems allows a patient to behave appropriately to environmental circumstance, despite loss of awareness. Additional brain damage can, however, impair behavior. The damage is usually forward and medial to that which impairs awareness. In humans, such damage results in a denial of loss of awareness. In animals, instrumental behavior guided by allocentric or ego-centric cues becomes impaired. It is the "paradox" — the fact that animals' and humans' instrumental behavior remains intact despite damage to the "primary" sensory receiving systems and, further, that behavior is disturbed by more forward lesions — that led many eighteenth century neuroscientists to mislocate these primary systems (see the disputes between Ferrier, Goltz, Munk; reviewed by Ferrier 1876).

5.2 *Object centered frames of reference*

The more forward located systems involve the experiencing of entities. Allocentric and egocentric "spaces" constitute frames of reference within which behavior becomes organized. But these two are not the only frames for which separately localized brain systems can be identified. Another set of systems deals with constancies, the invariant properties that make possible the perception of entities. In vision these are e.g. objects and color; in audition they are e.g. phonemes and tones. Characteristic of entities is that they remain invariant over transformations. For example, object constancy derives from operations that can be described in terms of mathematical group theory (Hoffman 1978; Pribram 1991). Color constancy derives from operations on double opponens processing (DeValois & DeValois 1993; Zeki 1993).

I did not realize the devastating effect on conscious experience that damage to a constancy system would produce until I read "The Case of the Colorblind Painter" presented by Oliver Sacks in *An Anthropologist on Mars* (1995). The painter, whose color constancy system was selectively damaged, was not left with just a colorless black-white visual world; he was left with a muddy, hazy experience. Should the damage be to *object* constancy, the visual world appear to be devoid of entities such as telephone poles or arms (Alice doesn't live here anymore).

When we performed an experiment on size constancy, Ungerleider, Ganz and I (1977) showed that monkeys who had their peri- and prestriate cortical systems removed responded to the retinal image size of a pattern (a square) and failed to take the distance of the pattern into account. Extrapolating to object constancy, one would expect that a person would fail to recognize an object when its perspective changed. Turnbull (Turnbull & McCarthy 1996; Turnbull 1997; Turnbull, Carey & McCarthy 1997) describe just such a patient. For this patient, every perspective of an entity entailed its own "meaning", separate from any relationship to other perceptions.

5.3 *Other reference frames and the relations between them*

Taken a step further, other frames of reference can be identified. A categorical and a propositional frame are the most obvious. Just as perspectives are grouped to construct invariances that are identified as entities, so entities can become grouped into categories. Eleanor Rosch (1975) has performed a series of experiments showing how categories are constructed around a kernel, a prototype. And Martha Wilson (1987) has shown, using monkeys, that with respect to visual entities, the inferotemporal cortex lying anterior to the peri- and prestriate regions, is critical to the formation of prototypes. Furthermore, she has provided a model for the operation of this prototype system (see also the review by Pribram 1991, Lecture 7).

Edelman (1989) has constructed his theory of consciousness around the operations that produce categories. Others (e.g. Freud 1895; Eccles 1958) have invoked propositional utterances as the basis of conscious experience. A propositional frame of reference uses entities and categories to construct proposals, naming entities and categories and predicating their relationship to one another.

At this propositional level of experience we can go back and identify the distinction between allocentric and egocentric frames and suggest that this distinction underlies Brentano's (1973) conceptualization of "intentional inexistence" or as it is usually called, "intentionality". Intentionality is the experiencing of 'aboutness' — experiencing the distinction between self and other, where *both* experiences are about entities, an egocentric 'me' and an allocentric 'other'. Note that when operating in the propositional frame, the ego and allocentric frames are embedded — but note also that the embedding is reciprocal and interpenetrating, not just hierarchical.

This reciprocal embedding can be accounted for by a multidimensional model where dimensions are extended into a more encompassing domain. Hertz named such operations holonomic (*holos*, whole; *nomos*, lawful), What I have in mind is a shift much as occurs from a representation in Euclidian geometry to Riemanian, or from viewing a scene in two-dimensions to viewing it in three. Essays into such hyperspaces are being explored (see e.g. *Hyperspace*, by Michio Kaku 1994) in physics but as yet have not been applied to understanding the variety of frames of reference in our conscious perceptual experience and their relation to one another. I believe this to be a most fruitful direction to pursue in consciousness research and wish I had the mathematical and intellectual tools to do so myself. However, this much appears to be necessary: In a massively parrallel system, each of the variables (dimensions) can be encoded in its own synaptodendritic domain (or segment of the network) and the entire ensemble scanned simultaneously. Any significant change in any one or in several of the dimensions would change the profile of the ensemble and thus the output to the scanner which determines the frame of reference.

Earlier I noted that with deeper brain damage, a failure in awareness of a loss of awareness results. Such denials can become complex in that they are often situation dependent. Ramachandran (1995) has described in detail such complexities. These context (situation) dependent second order impairments of conscious experience are dispositions that lead to meta-consciousnesses. At the same time, when unimpaired, such dispositions operate outside of awareness and therefore partake of unconscious processing. For that matter, the *processing* that allows us to experience entities and frames — e.g., allo- or egocentrically, categorically, or propositionally — is always unconscious. We experience only the result of processing as the contents of consciousness. And even these escape intentionality, aboutness, under most circumstances when processing has become automatic. Only when a situation is new (as when we are learning to drive, or when automaticity is disrupted) do we need to mind, to "pay" attention, to monitor and become consciously aware that we are processing the contents of consciousness.

6. Experiences that monitor the episodes that construct a "narrative I"

There are other systems with functions different from those so far considered that are located, in a sense, at the opposite "end" of the brain. The systems include the anterior poles of the frontal and temporal lobes and the limbic formations on the medial part of the cerebral hemispheres that connect the two poles (Kaada, Pribram & Epstein 1949; Pribram 1961). Whereas the posterior convexal systems organize our experience (minding) within a complex of reference frames, these frontolimbic systems organize our experience into a "narrative" composed of episodes and events that occur within these episodes. Again a case history highlights the issues (modified from a thesis written by Richard Ahern 1998):

> TK [an eight-year old boy] had an agenesis of the corpus callosum with a midline cyst at birth. During the first six months of his life, two surgical procedures were carried out to drain the cyst. Recently performed Magnetic Resonance Imaging (MRI) showed considerable enlargement of the frontal

> horns of the lateral ventricle — somewhat more pronounced on the right. The orbital part of the frontal lobes appeared shrunken as did the medial surface of the temporal poles.
>
> TK appears to have no ability for quantifying the passage of time [what Bergson (1922/65) called durée] and no experiential appreciation of the meaning of time units. For example, a few minutes after tutoring begins, he cannot say — even remotely — how long it has been since the session started. He is as apt to answer this question in years as in minutes. He does always use one of seven terms of time quantification (seconds, minutes, hours, days, weeks, months or years) when asked to estimate the duration of an episode but uses them randomly. He can put these terms in order, but does not have any sense of their meaning or their numerical relationships to one another.
>
> When TK returned from a trip to the Bahamas he did recall that he had been on the trip; however, the details he could recount about the trip numbered fewer than 5. His estimates of how long it had been since his trip, were typical in that they were inaccurate and wildly inconsistent on repeated trials. Also, the first five times back at tutoring he stated that he had not been at tutoring since his trip. It appears that he is unable to place in sequence those few past events that he can recall. Nonetheless, he can answer questions correctly based on his application of general knowledge, e.g. he knows he was a baby before he could talk because "everyone starts as a baby". But, one day he asked his tutor if he knew him when he was a kid, indicating his incomprehension of the duration of each of these developmental periods and his unawareness of what events constituted such a period for him.

TK has no difficulty whatsoever in processing entities or allocentric and egocentric space. He has learned to read despite his considerable brain damage. His categorical and propositional skills are so well developed that he can use these "semantic" processes to veil his deficit in "episodic" processing to such an extent that one would not, during a particular encounter, realize the severity of his difficulty.

Episodic processing organizes experience not according to invariancies that organize frames but according to covariations among events. Covariations are "parsed" into episodes, (de)marked at both ends by a "stop" constituted of an orienting response. Orienting is ordinarily accompanied by visceroautonomic arousal, arousal which fails to occur after amygdalectomy (Pribram et al. 1979; Pribram 1991, Lecture 8). In the absence of this visceroautonomic arousal, habituation of the orienting response fails to occur, and the organism (monkey or human) continues orienting to a repetition of the event. There are no boundaries; experience is ever novel and never familiar.

Seizures originating around the amygdala produce experiences such as deja vue (a feeling of familiarity in a strange place) and jamais vue (a feeling of estrangement in what should be a familiar place). When the seizures are prolonged, an entire experienced episode fails to become encoded into the person's retrievable life story. As an example, one Friday I was accompanied by a young psychologist to my car after having lectured at Napa State Hospital in California. I wished her a happy weekend, and she said that she looked forward to it because of a party the group was having. The following week, she and others of the group were again accompanying me to my car, and I asked how this young lady had enjoyed the party. She answered that she had become overly tired and had fallen asleep and not gone to the party. The others in the group turned to her in surprise — they had all seen her, seemingly enjoying her attendance, "a bit spaced-out because, perhaps she had had a bit much to drink". On examination it turned out that the young lady had psychomotor seizures due to an epileptic focus in the region of her medial temporal lobe. In extreme, when this part of the brain is not just temporarily out of commission, but is permanently injured as in TK, experience simply never engenders the feeling of familiarity.

As to how a "stop" process that marks an episode might operate, I have for years suggested to my laboratory colleagues that the marking could work somewhat like pagination in a computer program, or setting a bandwidth in a content-addressable holographic-like memory. This would account for the effect of priming and the intrusive retrieval of material by a subject with "memory loss" due to excessive alcoholism as in Korsakoff's syndrome or in HM who has had both amygdala and hippocampus bilaterally removed (Weiskrantz, Warrington et al. 1974). The suggestions need to be modelled in a PDP type program to understand more fully the observations.

7. The frontal executive system

To this understanding must be added what we know about the role of the anterior frontal cortex in organizing executive working memory (reviewed by Pribram 1991, Lecture 10; Pribram 1997). This part of the frontal lobe is anatomically intimately related to the parts of the brain so severely damaged in TK, the amygdala and hippocampal systems. The connection to the amygdala via the uncinate fasciculus and to the hippocampal formation by way of the adjacent cingulate cortex (Papez circuit: hippocampus → septal region [*n. accumbeus septi*] → mammillary bodies of the posterior hypothalamus → tract of VicDazir → anterior thalamic nuclei → cingulate cortex). Essentially, the executive working memory provides flexibility in processing experienced episodes and events. This is accomplished by connections with the rest of the brain to allow monitoring of what is going on — by inducing the delay in processing necessary for the signals in a circuit to engage extended parts of other circuits.

An experiment by Fuster (1997) demonstrates this delay function. Using the delayed matching from sample technique, Fuster recorded from neurons in the inferotemporal cortex (as noted earlier, this is part of the reference frame system critically involved in making visual choices (see Pribram 1991, Lecture 7 for review). He found neurons to be active at all stages of the task — different neurons for different stages. He then temporarily deactivated the frontal cortex by cooling it. Now he found *no* cells active during the delay — only during the initial (sample) and final (matching) stages. Monitoring is thus achieved by virtue of the operations of the anterior frontal cortex but not within it. Rather the anterior frontal cortex apparently actively *facilitates delay* within the circuits that are critical to the performance of a task, making it possible for alterations in that circuitry to occur. In computer language, the executive routine influences (e.g. sets up delays within) ongoing programs and the relations (such as priorities) between them.

In 1966 I described a process by which such delays and priorities become assigned under the heading "The Temporal Hold" (which is in the same paper in which I suggested the holographic metaphor). The paper was entitled "Some Dimensions of Remembering: Steps Toward a Neuropsychological Model of Memory", pp. 179–188:

> This "temporal hold" is assumed to be accomplished through an operation similar to that which gives rise to a temporary dominant focus in the experiments of Ukhtomski (1926), Rusinov (1956), and Morrell (1961). Without regulation by such a hold mechanism, the organism would fluctuate inordinately among possible temporal codes and thus produces only a jumble of neural patterns. In such circumstances even temporary combinations, i.e., moiré effects necessary to the registration of interference patterns as holograms cannot be achieved. Support for some sort of temporal hold process emanating from the frontolimbic portions of the brain comes from electrical recordings made in man:
>
> When conditional and imperative stimuli are presented, a remarkable change appears in the frontal brain response; a negative potential appears immediately after the conditional response and endures until the imperative response, when it declines rapidly to zero or becomes positive. This has been described as the "Contingent-Negative Variation" or Expectancy Wave (Walter et al. 1964). In conditions such as those described, the E-wave is the most constant and stable of all electrocerebral phenomena in normal adults … and represents depolarization of the apical dendritic plexus. (Walter 1964: 310–313)

Episodic processing and its working memory component (especially when considered as short term memory) have often been considered in a somewhat post-modern spirit, to precede semantic processing (what has been discussed here as processing [minding] that involves reference frames). The clinical evidence (TK) presented earlier indicates, however, that episodic and semantic (referential) processing can effectively proceed independently of one another indicating that experienced reference to a "real" world may indeed proceed independently of the stories we tell about the experiences. Of course, the brain systems that organize these processes do, as indicated by the Fuster and my electrical stimulation experiments, ordinarily interact (see p. 139). Thus ordinarily, episodic awareness uses referential systems and referential systems become modifiable by virtue of input from the episodic systems.

The variety of brain systems involved in organizing conscious (and unconscious) processes leads to a pluralistic rather than a dualistic epistemological stance. Thus in cognitive neuroscience such conceptualizations as the Society of Mind (Minksy 1986) and its modularity have become popular.

8. Processing structure as the basis of monism

However, there is another dual that I have so far not considered. This dual relates to conscious versus automatic or unconscious processing. Any model we make of conscious processes must thus take into account both the importance of subjective experience, and the fact that there are influences on behavior of which we are not aware. Instrumental behavior and awareness are often opposed — the more efficient a performance, the less aware we become. Sherrington noted this antagonism in a succinct statement: "Between reflex action and mind there seems to be actual opposition. Reflex action and mind seem almost mutually exclusive — the more reflex the reflex, the less does mind accompany it."

The reciprocal relationship between awareness and behavior is perhaps best iluminated by the psychological processes of habit and habituation If an organism is repeatedly exposed to the same situation, is placed in an unvarying environment, two things happen. If he consistently has to perform a similar task in that environment, the task becomes fairly automatic, i.e., he becomes more efficient. The organism has learned to perform the task; he has formed *habits* regarding it. At the same time the subject habituates: he no longer produces an orienting reaction; he no longer notices the events constant to this particular task in this environment. His verbal reports of introspection, his failure to move his head and eyes in the direction of the stimulus, and electrophysiological measures such as galvanic skin response, plethysmography and EEG, all attest to the disappearance of orienting when unvarying situation is repeated. However, habituation is not an indication of some loss of sensitivity on the part of the nervous system but rather the development of a neural model of the environment, a representation, an expectancy, a type of memory mechanism against which inputs are constantly matched (Sokolov 1960; Pribram 1971; Thompson 1986; Grandstaff & Pribram 1972). The nervous system is thus continually tuned *by* inputs to process further inputs.

The habitual performance of the organism also results (of course) from neural activity. So the question is: What is the difference between the two kinds of neural activity that make awareness inversely related to habit and habituation?

Nerve impulses and graded potential changes (hyper- and depolarization) occurring within a dendritic web are two kinds of processes that could function reciprocally. A simple hypothesis would state that the more quickly the patterns of signals arriving at synapses are transduced into patterns departing from the web via axons, the shorter the duration of the design occupying the processing web. Once habit and habituation have occurred and a throughput has been established within the processing web, behavior becomes "reflex". By contrast, the more persistent designs of graded polarizations are coordinate with awareness. The hypothesis carries a corollary: Nerve impulse patterns *per se* and the behavior they generate are unavailable to immediate awareness. Thus, even the production of speech is "unconscious" at the moment the words are spoken.

The distinction is between neural circuits composed essentially of axons and microprocessing in the dendritic web. Neurons are ordinarily conceived to be the computational units of the brain. Thus the majority of processing theories since the seminal contribution of McCulloch and Pitts (1943) have taken the axonal discharge of the neuron, the nerve impulse, as the currency of computation.

However, there is more to processing than these models indicate. Not only are axonal-dendritic synapses that connect neurons subject to local influences in these networks, but innumerable dendro-dendritic synapses provide an initially unconstrained high connectivity needed to account for the spatial and temporal richness of experience (Bishop 1956; Pribram 1960b, 1971; Schmitt, Dev & Smith 1976). Presynaptic dendrites are found in many locations in the sensory and central nervous system (see Table, p. 9, in Shepard 1981). As summarized by Szentagothai (1985: 40):

> The simple laws of histodynamically polarized neurons ... indicating the direction of flow of excitation ... came to an end when unfamiliar types of synapses between dendrites, cell bodies and dendrites, serial synapses etc. were found in infinite variety ...

Junctions (axodendritic and dendo-dendritic) between neurons in the form of chemical synapses, electrical ephapses, and tight junctions occur within overlapping dendritic arborizations.

These junctions provide the possibility for microprocessing within each neuronal circuit as opposed to the mere transmission of signals. The term neurotransmiters applied to chemcials acting at junctions is, therefore, somewhat misleading. Terms such as neuroregulator and neuromodulator convey more of the meaning of what actually transpires at synapses.

Nerve impulse conduction thus leads to a variety of dendritic microprocesses. When a nerve impulse courses down an axon it becomes attentuated both in amplitude and speed of conduction as the axon branches into teledendrons. This is because the amplitude and speed of conduction are proportional to fiber size diameter. When nerve impulses arrive at synapses, the reduced fiber size diameter reduces the impulse into presynaptic polarizations. These are never solitary but, as noted, constitute arrival patterns. The patterns are constituted of sinusoidally fluctuating hyper- and depolarizations which are ordinarily insufficiently large to immediately incite nerve impulse discharge in the post-synaptic dendritic web. These ordered sinusoidal fluctuations can last for a variable period of time. It is this delay that affords opportunity for computational complexity.

Neurons are thresholding devices that sample the results of the dendritic microprocess and form discrete packets of nerve impulses for communication and control of other levels of processing. These packets are more resistant to degradation and interference than the graded microprocess. However, they constitute the channels of communication, not the processing elements. The following quotation from *Brain and Perception* (Pribram 1991) and from Thatcher & John (1977) summarize what appears to be occurring:

> The holonomic brain theory is based on the Fourier and Gabor relationships. As noted, Fourier's theorem states that a pattern can be decomposed into components representing the relationships among sets of regular (i.e., periodic) oscillations each of which has been further decomposed into oscillations 90° out of phase. Components encode frequency, amplitude, and phase (the relations between oscillations). These components are quantified as Fourier coefficients. The ensemble of such coefficients, when embodied in physical form, becomes palpable as an optical hologram. When coefficients of identical value are connected as in a contour map, the resulting schema is what in the holonomic brain theory is called a holoscape. The contours forming such a holoscape are embodied in the microprocess of polarizations occurring in denditric networks, thus constituting a sub- and transneuronal manifold (Pribram 1991: 28–29)

The spatiotemporal patterning of these cooperative processes … [involve] ionic shifts … with extrusion of potassium ions and ionic binding on extracellular mucopolysaccharide filaments. If we focus our attention not on the membranes of single neurons, but upon charge density distributions in the tissue matrix of neurons, glial cells, and mucopolysaccharide processes, we can envisage a complex, three-dimensional volume of isopotential contours, topologically comprised of portions of cellular membranes and extracellular binding sites and constantly changing over time (Thatcher & John 1977: 305–306).

There is more. Dendrites are fitted with spines that resemble little cilia, or hairs, protruding perpendicularly from the dendritic fiber. These spines have bulbs at their endings, knoblike heads that make contact with teledendrons, the branches of axons and with other dendrites to form synapses. Activity in teledendrons and in dendrites such as those stemming from axonless neurons produce depolarizations and hyperpolarizations in the dendritic spines. The postsynaptic effects are ordinarily invoked chemically and can be modified by other chemicals that act as regulators and modulators (see Candace Pert 1997; Jibu, Pribram & Yasue 1996).

Shepherd, Rall, Perkel, and their colleagues[1] (see, e.g., Coss & Perkel 1985; Perkel 1982–1983; Perkel & Perkel 1985; Shepherd, Brayton, Miller, Segey, Rindsel & Rall 1985) modeled the process whereby these postsynaptic events occurring in spine heads interact. The issue is this: The stalks of the spines are narrow and therefore impose a high resistance to conduction (active or passive) toward the dendritic branch. Spine head depolarizations (as well as hyperpolarizations) must therefore interact with one another if they are to influence the action potentials generated at the axon hillock of the parent cell of the dendrite. The interactions (dromic and antidromic) among dendritic potentials (by means of which the signal becomes effective at the next stage of processing) thus depend on the simultaneous activation of both pre- and postsynaptic sites. According to Shepherd and colleagues (1985) several advantages accrue from this form of activation:

> First the relative efficacy of distal dendritic inputs would be greatly enhanced. Second, … the transients within the model spines and dendrite are rapid and do not have the slow, low amplitude time course of synaptic potentials recorded experimentally at a distance from the cell body. Within the distal dendrite, information might thus be processed through precise timing of specific inputs to different neighboring spines … These precise interactions would greatly increase the complexity of information processing that can take place in distal dendrites. (p. 2194)

The activation of interacting polarizations occurs in parallel, is distributed and discontinuous: "Thus, the active propagation. . . was discontinuous and resembled in this respect the saltatory conduction that takes place from node-to-node in myelinated nerve" (Shepherd et al. 1985: 2193).

When we map these microprocesses as surface distributions occurring in dendritic arborizations, we find that they can be described in terms of Gabor functions, a wavelet representation in a class of four (or more)-dimensional informational hyperspaces based on Jacobi delta functions or Wigner distributions (Wechsler 1991; Reviewed by Pribram 1991, Lectures 1 and 2). Gabor wavelets are composed of sinusoidal oscillations constrained by Gaussians that can operate either in the spectral or the space–time domain. I have reviewed the implications for neuropsychology of these Gabor functions (Pribram 1995).

For philosophy, the Gabor function has the following import: Gabor noted that he used the same mathematics (Hilbert phase space) as had Heisenberg in describing the micro-organization of matter. He, therefore, labelled his unit a quantum of information — the maximal compressibility of a communication before the indeterminacy of the uncertainty comes into play. The unit is a limit of Shannon's information measure of the reduction of uncertainty.

Gabor developed his descriptions for solving the problem of maximum compressibility of a telephone message to be sent across the Atlantic cable. During the early 1970's many laboratories, including mine, showed that Gabor functions served as excellent descriptions of dendritic receptive fields in the primary visual cortex, and since then it has been shown that they also describe fields in the auditory and somatosensory systems.

A Gabor wavelet thus describes both the material receptive dendritic field of sensory cortical neurons in the brain and the maximum usable compressibility of a psychological message sent across the Atlantic Cable. Thus the quantal structure of the wavelet describes the physiological structure of the elementary brain processes basic to perception and, at the same time, the elementary nature of telecommunication (a mental, psychological process).

In summary, there are advantages to both dualistic and monistic thinking. It is difficult to understand many concepts except in relation to other concepts. As noted, there can be no up without a down, no light without dark, no happiness without sadness. On the other hand (a dual), there is a unity that underlies each dual: in the above examples, space, illumination, emotion. Mind and brain are duals that, as we have seen, are better characterized epistemologically as plurals. What constitutes their underlying ontological commonality? I opt for order, pattern — that is, informational structure.

The term 'structure', as used here, is applied to the arrangement of the relationships within a process such as linguistic communication, a computer program or a plan. As can be seen from the foregoing, structure is neither exclusively material nor exclusively mental. Structure therefore serves a neutral monism in the mind-brain relationship. But the question immediately arises as to the structure of 'what'. I have ventured that at bottom, it is the structure of energy, its negentropy, or in the language of communication theory, information, the form within. The concept order, in-formation, the form within, thus heralds a holism that supervenes both behaviorism and cognitivism by taking into account the spiritual nature of mankind (Pribram 1985b).

9. Quantum theory in cognitive neuroscience

The ubiquitous role of quantum formulations in neurobiology is becoming more and more obvious. Every time a photon enters the eye, an energy transaction obeying the law $E=\hbar$ takes place. The possibility that processes in the brain's processing web may result in the transmission of photons of frequencies in the 10^{13} Hz, i.e. far-infrared range, was suggested by Fernandez-Moran in 1951, and has been increasingly borne out. In 1960 Wiener wrote:

> ... the active bearer of the specificity of a molecule may lie in the frequency pattern of its molecular radiation, an important part of which may lie in the infrared electromagnetic range or even lower. (52)

Since the late 1960's Fröhlich's researches have confirmed collective behavior of assemblies of biomolecules resulting in long-range coherent radiation in the 10^{11} Hz range. The quantum role is further addressed in the papers of Jibu, Yasue and Pribram (Jibu et al. 1993, 1996). Until recently, the tendency in quantum mechanical as well as neuroscientific circles has been to ignore the phase of the de Broglie wave, and attribute significance only to its frequency, wavelength, and the non-negative square of its amplitude. Aside from a few great physicists such as Born, Dirac and Feynman, the common attitude has been to dismiss rather naively the de Broglie wave as a mathematical "tool".

In neuropsychology and neurophysiology as well, the importance of phase locking has been underestimated. Caelli & Hubner, however, showed that amplitude encoding was insufficient in veridically processing an image (see Pribram 1991). Bell and Sejnowski (1996) confirm the Caelli and Hubner findings and summarize the advantages of an independent component analysis (over a principal component analysis) to achieve this results:

> The failure of correlation-based [processing] is most clearly shown by the filters they produce when trained on stationary ensembles of signals. The filters are typically *global* …, sensitive to different spatio- or temporal frequencies, but with non-zero weights extending throughout the filter. They reflect only the amplitude spectrum of the signal and ignore the phase spectrum where most of the suspicious *local* coincidences in natural signals take place. An edge in an image, for example, is a coincidence in the phase spectrum, since if we were to Fourier analyse it, we would see many sine waves of different frequencies, all aligned in phase where the edge occurred …
> To illustrate formally that second-order statistics only carry information about the amplitude spectrum, consider the autocorrelation function of a signal, which contains all its second-order structure. The Fourier transform of this is the power spectrum, which is the square of the amplitude spectrum. Thus the two carry identical information.
>
> To demonstrate intuitively that what we consider as the informative part of a natural signal is captured in the phase spectrum, Fourier transform the signal, remove the phase information, and transform it back to the space or time domain. It will then look or sound like noise, typically with a $1/f$ amplitude spectrum. All the visual or auditory features that our perceptual system thinks of as 'signal' will be lost. On the other hand, if we remove the amplitude information, and preserve the phase, the signal will be distorted but remain recognisable (*sic*).
>
> This points to a curious paradox: correlation-based learning algorithms are sensitive to exactly the part of natural signals which we regard as least meaningful (amplitude), and ignore the part of the signal which we find most meaningful (phase). To encode the phase of signals, we need an algorithm that is sensitive to higher-order statistics. (261–262)

Independent component analysis, by being sensitive to higher order statistics provides the procedure necessary for recording phase encoding in electrical recordings of brain activity — an essential requirement if cortical processing can be represented mathematically in terms of complex wavelets, in a quantum holographic fashion.

10. A holonomic universe

It was the pioneering thought of Haldane (1934) that *the full-fledged de Broglie wave (with frequency, wavelength, amplitude and phase) is involved in all phenomena in the universe*, and thus the phase of the de Broglie wave is most germane to the understanding of cognitive processes.

The central theme of Haldane's proposal is that the wave-process of de

Broglie and Schrodinger can explain the phenomena of both life and mind. He notes as limiting extremes the billiard-ball atomism of Lucretius and Newton on the one hand, and, on the other, the ideal world of Plato, these limits being attained as the mass-energy of the system is allowed to tend to zero or infinity, respectively. The fact that the universe is in-between these extremes is what makes life and mind possible.

From Haldane:

> In a degenerate system degrees of freedom are lost because certain periodic systems oscillate together instead of independently. This resonance gives rise to various observable phenomena. It is responsible for certain terms in the energy of a material system. As the resonators are removed from one another, the energy falls off very rapidly. Haldane (1934), p. 97

Haldane points to some biological phenomena that exhibit the same sort of behavior. (a) During reproduction the gene loses its identity: it is hard to tell parent from daughter. (b) Quantum resonance is behind the larger molecules, and larger building blocks of organic matter, e.g. the joining of amino acids that produces the protein molecule and chains thereof. Such resonance is what accounts for the self-regulatory and reproductive aspects of life.

In my own work, my colleagues and I (Spinelli & Pribram 1966; Pribram, Lassonde, Ptito 1981, etc.) have shown that posterior and frontal lobe stimulation of the brain can bring about tendencies toward the extremes of conscious processing. These extremes can be formulation in more global terms, as follows:

At least since the time of Newton and Leibniz, two rather different conceptual schemes have dominated thinking. Both are concerned with the lawful relation between observed events. But the Newtonians express these relations in terms of the relations among material entities, whereas the Leibnizians explain them in terms of the constructive effect of oscillations.

1. The received view: Brain, by organizing the input from the physical and social environment as obtained through the senses, constructs mental phenomena.
2. The Leibnitzian view: A pervasive organizing principle of the universe is a hierarchy of monads. All monads are informed, but with different degrees of clarity. Mental processes are able to discern the pattern of the cosmos by virtue of the brain's intunement (albeit imperfect) with the forms inherent in the universe.[2]

Almost all behavioral- and neuro-scientists would today subscribe to some form of statement one, while statement two reflects the belief of many theoretical physicists such as Einstein, Dirac and Schrödinger, Wigner and others. Important are the dynamics described in Leibniz's *monadology*. Just as the mechanics of matter could be built á la Newton on the basis of the ideal concept of the *point mass*, so Leibniz held that the mechanics (or as he preferred to say, *dynamics*) of the spirit could be built on the ideal concept of a *point-mind monad*. Each monad, like a tiny mirror, produces its own image of the universe. Point masses can vary: the mass can range over the set of positive real numbers. Likewise for monads. For although Leibniz offered no unit of perceptual range and clarity, he maintained that the range and clarity of the perception or vision of a monad can vary from the very short-ranged and very blurred, to the very long-ranged and sublimely sharp. (Today we know that Gabor wavelets have just these attributes and can, therefore, serve as point-mind units — See Pribram 1993, Epilogue.)

How does this conception of the world fare when judged by the modern development of quantum holography? As Wiener noted in 1930 "... the interposition of a ground-glass screen or photographic plate ... will destroy the phase relations of the coherency matrix of the emitted light, replacing it by a diagonal matrix with the same diagonal terms" (194).

Were we to be able to examine the universe without recourse to such photometric processes, we would witness a hologram, that is, a huge interference pattern embodying all phase relations as in the example of the surface of a pond. In this *implicate order* (to use a term due to David Bohm), each organism, like a Leibnizian monad, re-presents the universe, and the universe reflects, in some manner, the organism that observes it. The perceptions of an organism cannot be understood without an understanding of the nature of the physical universe and the nature of the physical universe cannot be understood without an understanding of the perceptual process.

From the discussion in the earlier sections of this essay, it would appear that the insights we have gained into the nature of the brain is broadly supportive of the Leibnizian point of view. When we bring to bear the new insights offered by quantum theory since the mid-1920's, the Leibnizian position gets significantly reinforced, but remarkably in a way in which the space–time and spectral perspectives get reconciled and appear to be no more divisive than the two faces of the same coin. This occurs via Planck's constant $\hbar$, which opens up a bridge between space–time locatable concepts such as mass and undulatory concepts such as energy measured as frequency, wavelength, amplitude and phase. On the basis of such reasoning, the brain is seen to be the medium for transformations into and out of a potential distributed energetic and an experienced spacetime order.

References

Bell, A. J. and Sejnowski, T. J. (1996) Learning the higher-order structure of natural sound. *Computation in Neural Systems* 7: 261–266.

Bishop, G. (1956) Natural history of the nerve impulse. *Physiological Review* 36: 376–399.

Brentano, F. W. (1973) *Psychology From an Empirical Standpoint*. Routledge and Kegan Paul.

Coss, R. G. and Perkel, D. H. (1985) The function of dendritic spines: A review of theoretical issues. *Behav. Neural Biol.* 44: 151–185.

DeValois, R. L. and DeValois, K. K. (1993) A Multi-Stage Color Model. *Vision Research*, Vol. 33, No. 8, pp. 1053–1065.

Eccles, J. C. (1958) The physiology of imagination. *Scientific American* 199: 135–146.

Edelman, G. (1989) *The Remembered Present*. New York: Basic Books.

Ferrier, D. (1876) *The Functions of the Brain*. London: Smith Elder and Co.

Freud, S. (1895) *Project For a Scientific Psychology*. (Stand Ed., Vol. 1, pp. 281–397). London: Hogarth.

Fuster, J. (1997) Frontal and Temporal Lobe Interaction. In Sakata, H., Mikami, A. and Fuster, J. M. (Eds.) *The Association Cortex: Structure and Function*. New York: Gordon & Breach Publishing.

Grandstaff, N. and Pribram, K. H. (1972) Habituation: Electrical changes in the visual system. *Neuropsychologia* 10: 125–132.

Haldane, J. B. S. (1934) Quantum mechanics as a basis for philosophy. In *Philosophy of Science*, Vol. I, pp. 78–98.

Jibu, M., Hagan, S., Hameroff, S. R., Pribram, K. H. and Yasue, K. (1994) Quantum Optical Coherence in Cytoskeletal Microtubules: Implications for Brain Function, *BioSystems* 32: 195–209, Elsevier Science Ireland Ltd.

Jibu, M., Pribram, K. H. and Yasue, K. (1996) From conscious experience to memory storage and retrieval: The role of quantum brain dynamics and boson condensation of evanescent photons. *International Journal of Modern Physics B*, Vol. 10, Nos. 13 & 14, pp. 1735–1754.

Kaada, B. R., Pribram, K. H. and Epstein, J. A. (1949) Respiratory and vascular responses in monkeys from temporal pole, insular, orbital surface and cingulate gyrus. *Journal of Neurophysiology* 12: 347–356.

Kaku, M. (1994) *Hyperspace*. New York: Oxford University Press.

Köhler, I. (1964) Psychological issues. In G. Kleine (Ed.), *The Formation and Transformation of the Perceptual World*. New York: International Universities Press.

McCullough, W. S. and Pitts, W. (1943) Logical calculus of the ideas immanent in nervous activity. *Bulletin of Mathematical Biophysics* 5: 115–133.

Miller, G. A., Galanter, E. and Pribram, K. H. (1960) *Plans and the Structure of Behavior*. New York: Henry Holt, 1960. (Russian trans; also in Japanese, German, Spanish, Italian.).

Mountcastle, V. B., Lynch, J. C., Georgopoulos, A., Sakata, H. and Acuna, C. (1975) Posterior parietal association cortex of the monkey: Command functions for operations within extrapersonal space. *Journal of Neurophysiology* 38; 871–908.

Peirce, C. S. (1934) *Collected papers*. Cambridge, MA: Harvard University Press.

Perkel, D. H. (1982–1983) Functional role of dendritic spikes. *Journal of Physiology Paris* 78: 695–699.

Perkel, D. H. and Perkel, D. J. (1985) Dendritic spines — role of active membrane in modulating synaptic efficacy. *Brain Research* 525: 331–335.

Pert, C. (1997) *Molecules of Emotions: Why You Feel the Way You Feel*. New York: Scribner Press.

Pribram, K. H. (1960a) A review of theory in physiological psychology. *Ann. Rev. Psychol.* 11: 1–40.

Pribram, K. H. (1960b). The intrinsic systems of the forebrain In J. Field, H. W. Magoun and V. E. Hall (Eds.) *Handbook on Physiology, Neurophysiology II*. Washington, D. C.: American Physiological Society, pp. 1323–1344.

Pribram, K. H. (1961) Limbic system. In D. E. Sheer (Ed.), *Electrical Stimulation of the Brain*. Austin, TX: University of Texas Press, pp. 563–574.

Pribram, K. H. (1962) Interrelations of psychology and the neurological disciplines. In S. Koch (Ed.), *Psychology: A study of a science*. New York: McGraw-Hill, pp. 119–157.

Pribram, K. H. (1966) Some dimensions of remembering: Steps toward a neuropsychological model of memory. In J. Gaito (Ed.), *Macromolecules and behavior*. New York: Academic Press, pp. 165–187.

Pribram, K. H. (1967) The new neurology and the biology of emotion. *American Psychologist* 10: 830–838.

Pribram, K. H. (1971) *Languages of the Brain: Experimental Paradoxes and Principles in Neuropsychology*. Englewood Cliffs, NJ: Prentice-Hall; Monterey, CA: Brooks/Cole, 1977; New York: Brandon House, 1982. (Translations in Russian, Japanese, Italian, Spanish).

Pribram, K. H. (1985a) Mind and brain, psychology and neuroscience, the eternal verities. In S. Koch and D. E. Leary (Eds.), *A Century of Psychology as a Science*. New York: McGraw-Hill, pp. 700–720.

Pribram, K. H. (1985b) 'Holism' could close the cognition era. *APA Monitor* 16: 5–6.

Pribram, K. H. (1991) *Brain and Perception: Holonomy and Structure in Figural Processing*. New Jersey: Lawrence Erlbaum Associates, Inc.

Pribram, K. H. (Ed.) (1993) *Rethinking Neural Networks: Quantum Fields and Biological Data*. New Jersey: Lawrence Erlbaum Associates, Inc.

Pribram, K. H. (1995) Brain in Perception: From Köhler's Fields to Gabor's Quanta of Information, *Proceeding of the 39th Congress of German Society for Psychology, pp. 53–69.*

Pribram, K. H., Lassonde, M. and Ptito, M. (1981) Classification of receptive field properties in cat visual cortex. *Exp. Brain Res.* 43: 119–130.

Pribram, K. H. and Mcguinness, D. (1975) Arousal, activation, and effort in the control of attention. *Psychol. Rev.* 82: 116–149.

Pribram, K. H., Reitz, S., McNeil, M. and Spevack, A. A. (1979) The effect of amygdalectomy on orienting and classical conditioning. *Pavlovian J. Biol. Sci.* 14: 203–217.

Ramachandran, V. S. (1995) Illusions of body image in neurology: What they reveal of human nature. Decade of the Brain lecture given at the 25th annual (Silver Jubilee) meeting of the Socity for Neuroscience. Published in *The Mind Brain Continuum.* Ed. R. Llinas and P. Churchland. MIT Press (1996).

Rosch, E. (1975) Cognitive representation of semantic categories. *Journal of Experimental Psychology* 104: 192–233.

Sacks, O. (1995) *An Anthropologist on Mars*. Schmitt, F. O., Dev, P. and Smith, B. H. (1976) Electronic processing of information by brain cells. *Science* 193: 114–120.

Shepard, R. N. (1981) Psychophysical complementarity. In M. Kubovy and J. Pomerantz (Eds.), *Perceptual organization* (pp. 279–341). Hillsdale, NJ: Lawrence Erlbaum Associates.

Shepherd, G. M., Brayton, R. K., Miller, J. P., Segey, I., Rindsel, J. and Rall, W. (1985) Signal enhancement in distal cortical dendrites by means of interactions between active dendritic spines. *Proceedings of the National Academy of Science* 82: 2192–2195.

Sokolov, E. N. (1960) Neuronal models and the orienting reflex. In M. A. B. Brazier (Ed.) *The Central Nervous System and Behavior*. New York: Josiah Macy, Jr. Foundation.

Spinelli, D. N. and Pribram, K. H. (1966) Changes in visual recovery functions produced by temporal lobe stimulations in monkeys. *Electroenceph. Clin. Neurophysiol.* 20: 44–49.

Stratton, G. (1896). Some preliminary experiments on vision without inversion of the retinal image. *Psychological Review* 3: 611–617.

Szentagothai, J. (1985) Functional anatomy of the visual centers as cues for pattern recognition concepts. In D. Chagas, R. Gattass and C. Gross (Eds.), *Pattern Recognition Mechanisms*. Berlin: Springer-Verlag, pp. 39–52.

Thatcher, R. W. and John, E. R. (1977) *Functional Neuroscience, Vol.* . Hillsdale, NJ: Lawrence Erlbaum Associates.

Thompson, R. F. (1986) The neurobiology of learning and memory. *Science* 233: 941–947.

Turnbull, O. H. (1997) A double dissociation between knowledge of object identity and object orientation. *Neuropsychologia* 35(4): 567–570.

Turnbull, O. H., Carey, D. P. and McCarthy, R. A. (1997) The neuropsychology of object constancy. *Journal of the International Neuropsychological Society* 3(3): 288–298.

Turnbull, O. H., McCarthy, R. A. (1996) When is a view unusual? A single case study of orientation-dependent visual agnosia. *Brain Research Buletin* 40(5–6): 497–503.

Ungerleider, L., Ganz, L. and Pribram, K. H. (1977) Size constancy in rheusus monkeys: Effects of pulvinar, prestriate and inferotemporal lesions. *Exp. Brain Res.* 27: 251–269.

Wechsler, H. (1991) *Computational Vision*. New York: Academic Press.

Weiskrantz, L., Warrington, E. K., Sanders, M. D. and Marshall, J. (1974) Visual capacity in the hemianopic field following a restricted occipital ablation. *Brain, 97*(4): 709–728.

Wiener, N. (1930) Generalized harmonic analysis. *Acta Math.* 55, pp. 117–258.

Wiener, N. (1960) Possibilities of the use of the interferometer in investigating macromolecular interactions" in "Fast Fundamental Transfer Processes in Aqueous Biomolecular Systems", ed. F. O. Schmitt, Department of Biology, MIT, Cambridge, Mass., pp. 52–53.

Wilson, M. (1987) Brain mechanisms in categorical perception. In S. Harnad (Ed.), *Categorical Perception*. New York: Cambridge University Press. 387–417.

Zeki, S. (1993) *A Vision of the Brain*. Blackwell Scientific Publishing.

What is consciousness?

An essay on the relativistic quantum holographic model of the brain/mind, working by phase conjugate adaptive resonance

Peter Marcer and Edgar Mitchell

Abstract

The quantum holographic model described provides mathematically founded specifications in terms of physical laws for the nature of information, knowledge, qualia, intelligence, the self and consciousness. It explains how a brain/mind, its neurons, dendrites, synapses, etc may be postulated to work, so as to explain the well known binding problem. It sheds light on the fact that brains can be so much more versatile, competent, and efficient than their digital information processing counterparts, in relation to perception, cognition, language and intelligence. Further, it provides a methodology, by means of which to predict the information processing morphology and signal dynamics of such brains, i.e. their neuroinformatics on various scales, so as to be validatable against the experimental facts of neurophysiology, neuropsychology, etc. The paper begins with an explanation of general scientific principles and concepts associated with the model, and supporting evidence is described. It ends with a proposal by means of which it can be further experimentally validated. This proposal concerns predicting the existence and the properties of microtubules internal to the axon of the neuron. Such a prediction provides an independent confirmation of the long held, but still controversial hypothesis of Hameroff and Penrose, that such axonal microtubules are a quantum mechanism fundamental to consciousness in higher organisms, such as humans.

Introduction

It is a premise of the present paper that the natural intelligence of conscious human nervous systems is vastly more versatile, competent, and efficient than the artificial intelligence of digital computers [the European Science Foundation Neuroinformatics Network wording, see http://www.esf.org]. After the restoration of the scientific respectability of the concept of a science of consciousness, and the very extensive, largely verbal and philosophical debate that has followed, we believe that further progress in understanding consciousness, can only come by advancing the hard science of the brain. By this we mean, establishing a mathematical explanation in terms of the laws of physics, of how exactly the brain works. This model must account for the facts of the brain's morphology, dynamics, chemistry etc, as known through neurophysiology, neuropsychology, etc, and should ultimately make verifiable mathematical predictions about the brain, so as to establish the model's scientific validity. Since the human brain is the most complex biological system which we know of in the universe, this seems like a tall order. We are convinced, however, by the research program we have participated in so far (Marcer 1988), that science has now advanced to the point, where such an enterprise is both possible and practical.

The program has reached the stage where it explains the general features of the brain's information processing morphology and dynamics, and that of other biological systems, in answer to the leading question "Why are these features quite unlike any information processing system currently known, and what are the general scientific principles and concepts, by which they can be understood?". The answers to this question lead towards an inevitable choice for a particular model, and to the mathematically founded quantum physical explanations of mind and of consciousness. The model predicts the existence of a separate mind/memory process or self, and it explains how "first person data" — conscious experience — relates to the "third person data" of brain processes, behavior, and interaction with the environment, so that for each unique individual, there is something it is like to be that individual. A basic role is attributed to the holographic record of the actual physical holographic data of the individual's sensory experience, which maybe consciously or unconsciously processed. Consciousness, as phase conjugate adaptive resonance, is a process of adaptive amplification characteristic to quantum holography (see Sections 2.4 and 2.5). It is the primal source of human causal efficacy in thought, during learning, for initiation/termination processes in the human brain, in physical behavior, etc. It includes, intelligence, free will and creativity.

The reader is asked to bear in mind that what follows is a model based on theoretical physics intended to describe actual phenomena, which are the experimentally established facts. For clarity, it is felt necessary to make explicit the distinction between mathematically derived propositions and facts, since in physics, it is the experimental facts, which are the sufficient condition to ultimately validate a mental model or thought experiment, not the correctness of the logic from premise to conclusion; the latter simply being a necessary condition. Less technicality inclined readers may prefer to begin at Part 2, summarizing the workings of the Quantum Holographic Model. Part 1, the General Scientific Principles and Concepts, which describes the technical reasons for selecting this particular model, could then be consulted as required or returned to later. To aid readers, some forward and backward references of the form (2.1) meaning see Section 2.1, are given, and some important technicalities are dealt with in sections in brackets { }, which again the reader may choose to skip over.

1. General scientific principles and concepts

1.1 *The physical* nature *of information*

To answer the leading question, we must embrace the fact that the nature of information used by nature is physical and not mathematical. It need not, as in the classical computer science of ubiquitous digital computation, consist of bits. For bits and indeed qubits (the quantum mechanical generalized computational analogue of bits) are simply physically realizable mental models for the carriage/transmission of symbolic data. This may or may not convey any meaning and is subject to the known processing limitations of formal systems, such as Gödel's theorem, the Halting Problem, errors and paradoxes of type, etc, as well as to the well known difficulties of devising program algorithms and of validating software.

Data, however, in the form of the 3 dimensional properties of objects with respect to illumination, is physical, as the physical processes of holography prove (see 2.1.4 for a description). It exists in all forms of illumination (be this, electromagnetic, acoustic, etc) following that illumination's incidence on the objects in question. Such 'holographic' data (which exists prior to any mental model ie any human agency and by implication prior to the origination of all life) is actual knowledge about the three-dimensional objects, which (as revealed by the mathematical (ie mental) models of holography) is contained in the local amplitude and the phase of the illumination. It may, the physical processes of holography prove, be encoded and decoded, into and from holograms. It is actual physical potentially meaningful/semantic information about the three-dimensional objects of the real physical world and the physical nature of that world's illumination determining object qualia, and not simply a mental model of that world as constructed by human beings.

The ability of a holographically working brain to totally reconstruct the object image bearing illumination, includes the properties of the objects with respect to their incident illumination, allowing a construction of object qualia, where it is clearly advantageous or even necessary in the interests of survival for an observer to observe such object qualia (the observed) as they really are.[1] Such semantic processing could explain the brain's effectiveness, in relation to perception and cognition, despite the slowness of its signal transmission capabilities. For brains with the potentiality to use the whole of the information 'encoded' in its sensory illumination (at both phase and amplitude), would be at a definite evolutionary advantage to others that did not. Holography enables such brains to perceive the world initially as wholes, prior to filtering these wholes into a sum of their parts for the purposes of cognition, according to the brain/organism's experience and the properties of its sensory modalities. Such wholes, where the sensory illumination contains three-dimensional object imagery, coincident with the objects themselves (i.e. phase conjugate imagery) are the very essence of human visual experience. Just take a consciously controlled look out of your eyes to see that this is so! Holography, specifying a top down (encoding), bottom up (decoding) approach to 3 dimensional pattern recognition, potentially specifies a wholly practical way for brains to work, including holographic redundancy and associative memory; as is explained later.

1.2 *Information processing as a* physical *Process: A case for a scientific paradigm change*

But not only is information a physical quantity. The following facts emergent from the new interdisciplinary area of quantum information processing (Brookes 1999), preview the same corresponding major paradigm change for science as a whole, for:

a. in computer science, a physical theory — the quantum theory of computation discovered by Deutsch (1985) — is now to be regarded as the theory of computation replacing the mathematical/Turing theory (Turing 1936), as the correct one,
b. the nature of information is further extended by the concept of quantum information (Sudbery 1997), beyond what has generally in science been accepted to be the case. For as experiment shows (Bouwmeester et al. 1998), quantum teleportation involves two processes, quantum and classical. The former is instantaneous transmission from A to B, (unlimited in relation

> to distance as far as it is known) but it cannot be used without the latter, which is transmission by conventional means at the speed of light or lower.

Information therefore becomes a concept on a par with the accepted concept of energy, needing incorporation in physics, and as already demonstrated in the laboratory (Judson & Rabitz 1992), the incorporation of quantum information (Dahleh, Pierce et al. 1990), radically changes the scientific understanding of how chemistry may be performed — specifying new designs for chemical systems (Rice 1992). These designs employ optimally controlled quantum signal induced rather than approximately thermodynamically induced chemical reactions. They thus offer a definite evolutionary advantage over those which do not, for thermodynamic chemistry like cooking, lacks such precise control; precise control such as is found in biological systems.

This new information paradigm, where the recent experimental validation of quantum teleportation (Bouwmeester et al. 1998) is a striking affirmation of the holistic nature of all physical reality revealed by quantum mechanics, concerns a wholly quantum world operating over all geometric scales (not merely the microscopic). Here classical physics and computation are simply a class of invariant behaviors and processes of the quantum model (see Section 6 for a more technical specification of this fact). They concern, quantum holography says, globally square integrable Lie group representations whenever these occur (Schempp 1986, 1992, 1993, 1998). This expresses a modern form of the quantum correspondence principle, which has been historically used to construct quantum mechanical models from their classical counterparts.

Thus, current understanding of all disciplines where the concept of information plays a leading role — such as molecular biology, biology, neurophysiology, cognitive science, medicine, etc. — must be reassessed in the light of this paradigm change. For unknown quantum mechanisms almost certainly exist, inseparable from the known classical mechanisms, so as to yield a more complete understanding and explanation. For example, such a needed reassessment concerns the 1952/3 experiments of Miller and Urey into the origins of life, where within a closed flask, electric discharges through a 'primordial Earth atmosphere' for many days produced an aminoacid containing chemical soup. It indicates that these were essentially correct, except that the possibility of optimally controlled quantum signal induced chemistry (Dahleh, Pierce et al. 1990), then unknown, should have been used, and would be at the heart of the chemistry of living systems, and life's evolution.

1.3 *A new proof strategy and a model of the quantum self*

In this new paradigm, even the nature of proof has changed. The only valid proofs now are "engineering solutions" i.e. physical apparatus, be they manmade or biologically evolved, which demonstrate the process in question, as mathematically described. An example is physical apparatus demonstrating the processes of holography referred to above, so as to experimentally validate the mathematical description of the holographic processes, showing this description to be a good model. Similarly brains are "biologically engineered" solutions, which as "chemically based computer design" perform knowledge processing operations that are astounding from the engineering/technical viewpoint. They serve as a living existence proof that carbon-based analogue computation does work. Another example is Schempp's relativistic quantum holography (Schempp 1992), which is furnished with a manmade engineered solution, functional magnetic resonance tomographic imaging (Schempp 1998), already in world-wide production use for medical diagnosis.

Reflections on the latter suggested to Walter Schempp and myself, in accordance with the successful use of symmetry groups in quantum physics, that his theory of relativistic quantum holography, based on the three dimensional Weyl-Heisenberg nilpotent Lie group (Schempp 1986), would be a strong candidate to explain the knowledge processing morphology and dynamics of brains. This group, which has a three dimensional matrix representation, was discovered in 1928, by Weyl, a colleague of Heisenberg's, very soon after Heisenberg discovered his matrix representation of quantum mechanics, which allows for the successful use of symmetry groups. The 3 dimensional Weyl-Heisenberg group approach, is appropriate to describe quantum holography. It leads to the same background mathematics (Schempp 1993) in terms of Hilbert-Schmidt operators, which describes optimally controlled quantum signal induced chemistry referred to above. This chemistry has been demonstrated in the laboratory, by what has been independently cited as "quantum state holography" (Schleich 1999; Leichtle, Schleich et al. 1998).

Such a thesis is actively supported by the following list of publications, each of which correctly predicts the general features of the information signal processing morphology and dynamics of the corresponding living biological systems, so as to explain how it would work quantum holographically, on particular scales. These biological systems are:

- the brain as a conscious system (which is discussed in more detail below) (Marcer & Schempp 1998),

- the neuronal working (including, the neuron's dendritic structure, the neural body, axon, synapse, synaptic vesicles, hexagonal presynaptic vesicular grid and synaptic cleft) (Marcer & Schempp 1997),
- the simplest (prokaryote) living cells (Marcer & Schempp 1997), and
- the structure of DNA (Marcer & Schemmp 1996; Clement, Coveney et al. 1993; this details the morphological 3 dimensional structure, that the quantum holographic model predicts, if DNA is a quantum holographic encoding of the 3 dimensional morphological structure and dynamics of the embryo of its organism).

This last prediction correctly accounts for the double helix structure and the flat planes (de Duve 1984) on which chemical base pairings, labelled (A, U/T) and (G, C) in the genetic code, occur. It says that these are the hologram planes for encoding 3 dimensional geometric information about the embryo, such that in the quantum physical world, a complete set of 3 dimensional holographic virtual images of the embryo exists, in the embryo's DNA, from the moment of this DNA's conception. This virtual image set, each of which is coincident with the actual embryo/foetus at each step of its development (the meaning of a phase conjugate object image being that it coincides with that of the object itself), would terminate in that of the whole embryo. This whole embryo virtual image, particular to the specific individual organism's DNA in question, can be therefore be designated as the organism's Self. For in quantum mechanics, it can produce actual observable physical effects. That is, DNA is a complete chemically based quantum holographic 3 dimensional information processing design, which exists for each stage of the DNA's self (and so phase conjugate-adaptively resonant) incremental decoding/development up to and including the completed embryo of the organism. Thus, during the whole of the quantum holographic decoding process (assuming the DNA encodes a potentially healthy whole embryo) each living cell "knows" its place (and its function) at each stage of the decoding, relative to all its sister cells, and when to terminate the decoding process. This implies that the human Self and (see 2.1), human consciousness are properties of the chemically based (and therefore quantum) complexity of the whole living human organism's design. For, as Feynman, for example, tells us, there can be no chemistry i.e. chemical molecules, reactions, or other forms of chemically based design, without quantum mechanics.

1.4 *How precisely does this newly adopted proof strategy work?*

Quantum holography is based on the (Weyl-)Heisenberg Group. This is a nilpotent Lie Group (Schempp 1992), within which the embedded metaplectic group and its embedded group structures determine the symmetries, group representations and mechanisms, essential to the quantum coherence necessary for the quantum holographic processes; as, for example, is set out in the model of the neuron working by quantum holography (Marcer & Schempp 1997). The question then is if this description fits with the known neurophysiological fact of how biological neurons actually work. If the answer is no, the model is incorrect. If the answer is yes, however, the symmetries and mechanisms do describe the general features of the workings of the neuron on a particular scale, then the model can be said to be a good model. Further, since quantum holography cannot take place without quantum coherence, the applicability of the model would entail that such coherence indeed exists within biological neurons. This is given credence by another example, functional magnetic resonance imaging machines, extensively researched by Schempp (Schempp 1995). There is extensive evidence that such imaging machines do work by quantum holography, since, for example, it is easy to show that output diffraction patterns with respect to the brain slice images are indeed the holograms that quantum holography predicts, and therefore there is the quantum coherence necessary for the holography. Moreover, the quantum holographic model for the neuron predicts (Eccles 1986, 1989) among other features, one truly remarkable mechanism of actual biological synapses. It says that such synapses, must be resonant cavities, containing a hexagonal hololattice, that will on neural firing expel a single quantum probabilistically to provide the synaptic gain/amplification across the synaptic cleft. This is exactly as found in actual synapses (Eccles 1986), which are indeed cavities, where a single synaptic vesicle is expelled probabilistically from a hexagonal presynaptic vesicular grid.

1.5 *Is quantum mechanics an effective pattern recognition and problem solving methodology?*

Independent confirmation that quantum holography provides the effective model, which brains would need for perception and cognition, comes, for example, from the following research:

a. Chapline (1999) has shown that quantum mechanics can be re-interpreted as a canonical method for the solving of pattern recognition problems. He begins with the Wigner-Moyal formulation of quantum mechanics, which can also be given "physical" interpretation as the Weyl(-Heisenberg) quantization of the complete holographic representation of a surface. His mathematically well set out hypothesis is that theoretical physics in the form of quantum mechanics, re-interpreted as a theory of pattern cognition, defined through holography, embraces the

To contact the seller, go to Your Orders in Your Account. Click the seller's name under the appropriate product. Then, in the "Further Information" section, click "Contact the Seller."
Ship To:

AMZ Order -APTP - 1033844-1-0276
Main Address
800 Avondale Ave
1033844-1-0276
Grandview Heights, OH 43212

Buyer PO #: 1033844-1-0276

Order ID: 113-3916150-1837023

Thank you for buying from Recycle Bookstore, San Jose on Amazon Marketplace.

Shipping Address:	Order Date:	Tue, Sep 15, 2026
AMZ Order -APTP	Shipping Service:	Standard
Main Address	Buyer Name:	CollegeBooksDirect
800 Avondale Ave	Seller Name:	Recycle Bookstore, San Jose
1033844-1-0276		
Grandview Heights, OH 43212		

Quantity	Product Details	Unit price	Order Totals
1	**The Physical Nature of Consciousness (Advances in Consciousness Research) [Paperback] [2001] Van Loocke, Philip** **SKU:** 1031506 **ASIN:** 9027251495 **Condition:** Used - Very Good **Order Item ID:** 169828101243601 **Condition note:** Book has light scuffing and scratching to cover, slight bow. Otherwise an attractive copy. Tight binding, unmarked pages, no tears or stains. Very Good.	$39.95	**Item subtotal** $39.95 **Shipping total** $4.99 **Item total** **$44.94**

Grand total: $44.94

Returning your item:

Go to "Your Account" on Amazon.com, click "Your Orders" and then click the "seller profile" link for this order to get information about the return and refund policies that apply.

Visit https://www.amazon.com/returns to print a return shipping label. Please have your order ID ready.

Thanks for buying on Amazon Marketplace. To provide feedback for the seller please visit www.amazon.com/feedback. To contact the seller, go to Your Orders in Your Account. Click the seller's name under the appropriate product. Then, in the "Further Information" section, click "Contact the Seller."

whole of mathematics, and membrane string theory in cosmology. His claim is that it is a theory of Everything, explaining “the unreasonable effectiveness of mathematics” in physics.

b. This theory has the same mathematical specification as Walter Schempp’s quantum holography (as a creation/annihilation model, see Appendix) (Schempp 1992, 1993) used to describe the workings of synthetic aperture radars, and functional magnetic resonance imaging machines. Such fMRI machines as “engineered solutions” demonstrate both the pattern recognition and holographic nature of the image extraction process, as well as the nature of the Weyl geometric quantization of a surface, which Chapline describes. Schempp’s theory concerns phase conjugate adaptive resonance, while Chapline draws upon the mathematical model of adaptive optics.

c. Such a quantum mechanical model of holographic pattern recognition is currently implemented on existing computer technology by the AND Corporation (Sutherland 1999). This implementation is analogous to that, for example, which maybe used to demonstrate the principle of superposition as a basis for quantum qubit computing. The AND Corporation’s approach has given rise to a powerful commercial technology for pattern recognition, for example, for 3 dimensional human face pattern input encoding, storage, and recognition with impressive properties as to accuracy, speed, and practicality. The AND Corporation model is a second order biological conceptual approach, modelled on the whole of the neuron/axon/dentrite structure, rather than a first order one of the synapse as a weighting function, as in current neural nets. It represents signal input/outputs as complex amplitudes $\lambda\exp(i\theta)$, behaving according to quantum mechanical rules. This is in accord with the facts that in holography, the phase θ is the quantity of physical significance encoding geometric information, and that in quantum mechanics, the Berry/geometric phase is demonstrably the observable of some state vector, rather than the usual quantum eigenvalue of some operator. The Berry phase of any quantum system maintains a record of where the quantum system has been in 3D geometric space, how long it has been there, and what other quantum states it has passed through, i.e. is effectively an historical incremental process record of the system’s behaviour. An example of the Berry phase is the Aharonov-Bohm effect in relation to say a completely shielded electromagnetic field, such that there can be no classical electromagnetic forces at work outside the shield. Yet if a detector consisting of polarised light in an optical fibre is wrapped around the outside of the shield and the electromagnetic field inside is turned off, the phase — the observable Berry effect — of the polarized light changes. And similarly if the source of the electromagnetic field is moved. Even gravitational fields produce such effects. It maybe asked how a single complex number can serve as a complete historical record. The answer consists in the fact that values of such numbers form an infinite transcendental universally embedding totally ordered field, and as such can always contain a finite history, however large.

d. It has also been shown by Perus (1996), that there is a mathematical identity between neural net formalism and quantum systems formalism, where the first concerns real quantities, and the second concerns complex quantities. As is seen to be the case, in the AND Corporation model.

e. The thesis first set out in the '70s by the well known Stanford experimental neurophysiologist, Karl Pribram, that the brain works holographically. It was based on the brain's undue effectiveness, when subject to damage. That is, it has redundancy analogous to that found in holographic systems. This led Pribram and his Japanese theoretical physics coworkers, Jibu and Yasue (as, for example, is extensively detailed in Pribram's (1991) book, Brain and Perception) to modeling the brain using the Quantum Brain Dynamics of Umezawa (see Jibu & Yasue 1994), in order to account for the findings of experimental neurophysiology.

2. What this quantum holographic model says about the workings of the brain

2.1 *A mathematical model of the mind and consciousness*

In holography, phase is the essential quantity of physical significance, such that quantum holographic knowledge processing/pattern recognition is carried out by means of phase gates (as for example in the AND Corporation model above, where the biological neuron is conceived as such a phase gate). The basic principles concern whether signals in the form of waves are in phase or out of phase, so as to reinforce or attenuate each other. Wave interference patterns constitute hologram encodings for the three-dimensional object image bearing illumination. Therefore, they include the three-dimensional shape and properties of objects.

Relativistic quantum holography describes generalized holography applicable to any kind of physical wave phenomenon, by means of the standard quantum mechanical formalism (Schempp 1992), compatible with the transactional interpretation (Cramer 1986) and harmonic analysis over the Heisenberg Lie group (Schempp 1986), so as to incorporate signal theory (of the observed relative to an observer) into quantum physics. By this means, it has been possible to conclude (1.3) that the analogue/physical information processing controlling the human organism has reached an evolutionary stage, where it operates by means of quantum non-local coherence/teleportation on many scales. This is related to the fact that, in quantum holography, the same fundamental core process, phase conjugate adaptive resonance, applies to the description of the processes of both evolution and learning (see Sections 2.6 and 2.7 that follow).

Many scientists unaware of the properties of time reversal invariance, will object at this point, saying that the brain is a hot, noisy system, where quantum holography, could not take place. This is however incorrect, a fact easily demonstrated by analogy with classical acoustic wave systems. Here, time reversal invariance (Fink 1997) produces a focusing rather than the expected scattering of the acoustic waves following the introduction of a random configuration of rods, representing the element of noise. In actual brains, this phenomenon is called stochastic resonance (Moss & Pei 1995). In fact, such focussing of acoustic waves is so good, that it is used to crack and remove gallstones within human bodies (Fink 1997).

Thus, in a description based on the quantum holographic emitter/absorber model of quantum mechanics, where time reversal invariance in the form of phase conjugation applies to the whole brain and its sensory systems (i.e. the whole body), quantum non-local coherence/teleportation applies from the whole brain down to what is traditionally the quantum level culminating in a Berry phase (Berry 1988; Anandan 1992). Thus if the human organism is a quantum coherent whole as quantum holography requires, then this represents not only a solution to the well known binding problem, but the organism's geometric/Berry phase, consisting of a complete mental (process) record of the history of the organism from its conception, constitutes a model for the mind.

According to this model, mental/mind events and processes (thought), may control neural events. Such an hypothesis of mind/brain interaction calls on the quantum mechanical fact that in relation to the Berry phase (Resta 1997), observables maybe the quantum phases of some quantum state vector (in this case of the whole mind/body). Thus, in such a quantum mind, mental processes can give rise to observable effects. The mind acts like a quantum non-local operating system with access to a labeled "program library" of activities, the holographic dynamical mental processes, which the brain has learnt by adaptation (the detailed nature of mind-brain interaction is dealt with in the sections below, in particular in Section 5).

2.2 *The quantum holographic model of the brain*

In such brain/mind, in such quantum control loops, the neurons, acting as phase gates, fulfil the dual functions of analysis and synthesis, filtering and combining respectively sensory holographic data and thought to produce, it has been shown (Marcer & Schempp 1998),

a. a frequency oriented paged holographic associative memory in the form of synchronously partitioned dendritric arboresences, and
b. the incremental stream of conscious perception and cognition, we all experience, as phase conjugate adaptive resonance.

That is, the principal modes of phase conjugate adaptive resonance (see Section 2.4) of quantum holography determine the stream of consciousness, while the less dominant modes proceed unconsciously, so as to filter and taxonomize the data of sensory experience and thought onto the paged memory in accordance with sharp frequency adaptive coupling conditions. These modes expand and contract the neural and dendritic arboresences as sensory experience (i.e. neurally controlled processes) and thought (mentally controlled processes) dictate. Simultaneously, the quantum Berry phase of the whole organism (its mind), as the total historical record of all the organism's activity including all sensory experience and thought, is automatically updated. The Berry phase therefore provides a complete redundancy of memory often essential to survival in biological systems separate from the usual connectionist/dendritic memory.

It is worth emphasizing that quantum mechanical descriptions of physical systems concern complex quantities, having two mathematical parts, where both parts can have observable/real physical consequences. In quantum holography these may concern real and virtual holographic images (see 1.4. of part II). It could therefore be argued, following the line of Bohm's concept of explicate and implicate order (Bohm 1980), and given the fact that the Berry phase corresponds mathematically to an imaginary part of a complex quantity with observable consequences, that these two parts, one real and one virtual, could be identified with the physical and the psychical respectively so as to provide an explanation of the respective phenomena.

2.3 *How such quantum brains differ from their classical counterparts*

The working within the whole neural system, described by quantum holography (Schempp 1992, 1993), implies that the activity/action potential of the neurons (and the brain as a whole) correspond to the group of symmetries,

$$X(v) : C_G(0, 0, z) \rightarrow \exp(2\pi ivz) \quad (1)$$

which define the central character X(v), frequency $v \neq 0$ of the Heisenberg group G's one dimensional center C_G of unipotent matrices (0, 0, z) where (x, y, z) stands for

$$\begin{pmatrix} 1 & x & z \\ 0 & 1 & y \\ 0 & 0 & 1 \end{pmatrix}$$

the three dimensional matrix representation of G, $i=\sqrt{-1}$, and x, y, z have the usual meaning of spatial measures. The z axis and the one dimensional center C_G of G, can thus be identified with the axon of the neuron (and the brain stem and spinal cord), so that for any phase conjugate resonant frequency $v \neq 0$,

$$U(v)/C_G = X(v) \text{ and } U^*(v)/C_G = X(-v) \quad (2)$$

define the center character representations modulo C_G. Here U(v) is, up to a unitary isomorphism, a unique infinite dimensional irreducible linear representation of the Schrödinger type of G, and $U^*(v)$ is the feedback/back-projection representation of G associated with U(v).

In (2), appropriate to this quantum feedback mechanism, the subscript −v in relation to X(−v) indicates time reversal symmetry. This is an important formal property, since it

- is applied and used in explanations of quantum teleportation;
- is necessary to give rise to the sharp frequency adaptive coupling conditions responsible for the paged memory;
- gives rise to stochastic resonance, where noise has a focusing rather than a scattering effect
- such that the brain (and each neuron) can work as a quantum coherent whole, with a Berry phase.

In this way, in this model of the brain/mind employing quantum feedback, neural processes may control mental processes and vice versa, and

a. as shown above, the action potentials of the neurons encode phase, the quantity of physical significance in holography, such that the neurons act as phase gates of the reversible fan in/fan out assembly the holographic associative memory requires. This assembly filters and combines the data, which consists of holographic interference patterns P_j resulting from sensory input and thought, so that, for example, the brain or a sub-assembly of neurons may, for the purposes of cognition, function as a square law detector in relation to the Hilbert space $H=L^2(R)$. That is, the closest pattern P_j, $j=k$, to that newly input, will be incrementally amplified by adaptive resonance, while the remaining stored patterns P_j, $j=1$ to n, $j \neq k$ are simultaneously attenuated, and

b. the model has the advantage of allowing the brain/mind to utilize quantum non-local coherence to achieve massive parallelism. This is quantum parallelism. It allows, for example, simultaneous activity in geometrically separate brain segments, and the instantaneous affecting of a "change of mind" (i.e. the shutting down of activity in one set of segments and replacing this by that in another set), to be carried out without the use of co-ordinating signals from a central control or switching center as in a classical machine. That is, the brain/mind is a fully distributed, synchronously partitioned, massively parallel processor and quantum holographic associative memory.

See the appendix, for an explanation of how, quantum holography says, the symmetries and equation (1) enable the brain and its neurons to perform the mappings, essential to problem solving and intelligence, so as to be able to overcome the combinatorial explosion rising from complexity in the real world.

2.4 *The importance of phase conjugation to the brain's survival, and why the brain has two hemispheres*

In holography one records not the optically formed image of an object, but the object (image bearing) wave itself, i.e. the whole of the illumination. This is done by mixing the wave with a separate coherent (usually non-object image bearing) wave or beam. Illumination of this hologram/record with the corresponding (non-object image bearing) 'anti-wave or beam' reconstructs the original object illumination including the object imagery. This imagery is practically indiscernible from the original object imagery including three dimensional parallax effects, and such that the context of the illumination defines other properties of the image i.e. the object qualia. Of particular interest in quantum holography is phase conjugation, the condition whereby the object wave is returned in real or virtual form along its path, so that the object image and the original object coincide. That is to say there is an almost exact analogy with an ordinary mirror, except that in a so called active phase conjugate mirror, the rays arriving at the mirror emanating from a point on a three-dimensional object, are reflected back to or seen as emerging from that point. Such active mirrors are used for targeting as part of weapons systems for example.

This phase conjugation condition is of fundamental importance in quantum holography, because it produces an adaptive *resonant signal* i.e. *effectively an amplification* allowing detection. It might be objected that the brain/mind does not employ phase conjugation. However two simple perceptual experiments serve to show that it does:

a. snap one's fingers and ask where the brain/mind creates the acoustic image of the snap. It is outside the head, *coincident with the snap*, as a phase conjugate image must be; similarly
b. reach out for a nearby object. Not only do the visual and tactile object images the brain/mind creates, each coincide with the object, but this coincidence also occurs *outside the head in every 3 dimensional geometric particular* with reference to the scale of resolution of which the senses are capable, as it would in holography.

Phase conjugation must be of vital importance to the processes of image formation in the brain/mind or imagemaker, since the survival of the imagemaker is completely dependent on locating objects where they actually are, whether it be by vision, sound or touch or even by taste or smell; that is, of sensing the world "the way it actually is". Such a statement is justified since phase conjugation ensures an ontological and epistemological equivalence.

Phase conjugation is also essential to communication between imagemakers. For what an imagemaker cognizes objects to be, depends entirely on the imagemaker's history of experience. This history is unique, since each imagemaker follows its own unique position or world line of motion and no two can be exactly the same. However what such imagemakers share in common on their own scale, is the objects of that scale and their positions relative to one another in the Cartesian theatre the objects define. Thus, according to this model, bats see acoustically "the same geometric reality" we see visually but they attach totally different meanings to the objects seen, as a result of their different genetic constitution, sensory apparatus, and their individual history of experience. Quantum holography therefore provides a clear definition of objectivity and subjectivity with respect to the qualia of objects, where it is the objects themselves, that implicitly label all aspects of experience in a universal way for all observers on that scale. Objects, the observed, therefore provide a common labelling for the basis of communication between such observers with a common genetic heritage and sensory apparatus.

Languages are therefore shared arbitrary labellings of objects and their properties such that

each holographic encoding of an icon or object,	maps to and from $\longleftrightarrow$	the holographic encoding of the arbitrary label for that icon or object.

It can therefore be postulated that the morphology of the human brain contains an instantiation of such mappings (Marcer & Schempp 1998). That is, the two brain hemispheres and corpus callosum (which joins them) are where these encodings reside and the maps (to and from) are realised. The right hemisphere containing the holographic encodings of the real world is the artistic brain, and the left, containing the arbitrary labellings for the real world objects and their properties is the logical brain. Here, in the latter, an essential element of such labelling of objects includes numbers and sets and their logical relationships or mappings one to another, where these must be acquired by learning/adaptation. Thus in quantum holography, phase conjugation specifies the mappings necessary to both geometry and logic, providing the canonical labelling any model of information processing must have if it is to formally and correctly constitute computation. That is to say brains possess a complete hemisphere (the right) plus a mapping morphology (via the corpus callosum and connecting the right hemisphere to the left, 'digital' hemisphere) absent from digital systems, as well as quantum information processing capabilities. This tells us, that in the human brain, it may be the right artistic hemisphere and the corpus callosum, that effectively overcomes the limitations, like Gödel's theorem, of the formal systems "encoded" in the left hemisphere, since this left hemisphere is the analogue of the digital computer.

The surface of these hemispheres (the sensory cortices) are, quantum holography says, hologram planes, where the holographic sensory data, described in terms of the Fourier-Wigner quantum holographic transform, is encoded and decoded, such that the brain itself is a phase conjugate resonant cavity. Similarly the eye is a resonant cavity, where the retina is the hologram plane containing an array of detectors working by phase conjugation. Thus it will appear to the eye/brain as if the real phase conjugate incoming object image bearing beam, is an actual (rather than the virtual phase conjugate) outgoing beam, which coincides with the object or objects from which the sensory signal originates, as was originally proposed by Plato, and as pointed out in the simple perceptual experiments already described.

2.5 *The nature of the stream of consciousness*

Since phase conjugate adaptive resonance is, quantum holography says, the product of the creation/annihilation or emitter/absorber model of quantum mechanics, the nature of the stream of consciousness may be envisaged as having the format of a three-dimensional movie, which the brain produces (as the energy source/projector). Here each movie frame will be the consequence of the process of holographic decoding, i.e. an emission. It will consist of a set of three-dimensional sensory object images coincident with the objects themselves in the three-dimensional Cartesian theatre these objects define. Data input to the brain/mind thus corresponds to a subsequent absorption or process of holographic encoding resulting in a stationary quantum interference pattern, such that adaptation occurs, so as to allow the brain/mind to model the relative motion of objects and other aspects of environmental change.

That is, the senses or sensory apparatus are the means by which the brain/mind experiences the material world as it really is, as a consequence of the condition of phase conjugation, such that the brain/mind's conscious perception will include:

i. an arrow of time,
ii. a present advancing in the direction of that arrow,
iii. a fixed unalterable past,
iv. a present filled with three-dimensional objects in relative motion to one another and the brain/mind itself in space and where the relativistic invariance of quantum holography says that space–time is the universal property of such relative motions.

These conclusions are based on (a) the premise that for the purpose of survival, the brain/mind's experiental record must phase conjugately mimic reality (so that objects are 'seen' as located where they actually are), and (b) the premise that reality itself must also be describable by such creation/annihilation model (and hence as a three-dimensional phase conjugate adaptive resonant stream), and thus is subject to a globally irreversible incremental evolution over time, following as a consequence of that evolution's own historical record (as contained in its Berry phase).

{*Technicality*: (iv) requires an explanation of how such phase conjugate imagery, where actual objects may stand at any distance from the observer to the horizon, may be so readily compared? The answer follows from the representations of the Lorentz group which are intrinsic to the specification of relativistic quantum holography. That is, it is an embedded group, which describes the signaling of the observed with reference to the observer, i.e. the observer's holographic perspectives of the observed. Such quantum signaling (ie teleportation) corresponds to supraluminal Lorentz representations (Nibart 1999); classical signaling corresponds to luminal Lorentz representations (better known as special relativity) and those of phase conjugate quantum signaling correspond to the Lorentz representations, which fall on the wave (light) cone itself. This shows that phase conjugate holograms (the formation of which involves all three Lorentz representations) all concern the Minkowski wave cone as a common signal reference frame, and so can be directly compared, and act as filters for such comparisons.

This was already seen to be the case in quantum holography in relation to equation (1) above, where the symmetry ensures that phase conjugate signals are output from neurons and from the brain as a whole. It shows that phase conjugation defines the condition which acts as the bridge between quantum and classical signal processes, in the quantum world. It strongly suggests that the reason why phase conjugation gives rise to adaptive resonance, is the same as why $E=mc^2$! This may well also concern a fourth Lorentz representation associated with the vertex/origin of the wave cone, which in quantum holography concerns the source of the radiation/illumination. These sources are described by point orbits in terms of actions on the nilmanifold of the Heisenberg group G. These have been used to model the prokaryote cell quantum holographically (see Marcer & Schempp 1997)}

This stream of consciousness, consisting of the sum of histories of its movie frame objects in motion, may be cognitively filtered holographically into the separate histories of its component objects and their properties with respect to their sensory illumination, so as to allow the mind to select, say, the history or paths of those objects, which are red. That is, such quantum holographic pattern recognition, allows the taxonomization, filtering and storage of information including qualia.

Thus this brain/mind is quantum mechanically a "Feynman machine" (Feynman 1990), i.e., a machine capable of storing the histories of the objects of the totality of its sensory experience and thought in holographic form, including the geometric information about their morphology and relative locations over time (as a product of change) in the three dimensional Cartesian theatres which the brain/mind and the relative motion of objects define. Thus following Feynmann's quantum mechanical prescription (Feynmann & Hibbs 1965; Feynmann 1990; Schempp 1993) or sum of histories approach to quantum mechanics (as applies in quantum holography), such a machine is able to quantum mechanically compute any appropriate sum of histories from its experience and thought in order to formulate its behavior. Thus, the possible incompleteness of the history of an individual's experience, and thought, in a particular context may place limitations on the accuracy of prediction by this means.

2.6 *How intelligence may be mathematically and physically defined and explained*

Intelligence is defined here in terms of the mechanism of the pattern recognition problem solving ability of quantum holography, the properties of which can be illustrated in terms of the following three metaphors of (1) the jigsaw, (2) the elephant, and (3) the lighthouse[2]. Quantum holography, says that:

1. the unique perspectives, with respect to the observed from the viewpoint of an observer, together make up a whole 3D-picture. These perspectives may therefore be thought of as the pieces that make up a jigsaw as a whole, such that
2. such perspectives may be compared to the three blind philosophers taken to feel an elephant, who respectively describe the tail, a leg, and a tusk; leading each to an observation apparently at odds with the others, but which, in fact, is a consistent aspect of the whole — an elephant, and
3. now consider an observer walking on the seashore on a dark night with thick, low cloud, who sees only a faint light reflected from the surface of the waves. Such an interference of light with water waves is a hologram. It is an encoding which could be decoded, if one could control the source of the water waves, so that the surface of the sea becomes flat; that is, like a mirror in which one sees the image of source of the light waves — a lighthouse — the source of the illumination in this case. This metaphor is almost an exact analogy for the holographic encoding and subsequent decoding of a hologram, or for the encryption/decryption of a message, where the original wave interference is, in fact, an exponential map or 'disordering', and so is seen as random; although clearly in fact, it is not, for it can be decoded and therefore has an inverse logarithmic mapping (Marcer 1998)! This inverse mapping is its semantics or meaning, for example, the encoded meaning/message in a cryptogram, which ensures such an inverse mapping exists, such that it can be decoded.

{*Technicality*: In quantum holography based on the Heisenberg nilpotent Lie group G, it is the Lie nature of the group G which ensures the existence of this inverse. For the natural Lie diffeomorphism — the exponential map — is a differentiable map with a differentiable inverse ie an logarithmic map, so that in relation to every apparently exponential disordering/combinatorial explosion, there exists a inverse map, which solves the problem. That is, the constructive quantum mechanical holographic formulation of a problem, quite naturally carries within it, the solution to that problem! Indeed, the diffeomorphic nature of the Lie group says that this will always be the case, even if there is an exponential tower of complexity, and that the transformational methodology discovered by Sophus Lie, constitutes the general problem solving strategy for such problems (Fatmi, Jessel et al. 1990). It says that such problem solutions can be reached through the the Lie algebra g of G, so allowing the problem to be linearized, and thus in principle facilitating the problem solution in real time, which is a prerequisite for the survival of intelligent machines, such as brain/minds are in a complex world. For if L_i are the associated infinitesimal transformations of a Lie algebra L, then the Lie commutator/product or Lie group germ determines a Lie group G_L which is a topological group, such that by Lie's second fundamental theorem (Cohn 1956),

$$[L_i, L_j] = L_iL_j - L_jL_i = c_{i,j,K}L_k \text{ over all k belonging to } G_L$$

where $c_{i,j,K}$ are constants/invariants of the problem dynamics. Such invariants concern in the case of G the constancies of shape, size, and the properties of object and invariant path curves, which typify object motion and behaviour. These, taxonomizing objects, are, of course, the very meat and drink of human perception and cognition. The constant features of the world, by means of which we are able perceive and recognize it. Very remarkably in quantum holography (Schempp 1992), the Lie algebra g of G, specifies the commutators which define the Heisenberg uncertainty relations. This says that while these relations will continue to hold, they constitute the very means by which in the emitter/absorber model of quantum holography (see Appendix), computation can be carried out! That is, to say, the state vector of an emission/absorption, exp(iHΔt) where H is the Hamiltonian and Δt is the time interval, may be thought of as representing a computational quantum phasegate, such that Δt is the switching time by analogy with conventional computer gates, for which the energy H is applied, so as to compute, in the case of quantum holography, the desired (resonant) output.}

This tells us that in quantum holography:

a. quantum information processing concerns quantum measurement/output, where this is performed using an exchange of resonant energy and where the parameters are chosen in such a way that this resonant exchange is fully reversible, and imposes no uncertainty limitations on the output, such that
b. entropy is both an information metric (as shown by Zurek 1989) and a measure of disorder. That is to say, entropy production can be used respectively to both create and destroy machine states, so enhancing or degrading the behavior of the machine. An example is the well-known Maxwell demon (Clement, Coveney et al. 1999), or holes/communication channels in biological membranes, where receptors govern a whole range of chemical behavior, between the inside and outside of the cell (Marcer & Schempp 1997). Such reversible quantum holographic measurement is quite different from the deterministic evolution governed by the Schrödinger equation. It follows from the new awareness that exploitation of quantum interference

effects (in this case attributable to holography) inherent in the quantum mechanical description of systems can be used to guide system evolution (Rice 1992) including the interaction of a systems with itself, i.e. self reference (Marcer 1995, 1996)

{*Technicality*: Returning to the metaphor of the lighthouse, it tells us, as can be shown, that such holographic problem solving concerns the ability to find a Heaviside operator B (or a corresponding Green's function, see Clement, Coveney et al. 1999) to describe the encoding/decoding process, so that in some finite domain, in the case of an area of sea, this operator B is zero specifying the flattening of the waves to make the sea like a mirror, while outside this domain B = 1. This satisfies the Fatmi/Young definition of intelligence published in Nature (Fatmi, Young et al. 1970), that intelligence is the perception of order, where none was previously perceived. And in 3 dimensions, such a Heaviside operator/Green's function corresponds to the well known Dirac Delta function of quantum mechanics. Such a model is dialectic, so that a scientific investigator should never say that another is wrong, and that he/she is right, for this may only be true in some domain of experience i.e. where B = 1. But as shown B always possesses an inverse B* such that B* = 0 in the domain where B = 1, and is itself 1 outside this domain. That is, a better solution is to combine the experience of their joint understanding so that for a new operator B** = 1 in both domains. That is, employ a non-zero rather than a zero sum strategy.}

2.7 *An explanation of the nature of creative acts and of free will?*

Quantum holography is an adaptively resonant creation/annihilation model of quantum mechanics, which maintains an historical record, the Berry phase. This does not fully determine future quantum system states (i.e. there is a potentiality for free will in conscious systems as the brain/mind as modelled here). That is to say, there will be events some of which are predictable in view of the systems past history, and some unpredictable. This allows a brain/mind some freedom of action, because the course of some future events is undetermined at this point in evolution; a freedom which can also lead to the wrong action, even when the course of future events is determinable, but was not known, or could not be made in time. Even so, such quantum mechanical systems or wholes, have, it can be shown, a unique global evolutionary development, where system entropy may play the role of an information metric as well as a measure of disorder (Marcer 1997). This says that such systems do indeed obey both the Third and the Second Laws of Thermodynamics i.e. they cannot because of their historical record return to their original state, but rather than 'running down' to produce ever increasing disorder, they evolve so that they are 'running up' producing ever increasing order. As Dawkins (1989) has pointed out living systems do this through their genes/DNA by means of, quantum holography predicts (1.3), acts of annihilation/creation or processes of encoding/decoding.

This model presupposes an event or very initial creative act, for which quantum holography provides a mathematical description in terms of point orbits which describe the sources of the illumination. At such sources there exists both the spatial and temporal coherence necessary for the quantum holography to take place phase conjugately such that the system will be adaptively resonant. That is, these conditions specify an initial creative act to define the existence of order, where none previously existed, for example, in thought, the Eureka moment of entirely new understanding, or the birth of an entirely new idea; or within a species, the birth of each unique individual, etc. That is, it explains the nature of creativity and equally the Creation of the Universe (Marcer 1992, 1995, 1996) in line with Chapline's postulate (see 1.5a). Here there will be an initial resonant amplification of holographic signal energy (i.e. big Bang). However this adaptively resonant signal not only corresponds to energy/matter, but is a holographic encoding of the 3 dimensions of space for which relativistic quantum holography specifies definite metrics. That is, it can be postulated that this is a creation of Everything from Nothing (Puthof 1990)/Self-Creation (Marcer 1996), in line with quantum holographic law, such that energy and space/time are complementary, each to the other. This would sustain an adaptively resonant evolution, where the condition of phase conjugation says that such a quantum universe, as all that exists, is such that as a whole, it maps itself onto itself, ie automorphically, adaptively changing itself at each step of the evolution ie at each 3 dimensional movie frame as described above; and where this is from Nothing because prior to this initial creation, the quantum holographic universe can have no recorded history. Such a process as described above would therefore be a self-organizing one (Marcer 1998), where under the appropriate circumstances, life, DNA, living units (observers of their environment (the observed)), societies of living units (observers of their environment (the observers, themselves)), biospheres; nervous systems, brains, consciousness, language communication, formal symbolic systems, mathematics are all inevitable emergent consequences of physical law.

2.8 *Can the so-called paranormal now begin to be given a scientific explanation?*

As was described, quantum holographic descriptions concern phase conjugate images outside the head coincident with the objects of the physical world. Further, the senses in part work and communicate quantum mechanically employing non-locality/teleportation. Therefore, this model may imply quantum non-locality of a brain/mind with non-living material objects, and with other brain/minds. That is the compatibility of their 'synchronicity' with that of other systems, including the Universe itself as quantum coherent phase conjugate self-organizing system. As already cited above, there are two inseparable fundamental modes of signal transmission, corresponding to supraluminal (ie quantum teleported), and luminal (i.e. classical) signal transmission possibilities. Thus, for example, normal vision is the reception by the eye of a light signal, simultaneous with the phase conjugate mental/virtual projection of that light signal back to the object from which the light signal originated. It may be hypothesized therefore that 'remote viewing' is a similar process, but rather where now it is the phase conjugate mental/virtual projection onto an object (beyond the viewer's normal visual horizon), which initiates the remote view of the object in the brain/mind such that, say, the brain is able to learn to transduce this novel viewing process into a real signal — the remote view.

The scientifically founded possibility of a quantum holographic model of the brain, and of quantum teleportation of information between brains, provides a model which justifies the exploration of this possibility in relation to phenomena such as extra sensory perception, i.e. in the case when the observed is another human observer. Similarly, in case of telekinesis, the observed is simply a material object, for which quantum teleportation could allow a change of the state of motion. It opens the model to the possibility of describing scientifically what is conventionally considered to be the province of the paranormal (Mitchell 1999). It includes the possibility of the control by mind (i.e. mental) over brain and body (i.e. physical) processes, especially since it predicts that mind memory includes the sum of histories of the development of the human embryo from each individual's conception as blueprinted in the individual's DNA. This indicates a potentiality for healing (making whole) of the unhealthy body (i.e. such a body's reconstruction by the mind) according to an individual's will, via the process record of its embryonic/foetal development, as held in the mind. There is an extensive experiential record of this happening throughout human history, and in many simpler organisms, like worms, where whole sections of the body can be renewed to create two entirely separate organisms. This potentiality is at the heart of much of alternative and complementary medicine. It could therefore provide an explanation for their effectiveness, putting them on a scientific footing. Further, the model of the quantum mechanical self could be fundamental, the quantum holographic model of DNA says (1.3), to the workings of the body's immune system. For it could allow the organism to know where and when the health of the body is out of kilter with its healthy design blueprint/

design plan and to instruct the brain/mind unconsciously to initiate the required remedial actions. For the word health derives from "making whole", and do we not say of an unhealthy person that he/she is not looking his/her self today? Indeed the immune mechanism is central to all medicine, which at best can only aid, enhance and restore the body's ability to maintain and heal itself. For without this capability no complex organism like ourselves can remain alive for any extended time when in contact with the biological environment.

2.9 *Further evidence and next steps*

Further mathematical and physical evidence in favour of the brain working quantum mechanically, comes for example from:

a. Noboli who published two seminal papers "Schrodinger Wave Holography in the Brain Cortex" (1985), and "Ionic Waves In Animal Tissues" (1987) to account for the function of the glial cells which overwhelmingly surround the brain's neural structure, and who cites the fact that wherever holography is performed by the excitation of stationary modes inside a wave-propagating medium with reflecting boundaries, that phase conjugation occurs spontaneously such that both virtual and real images of the recorded information are elicited by wave diffraction. This is a mechanism essential to the methodology set out above, and one already confirmed with respect to fMRI tomography.
b. Penrose, Hameroff and their coworkers. Their mathematical and very extensive work into the science of consciousness, in relation to which the Penrose book, the Emperor's New Mind (Penrose 1990) was seminal in establishing this science's respectability. Together with Hameroff's equally important work on the quantum mechanical role that microtubules could play in the emergence of consciousness in the human brain (Penrose 1998; Hameroff 1998), it has lead to the establishment of an new Institute for Consciousness Studies at the University of Arizona, together with a too numerous to cite important list of scientific publications and programmes (see www.consciousness.arizona.edu).

The next step is therefore to use the new proof methodology to predict the internal morphology and dynamics of the axon working by quantum holography at the level of the scale interior to the axon, so as to reveal the existence and role of the microtubules, which are known as a fact of neurophysiology to exist there. For if the quantum holographic model does not predict their existence and role, then it is wrong. But if it does, then in accordance with the quantum mechanical workings of the axon already cited above, this would provide an independent confirmation of the still disputed Hameroff/Penrose hypothesis concerning the microtubules' quantum mechanical working and role (Penrose 1998). It would establish a bridge between their work, and the quantum holographic model to the great mutual benefit of both. It can further be expected to resolve the dichotomy between their work and that of Tuszynski (Tuszynski, Brown et al. 1998), where the claims are that the behavior of microtubules can be explained quantum mechanically and classical respectively, since in the quantum holographic model both will be true.

Notes

1. This aspect of the quantum holographic model is not further discussed as it would take a whole paper in itself. It involves the relationships (i.e. symmetry group properties) between phase and frequency, etc. and is still being researched.
2. The author wishes to thank Michael Brown for suggesting this metaphor
3. The fact that phase information is not lost, but amplitude maybe, means that as is known in holography, there can be a complete global image with a possible loss of resolution. Amplification of such signals can therefore be performed so as to restore amplitudes.

Appendix: A mathematical outline of the creation/annihilation model of quantum holography

This Appendix summarizes the formal argument in Schempp (1998). The multiplicative group G of all unipotent real matrices

$$\begin{pmatrix} 1 & x & z \\ 0 & 1 & y \\ 0 & 0 & 1 \end{pmatrix} \quad \text{written as } (x, y, z) \text{ for convenience}$$

with unit element (0, 0, 0) is a simply connected nilpotent Lie group diffeomorphic to the differential manifold $(R \oplus R) \times R$ with one dimensional center $C_G = \{(0, 0, z) \mid z \in R\}$. G is a realization of the three-dimensional Heisenberg Lie group. The Haar measure of G is the Lesbesgue measure $dx \otimes dy \otimes dz$ of the underlying manifold R^3 and the Lie algebra of G is formed by the upper triangular matrices $\{(x, y, z)-(0, 0, 0) \mid x, y, z \in R\}$. In terms of the canonical basis $\{P, Q, Z\}$ of g given by the matrices,

$$P := \begin{pmatrix} 0 & 1 & 0 \\ 0 & 0 & 0 \\ 0 & 0 & 0 \end{pmatrix} \quad Q := \begin{pmatrix} 0 & 0 & 0 \\ 0 & 0 & 1 \\ 0 & 0 & 0 \end{pmatrix} \quad Z := \begin{pmatrix} 0 & 0 & 1 \\ 0 & 0 & 0 \\ 0 & 0 & 0 \end{pmatrix}$$

the Heisenberg commutation relations read as follows,

$$[P, Q] = PQ - QP = Z; \ [P, Z] = 0; \ [Q, Z] = 0$$

and thus the centre c of the Heisenberg Lie algebra g, modelled by Z, is one dimensional and satisfies $\exp(c) = C_G$ under the natural Lie diffeomorphism /mapping. The classic uncertainty principle takes the form of the Robertson relation

$$\Delta U_v(P) \,.\, \Delta U_v(Q) > \tfrac{1}{2} \mid U_v(Z) \mid \ (v \in R,\ v \neq 0)$$

where U_v is, up to a unitary isomorphism, a unique infinite dimensional irreducible linear unitary representation of the Schrodinger type of G in the standard Hilbert Space $H = L^2(R)$; Δ is the standard root mean square deviation and v is the frequency. That is, the standard quantum mechanical commutators of the group of symmetries of G are the structure relations of g, its Lie algebra, as was known to Weyl in 1928.

Introduction of the usual complex mode co-ordinates

$$T = 1/2\ (P + iQ) \text{ and } T^* = 1/2(P - iQ)$$

permits the different alternatives at the photon level that can co-exist in quantum linear superposition to be expressed in terms of the annihilation and creation operators of a emitter/absorber model

$$a = U(T);\ a^* = U(T^*)$$

through the linear Schrödinger representation U of G, where in terms of the number states $|n_k>$ which are quantum states with n_k quanta occupying the mode k. These number states are the eigenstates of the number operator

$$N_k = aa^* \text{ and } [a, a^*] = p$$

is the bosonic commutation relation. Thus if $H_v(\varphi, \phi;\ x, y)$ expresses the probability of detecting a wave quantum (for example, a photon) of energy hv within a unit area attached to (x, y) in $R \oplus R$, the hologram plane, where wavelet mixing $\varphi \otimes \phi$ takes place, then $H_v(\varphi,\phi;\ldots)$ and $\overline{H}_v(\varphi,\phi;\ \ldots)$ respectively can be considered as the wavelet transform of the retarded signal $\varphi \in L^2(R, dt)$ with the respect to the advanced reference response wavelet $\phi \in \overline{L}^2(R, dt)$ and vice versa, so that time averaging performed by integration along the whole real line R by superposition of the net wavelets (expressed in the modular scalar product $\langle | \rangle$ of the complex Hilbert space $L^2(R, dt)$) effectively freezes the time t of the advanced signal wavelet packets and the retarded response signal wavelet packets into the spatial synchronization variables (x, y) of the symplectic hologram plane $((R \oplus R),\ \Omega_{v'}(dx \wedge dy))$, where Ω_v is the symplectic frame and $v \neq 0$ is the frequency. This spatial encoding of the relative phase avoids the loss of phase information under wave packet reduction,[3] and knowledge of the coordinates (x, y) with respect to the symplectic frame allows the identification of the split quantum (i.e. photon in the case of light) channels in accordance with the non-local quantum property of individual quanta passing by different pathways, ie locally recording (x, y) makes the multiplexing coherent wavelet packet densities $\varphi(t')dt'$ and $\phi(t)dt$ indistinguisable by relative time and phase corrections to the respective pathways. This conservation of information on wave packet reduction is the truly remarkable feature of quantum holography and of gating in this way by phase. It allows the brain/mind to function as a fully distributed, synchronously partitioned massively parallel processor and holographic associative filter bank and memory as already described.

The natural Lie diffeomorphism (i.e. differentiable mapping with a differentiable inverse) of G is such that

$$\exp g \to G \text{ and } \log G \to g$$

and $\exp c = C_G$ and $\log C_G = c$ (B) i.e. this form of holographic encoding, decoding and transmission of signals allows the treatment of arbitrary or exponential towers of complexity. It implies the essentially unlimited compression of holographic data with regard to signal transmission and memory, because at its most primitive level, the two, as in the brain/mind's dendritic arboresences, are, quantum holography predicts, one and the same.

Equation (B) taken in conjunction with equation (A) in 2.3, explains how problem solving ability/intelligence (see 2.6), follows as a natural consequence of the symmetries, which (A) determines, and which quantum holography says, must hold in relation to neuron/axon structure and across the whole brain. (A) demonstrates the importance of phase θ, which is the essential quantity of physical significance in quantum holography, where it is seen from the main text that exp(iθ) literally symbolizes:

i. the nature of the quantum holographic signal, including quantum teleportation
ii. a quantum computational/informatics gate
iii. the quantum Berry/geometric phase or process memory, which is a natural quantum observable of a state vector, as well as
iv. the Fourier transform action / harmonic analysis over the Heisenberg Lie group by means of which the quantum information processing is realized

that is, it symbolizes the universal mathematical element in quantum holography, such that $i=\sqrt{-1}$ expresses the natural duality of the representations of the theory; so that for example (x, y) in R⊕R the hologram plane, as appears above, constitute a Fourier duality pair embedding the complex plane in G. It emphasizes, as has already been found by a substantial body of research, the importance of phase in relation to the workings of the brain.

References

Anandan, J. (1992) The Geometric Phase, Nature, 360(26): 307–313.

Atiyah, M. (1990) The Geometry and Physics of Knots, Lezioni Lincee, Cambridge University Press, Cambridge.

Berry, M. V. (1988) The Geometric Phase, Scientific American, December, 26–32.

Bouwmeester, D. et al. (1998) Experimental Quantum Teleportation, Nature, 390, 11th December 575–579.

Brookes, M. (1999) Quantum Computing and Communications, Springer Verlag, London.

Chapline, C. (1999) Is Theoretical Physics The Same Thing As Mathematics?, Elsevier Physics Reports, 315, 95–105.

Clement, B., Coveney, P., Marcer, P. (1993) Surreal numbers and optimal encodings for universal computation as a physical process: an interpretation of the genetic code. CCAI Journal, 1, 1/2, 149–164.

Clement, B., Coveney, P., Jessel, M. and Marcer, P. (1999) The Brain as a Huygens' Machine. Informatica, 23, 389–398.

Cohn, P. M. (1956) Lie Groups, Cambridge Tracts in Mathematics and Mathematical Physics, 46, Cambridge University Press, Cambridge.

Cramer, J. G. (1986) The Transactional Interpretation of Quantum Mechanics, Reviews of Modern Physics, 58, 647–687.

Dahleh, M., Pierce, A. P. and Rabitz, H. (1990) Optimal Control of Uncertain Quantum Systems, Physics Review A, 42(3): 1065–1079.

Dawkins, R. (1989) The Selfish Gene. Oxford University Press.

de Duve, C. (1984) A Guided Tour Of The Living Cell. Vol. 2, Scientific American Library, Rockefeller University Press, New York.

Deutsch, D. (1985) Quantum Theory, The Church-Turing principle and the universal quantum computer, Proceedings Royal Society of London A400: 97–117.

Eccles, J. (1986) Do Mental Events Cause Neural Events Analogously To The Probability Fields Of Quantum Mechanics? Proceedings Royal Society London, B227, 411–428. See also, 1989, The Evolution of the Brain, and the Creation of the Self, Springer Verlag, London.

Fatmi, H. A., Jessel, M., Marcer, P., Resconi, G. (1990) Theory of Cybernetic and Intelligent Machines based on Lie Commutators, International Journal of General Systems, 16, 123–164.

Fatmi, H. A., Young, R. W. (1970) A Definition Of Intelligence, Nature, 228. 3rd October, 97.

Feynman, R. P. (1990) QED. Penguin Books, London.

Feynmann, R. P. and Hibbs B. J. (1965) Quantum Mechanic and Path Integrals, McGraw-Hill, New York.

Fink, M. (1997) Time Reversed Acoustics, Physics Today, March, 34–40.

Hameroff, S. (1998) Quantum Computation In Brain Microtubules? The Penrose-Hameroff 'Orch OR' Model of Consciousness, Philosophical Transactions: Mathematical, Physical and Engineering Sciences, Royal Society of London, 356, 1743, 15th August, 1869–1896.

Jibu, M. and Yasue, K. (1994) A Physical Picture of Umeawa's Quantum Brain Dynamics, Cybernetics and Systems Research '92, Vol. 1, Edited by Robert Trappl. World Scientific Publications, Singapore, 2–9.

Judson, R. S. and Rabitz, H. (1992) Teaching Lasers to Control Molecules, Physics Review Letters, 68, 10, 9th March, 1500–1503.

Leichtle, C. and Schleich, W. P., Averbukh, I.Sh. and Shapiro, M. (1998) Quantum State Holography, Physics Review Letters 80(7): 1418–1421.

Marcer, P. (1992) A Specification of the Unified Field, 161–164; Dubois, D. and Marcer, P. An Outline Model of Cosmological Evolution, 157–160, 13th International Congress of Cybernetics, Namur, Belgium, 24–28th August, Symposium VII, New Concepts in Cybernetics.

Marcer, P. (1995) A Proposal For A Mathematical Specification Of Evolution And The Psi Field, World Futures Journal of General Evolution, 44, 149–159.

Marcer, P. (1996) From The Self-Creation To The Creation of The Self. Proceedings of the ANPA 18 Conference, Cambridge, September, editor Etter T.L, 172–189.

Marcer, P. (1997) A mathematical definition of intelligence, Proceedings of the 5th Annual Greenwich Symposium, The Outer Limits of Computation, May 24th. University of Greenwich, eds. Fedorec A., Marcer P. 62–71.

Marcer, P. (1998a) The Jigsaw, the Elephant and the Lighthouse, Proceedings of the ANPA 20 Conference, Cambridge, 3–8th September, editor Bowden, K. G. 93–102.

Marcer, P. (1998b) Wider Perspectives — Nature, Cognition and Quantum Physics, Proceedings of ANPA 20, Cambridge, September, ed. K. Bowden, 87–92; see also www.bcs.org.uk/cybergroup.htm.

Marcer, P. and Schempp, W. (1996) A Mathematically Specified Template For DNA And The Genetic Code, In Terms Of The Physically Realizable Processes Of Quantum Holography, Proceedings of the Greenwich Symposium on Living Computers, editors Fedorec A. and Marcer P., 45–62.

Marcer, P., Schempp, W. (1997) Model of the Neuron working by Quantum Holography, Informatica 21, 519–534.

Marcer, P. and Schempp, W. (1997) The Model of the Prokaryote Cell as an Anticipatory System Working By Quantum Holography. Proceedings of the 1st International Conference On Computing Anticipatory Systems, Liege, Belgium, August 11–15, editor Dubois D. 307–313.

Marcer, P., Schempp, W. (1998) The brain as a conscious system, International Journal of General Systems, 27, 1/3, 231–248.

Mitchell, E. and Williams, J. (1996). The way of the explorer. G. P. Putnam's Sons, New York.

Mitchell, E. (1999) Nature's Mind, the Quantum Hologram, ISCAS 295–312.

Moss, F. and X. Pei (1995) Neurons in Parallel, Nature 376: 211–212.

Nibart, G. (1999) A Relativistic Model of A Particle-Antiparticle Pair May Break Up the EPR Paradox. ISCAS Proceedings.

Noboli, R. (1985) Schrödinger Wave Holography In The Brain Cortex, Physical Review A 32(6): 3618–3626.

Noboli, R. (1987) Ionic Waves In Animal Tissues, Physical Review A 35(4): 1901–1922.

Penrose, R. (1990) The Emperor's New Mind. Vintage, Random House, London.

Penrose, R. (1998) Quantum Computation, Entanglement, And State Reduction, Philosophical Transactions: Mathematical, Physical and Engineering Sciences, Royal Society of London, 356, 1743, 15th August, 1927–1939.

Perus, M. (1996) Neuro-Quantum Parallelism in Brain-Mind and Computers, Informatica 20, 173–183. see also, All In One, One In All, Brain and Mind in Analysis and Synthesis, DZS d.d. General Publishers, Ljubljana.

Pribram, K. H. (1991) Brain and Perception; Holonomy and Structure in Figural Processing, Lawrence Eribaum Associates, New Jersey.

Puthoff, H. (1990) Everything for Nothing, New Scientist, 28, July, 52–58.

Resta, R. (1997) The Berry Phase, Europhysics News, 28, 19.

Rice, S. A. (1992) New Ideas for Guiding the Evolution of a Quantum System. Science 258: 412–413.

Schempp, W. (1986) Harmonic Analysis on the Heisenberg Group with Applications in Signal Theory, Pitman Notes in Mathematics Series, 14, Longman Scientific and Technical, London.

Schempp, W. (1992) Quantum holography and Neurocomputer Architectures, Journal of Mathematical Imaging and Vision 2: 279–326.

Schempp, W. (1993) Bohr's Indetermincy Principle In Quantum Holography, Self-adaptive Neural Network Architectures, Cortical Self-organizatrion, Molecular Computers, Magnetic Resonance Imaging and Solitonic Nanotechnology, Nanobiology 2: 109–164.

Schempp, W. (1998) Magnetic Resonance Imaging, Mathematical Foundations and Applications, John Wiley, New York.

Schleich, W. P. (1999) Sculpting a Wavepacket, Nature, 397, 21st January, 207–208.

Sudbery, T. (1997) The Fastest Way from A to B. Nature, 390, 11th December, 551–552.

Sutherland, J. (1999a) AI@Work — Automated Cardiac Monitoring using Holographic/Quantum Neural Technology, PCAI Journal, Septemer/October, 20–22.

Sutherland, J. (1999b) Holographic/Quantum Neural Technology, Systems and Applications, ISCAS 313–334.

Turing, A. M. (1936) On Computable Numbers with Reference to the Entscheidungsproblem, (i.e. Godel's theorem/Halting problem), Proceedings of the London Mathematical Society, 42, 230–265, and 544–546.

Tuszynski, J. A., Brown, J. A. and Hawrylak, P. (1998) Dielectric Polarization, Electric Conduction, Information Processing and Quantum Computation In Microtubules. Are They Plausible? Philosophical Transactions: Mathematical, Physical and Engineering Sciences, Royal Society of London, 356, 1743, 15th August, 1897–1926.

Zurek, W. H. (1989) Thermodynamic Cost of Computation, algorithmic complexity, and the Information Metric, Nature, 341, 14th September, 119–124.

Zurek, W. (1989) Algorithmic Randomness and Physical Entropy, Physical Review A 40(8): 4731–4751.

Thinking together quantum brain dynamics and postmodernism

Gordon Globus

Abstract

I "think together" quantum brain dynamics (QBD) and postmodernism (appropriated to include Heidegger). In particular, the world thrownness of Heidegger, the sovereignty of Bataille and the differance of Derrida can be talked about in terms of QBD. This effects a rapprochement between the QBD revolution against classical neural network brain theory and the postmodern revolution against modernity and the metaphysical tradition. Such a grand millenial rapprochement brings together science in the guise of quantum neurophysics and postmodernism against their respective wills. Discussion of the problem of "consciousness" and brain has been so stalemated and seemingly interminable that if progress is to be made, a great conceptual wrenching is only to be expected. My formulation relinquishes consciousness and the quotidian world-in-common in favor of existence and parallel world-thrownnesses.

1. Introduction

Before attempting to think together such strange bedfellows as quantum brain dynamics (QBD) and postmodernism, a way must be cleared. There is antagonism from both sides to such an endeavor. Science disregards postmodernism, and curls its lip to postmodernism insistence. Postmodernism is equally scornful of science; already in Heidegger (1977) we find a deconstruction of science-imbued modernity, which is the current phase of the Gestell, the technoscientific context that goes unquestioned at the Millenium. This metaphysical Gestell goes back to the Socratic philosophers of ancient Greece, and now this framework is technoscientific. So postmodernism and brain science confront each other with equal scorn, I think, or more typically, withdrawing from the confrontation, postmodernism and brain science remain quite indifferent to one another. All this conflict/indifference makes it difficult to think together quantum brain dynamics and postmodernism. So my attempt to say QBD and postmodernism in the same breath is unconventional.

More way-clearing: My exemplars of postmodernism are Bataille (1988–90) and Derrida (1974, 1978, 1982, 1989) … and Heidegger (1962, 1972). Of course, postmodernists do not typically admit Heidegger to membership. I think there is a very deep failing in postmodernism's ontological shift away from Heidegger. Derrida considers text, whereas the presence of world, the very appearing of marks on a page, goes by and large unremarked. This is completely different from Heidegger who thematizes presence, and laments the Seinsvergessen of modernity, that it forgets Being, forgets the presencing of world. In early Heidegger Dasein provides a Lichtung, a lighted place, where world is disclosed. Heidegger wonders about this lighting process (in which, for example, Derrida finds himself thrown amidst legible texts rather than in the dark). Postmodernism properly tried to deconstruct the metaphysics of presence in texts but went too far. Heidegger must be brought back in, I think, to appreciate that the presence of the world is problematic. So when I use the term "postmodernism", I have effected an appropriation and welcomed Heidegger back under the postmodern umbrella, at least in the present region of discourse.

A very difficult to clear way: Now, "consciousness" is currently under great study — the discipline of "consciousness studies" is widely accepted-whereas talk of consciousness drops out of postmodern thought. I think that the current insistence on "consciousness" is an enormous obstacle to progress. To deny consciousness is not to be some kind of cranky materialist, behaviorist or operationalist, or wild postmodernist. The focus shifts from consciousness to existence, to finding ourselves already thrown, situated, amidst the world, a world whose taken for granted presence is deconstructed.

Down at the bottom of the tangled pile, "consciousness" is a theoretical construct used to explain presence (Globus 1998). For common sense the world is there, present, any fool can see, and we know of that world out there through our "consciousness". The world is self-subsistingly there and we become conscious of it, commonsense has it. Worldly presence is dealt with by common sense, but at the cost of an intractable consciousness/brain problem. QBD has the resources, however, to account for presence without any resort to "consciousness".

The so-called "hard problem" of qualia dissolves from this point of view; qualia, too, are theoretical entitities (Sellars 1963). If I stub my toe, the pain is in my toe, not my mind. My toe is part of the world. A tomato part of the world looks red and a toe part feels painful. These are different world *qualities*. There is no experience of a red image, sensation or quale in my mind in addition to the red tomato there in the world. There is no pain sensation in addition to the toe that hurts. All the pain's in my toe, Heaven's sake! There are only the *qualities* of world objects. The notion of a *quale* (pl. *qualia*) is purely theoretical, formulated to explain how world entities are represented to the mind, and deeply embedded in ordinary language (Globus 1998).

So the following is definitely not a discussion of consciousness, and any attempt to understand what follows in terms of consciousness will result in a deep misunderstanding of my endeavor. To relinquish consciousness is to avoid interminable discussion. Instead of consciousness I shall speak of existence as sovereign, situated, world-thrownness.

A bit of motivation: There is a large literature on consciousness and quantum neurophysics, but there's something out of balance here… Quantum physics is truly a revolutionary physics and quantum neurophysics is a revolutionary theory of brain functioning. But there is nothing revolutionary about "consciousness", whose provenance lies in Descartes. A theory as revolutionary as QBD (compared to classical neural network computation) calls for revolutionary concepts on the immaterial side. Classical "consciousness" may not be a fit candidate to think together with QBD, but how about postmodern existence? Could the quantum brain be postmodern? We need to think in revolutionary ways to undo the "world knot" of mind/matter relationships.

2. Quantum neurophysics

I want to try and convey something of the beauty of quantum neurophysics. I think that an intuitive sense of the brain's workings facilitates the process of thinking brain together with postmodernism. I will take as my underlying quantum theory the quantum brain dynamics (QBD) of the Umezawa school of quantum field theory (e.g., Jibu et al. 1994; Jibu & Yasue 1998; Umezawa 1993; Vitiello 1995).

To give an illustration of the emergence of quantum degrees of freedom in brain systems, we reduce our scale down to the nanolevel, ten to the minus nine meters, incredibly small … Lets focus down on certain nanolevel structures within neurons, the famous microtubules, which are mini-mini-miniscule hollow tubes. These tubules have walls made of protein isomers called tubulins, and the tubulins vibrate between two states at an incredibly rapid rate, in the nanosecond range. This is a remarkable structure: A nanolevel tube of vibrating tubulins filled with water molecules! And there is more structure: Because of the physical properties of water molecules under these conditions, they loosely arrange themselves into a lattice structure, a quasi-crystal, which is called "ordered water". So the neuron contains incredibly tiny locally vibrating tubules with ordered water inside.

Now, the ubiquitous water molecule which we take for granted has remarkable physical properties. The water molecule has a positive and a negative pole; such a structure is called a dipole. The molecules spin around their dipoles. So we have this quasi-crystal of spinning dipoles inside the locally vibrating microtubules. The Umezawa school has shown that out of the *physics* of this biological situation, quantum fields emerge at the macroscopic level of everyday life. This is one of Umezawa's achievements, showing how to get macroscopic fields out of microscopic quanta, by Bogoliubov transformation of the quantized field.

Pardon my enthusiasm, but this is remarkable: quantum field theory tells us that in living brain tissue macroscopic quantum fields emerge. Doesn't happen in silicon. No, the computer is completely inept at upholding such a thing. Sure, a computer has a quantum description, like any object, but no quantum fields emerge from the metally depths of the computer.

Quantum fields occur in the rest of our tissue as well. All our cells have microtubules and macroscopic quantum fields are formed in watery quasi-crystals inside the microtubules. Jibu and Yasue (1995) suggest that the field energy here is the *chi* of oriental medicine; *chi* is the nonlocal quantum energy of living tissue.

Brain cells have specialized microtubules, and the organization of cells is vastly different between brain and, say, liver. The brain is recursively organized into systems — systems embedded within systems embedded within systems, and so on — and the various brain systems have the option of participating in interactions with other brain systems, a "variable participation". The brain specializes in hoisting quantum field interactions. For the computer, no way. For the liver, maybe a smidgin.

Now, these spinning dipoles can be pointing every which-way — this is called incoherence — or they can all line up like synchronized swimmers. This case is "coherent", a form of which is the famous Bose-Einstein condensation. If you think of the quanta of the field as waves, coherence means that all waves are in phase (or maintain constant phase differences).

Usually coherence in a quantum system is rapidly lost because of interaction with its environment. It takes extreme technological conditions to maintain Bose-Einstein condensation in the laboratory. But in living neural systems, coherence can be maintained at modest biological temperatures and energies. These living systems also protect against thermal noise and dissipation. I want to bring in a beautiful term of Maturana and Varela (1980) here: autopoiesis, which refers to systems that are self-forming, self-maintaining and self-organizing. In the evolution of life, autopoietic systems sustain a quantum realm called the water dipole field, and in the evolution to neural tissue, the water dipole quantum field comes under nonlocal control.

Note that this rescues us from panpsychism in which ontological status is given to consciousness (*contra* Chalmers [1996] and Hameroff and Penrose [1996] who put consciousness into their fundamental ontology). Mind isn't universal, it's only where there are emergent macroscopic quantum fields that variably participate in interactions. *Existenz is unique*!

This water dipole field emergent in living neural tissue does not stand alone, it interacts with the ubiquitous quantized electromagnetic field. The dynamics of that interaction is described by quantum brain dynamics. That is, the interaction of water dipole field and quantized electromagnetic field is described in QBD. A form of coherence within the microtubules is beautifully termed "superradiance" (Jibu et al. 1994).

Ordered water and superradiant light in the microtubules! Water and light ... working together down there at the nanolevel in living neural tissue! [The hippies got it right ... it's all water and light.] Could there be an emergent quantum brain dynamics in living neural tissue based in water and light? If Dasein's brain were such a thing, maybe Dasein would fit his brain at last!

It's not all water and light though; there's also a web, a pervasive web spreading throughout a given neural system, both inside and outside of neurons and the even more numerous neuroglia, not respecting cell membranes, extended within and between cells, a densely filamentous nanolevel web of protein strands. This is a pervasive distributed system, and its logic is quantum.

So there is another system hidden behind the classical system of local neurons interacting across local synaptic junctions. The microtubules just discussed are in fact a specialized region of this nanolevel filamentous web. Out of the pure physics of this situation, quantum capabilities appear, which don't appear in salt or silicon. Solitons go whizzing through the filaments...these are lone traveling waves that arise out of the whole. The primacy of the whole is characteristic of quantum systems; it is called "nonlocality". Coherent waves called Froehlich waves also propagate through the filamentous web, in response to incoming energy pumping it (Froehlich 1968).

It is clear that Dasein's brain has lots of resources that the computer on your desk doesn't have. This difference between neural and technological will remain even when quantum computers become available. Quantum computers will process information in incredible ways, but the quantum brain deep down isn't computing. It's doing different kinds of things, which I suggest make it possible to think the quantum brain together with postmodernism.

Lets go a little more closely into quantum brain functioning: There is a relationship between a certain part of the filamentous nanolevel web and the water quasi-crystal. Certain filaments called MAPS *tune* local regions of the microtubules, according to Hameroff and Penrose (1996); they bias the Bose-Einstein condensate of coherent waves. So we have inside the microtubules a continually *tuned* quasi-crystal that sustains variable macroscopic quantum coherence. The tubulin walls of the microtubules carry order from the classical system of neurons to the tuned water dipole field which becomes coherently excited. The water dipole field interacts with the quantized electromagnetic field and laser-like activity is induced within the microtubules at biological temperatures and energies.

Tuned for what? The watery quasi-crystal is tuned for what might be outside the brain. Or in a Heideggerian spirit, tuned for the interaction with the surrounding reality's gift, ready to accept the gift gratefully. This fluctuating attunement situates for reality. I am claiming that Dasein's situatedness is a varying quantum attunement mediated by MAPS. Furthermore, Dasein's situatedness cannot be reduced to digital logic because it is nonlocal. Nonlocal control has the characteristics of "I" as agent. (In Cartesian interactionism, the subject is specifically nonlocal with respect to *res extensa* and is taken to be nonphysical, hence Cartesian dualism, but in the quantum framework nonlocal has a physical meaning, so there is ontological monism.) So each of us might properly say: *I am nonlocal control.*

So we have an interaction between a quantum flux representing real invariances and a shifting quantum attunement that situates for the reality represented. Both quantum representation and quantum attunement are irreducibly nonlocal; here the undivided whole becomes ontological. There is a nonlocal interaction that classical mechanism cannot fit, with its tedious local interactions. The whole is not emergent from interacting parts but is primary, and the parts derivative.

There is another level to Umezawa's ontology. He posits a *tilde* domain which is the time-reversed mirror image of the standard quantum domain, and on this basis is able to bring in thermodynamic considerations and develop thermofield dynamics and quantum biodynamics. Vitiello (1995) exploits the *tilde* domain emergent in living brain tissue to explain memory, and I suggest cognition too. There is an interaction going on in the vacuum states supported and protected by living neural tissue, in which the flux of input order representing physical reality comes to meet the shifting attunement, an interaction in which memory, cognition and reality meet.

Lets try to understand some functions of this quantum brain. Think of the quantum brain as holding up a special kind of plenum to the interaction with reality. The brain brings quantum richness to the interaction with quantum reality. This *tilde* plenum is filled richly with possibilities but not like Pandora's box of individual butterflies; instead the possibilities are interpenetrated, entangled, what physicists call "superposed". The plenum is a superposition of possibilities, an "implicate order" (Bohm 1980).

The possibilities are not all equally likely to become actual. Some of the possibilities are more probable than others; each possibility has a p value, a probability value. Tuning adjusts the p values, so some are likely and the great majority unlikely. The attunement brings certain possibilities to the forefront of the plenum and the rest are very low probability. When walking through the hot late afternoon chaparral, we are attuned as rattlesnake possibilities but not when walking through the snow in Alaska, when we are attuned for grizzly bears. An ontology of nonlocal possibility is probabilized here.

So the quantum brain faces the interaction with its surrounding reality as tuned interpenetrated possibility, an implicate order which continually varies. The surrounding reality enters via a quantum representation that conserves the symmetries of the surround, that is, the invariant properties over time of the surround. This invariance representation is in a state of continual flux. Symmetry-conserving quantum representatives of quantum reality interact with continually tuned quantum possibility.

Now in that interaction between quantum reality and quantum possibility, if a certain kind of match is made, then something very cool happens. Suppose this match is a conjugate match, such as the match between the complex number $a+bi$ and its complex conjugate $a-bi$, where $i=$ the square root of minus one. When a complex number is multiplied by its complex conjugate, the i-term drops out, leaving a real number, which is associated with observables. The imaginary dimension of a complex space collapses in the match, leaving good old familiar Cartesian space. I think the quantum brain is arranging that kind of match, mathematically the match between complex and tilde complex conjugate numbers.

So the brain brings a tuned implicate order to the interaction with reality's quantum representatives, and in making a *tilde*-conjugate match, a world appears. Presence comes out of the conjugate matchings sustained by living brain tissue. We always find ourselves already thrown amidst the world because our brains continuously support a tilde-conjugate match between quantum attunements and quantum representations of reality.

3. A category mistake?

It appears that a category mistake has been made in my formulation: World presence with its various qualities seems intuitively incompatible with quantum happenings … the red of the tomato is simply not in the same league as Bogoliubov transformation of the quantized field. This quantum field formulation is just as far away from world qualities as Boolean logic. So it seems like the same category mistake made when presence is identified with neural network computations.

As a first step in undermining the alleged category mistake, we must forgo an extrinsic bias. My discussion of brain functioning with quantum degrees of freedom has tacitly assumed that we are scientific observers of the brain. But to comprehend world presence, we must shift to an intrinsic perspective, the case of actually *being* a human brain with quantum degrees of freedom.

What is it to be a body-embedded human brain with quantum degrees of freedom (brain-Q)? It is to exist. *To be brain-Q is to exist.* If this claim is correct, then quantum brain dynamics ought to be speakable with existence (*Existenz*), sympathetic to the ontological structure of existence: situated and world-thrown (Heidegger), sovereign (Bataille), discursive (Derrida).

The category mistake is to fuse an extrinsic perspective on brain-Q with existence. Although we all might have extrinsic perspectives on world objects, we do not have an intrinsic perspective on any world object, with one exception, our own brain. What I have attempted is fusing an intrinsic perspective "on" brain-Q with existence. The next three sections think together some postmodern thinkers and QBD. If that can be done, then we can take for serious consideration the claim that being brain-Q is existence. The perspectives are compatible here so no category mistake is made.

4. Some connections to Heidegger

It now becomes clear why Dasein provides the *Lichtung* in early Heidegger. It is because Dasein's brain is arranging for quantum field interactions in which the imaginary dimension collapses when *tilde*-conjugate matches are made, and *mirabile dictu*, there is presence, Dasein finds himself amidst a world. Apart from Dasein and related species, there is only the quantum darkness of the undisclosed. (In quantum mechanical formulations, my "quantum darkness" is called "unitary evolution of the Schrödinger wave function".) Since "darkness" implies a kind of presence — we see the dark — I shall say "quantum beyond darkness of the undisclosed".

There is something highly counterintuitive here, and scary. If Daseins are these little monadic bubbles of light where world presence is disclosed...why there is no world in common, only worlds in parallel. The parallel worlds are explicate worlds unfolded from the implicate order in a conjugate match sustained by each Dasein's brain. It's not that there is truly one world-in-common that we differently interpret. There are many worlds in parallel, each upheld by Dasein's brain.

More or less same situatedness across Daseins, and more or less same surrounding reality, then more or less same worlds unfold. In that comparable worlds unfold across Daseins, *maya* is sustained, there is an *illusion* of a world in common. It works just fine that we commonsensically believe in a self-subsisting world in common but actually there are synchronous parallel worlds, *Lichtungen* floating in a dark quantum sea, world thrownnesses continuously generated out of quantum field interactions arranged by Daseins' brains.

So we are maya-rapt bubbles of world thrownness floating through a quantum void.

I have been appropriating early Heidegger and thinking this appropriation together with quantum brain dynamics. One reason Heidegger is possible to connect is because underneath it all, he is a dynamical thinker, even Heraclitean. There is a core eruption in Heidegger, the *Ereignis*, a fundamental dynamic of which being and time are derivative—being and time are not primitive in late Heidegger. Being and time furthermore have a special relationship, they are eye-to-eye, they encounter each other. What's primitive is the dynamic of *Ereignis*, in which Being and time encounter each other. Recall Heidegger (1972): *Es gibt Sein. Es gibt Zeit*. The "Es" which is giving being and time is none other than the dynamical Ereignis.

"Thrownness" means lack of foundation, a sourceless irruption in which (unless we're in an altered state of consciousness) world presences to Dasein's involvement. *Ereignis* is anything but founded and mechanical; *Ereignis* at the depth of Heidegger's ontology is spontaneous and "sovereign" (Bataille 1988–90). Our world-thrownness erupts from a spontaneous sovereign quantum brain dynamical process.

My quantum formulation makes one important change from Heidegger. For Heidegger in this quote, *Es gibt Sein. Es gibt Zeit. Sein* means presence... the marvel that there is something, rather than nothing, that entities appear. For me, what Es gibt is Unpresent, lets call it *Un-Sein. Un-Sein* is the quantum form, which is unpresent, and which requires complex numbers for its mathematical description. I am echoing a postmodern stance here...the unpresent is characteristic of Bataille's general economy. So I say: *Es gibt Un-Sein*. I appropriate *Zeit* as an attunement, including the stretching of a past, a now and a future. *Es gibt Zeit*, it stretches an attunement. So differing from Heidegger: *Es gibt Un-Sein. Es gibt Zeit. Sein* as such comes out of the *tilde*-conjugate match between *Un-Sein* and *Zeit*.

5. Bataille's general economy

Lets finally turn from Heidegger to Bataille, whose "general economy" is fully postmodern. The texts I primarily rely on are Plotnitsky's (1994) complementarity book and Derrida's (1982) chapter, "From Restricted to General Economy: A Hegelianism with Reserve". I think the conjugate match just described between quantum situatedness and quantum reality fits Bataille's process of sovereignty. Let me try to work out the idea that a quantum brain has sovereignty. The ladder we will climb, and then throw away, is that of Being, presence. Presence is the way of getting to the point of leaping to the unpresent of sovereignty.

Presencing is a product of underlying quantum processes. Presence unfolds out of the matching process between quantum situatedness and quantum reality. Presence unfolds in the *tilde*-conjugate match.

Sovereignty is so different, completely alien to presence. Sovereignty does not seek to be recognized, Derrida says; it abides in nothing. A nothing which is not a negative — the negative has a relationship to the positive — but instead a kind of black hole, a singularity in the knowable, lacking all relationships. The very thought of sovereignty induces Borgesian vertigo.

The general economy, Plotnitsky says, is "a theoretical framework and a textual practise — by means of which one can relate to the production, material or intellectual, of excesses that cannot be utilized." (p. 19) The dynamics of such excess show up in my formulation of quantum brain dynamics.

Lets put my formulation into David Bohm's (1980) terminology. The dynamic is the continual unfolding of everyday explicate order from an unpresent implicate order of tuned interpenetrated possibilities. Bohm called this kind of physical process the *holomovement*. What I am talking about is a holomovement emergent from living neural tissue, a neural holomovement in which explicate orders continually unfold in a *tilde*-conjugate match. Here a holoworld of interpenetrated possible worlds meets representatives of a surrounding physical reality and world thrownness unfolds, a world becomes actual.

But something else takes place in the neural holomovement, something is lost. What's lost is all the other unmatched possibilities. In the movement of explication the unrealized possibilities are an excess that cannot be utilized. New possibilities replace them in the ongoing eruption of possibility. Whatever world thrownness is realized, there is an excess of quantum possibility that is not utilized, which is characteristic of Bataille's general economy.

Bataille emphasizes that the loss of the excess is "without the slightest aim", and having no aim, the loss is meaningless. It is a useless senseless loss, says Bataille, and calls it sovereignty. This is like what we have found in quantum brain dynamics. There is a continual eruption of tuned possibility that is fully spent in but one actuality, without reserve. The eruption expends its richness in the collapse of the conjugate match onto world thrownness.

This expenditure without reserve is what Bataille means by "sovereignty". It is not possible to get behind this loss to some Hegelian place of absolute knowledge. There is only the dynamical *Ereignis* in neural tissue, in which *Un-Sein* and *Zeit* have an encounter in which presence and useless unknowable loss are yoked. What *Zeit* brings to the encounter is an unknowable sovereign exuberance that is lost in the collapse onto presence in the tilde-conjugate match. Sovereignty is exactly *not* the sovereignty of an absolute Hegelian subject. Sovereignty is the ungrounded freedom of an unpresent unanalyzable nonlocal whole that is continually spent without reserve.

6. Derrida's differance

I think that *differance* as the movement of difference/deferral—Saussurian difference and Freudian deferral (Derrida 1982) — can be thought with quantum brain dynamics. Of course *differance* is more than difference/deferral...but these are closest to the name *differance*, so they are a good incision point. My idea is that the movement of the tuning process both differentiates and defers. We can discern both difference and deferral in quantum brain functioning, just as we discerned sovereignty and the general economy.

First, differance: Without possibilities, there can be no matchings and thus no differing presences. That is, possibility is the condition for the possibility of different presences. Presence comes *out of* interpenetrated possibilities; possibility is transcendental to presence. Each possibility has different relationships with other possibilities, relationships that depend on past entanglements and shared symmetries. So the difference of *differance* is probabilized interpenetrated possibilities, from which different presences can be unfolded.

Now deferral: Deferral also derives from the movement of the tuning process. Certain potential presences can be deferred because their possibility is by and large tuned out. In Freud's Oedipal wish, for example, the attunement is such that thoughts of killing father and marrying mother cannot be present; they are endlessly deferred by the defensive Oedipal attunement. Freud's unconscious wish is an unpresent attunement modified by defense mechanisms into a defensive unpresent attunement out of which the presencing of direct instinctual gratification is highly unlikely, not permitted by the realm of interpenetrated possiblity.

There is a piece I need to fill in here before finishing with Freudian deferral. We can become conscious of certain of our attunements. In reflection I find that I am attuned to write a paper, I knowingly operate within this horizon. If I have a naked Oedipal wish, I am attuned to kill my father and marry my mother, I operate within this horizon. If I have a defended Oedipal wish, I am attuned say, to rebel against authority and be drawn to nurturing women. The Oedipal wish is retuned in the resolution of the Oedipus complex. This tuning out of the possibility of certain presences is the deferral of *differance*. Tuning controls the flow of the interaction with reality, delays certain presences, or forever forbids them by setting and maintaining the p-values of their possibilities at almost zero. This tuning is, in effect, a cybernetics, a nonlocal control process, a quantum helmsman on the encounter between possibilia and reality's representatives, steering by adjusting the probabilities of the interpenetrated possibilities. So the difference/deferral of differance can be thought together with the unpresent interpenetrated interrelated possibilities and thought together with their attunement which defers certain presences. The movement of the quantum brain partakes of *differance*.

My overall claim, which thinks together QBD and postmodernism, in a nutshell: The quantum brain is sovereign, differs/defers, and continually unfolds presencing worlds.

7. Dogleg

This "dogleg" provides a fresh angle on the above proposal by applying it to the well-known "measurement problem", which continues to vex quantum theory. Following Penrose's (1995) lucid discussion, two quantum descriptions are distinguished: U and R. U describes the unitary evolution of the Schroedinger wave equation. Here possibilities are superposed yet each possibility retains its independence in the evolution of the wave function. In Schrödinger's quantum cat gedanken experiment, the poor cat's suspended in a (politically incorrect) dead#alive superposition. (I use the symbol '#' to indicate interference.) If a measurement is made by some mechanical apparatus, M, then a more complicated superposition is formed: dead#alive#M. Continued measurements comprise the "von Neumann chain" in which the original quantum system and the various measuring apparati become "entangled". (In the von Neumann/Wigner view, this chain of entanglements is only broken by the consciousness of the observer...without consciousness there is only continuous and deterministic evolution of the wave function.)

R is a completely different, discontinuous and probabilistic, description that the U description jumps to. Under R the superposed state of possibilities is abruptly reduced to one classical level actuality. Schrödinger's cat is either dead or alive, not a superposition of both. This is called "state-vector reduction" or "collapse of the wave function". Without R, "the universe is just one incredibly complicated quantum-entangled mess that bears no relationship to the classical-like world that we actually observe" (Penrose 1995: 300). The vexing mystery for quantum physics is the account of R in which U collapses onto description in terms of a statistical ensemble of classical states.

Many different accounts of R have been proposed. In the "many-worlds" explanation, there is no reduction of possibility to one actuality. Each possibility becomes actual in the various branches of the wave function. Thus there is a world in which the observer finds the cat dead and another orthogonal world in which the cat is found alive.

Bohr insisted that the wave function is epistemic, not ontological. U describes the observer's *knowledge* in terms of possibilities and R describes the observer's *knowledge* of an actuality. With the advent of quantum brain theory, Bohr's account gets a new life, for knowledge is a brain function and accordingly has a quantum explanation. Here Bohr might recover an ontology.

Another set of accounts explains R as describing a natural event, something like the decay of an unstable particle. Penrose (1995) thinks gravitational effects bring about R whereas the Ghirardi-Rimini-Weber (1986) scheme introduces an arbitrary event in which the wave function is multiplied by a Gaussian function which collapses the wave function. Zurek (1991) finds coherence highly unstable; inevitable interactions between alive#dead#M and the environment quickly reduce the U description of superposed possibilities to the R description of classical actuality.

Now, all of these various accounts of R suffer a gaping hole in their explanation, where that most uncommonsensical of physical theories, quantum physics, suddenly relies on commonsense, which ought to give us great pause. R, strictly speaking, gives us a statistical ensemble of outcomes of measurement. R tells us only that *if we make an observation* of Schroedinger's cat apparatus, half the time we will find the cat dead and half the time we will find the cat alive. The *actual* state of affairs remains unknown until an observer comes along and takes a look inside the box. Standard quantum theory on its own doesn't connect to world presence.

This gap in standard quantum theory, better, this *wrenching* of quantum theory in which common sense is all in a rush admitted, arises in relying on a commonsense theory of perception to get from possibility to actuality. A quantum description of macroscopic objects doesn't do it. "Macroscopic objects" here doesn't imply actually present. When Umezawa (1993) derives macroscopic objects by Bogoliubov transformation of the quantized field he effects a scale change from *Microwelt* to *Mitwelt*. But this doesn't explain world's actual appearance, so quantum theory has to dangerously default to common sense.

It is an act of faith, indeed, to think that the cat is *in fact* either dead or alive, and conscious observation simply tells us which outcome has occurred. Quantum theory as such does not provide facticity, only probability. Furthermore, conscious observation lies outside the nomological network of traditional quantum physics. Quantum theory provides no account of the connection between the presumed state of affairs (in which the cat is in fact dead or in fact alive) and the conscious observation that finds out just what the presumed case actually is. Perception lies outside the scope of traditional quantum physics... perception is left to other disciplines—classical disciplines like brain science, psychology, cognitive science, philosophy of mind, and good old common sense. *Quantum physics is stunningly incomplete* across the various solutions to the measurement problem. Quantum physics doesn't have the resources to give you world presence, only a statistical ensemble of possibilities. But if the brain has quantum degrees of freedom, then perhaps quantum theory can close this glaring explanatory gap.

I have tried to close this gap in the account I gave above, where the living brain supports coherent states and protects them against decoherence (Jibu et al. 1994). Here sustainable coherent states come under non-local control. This coherence is tuned for participating in an interaction with coherent states under external control (via sensory input). Quantum intrinsic and quantum extrinsic meet...there is the continual flowing together of intrinsic and extrinsic...and the sustaining of coherence at biological temperatures and energies. The flowing interchange of outside and inside brings optimized matches between them, when there is a balance between non*tilde* and *tilde* in lowest energy vacuum states supported by living brain tissue. World presences in the match.

For just about everywhere in the reality described by the equations of physics, the U description suffices. At scattered locations, however, something quite miraculous takes place. Living brain systems sustain quantum coherence and permit interactions, and in the *tilde*-conjugate match taking place in the brain's vacuum states, living brain systems offer world thrownness. Dasein in early Heidegger provides a *Lichtung*, a clearing, a lighted place, because (I claim) Dasein's brain supports making a *tilde*-conjugate match between what's coming in and what the brain is tuned for, and world only lights up in this match. Everyplace else is the quantum beyond-darkness. The quantum beyond-darkness of U is punctuated by bubbles of light where world-thrownness is realized. R at these places describes a *tilde*-conjugate match.

* * *

I have tried to complete quantum theory utilizing quantum neurophysics (in particular, quantum brain dynamics). I have attempted to give an account of world presence, such as meter readings, in quantum neurophysical terms. If successful, then quantum neurophysics completes the quantum account — and if all this connects up with post-modernism, as I tried to show, then the more the merrier.

References

Bataille, G. (1988–90) *The accursed share,* 3 vols. Translated by Robert Hurley. New York: Zone.

Bohm, D. (1980) *Wholeness and the implicate order.* Boston: Routledge and Kegan Paul.

Chalmers, D. (1996) *The conscious mind.* New York: Oxford.

Derrida, J. (1974) *Of Grammatology.* C. G. Spivak, trans. Baltimore: Johns Hopkins.

Derrida, J. (1978) *Writing and difference.* A. Bass (trans.) Chicago: University of Chicago.

Derrida, J. (1982) *Margins of philosophy.* A. Bass (trans.) Chicago: University of Chicago.

Derrida, J. (1989) *Of spirit: Heidegger and the question.* G. Bennington and R. Bowlby (trans.) Chicago: University of Chicago.

Ghirardi, G. C., Rimini, A. and Weber, T. (1990) 'Unified dynamics for microscopic and macroscopic systems.' *Phys.Rev.* D34: 470.

Globus, G. (1998) 'Self, cognition, qualia and world in quantum brain dynamics.' *J. Csness. Stud.* 5: 34–52.

Froehlich, H. (1968) 'Long-range coherence and energy storage in biological systems.' *J. Quantum Chem.* 2: 641–649.

Hameroff, S. and Penrose, R. (1996) 'Conscious events as orchestrated space–time selections.' *J. Csness. Stud.* 1: 91–118.

Heidegger, M. (1962 [1927]) *Being and time.* J. Macquarrie and E. Robinson (trans.) New York: Harper and Row.

Heidegger, M. (1972) *On time and being.* J. Stambaugh (trans.) New York: Harper and Row.
Heidegger, M. (1977) *The question concerning technology and other essays.* W. Lovitt (trans.) New York: Harper and Row.
Jibu, M., Hagan, S., Hameroff, S., Pribram, K., Yasue, K. (1994) 'Quantum optical coherence in cytoskeletal microtubules: Implications for brain functions. *Biosystems* 32: 195–209.
Jibu, M. and Yasue, K. (1995) *Quantum brain dynamics and consciousness.* Amsterdam and Philadelphia: John Benjamins.
Maturana, H. and Varela, F. (1980) *Autopoiesis and cognition: The realization of the living.* Dordrecht: Reidel.
Plotnitsky, A. (1994) *Complementarity: Anti-epistemology after Bohr and Derrida.* Durham: Duke University.
Sellars, W. (1963) *Science, Perception and Reality.* New York: Humanities Press.
Stapp, H. (1993) *Mind, Matter and Quantum Mechanics.* New York: Springer Verlag.
Umezawa, H. (1993) *Advanced Field Theory: Micro, Macro and Thermal Physics.* New York: American Institute of Physics.
Vitiello, G. (1995) Dissipation and memory in the quantum brain model.' *Int. J. Modern Physics* B 9: 973–989.
Zurek, W. H. (1991) 'Decoherence and the transition from quantum to classical.' *Physics Today* 44: 36–44.

Consciousness and non-hierarchical physics

Chris Clarke

Abstract

An example is presented of a model of consciousness based on a description of the world which integrates the material and psychological aspects from the start. An indication is given of work under way to test the model.

1. Orientation

A fundamental problem in the study of consciousness (essentially the "hard problem" of Chalmers (1995)) is the connection of the apparently incommensurable worlds of lived experience and formal objective scientific observation; the difference, that is between "what it is like to be" a person (cf. Nagel 1974) and what a person is as far as external physical description is concerned (where I include as "external" the examination of physiological functions that are spatially internal but observed externally). The essence of human consciousness, of what it is like to be a person, lies in the awareness of qualia (the elementary irreducible aspects of perception) and in the exercise of free will.[1]

My elucidation of qualia and of free will involves three points (the first two of which were briefly signalled in Clarke (1995)).

1. Qualia arise from an "entanglement" between the state of a person and aspects of the thing perceived. This phenomenon is quantum-like but takes place at the macroscopic level.
2. Free will arises from our capacity through self-reflection to change the conceptual reference frame within which we are taking decisions. This change of frame is formally equivalent to the possibility of changing between complementary representations (e.g. wave and particle) in quantum theory.

3. The world is not a bottom-up hierarchy. The above properties of consciousness cannot be derived by "summing up" microscopic events (quantum events in the usual sense). Moreover, any interpretation of conventional quantum theory requires additional structures[2] derived from a higher level than the microscopic, reinforcing a non-hierarchical approach.

In order to expound these points we need a way of talking about things (people, atoms, pendulums) in a uniform language, so that their distinctive properties (consciousness, quantum theory, determinism) arise from their particular physical constitutions, rather than being built in through the prior choice of a different formalism in each case. This will make it natural to identify properties present in all systems, which become awareness when that system is percipient and self-reflexive, and conscious in the sense that we identify as human subjects when free will is operative.

The method to be used stems from the approach of Merleau-Ponty and the later phenomenolists who argue that "any … attempt to establish an intrinsic connection between the [physiological and psychological] is bound to fail" (Langer 1989: 28–9). I am, however, less pessimistic: I will argue that there is a way of analysing systems which is sufficiently flexible to bridge much of the gap between the physical and the psychological. I will concede that this gap may never be wholly bridged without the need for a jump from formal to experiential; but I would claim that the gap can be closed enough for the jump to be fairly secure and unproblematic.

The inspiration for the particular language and formalism used derives from quantum theory — though there is no suggestion here of being limited to the microscopic. The idea is to regard a system rather abstractly in terms, for instance, of the set of possible states that it may have, using a language that is applicable to atoms (when it becomes quantum mechanics) to planets and pendulums (when it becomes classical physics) to the internal life of people (when it becomes psychology). This may seem so "broad brush" and abstract as to of little practical use, but I will demonstrate (here and in a later paper) that it lends itself both to the experimental study of areas such as parapsychology that lie in the interface between the subject and the objective, and to the development of theories of qualia — the crux of the "hard problem".

The structure of the paper is as follows. The next section gives the philosophical background, which is provided to give more of a feel for the ideas (though the section is not formally part of my argument). The following section gives the proposed bridging language, in subsections describing the basic mathematical structure, the way in which systems amalgamate to form compound systems, truth values and the role of dynamics. Following this are sections on the two key properties of consciousness: qualia and free will; and the paper ends with pointers to other developments, including experimental areas.

To end this introduction I will indicate more closely the actual area that I have in mind when I talk of consciousness. A feature of the phenomenological approach is that the world, in the primary sense, *is* what subjects are aware of (though this does not, as we shall see, imply solipsism or idealism). It would thus become trivial to identify consciousness with awareness; Merleau-Ponty regards consciousness rather as "my actual presence to myself" (ibid.: xv), that is, the self-reflective aspect. On this view simple I-less awareness is not a faculty possessed by an organism (being-the object-of awareness is just the nature of reality) and so the question of its evolutionary origin does not enter. On the other hand consciousness as a self-reflective process involving free will, in the sense that I use it here, is a specific faculty which leads to a creative adaptation between the world and the organism, and makes a difference to what the organism does. I am not, however, primarily concerned with problem solving, pattern recognition and so on, although these fall within the range of phenomena under consideration.

I have enlarged Merleau-Ponty's definition to include qualia, because these provide a link between the phenomenological and materialist perspectives. On the latter the primary aspect of consciousness is the presence of *qualia*, in the restricted sense of the elementary, irreducible constituents of our perceptual experience, such as colours, musical timbres, tactile components such as roundness, pointedness, the basic tastes and so on (others will be added later). They are clearly identifiable and distinguishable one from another through their intrinsic natures, and not, as far as immediate experience is concerned, through any logical or structural discrimination. While we still lack any genuine understanding of what qualia *are*, I believe that progress can still be made in explaining their role in the organism (what qualia *do*) and their relation to the world as a whole. This involves in an essential way including certain aspects of *free will* within the area of consciousness.

The model that I am proposing will be based on physical principles that attribute awareness-like properties to a much wider range of phenomena than human consciousness as delineated above. In order to talk of *human* consciousness (or at least a healthily functioning consciousness) we need not only reflexivity (thinking about myself), which will be treated briefly, but in addition the presence of a 'me' as a distinguished area of subjectivity within the conscious field. This last will not be explicitly modelled here.

2. Philosophical background

My aim is a 'model' in the sense of a formalised set of mathematical structures and interpretations, whose individual components do not necessarily correspond, one-to-one, with the physical situation, but whose overall predictions are testable. (This is the sense as used by, for instance, Fowkes & Mahoney 1994). A model differs from a 'theory' in that in the latter all constituents are claimed to correspond to physical structures — though in practice, of course, these are merely extremes of a spectrum, and the distinction may become vacuous in psychology. The handling of qualia as described in the previous section is in the spirit of modelling rather than theory.

While my aim is thus scientific, not philosophical, it may help the reader's understanding if I briefly place my approach in its philosophical context. The first and most important influence is the phenomenology of Merleau-Ponty (1962) and Heidegger (1957). Phenomenology takes as its starting point the totality of the field of conscious awareness of a person, an awareness conceived not as a *representation* of the things in themselves but as something with an existential status in its own right that arises from an interaction (or, in psychological terminology, a dialogue) between the person and other entities. Perception is described by Merleau-Ponty as a "form of communing between the body and the world" (1962: 212). More vividly (p 214) he exemplifies this dialogue as follows:

> ... [a sensible quality, like the colour blue,] which is on the point of being felt, sets a kind of muddled problem for my body to solve. I must find the attitude which will provide it with the means of becoming determinate, of showing up as blue; I must find the reply to a question which is obscurely expressed. And yet I do so only when I am invited by it; my attitude is never sufficient to make me really see blue or really touch a hard surface. The sensible gives back to me what I lent to it, but this is only what I took from it in the first place. As I contemplate the blue of the sky I abandon myself to it and plunge into this mystery; it 'thinks itself within me'. I am the sky itself as it is drawn together and unified and as it begins to exist for itself; my consciousness is saturated with this limitless blue ...

The quasi-unity of the self and the percept, and the idea that the percept "thinks itself in me" is the core of my model. The unified person-plus-perceived-world expressed in this passage (which Heidegger and Merleau-Ponty call Being-in-the-world) is taken as the primary foundation of the universe. Its unitary character can hardly be overstressed: it is what distinguishes this approach from the traditional Cartesian one in which subject and object are separate and perception is a "*commercium* ... *between* a subject present-at-hand and an object ..." (H

132).[3] Once one has fragmented the phenomenon in this way "there is no possibility of putting it together again from the fragments. Not only do we lack the 'cement': even the 'schema' in accordance with which the joining together is to be accomplished, has been split asunder ..." (ibid.) Or, as Langer (1989: 29) paraphrases Merleau-Ponty, "Given the complete antithesis between a being which is purely 'in-itself' [as object] and one which is exclusively 'for-itself' [as subject], any meeting point is utterly inconceivable (cf Merleau-Ponty 1962: 431).

As it stands, Merleau-Ponty's approach poses many problems in a modern context. Which entities — humans, animals, stones ... — are "carriers" of worlds in this sense? How is a *common* world arrived at unless it grows from an objective realm of things-in-themselves? Merleau-Ponty presents an account that is essentially restricted to human organisms (he emphasises, for example, the role of language) and the question of the nature of the world before the advent of humans is excluded from the picture (1962: 432), making any serious connection with contemporary science almost impossible. The commonality of the world is elucidated through the way in which, "[p]rior to the process of becoming aware, the social exists obscurely and as a summons" (ibid. p 362) so that the body-subject forms, with others, a "single pre-reflexive intersubjective system" (Langer 1989: 100), but it remains difficult to link this with a broader scientific context. The approach of this paper aims to provide, at a formal rather than philosophical level, possible answers to these difficulties by using a generalised-logic formalism in which one can pass, back and forth, in a precisely specified manner, from a description where *things* are primary, to one where *perceptions* are primary and things are secondary. An influence on the whole approach has been the development of logic approaches to quantum theory, in which the "things" are, for example, states or wave-functions, and observations (or propositions, or projections) correspond (at a formal level) to perceptions.

A second philosophical influence has been the work of Whitehead, particularly the emphasis behind his *Concept of Nature* (revised ed., 1926). Here he starts with perceived worlds as momentary snapshots of simultaneity, and then constructs space and time by considering the overlaps between these perceived worlds, using a mathematically specified process of abstraction. The version given in *Concept of Nature* is, as it stands, untenable because it is linked in an essential way to *special* relativity and collapses entirely when the small modifications produced by general relativity are introduced. It is possible, however, to develop this in a more process-oriented way that does not suffer from this drawback (Clarke 1993). Whitehead's later views in *Process and Reality* (1929) enter here, while his idea that the interaction between all processes is ultimately perceptual in quality has influenced my conception that all beings undergo such interactions, even if it is only in humans and higher animals that they reach the level of complexity that warrants the use of "consciousness".

Finally, I should mention the influence of Voloshinov (1973), and in general the Bakhtinian school of Soviet philosophy, who add to the forgoing a lively appreciation of the role of society in forming the fabric of reality. This work is easily misunderstood because of its subordination to Marxist terminology (so that the whole of social psychology, for example, becomes the study of "ideology"; and Heidegger's *Zeug* become "the means of production"). A further source of misunderstanding arises because the atmosphere of the period was dominated by linguistics, so that the impression is given that consciousness is coextensive with language. It is clear from a closer reading, however, that "language" means the total array of "signs", expressed or unexpressed, which coordinate our transactions with the world, and that "society" encompasses all human-human interactions, so that it could include the mother–child dyad (Leiman 1992). Thought of in this way, Voloshinov is adding a vital interpersonal dimension to a philosophy which, at least in the early work of Heidegger, gives the impression of being excessively individualistic.

I will refer back to these influences in what follows (as well as adding others) and in the case of phenomenology I will use for reference the ideas of Heidegger rather than Merleau-Ponty, as the former better illustrates the way the ideas are embodied in my model.

3. Description of the basic structure

As already noted, I will be adopting a logical formalism in order to implement a form of phenomenology. This may seem paradoxical in view of Merleau-Ponty's explicit rejection of abstract thinking as opposed to historically and culturally embodied thinking.[4] I would argue, however, that there is a need to build a bridge between our fundamental perceptual awareness as disclosed by the phenomenological method, and the scientific structures that have become an essential part of our understanding of the universe. This model is that bridge. By drawing on formalisms from quantum theory, I hope to establish an essentially non-classical framework of analysis, within which both modern physics and consciousness (or rather, the general elements which, in human beings, become consciousness) have a natural place. In this section I will describe in turn the "generalised logic" to be adopted; its application to interacting beings/processes; and the dynamics appropriate to this application.[5]

3.1 *A generalised logic*

One of the by-products of quantum theory has been the suggestion that the description of a physical system can be carried out in terms of its logic. There is considerable controversy (in the particular case of quantum theory) over whether the logic alone is sufficient to describe the system, or whether additional structures are required. Much depends on the precise meaning attached to the concept of "logic". Here I am focusing on the core ideas, and in calling these a logic I do not mean to imply either that they correspond precisely to the traditional philosophical concept of a logic, or that they are necessarily complete. Placing the logic first is an essential step in making a bridge to the phenomenological programme of giving primary status to Being-in-the-world, as opposed to adopting a representational view of perception. The adoption of a form of generalised logic, rather than classical logic, is needed not only for quantum theory, but, more importantly here, for the later theory of free will and decision making, which in turn is required if consciousness is to be effective and not merely epiphenomenal.

I should stress that in using a logic-based approach I am not implying that the operation of conscious processes is, in psychological terms, of a logical (and hence linguistic) nature. Rather, this basic idea is that, at each moment, consciousness structures its world through a collection of pre-verbal concepts. Although these concepts are to be thought of in operational rather than verbal terms, their representations in the model will be called *propositions*. When expressed verbally, they will be concepts like 'there is a brown tree here' or 'I am angry'. Though we represent them verbally in order to describe them, the concepts are prior to the verbal description.[6] While I approach the logic in terms of human consciousness, I regard it as an abstract specification of what the world is like in relation to a particular context. Considered in this way a logic is more generally applicable than just to human mental processes: it defines any sort of physical context. *The Logic* associated with a particular physical/mental context (or what I shall later call a locus) is the set of propositions definable in that context together with the primitive logical relations between them. Note that I am viewing a logic as a formal language rather than as a calculus for truth-values; truth-values will be introduced as a separate function on the logic.

Technically, by a "generalised logic" I will mean as system of propositions having the structure of a lattice (not necessarily with a 1) in which are defined the (not independent) operations:

&	And
$\vee$	Or
$\rightarrow$	Implies
$\backslash$	but not

In this "&" is the usual conjunction and "$\vee$" is inclusive (either ... or ... or both). For the general background here, see, for example, Beltrametti & Cassinelli (1981), but note that their use of "logic" refers to a stronger concept of predication (see 3.4 below). The definition of a lattice is given in this paper in the Appendix, Section 1.1.

For classical logic, it is assumed that for each proposition a there is the contradictory proposition not-a (the complement of a, in mathematical terminology), which asserts the possibility of absolutely everything that is different from a. Now, it is an essential part of the conception of free will to be developed later that any system is potentially open to an indefinite extension of its possibilities, so that as far as the interpretation is concerned, we cannot interpret the idea of "everything" that the system might do — though, as I indicate in the Appendix, Section 8.2, at a purely formal (uninterpreted) level it may be possible to enlarge the system until this becomes the case. In place of the complement I need only the relative complement $b\backslash a$, interpreted as "b but not a" and defined only when $a \rightarrow b$. Relative complements have to be consistent, in the sense that $c\,\&\,(b\backslash a) = (c\,\&\,b)\backslash(c\,\&\,a)$ whenever $a \rightarrow b$ and I also require that the correspondence between a and $b\backslash a$ should be a true (ortho)complement on the sub-lattice $L(b)$ of all those as such that $a \rightarrow b$ (see Appendix Section 2).

Apart from the technicality of only having a relative "not" (which actually is of very little consequence), I have not yet indicated any difference from ordinary classical logic. If we were using classical logic then we would assume as an axiom the distributive law that

$$(a\ \&\ b) \vee (a\ \&\ c) = a\ \&\ (b \vee c) \tag{D}$$

(in which case we speak of a distributive lattice). In our case the introduction of relative complements automatically ensures that, for any a and b with $a \rightarrow b$, $(b\backslash a) \vee a = b$. This is the orthomodular condition used in quantum mechanics, and it implies that the distributive law (D) holds in the restrictive case where two of a, b, c in (D) are complements of each other (see Appendix, Section 3). I discuss in Appendix Section 4 the circumstances in which this makes the whole logic into a sublattice of an orthomodular lattice, as is the case for quantum theory.

3.2 *Reference frames*

In order to understand further the difference between the generalised logic and a classical logic, we note first that it is a consequence of the axioms used here that

$$(a \,\&\, b) \vee (a \,\&\, c) \rightarrow a \,\&\, (b \vee c). \tag{D*}$$

(See Birkhoff 1964: 5). For convenience write the left hand side as A and the right hand side as B so that this becomes $A \rightarrow B$

The distributive law (D) is $A = B$. But if A and B are not equal, as allowed for by (D*), then there is a possibly true proposition $B \setminus A$ representing their difference. For example, if a is "this ball is heavy" and b (respectively c) is "this ball is green (resp. blue)", then $B \setminus A$ describes a ball that is heavy and either green or blue, but which is not heavy and green, nor heavy and blue, a situation impossible in the classical logic to which properties of weight and colour properly belong. The only situation where we could consider this would be when "heavy" and "green" belonged to such different categories of thinking that it was impossible to ascertain both at the same time. In such a case "heavy and green" would become a nonsensical impossibility, even though we might happen to know that all balls involved were either blue or green with no other possibility. We could, however, say "heavy and either blue or green" as merely be a roundabout way of saying "heavy". I shall call the incompatible categories of thinking involved here (to be defined more formally in a moment) *reference frames*. I want to claim that they do in fact crop up very regularly in ordinary informal thinking, and even more in the general conceptualisation that precedes thinking.

To give a more picturesque example, and to illustrate how it applies to the formal structure in use here, consider the case where

a = {Angels are blessing my garden}
b = {My garden has a nitrogen-rich soil}
c = {My garden does not have a nitrogen-rich soil}

(To simplify the example I am assuming the special case where there is a full negation expressed by 'not' in the example, or equivalently a maximum element **1**, the identically true proposition, so that

$$[\text{not } a] := \mathbf{1} \setminus a.)$$

If (as might be the case, though it is not necessarily so) explanations in terms of immaterial beings of healing energy, on the one hand, and explanations in terms of biochemistry, on the other, belong to different reference frames then, as I have discussed, the conjunction of propositions a and b (or a and c) is the identically false proposition, **0** (because there are no circumstances under which both propositions could be entertained at once, and hence no circumstances under which they could both be true at once).[7] We can then evaluate the two sides of (D*) as follows:

$(a \ \& \ b) \vee (a \ \& \ c)$	$A \ \& \ (b \vee c)$
$= \mathbf{0} \vee \mathbf{0}$	$= a \ \& \ \mathbf{1}$
$= \mathbf{0}$	$= a$

We can see that, while the left hand side implies (→) the right hand side, the two are not the same, as they would have to be in classical logic.

Incompatible reference frames arise in our ordinary thinking not merely when, as here, there are plausible grounds for separating them into different logical categories, but where we have compartmentalised the different schemes and not yet made the mental jump of bringing them together into a synthesis. Much of our thought is occasion-specific, restricted to boxes waiting for a creative moment for them to be amalgamated into a bigger scheme.

A quite unambiguous application of this occurs in quantum logic. For instance, if we are talking about the direction of the spin of an electron and a = "the spin is pointing along the positive z-axis", b = "the spin is pointing along the positive x-axis" and c = "the spin is pointing along the negative x-axis" then we have precisely the situation just described.

To state this formally, a *reference frame* is any distributive sub-lattice of the logic. Two such frames will in general neither be completely compatible not completely incompatible; but we might expect that there will some combination of propositions from the two which fail to satisfy the distributive law. As I shall show later, introducing this idea is essential for understanding the role of qualia and of free will.

Later on (Subsection 3.4) we shall consider the sorts of valuation (i.e. assignment of True and False) applicable to this sort of logic.

3.3 *Interacting processes*

In the conventional quantum setting just described, a generalised logic is associated with each quantum system (with its linked observer). In quantum field theory, on the other hand, the logics are based on the algebras of observables that are associated with each region of space–time (Kay 1985; Isham 1994). These constitute the quantum version of the networks of overlapping processes referred to in connection with Whitehead, Section 1 above. Generalising and combining these two ideas, I will call any entity associated with a generalised logic a *locus*. Thus a locus might be a system-observer pair, or (if we are working strictly in conventional reductionist physics) a space–time region, or — the case we are really interested in for consciousness — the Being-in-the-world of a particular person. In this last case, a locus is *the world of an individual person* — both external and internal. The distinction between external and internal is determined by the extent of overlap with other loci: things in common between the worlds of many individuals could be regarded as external, while things exclusive to one individual (or to one and a few empathically related individuals) are regarded as internal.

The interacting aspect of loci arises from a specification of ways of combining loci to form unions and intersections just as regions of space–time combine in the formalism of local operator algebras, and events overlap in Whitehead's system in *The Concept of Nature*. We need to be able at times to widen the locus, to consider a society, a planet …, taking into account the way in which what emerges at each widening will be more than the sum of the parts. (Following Voloshinov, above, the locus of *society* is particularly significant.) We need to be able to narrow the locus, to the objective world that is held in common by many people, for example, or to the physical locus held in common by people and by systems of measuring instruments. In keeping with the phenomenological approach, we *do not assume that there is any single fixed ultimate reality on which these separate loci are perspectives.*

The place of "ultimate reality" is taken by the *objective world*, the world that is common to, that is, lies in the overlaps of, a large number of percipients. For us objectivity lies in the numbers of human percipients, but the stability of the objective world is constituted by the fact that a multitude of non-human, indeed non-living "percipients" (loci) also enter into its determination. The realness of the objective world is on this view not something that is given, but something that arises dynamically form the nature of the overlaps. I have discussed in detail elsewhere (Clarke 2000) the way this process works, using the quantum formalism of (Isham 1994).

Overlaps give rise to a partial ordering of logics, in the sense that where two loci overlap this is represented formally by the existence of a logic L' which can be injectively mapped into each of the logics of the overlapping loci, and which thus provides the correspondence between certain propositions of the two loci. (There may, of course, be situations where these ordered logics can, as a whole, be regarded as a logic (Isham, op. cit.), but we do not assume this here.)

What is, and what is not, a locus is itself dynamically determined, and speculations as to the nature of this dynamic would take us far beyond the scope of this paper. The considerations of the modern phenomenologist D. Abram

(1997) suggest that loci are considerably more extensive than humans. He describes how, with an extended personal awareness, he sees how "a large boulder reposes at the edge of these bushes, dialoguing with the old tree about shadows and sunlight" (ibid. p. 203). On this view, anything that can enter a dialogue with us should itself be regarded as a locus. On the other hand consistency with quantum mechanics strongly suggests that we need to include most macroscopic systems, even if they are non-sentient in the usual sense. In these cases, however, their participation in the human world (in which they are *Zeuge* in Heidegger's sense) may in part confer their status as loci. In the case of the "worlds" of macroscopic non-sentient loci, we can only speculate as to whether it is mere size, or complexity, that qualifies them for this status. The choice is important in order to resolve the Schrödinger's cat paradox: we need to allow the cat, and probably its box as well, to play a role in determining a specific state. In the case of the cat this could be quite a sophisticated role, corresponding to some rudimentary consciousness; in the case of the box it will be a mechanistic role of the sort envisaged by authors like Penrose (1994), a role for which the term consciousness is no longer appropriate.

An important experimental case arises from the consideration that, since all perception involves (as discussed below) an entanglement of states, it is reasonable to postulate that the sustained mutual perception involved in an empathic relationship between individuals will give rise to a common locus embracing the two. In making this interpretation of empathy I diverge from Heidegger, since he regards as mistaken the idea that empathy, in the sense of "understanding 'the psychic life of others'" (H124) could be (as here) "the first ontological bridge from one's own subject … to the other subject" (ibid.). The difference is partly one of terminology, in that my 'empathy' is not merely 'understanding the psychic life of others', but is much closer to Heidegger's 'Being-with'. But the difference is also due to the fact that I deal here with (to use his terminology) the ontical (the being-ness of particular things) rather than the ontological level (Being as such).

3.4 *Truth values and the Situation*

Many authors (e.g. Beltrametti & Cassinelli 1981), when speaking of a logic, imply that the propositions are predicates that are being asserted or denied in a particular situation; that is, for these authors, a logic is a lattice of propositions together with a system of truth-values and ways of handling them. Here I just refer to the lattice as the "logic", but we still need to discuss truth values.

Classical logic proceeds from a godlike view where every proposition is either true or false; but our experience of the world is not like that, and according to quantum theory (on most interpretations) the world itself is not like that. A not unreasonable representation of things, borrowed from quantum mechanics, would be to say that to each proposition a we can assign a number $S(a)$ ranging from 0 (definitely false) to 1 (definitely true), which we can interpret as the probability that future exploration will resolve the question in favour of the proposition. I shall call this assignment of a number the *situation, S.* Clearly for consistency we have to demand that

$$(a \to b) \Rightarrow S(a) + S(b \setminus a) = S(b).$$

In addition, we demand that classical propositional calculus should hold for those propositions whose status is certain in the given situation: in other words, if we define the certainty set of S to be

$$C(S) = \{a \mid S(a) = 0 \text{ or } S(a) = 1\}$$

then for propositions a, b in $C(S)$ the values of $S(a \,\&\, b)$, $S(a \vee b)$ and (where defined) $S(a \setminus b)$ are given by the usual "truth tables"[8] (Appendix, Section 3). This entails that $C(S)$ is a distributive sublattice, the *situational lattice* at the time in question.

On the basis of the situation, we can reasonably assign truth-values $\{T, F\}$ (True and False) to propositions where the probability is 1 or 0, respectively. For the other cases, we can either assign the value F whenever it is not T, or intro duce a third value of U (uncertain), or else simply withhold any assignment. The first is the usual approach of quantum logic. Since, however, the situation already contains all the information available, I shall not explore truth values further here, but instead use the situation, associated with each locus at any given time t.

The term 'situation' is Heidegger's (H 299), used to describe the totality of "items constitutive for the existential phenomenon"; but he applies it only to the most far-reaching acts of free will (discussed below) whereas I am generalising it considerably. The important point is that the 'situation' is *wider* than the 'what-is-in-fact-the-case' of the truth function.

3.5 *Non-deterministic dynamics*

Consciousness is an activity, not a thing. It is an ingrained habit of thought to look for an agent corresponding to every activity, but here I am regarding the activity itself as fundamental. For the purpose of building the model, the activity will be thought of as proceeding in a normal (Newtonian) linear time. But then, as a simplification, I will represent it as taking place in discrete steps. (We could make the process continuous, and the phases concurrent, in much the same way as recent work (Sudbery 1984) has made the process of quantum measurement continuous.)

Each step is divided into two phases. The first involves a reflexive aspect of consciousness. Consciousness observes itself, applying the logic L to the situation S so as to yield a revised situation S'. This phase is modelled on the usual quantum mechanical measuring process in its quantum logic (Gudder 1967) or consistent-histories (Zeh 1996) version,[9] and is essentially non-deterministic, S determining only the probabilities for the outcome. This is not, however, dependent on quantum mechanics: the same structure could be modelled by chaotic classical mechanics subject to thermal noise. The second phase is an evolution of L, through experience, or learning, altering one's concepts, adding new conceptual frames, recognising the compatibility of frames that were previously distinct, in response to the knowledge of the situation expressed through S'. We would expect this phase also to be non-deterministic; but, more importantly, it is not merely probabilistic: as I shall recount later, the qualia of consciousness, which are present through both phases, enter here in a creative manner. It seems likely that this step could not be modelled either classically or in terms of a quantum mechanics that used a fixed system of projections for measurements.

S' is evolved partly through the influence of the preceding S — the world is actually altered and formed by reflexive observation — but also as a result of its own dynamics, including the physics of matter. The dynamics of different loci have to be interrelated in a hierarchical manner, if those loci are to remain overlapping, and in particular the dynamics of physical loci influences the dynamics of the individual worlds of beings-in-the-world. This aspect follows precisely the usual operator algebra formalism for quantum field theory: whenever loci overlap, there is by definition a sub-logic common to both, and the dynamics of the sublogic are required to be compatible with the dynamics of each of the larger logics of which it is part, so that constraints are thereby placed on the behaviours of these larger logics.

4. Qualia

4.1 *The nature of qualia*

So far I have not justified this being a model *of consciousness*, in that I have not incorporated the essential aspects of qualia and free will (or creative will, as I would rather call it) nor have I explained how it is participatory. (Recall that in Section 1 I defined qualia as the irreducible components of experience, as being, so to speak, pure experientiality.) To do this requires further development.

To explore this further, we can first recognise that the field of our awareness at any given time is a unity, though embracing many more or less distinct components, with some sort of focus, or at least gradations in the degree of attention. Some components of this unity (colours have been mentioned already) seem irreducible, and for these the term 'qualia' has been introduced. The total field of experience is, however, more than a sum of qualia (in this restricted sense); and the same can be said of those components of this experience that are themselves compound. Thus the perception of a tree is not the perception of a leaf, and of a trunk, and of attachment ... and nothing more. At the very least it is the perception of these together with the result of that analytical, socially rooted process that fuses these into a particular construct with all its associated ideas (to which we may then, if we choose, attach the *word* 'tree'). Cognitive research focuses on the information processing that leads from the components to the whole tree, and for such a study any extension of the concept of quale to include anything like the 'quale of a tree' would at best be an irrelevance, at worst be nonsense.

For clarity, therefore, I will continue to restrict 'quale' to the sense just specified of irreducible components, and use the term 'experience' for the total field of awareness that embraces, but is not constituted by, its qualia. For simplicity I will talk mainly about these two extremes of extensiveness, but it will be important to remember the intermediate level of conceptualised objects such as trees.

Within an experience we can adopt Alexander's (1920) distinction between components that are *enjoyed,* in the sense of being experienced 'from the inside', so to speak; and those that are *perceived,* being experienced 'from the outside'. While this distinction roughly corresponds to that between the self and the external world (so that anger is enjoyed — in this technical sense! — whereas red is perceived) it is important to note that the distinctions do not coincide. When we empathise with another being then there is at least the possibility of experiencing it in the mode of enjoyment, whether that being is a beloved person, an animal ritually identified with (Eliade 1964) or a tool that is totally absorbed within ones own physical work. With particular reference to this last, Heidegger argues that enjoyment (*zuhanden sein*) is the primordial experience, and that a process of withdrawal relegates enjoyment to mere contemplation (*vorhanden sein*). Analytic studies of child development confirm this transition from total participation to a partial withdrawal of participation so as to form the world of not-self, which is perceived rather than enjoyed. But the withdrawal is only partial, and I shall argue that the characteristics of qualia derive from their origin in enjoyed experience.

4.2 *Where qualia come from*

Conventional Cartesian philosophy would hold that qualia are purely mental constructs, and that our perceptual world with its qualia is a distant model of reality. For the Kantian, that reality is totally unknowable. For the scientific realist, reality has the same geometrical structure as the experienced world but contains scientific entities that are associated with the qualia, though quite different from them. For example, the frequency of light in the scientific world corresponds to the quale of a colour in perception. This leaves the nature of the qualia quite unexplained, and makes it impossible to make any headway with the fundamental question of why, in Nagel's sense, there should be anything that "it is like" to experience something.

The phenomenological view which I am proposing turns this scientific realist model on its head. On the phenomenological view, the scientific picture is a model of our perceptual world, rather than vice versa, and the perceptual world, with its ramifications through all the different perspectives of sentient beings, is the only sort of reality we are going to get. Thus the qualia are manifestly part of the (real) world: we are as much, or more, entitled to assert that the qualia are "really out there" as we are to assert that electrons are. Velmans (2000) has demonstrated the propriety of regarding qualia as being at the place that they appear to be at (indeed, since qualia *are* appearances it would be improper to do anything else) but this leaves unexplained the problem of how this comes about: how is it that a quale located in an external object becomes part of "my" perception. Fortunately, the descriptive scheme I have adopted, inspired by quantum theory, provides a ready way of doing this.

Suppose I am looking at a brown tree and I want to reconcile my physical model of the process with the view that the brownness actually is a property of the tree, and is not just a by-product of mental processes that is projected onto the tree. In previous accounts (Clarke 1995) I pointed out that, if we use the language of physical (quantum) states, then, when I am observing the tree, the state of my nervous system is "entangled" with the state of the tree. By this I mean that the compound system admitted stable pure states which could not be expressed as the tensor product of separate states of the constituents — a situation which in this case arises when there is an interaction between the two (as has to be the case in an observation). The situation is similar to that obtaining in the Einstein-Rosen-Podolsky phenomenon (verified by Aspect), which will be referred to later, where a joint state cannot be decomposed into two separate states.

In terms of the description developed here, we need to express this in terms of loci. Formally this is easy: we require there to be an external situation in which the probabilities of propositions from the two constituent sub-loci are not statistically independent. When examined more closely, however, this formal equivalence breaks down, because the loci of myself and the tree are necessarily overlapping, and it is no longer possible to identify a separate locus for myself which does not overlap that of the tree — without abolishing precisely that observation which we are trying to describe! We cannot directly translate "entanglement". What replaces this concept is simply the overlap of loci. In other words, the determination of what are loci (which is not specified here) has to be such that, when there is a quantum mechanical basis, systems that are entangled have overlapping loci. Thus, if we were to use the language of states to talk about the tree, then because my state is entangled with the state describing the capacity of the tree to reflect light there is objectively nothing to separate out this aspect of the tree from the total locus, part of which is "me". So any experiential quality associated with my own locus must necessarily include aspects of the tree. Thus my perception of the tree, on this account, is an experiential participation in the actual brownness of an actual tree, mediated by the entanglement of states that is set up when my nervous system is interacting with the tree. This is the essence of perception: that qualia arise through an actual participation in external objects. The establishment of this participation is the process described by Merleau-Ponty in the quotation in Section 2.

We must, however, go beyond this account to get a credible picture of perception. First, we need to recognise the mutuality of a dynamic interaction as expressed by Merleau-Ponty. In the generalised logic picture, this is expressed by the fact that perceived objects arise from the overlaps between the loci of perceived, perceiver, and societal context, each with their own dynamic (described below).

The perceived object is very far from being a simple read-out of a pre-existing entity. It is this complex of interactions that I refer to in talking (above) of "participation" in the external object. (Note, by the way, that we have here implemented at the level of perception the basis of Heidegger's insistence that our understanding of a thing is not a representation of it, but a grasping of the thing itself: "To say that an assertion '*is true*' signifies that it uncovers the entity as it is in itself" (H 218).)

The second, and more serious, reason why more needs to be said, is because of the problem of illusion. The standard philosophical example of this is the phenomenon of the after-image. An after-image seen on looking towards a white wall is purely a mental projection, and yet it is momentarily indistinguishable from a greenish blob of paint on the wall. If there is in reality no blob of paint on the wall with which I can entangle my state, how does it come about that the quale of the perception is exactly the same as if there were such an external object? Does not this example instantly demolish my theory? The example in fact leads the theory forward in a most interesting way, by requiring us to take into account a form of memory, and illuminates Heidegger's "withdrawal" that we have noted as a mark of perception as opposed to enjoyment. We need to explain how qualia, for instance, are indeed grounded in participation in other loci, but without their being nothing but simple enjoyment of these.

A given neurological state associated with a perception may have been manifested on many previous occasions, each entangled with the state of a different locus. I propose to examine this in terms of the concept of *identity*. In classical physics the only things considered are objects, and any two object-instances are either identical or different. Moreover, if two object-instances are in different places at the same time, then even if the objects are indistinguishable, they have to be regarded as different. This last principle fails to hold in modern physics, where there is a sense in which things that are indistinguishable (notably fundamental particles of a given species) can be regarded as identical even though occupying different places. I would suggest that this quantum property should carry over to the neurological state of perceptions, and that the perception of a particular shade of green now could be the *same perception as*, that is, it is identical to, a corresponding perception a year ago. Put more carefully, it is more or less identical — we are not even bound to regard identity as a binary matter, but could allow a fuzzy concept of identity. If we take this step, then the quale of green, associated with a given neurological state, is built up, with each occurrence of the state, out of a succession of participations, thereby averaging out that common component from many different total experiential contexts. As a result this adds to the basic idea of participation what Zohar (1990) has called "quantum memory". *The quale engendered by this neurological state, as perceived rather than only enjoyed, is an abstraction (a sort of highest common factor) from the experiences represented by all these earlier states of other loci.* In this way (to borrow a metaphor from Sheldrake 1987) qualia are habits of nature rather than the manifestations of fixed laws.

Qualia entering into perception are thus built up through progressive experience, certainly from early childhood and even, in the case of such basic qualia as colour, through the course of the evolution of our species, since there appears to be nothing in the idea that limits it to a single individual. The quale of green, for example, would arise from such a vast sea of green objects that it would be stabilised at a very early stage of childhood, if not as a "race memory", and no subsequent development of the quale through life would be discernible. It would appear to be a fixed datum of our experiential world. Thus (to return to the problem of illusion) a given neural stimulation, whether veridical or illusory, will tap into a long line of previous such stimuli, out of which an associated quale has been built up through participation in a succession of real external objects (and a very few non-existent or illusory ones).

Let me summarise the conclusion of what has been a progressively exploring argument. When I perceive the quale 'green' it is external in the sense of being perceived rather than enjoyed; but it is none the less experiential — part of my experience and not at all, say, a count of vibrations per second — and it is moreover located in an external object in whose being I appear to be participating. What is happening is that I am extending my own enjoyment of that locus whose process is my own consciousness, to an abstraction of the enjoyed processes that have shared this colour green, distilling the enjoyment of such loci as leaves, of deep sea, and the rest.

5. The role of consciousness in the dynamics of loci: Free will

While the inclusion of qualia permit us to call what we are describing 'consciousness', it remains to be shown that it makes a difference to what goes on in the world. Without this, what we are saying would not be testable and so it could not be called a model; we would merely have an epiphenomenal theory of consciousness. For consciousness to *do* something we need a dynamic, which needs to be different from a dynamic acting through external forces. This happens through the exercise of what, I think misleadingly, is usually termed free will. To elucidate this I return to the outline of dynamics in Section 3.4.

There are several points at which free will might act:

1. in determining the situational lattice $C(S)$ (which is determinative of the "frame of reference" — the conceptual classical logical framework prevailing at the time);
2. in determining the value of S only on our internal states; thereby selecting, within a given frame of reference, between alternative and exclusive propositions in order to bring about one particular course of action, and
3. in the evolution of L to L', in enlarging the range of our conceptual categories.

I want to argue that, despite some superficial appearances to the contrary, it is in the first and last of these points that we should look for the action of will.

To understand this, I want to recall the fundamental philosophical problem that is associated with any account of free will. If we have sufficient grounds for making one particular choice then, it could be argued, our choice is determined by those grounds and is not free. On the other hand, if there are insufficient grounds for the choice then it would appear to be a purely random event and not a true choice or a rational act of will. Free will appears to be "free" only if it is not "will". There is a large literature concerned with strengthening the two horns of this dilemma and then extricating oneself from them (see McCall 1994, for a survey). The approach I take to it is to suggest that the dilemma stems form concentrating on step (2) above to the exclusion of steps (1) and (3).

Suppose we make a rational choice, thereby fixing the value of the truth function to be true on one intention rather than another (step 2). We are (on most interpretations of "rational") conscious of reaching such a choice. But then we are tempted to say that our consciousness is the agent of the choice; and this is an illegitimate deduction. The evidence of introspection (Jaynes 1993) is that at this stage we participate passively, not actively: we observe and report a decision process whose actual origin is non-conscious. Some (contested) evidence for this also comes from the work of Libet (1987) Consciousness does seem to be involved in the process of *attention* in which a certain range of propositions is assembled for the purpose of scrutiny and processing, and this act of attention and selection continues until a decision emerges. But the decision itself is not an act of consciousness. The purely logico-deductive part of decision-making (which for Descartes was the only part of consciousness that he regarded as unquestionably non-mechanical) is something that can be, and increasingly is, fully automated and so has little necessary connection with the conscious process.

So if logical argument from sufficient grounds is not the hall-mark of free will, are we left with randomness? In fact there is little evidence, either physiological or introspective, that human beings normally act as game-theory recommends by using a randomiser to resolve inadequate information. To make decisions we start off by trying a variety of (usually incompatible) rules of thumb, combined with a process of imagining possible outcomes of decisions and evaluating the nature of our emotional reactions to these outcomes. So far this is essentially the same as the construction of a chess-playing computer (except that the evaluation process is not called "emotions"). If a decision does not then emerge, we do not resort to a randomiser; rather, *we alter the rules of the game*. It is this that constitutes the essence of conscious human decision making. We might enlarge the domain $C(S)$ by asking, what would my Grandmother have done in these circumstances. More creatively, we might shift $C(S)$ within L: such a shift will entail a shift to a different distributive consistent domain, a shift of *reference frame*. For this a generalised logic rather than a classical logic is essential.

Beyond shifting reference frames, most creatively of all, we might change our logic L altogether, usually by moving to a larger system in which what were previously incompatible frames become reconciled, but in which there are new possibilities for incompatible frames. This step is the most likely one to involve consciousness, rather than mere intelligence. It is the possibility of enlargement of L that motivated the inclusion of relative complements in the logic rather than absolute complements, since the latter presuppose a fixed universe of discourse and hence limits its future enlargement.

To cite an example from a previous paper (Clarke 1995), what I call 'choosing' whether to eat quiche or nut roast for dinner (level 1) is in reality only my post hoc emotional reactions to a largely non-conscious decision process. A true exercise of free will (level 2) would be to enlarge the scope of possibilities, uniting what had previously been seen as incompatible, and respond by cooking a nut quiche.

I am here following the distinction of Heidegger, who regarded "will" of type 2 as strictly secondary. In such a sense "no positive new possibilities are willed, but that which is at one's disposal becomes 'tactically' altered in such a way that there is a semblance of something happening" (H 195). On the other hand I diverge from him as to the possible extent of will of type 3: Heidegger's "resolution", which is "precisely the … determination of what is factically possible at the time" (H 298) is only possible as a result of the existential act of grasping ones own Being-oneself. Though this is indeed the main significance of type 3 will, I would see it as physically present, if not so apparently recognisable, in much more trivial cases.

The creative process of shifting reference frames or enlarging L is neither deductive nor random and appears to involve consciousness essentially; but it remains for us to understand exactly *how* consciousness provides a suitable dynamic for this process. I have characterised consciousness through a proposed scheme for understanding qualia, noting that similar considerations will hold for the qualitative aspects of compound percepts, stressing that it is the participation in other loci that confer on percepts their "what it is like to be …" aspect. I now want to explore the possibility that the dynamic of free will arises from the way in which this aspect of percepts enables them to act as *symbols*.

In referring to the qualia as 'symbols', acting in the conscious domain I am diverging somewhat from some previous philosophical terminology. Within the phenomenological tradition the role of percepts as symbols is expressed through the concept of *significance*. E.g. “The relational totality of this signifying we call ‘significance’ This is what makes up the structure of the world.” (H 87) Here, however, I largely follow the work of S Langer (1951), in which a symbol is an artefact: an utterance, a piece of music, a work of art or whatever. She also emphasises that the formation of such relations of symbolisation is the result of a primary human drive towards symbol formation, which she regards as the characteristic attribute of the human species. This results in the construction of symbol-relations concurrently with every process of perception and starting at the earliest developmental stages. Indeed, she sees the linking together of numerous strands of percepts and affects into symbol complexes as an activity that proceeds with particular facility at these early, pre-verbal stages. On the approach I am presenting, the subjective aspects of qualia are composed from actual experiences, and so are particularly suited to symbolise those experiences. ‘Green’ contains the energetics of chlorophyll synthesis, and so naturally symbolises it. Moreover, if, as I am suggesting, the original state of the infant is one of enjoyment rather than perception, then this symbolic role will be built up from infancy in precisely the way that Langer describes. The participation of qualia and of compound percepts (as they appear to consciousness) in the actual events that exemplify them carries with it a natural structure of symbolic interconnectedness. This is rooted in the various loci that support actual events, and so in the world as it is, at an interpersonal level of reality. *The process of free will (or, better,* creative *will) is one of extending the logic and shifting reference frames by following these well-founded symbol systems that are expressed through the subjective experiences of consciousness.*

To study symbol manipulation, however, (as Langer points out) we need to look to the experts in the field: the poets and musicians. Thus the true task for the study of consciousness is to bring together the language of these artists, who can describe the operations of these symbol systems that are neither deterministic nor random, with the language of this mathematical model that shows how the enlargement of the logic fits within a universe influenced by quantum matter.

6. Future directions and experimental work

There remains, of course, a great deal to say in order both to flesh out the very bare bones given above, and also to develop the observational implications of the model. Work (supported by Fundaçao Bial) is currently under way in collaboration with Dr Peter Fennwick to test the idea that pairs of empathically related individuals manifest a common locus. This is a possible explanation of the observation by Jacobo Grinberg-Zylberbaum et al. (1993) and confirmed by Fennwick et al. (1998), that, when an auditory stimulus is applied to one member of the pair, then the appropriate evoked potential can be recorded from the EEG record of the other member. As noted earlier, the model here is applied by assuming that this empathic connection establishes a locus which overlaps both loci of the two individual subjects. The dynamics of the evolutions of their partial truth functions then become interlinked (the phenomenon is formally the same as that of the Aspect experiment) in a way that explains the observed result. A protocol is being implemented to repeat this experiment under different conditions to see whether the detailed predictions of the model are borne out. Full experimental and theoretical details of this application are being published separately.

This has been a first preliminary attempt to construct a testable scheme capable of accounting for the phenomena of consciousness in their experiential aspects. The viewpoint, while still needing a great deal of elaboration, is capable of being linked into practical life and experimentation. If verified, it would provide a theoretical underpinning for the way in which creative will, as experienced and exercised by people, can shape the collective world around us as well as our own interior lives.

Acknowledgments

I am grateful to the Editor, Philip van Loocke, for valuable assistance in enabling me to clarify many of the points in this paper.

Notes

1. I use free will in a somewhat onorthodox manner, as explained in Section 5.
2. E.g. a preferred basis for the many-minds approach of Zeh (1996), a specification of what interactions constitute measurement in the Copenhagen approach, a selection (out of the range of possible decohering histories) of which histories are "classical" in the consistent histories approach of Omnès (1999), etc.
3. Quotations from Heidegger (1957) are denoted by "(H ...)"
4. E.g. "Scientific thinking ... must return to the 'there is' which underlies it; to the site, the soil of the sensible and opened world as it is in our life and for our body ..." (Merleau-Ponty's *Eye and Mind* in Edie 1964).
5. The form of quantum theory that is in the background here is the consistent histories approach of Zeh (1998) with the application to consciousness based on the ideas of Stapp (1993), who

stresses their general applicability to the world including human beings as entire quantum systems. This approach should be distinguished sharply from that of Penrose (1994), where the focus is on quantum theory as a particular physical phenomenon. The presentation here is, however, independent of explicitly quantum considerations. The formalism is largely derived from (Mackey 1963; Gudder 1967; Beltrametti & Cassinelli 1981).

6. This is in contrast to Dennett (1991) who, by focusing on linguistic production rather than introspection as a source of data, is forced into a purely verbal conception of consciousness.
7. To clarify a point raised by a referee, note that this is a *semantic* issue of the application of the logic, not an additional formal property of the logic itself.
8. These are not truth tables in the usual sense since in the third case the values are not uniquely defined.
9. If we were to introduce the idea of the quantum state at this point (which is always possible as a gloss on the consistent histories appraoch) then this step would encompass both the Hamiltonian evolution and the probabilistic collapse. By not introducing the state, we avoid the questionable idea of collapse.

Appendix

1. Lattice definitions

1.1 *Basic definition*

The partial order axioms are (for any propositions, or "elements", a, b etc)

1. If $a \to b$ and $b \to c$ then $a \to c$.
2. It is always the case that $a \to a$, and if $a \to b$ and $b \to a$ then $a = b$.

The order is linked to the logical operations by the requirements that

1. $a \to a \vee b$, $b \to a \vee b$, and if c satisfies $a \to c$, $b \to c$ then $a \vee b \to c$
2. $a \,\&\, b \to a$, $a \,\&\, b \to b$, and if c satisfies $c \to a$, $c \to b$ then $c \to a \,\&\, b$

This results in the logical operations obeying the rules:

$$a \,\&\, b = b \,\&\, a,\ a \vee b = b \vee a$$
$$a \,\&\, (b \,\&\, c) = (a \,\&\, b) \,\&\, c$$
$$a \vee (b \vee c) = (a \vee b) \vee c$$

It is usual to require also that there exist special elements 0 and 1 such that, for any a, $0 \to a \to 1$, but only the existence of 0 will be assumed here. It is, however, always possible to add these elements to any lattice satisfying the other requirements.

1.2 *Orthocomplemented lattice*

Orthocomplementation is an operation on a lattice with 0 and 1 that associates with each element a the element $a^{\perp}$ (read as "not a"), such that

1. $a^{\perp\perp} = a$
2. If $a \to b$ then $b^{\perp} \to a^{\perp}$
3. $a \mathbin{\&} a^{\perp} = 0$ and $a \vee a^{\perp} = 1$

A lattice with an orthocomplementation is called an orthocmplemented lattice.

1.3 *Distributional law, orthomodularity*

Classical logic obeys the distributional law: for any three propositions *a, b, c,* we have

$$a \mathbin{\&} (b \vee c) = (a \mathbin{\&} b) \vee (a \mathbin{\&} c),\ a \vee (b \mathbin{\&} c) = (a \vee b) \mathbin{\&} (a \vee c)$$

together with the other relations obtained by permuting these elements among themselves. In an arbitrary lattice (not necessarily obeying classical logic) a set of three elements with these properties is called a distributive triple. An orthocomplemented lattice is called orthomodular if, for any elements a and b, the triple $(a, a^{\perp}, b)$ is distributive.

2. Generalised logics and complementation

In this section I examine whether the operation of relative complement can be extended to be a true orthocomplement. The essential tool here is the fact (Birkhoff 1964: 113) that any lattice L can be embedded in the larger lattice $\hat{L}$ of all *ideals* in L. An ideal J is a subset of L satisfying:

i. if a and b are in J then so is $a \vee b$
ii. if a is in J and $b \to a$ then b is in J.

$\hat{L}$ becomes a lattice when the lattice operations are defined by

$$A \mathbin{\&} B = A \cap B = \{\, a \mathbin{\&} b \mid a \in A \text{ and } b \in B \,\}$$
$$A \vee B = \{\, x \mid x \to a \vee b \text{ for } a \in A \text{ and } b \in B \,\}.$$

The embedding of L in $\hat{L}$ is defined by the map that associates with any $a \in L$ the *principal ideal* $L(a)$ of all $x \in L$ with $x \to a$.

$\hat{L}$ is *complete* in that the operations $\vee$ and & can be extended not only to finite sets but to arbitrary sets.

Suppose L is a generalised logic. The construction of the orthocomplement $c^{\perp}$of an element c proceeds as follows. Define

$$J_c = \{\, x \mid (\exists f)\ (x \to f \backslash c)\}.$$

It is then easily seen (using the orthomodular property of the sublattices) that J_c is an ideal. Let

$$\bar{L} = \{\, L(a) \mid a \in L \,\} \cup \{\, J_c \mid c \in \mathrm{L} \,\} \subseteq \hat{L}$$

On this set define $L(a)^{\perp} = J_a$, and $J_a^{\perp} = L(a)$. I then conjecture that this definition is consistent and that it extends uniquely to a complement on the smallest sublattice of $\hat{L}$ containing $\bar{L}$.

2.1 *Truth tables*

The standard "truth tables" for S (Section 3.3) as in classical logic are

$S(a \wedge b)$

$S(b)$ $S(a)$	0	1
0	0	1
1	1	1

$S(a \& b)$

$S(b)$ $S(a)$	0	1
0	0	0
1	0	1

$S(a \backslash b)$

$S(b)$ $S(a)$	0	1
0	0	1
1		1 or 0

(These are not truth tables in the usual sense since in the third case the values are not uniquely defined)

References

Abram, David (1997) *The spell of the sensuous.* Vintage Books, New York.

Alexander, Samuel (1920) *Space, Time and Deity.* MacMillan, London.

Beltrametti, Enrico G and Cassinelli, Gianni (1981) *The Logic of Quantum Mechanics.* Addison Wesley, Reading, Mass.

Chalmers, D. J. (1995) 'Facing up to the problem of consciousness.' *J. Cons. Studies* 2: 200–19.

Clarke, Chris J. S. (1993) 'Process as a primitive physical category'. In *Time and Process* (ed.) J. T. Fraser and Lewis Rowell, International Universities Press, Madison, Conn. pp. 53–69.

Clarke, Chris J. S. (1995) 'The non-locality of mind.' *JCS* 2: 231–240.

Clarke, Chris J. S. (2000) 'Construction and reality: reflections on philosophy and spiritual/psychotic experience' in *Psychosis and Spirituality: Exploring the New Frontier* ed. J. Clarke, Whurr, London.

Dennett, Daniel C. (1991) *Consciousness explained.* Allen Lane, London.

Edie, M. (1964) (ed) *The Primacy of Perception and other Essays.* Northwestern University Press, Evanston. Ill.

Eliade, Mercia (1964) *Shamanism: archaic techniques of ecstasy* trans. WR Trask, Routledge and Kegan Paul, London.

Fennwick, Peter; Vigus, Norman; Sanders, Sue (1998) "The transferred potential" (to appear: preprint, Institute of Psychiatry, London).

Fowkes, Neville D., Mahoney, John J. (1994) *An introduction to mathematical modelling.* Wiley, Chichester.

Grinberg-Zylberbaum, Jacobo; Attie, I; Delafor, M; Guevara, M; Gonzalez, M; Schettino, I; Cerezo, R; and Perez, T. (1993) "Electrophysiologia de la Communicacion Humana: Potencial Transferido" *Revista Mexicana de Psichologia* 10(2): 127–134.

Gudder, Stanley (1967) 'Systems of observables in axiomatic quantum mechanics.' *J. Math. Phys.* 8: 2109–2113.

Harman, Willis (1995) 'Towards an adequate epistemology for the scientific exploration of consciousness.' *JCS* 1: 140–148.

Heidegger, M. (1957) *Sein und Zeit* (Seventh edition) Quotations are from the English Translation by Joh Macquarrie and Edward Robinson, Blackwell 1962, and designated by "H n", where n is the seventh edition page number (used in the margin of the translation).

Isham, C. (1994) 'Quantum logic and the histories approach to quantum theory' *J. Math. Phys* 35: 2157–85.

Jaynes, Julian (1993) *The origin of consciousness in the breakdown of the bicameral mind.* Penguin.

Kay, Bernard S. (1985) "The double-wedge algebra for quantum-fields on Schwarzschild and Minkowsky spacetimes", *Comm. Math. Phys.* 100(1): 57–81.

Langer, Monica M. (1989) *Merleau-Ponty's Phenomenology of Perception, a guide and commentary.* Macmillan, Houndmills.

Langer, Susan K. (1951) *Philosophy in a new key.* Harvard UP. Cambridge, Mass.

Leiman, Mikael (1992) "The concept of sign in the work of Vygotsky, Winnicott and Bakhtin: further integration of object relations theory and activity theory", *British Journal of Medical Psychology* 65: 209–221.

Libet (1987) "Are the metal experiences of will and self-control significant for the performance of a voluntary act?" *Behavioural and brain sciences* 10: 783–786.

Mackey (1963) *The mathematical foundations of quantum mechanics* Benjamin.

McCall, Storrs (1994) *A model of the universe* Clarendon Press, Oxford.

Merleau-Ponty, Maurice (1962) *Phenomenology of perception.* trans Colin Smith, Routledge, London.

Nagel, T. (1974) 'What is it like to be a bat' *Philosophical Review* 83: 435–450.

Omnès, Roland (1999) *Quantum philosophy* Princeton University Press, Princeton NJ

Penrose, Roger (1994) *Shadows of the mind.* Oxford University Press, Oxford.

Sheldrake, Rupert (1987) *A new Science of Life.* Paladin, London.

Stapp, Henry P. (1993) *Mind, matter and quantum mechanics.* Springer-Verlag, Berlin Heidelberg New York.

Sudbery, Anthony (1984) 'The observation of decay', *Annals of Physics* 157: 512–536.

Velmans, Max (1990) (2000) *Understanding Consciousness*, Routledge, London.

Voloshinov, V.N., (1973) *Marxism and the philosophy of language.* Harvard University Press, Cambridge, Mass.

Whitehead, Alfred N. (1926) *The Concept of Nature.* Cambridge University Press.

Whitehead, Alfred N. (1929) *Process and Reality.* Cambridge University Press.

Zeh, H.D. (1996) in Giulini, D., Joos, E., Kiefer, C., Kupsch, J., Stamatescu, I.-O. and Zeh, H.D. (Eds.) *Decoherence and the appearance of a classical world.* Springer-Verlag, Berlin and Heidelberg.

Zohar, Danah (1990) *The quantum self.* Bloomsbury, London.

Time and the laws of nature

Ilya Prigogine

Abstract

The first part of this paper gives a summary of the philosophy of nature and of the view on time that follows from recent fundamental theories on complex systems. This part is followed by an interview-style part on the implications of this view for consciousness.

1. Time and the laws of nature

Time enters Newtonian physics as well as in quantum mechanics, but in a particular way. Indeed, the basic equations are time reversible. In other words, they remain invariant when $+t$ is replaced by $-t$. Moreover, they correspond to a deterministic description. Once the "state" of the system is given at some time to we can calculate this state for arbitrary times t both in the future and in the past. However everywhere around us we observe irreversible processes in which past and future play different roles. This is true on the microscopic level (consider e.g. radioactivity) as well as on the macroscopic level studied in thermodynamics. There the central quantity is entropy which increases with time till the system has reached equilibrium. Time symmetry is broken. Therefore A. Eddington has called entropy the "arrow of time".

The first to note the conflict between the time reversible view of nature and the evolutionary view based on entropy, was Ludwig Boltzmann (1872). Boltzmann looked for a microscopic dynamical interpretation of irreversibility. But this led to difficulties. Suppose that we invert the velocities of all molecules. This system would then go into its own past and entropy would decrease. To counter this argument Boltzmann added two ingredients: (a) "events" are determined not only by the laws of dynamics but also by initial conditions, (b) probabilistic reasoning; the probability of each macroscopic state is obtained by calculating the number of microscopic states that give rise to it. Entropy would be only applicable to macroscopic states.

Boltzmann's interpretation of irreversibility has been quite successful. The majority of physicists adhere to it. Still it is only applicable to highly dilude gases there are also difficulties. Let us enumerate some of them. Following Boltzmann, Feynman wrote in his Lectures on Physics: "For some reason, the universe at one time had a very low entropy ... that is the origin of irreversibility." I always found this argument somewhat strange. Whatever the past history of our universe, we observe today both reversible time symmetric processes (i.e. friction free pendulum, two body motion) *and* irreversible processes (such as heat conductivity, radioactivity ...). Our problem is to understand the difference which exists at present between these systems whatever our assumptions on the initial state of the universe. Moreover, the transition from the microscopic description to the macroscopic description would involve a loss of information, it corresponds to a "coarse graining". Then irreversibility would be the result of our approximations. Again this is strange, as we humans would introduce an arrow of time into a time symmetric world. This borders on anthropomorphism. Are we not the children of time, of evolution?

There is a third argument which was not known to Boltzmann. The arrow of time leads to new space–time structures in far from equilibrium situations. I called these structures "dissipative structures" to emphasize their difference with equilibrium structures such as a crystal. These new structures appear at "bifurcation points". At these points, there are generally multiple possibilities whose realization is ruled by probabilities.

The arrow of time has therefore a basic *constructive* role. It is currently assumed that the delicate structures we observe in nature (such as the biomolecules) involve irreversible processes. For all these reasons, I came to the conclusion that the usual formulation of dynamics has to be embedded in new mathematical structures which include the arrow of time already on the microscopic, dynamical level. In this description the basic objects are no more classical trajectories or quantum wave functions but probabilities. This is an ambitious program and before describing the main steps, I would like to make some remarks why this program was received with scepticism by the majority of physicists.

In short, I see three types of arguments:

1. Classical dynamics and quantum theory are "final". But is this true? As stated by the late Léon Rosenfeld every theory is based on idealizations and no physical concept is sufficiently defined without its domain of velocity.

2. Such an extension would go against the "royal road" followed in physics. For Leibniz, one of the great founders of dynamics, physics should bring men closer to a divine point of view. Now for God as traditionally conceived, there is no distinction between past and future, there are no doubts, only certitudes.
3. Is it really possible to construct an adequate mathematical formulation to express time symmetry breaking, in a consistent way?

As the result many physicists found this program too revolutionary, while on the other hand accepting highly speculative ideas such as multiple universes, or time travel into the past. Let me now explain briefly what we mean by "new" laws of nature. In classical dynamics, we deal with "point transformations". We follow a trajectory. The situation is quite different in quantum mechanics. There we deal with operators. Operators act on functions (through multiplication, derivation, etc.) and transform them therefore to different functions. However for a given operator there exist functions which remain invariant apart from a multiplicative factor. They are called the "eigenfunctions" associated with the operator, and the multiplicative factors are the eigenvalues. The set of eigenfunctions and eigenvalues gives the "spectrum" of the operator.

In classical mechanics a central role is played by the energy expressed in terms of coordinates and momenta. That is the "Hamiltonian". Similarly, in quantum mechanics, the central role is played by the "Hamiltonian operator" whose eigenvalues are the energy levels observed in atoms or molecules. But the spectrum depends on the class of functions we consider. Traditionally, one considers "normed" functions quite similar to ordinary vectors (to each function we can associate a length or norm, we also can define a scalar product). These "nice" functions form the so-called Hilbert space, in honor of the great mathematician David Hilbert, one of the founders of operator theory. Orthodox quantum mechanics is associated to the Hilbert space.

But what happens if one goes to more general functions spaces (we deal then with generalized functions also called distributions)? In a letter to G. Birkhoff, J. von Neumann wrote "I would like to make a confession which may seem immoral: I do not believe in Hilbert space anymore". In his later work, P. Dirac reached the same conclusion. Spectral theory outside Hilbert space has been studied in recent times by eminent mathematicians (specially Russians). The unexpected conclusion is that this recent field of mathematics solves the riddle of the time arrow. Let us emphasize the analogy with general relativity. It is by giving up Euclidean geometry that Einstein could include gravitation.

The operator method used in quantum mechanics can also be applied to classical systems. Instead of examining a single system, we can also study a collection of systems, an ensemble as Gibbs called it. Such an ensemble is described by a probability distribution ρ. Time change is then described by an operator acting on ρ. This description in terms of "populations" applies both to classical and to quantum systems.

It was always assumed that the ensemble description was equivalent to the individual description (in terms of trajectories or wave functions). But this is no more so precisely for the class of systems where we expect time symmetry breaking. Examples are chaotic systems or thermodynamical systems formed by a large number of interacting particles.

Of course, for simple systems Such as the frictionless pendulum, or the harmonic oscillator in quantum mechanics, we recover the usual results. However these are exceptions. In general, the fundamental quantity is probability. Probability is no more the consequence of ignorance but the result of the dynamical structure. In theoretical physics, this century was dominated by the discovery of quantum theory and relativity. When time symmetry breaking is included we obtain different formulations for classical and quantum dynamics (also for special relativity). These new formulations are "intrinsically probabilistic". That means that they cannot be reduced to trajectories or wave functions. This is an agreement with our observations. We have both time reversible planetary motion and irreversible chemical reactions. The world is much too diverse to be enclosed in a single formulation.

It is time to conclude. All objects in our universe age in the same direction, be it living beings, rocks or stars. The arrow of time is universal while the mechanisms of aging, are of course different. The arrow of time introduces a narrative element: nature is no more an automaton ruled by deterministic laws but a world in "construction" to which we may contribute. This conclusion gives hope to avoid the war of cultures which is going on in Western world. On one side "humanistic culture", in which time and history play an essential role, on the other hand, sciences, for which the arrow of time would be a man made artefact. We come now to the "End of Certainty" — this is the title of my recent book (Prigogine 1997). The end of certainty is necessary as it makes possible cosmic creativity and with that also human creativity.

2. Complex systems and consciousness

(This part is a short interview-style summary of the correspondence between the editor (PVL) and professor Ilya Prigogine; it deals with the implications on consciousness of his physics and his philosophy of nature).

PVL: In your books (for instance, in 'La nouvelle alliance' (1979), Entre temps et eternité (1988)), you conjecture at different places that the approach to physics (and chemistry) that recognizes irreversibility as a basic fact will help us explain how life has formed. Indeed, your books contain several examples illustrating self-organization in material systems. Suppose that, in line with the expectations, the physical/chemical description of the origin of life is achieved with ever more detail in the course of the years to come. It is usually assumed that, with the appearance of life, also consciousness has emerged, even if in a very primitive form. If a complete physical/chemical description of primitive life as a self-organizing system appears possible, then in particular its consciousness will be described in these terms. This raises the question if consciousness can play a causal role in addition to the role played by its material correlate. In other terms, why has consciousness, in addition to its material correlate, entered the scene? Does the explanation of the origin of life also explain the origin of consciousness, or is the latter an additional, more mysterious fact?

Ilya Prigogine: I believe indeed that life was a result of successive bifurcations as they appear in far from equilibrium systems. Consciousness is probably related to a later stage. As consciousness gives us a map of our environment, I think that one of the first states was motion — which requires transformation of chemical energy to motion. Certainly it seems to me that consciousness involves an additional fact. But I suspect that this fact does not escape physical theory.

PVL: As has been abundantly illustrated in your work, complex systems are highly sensitive to initial conditions. This sensitivity brings in indeterminism at least at an epistemological level. But it is correlated with properties like irreversibility and non-locality, which refer to ontological facts. Does this ontology have a place for free will?

Ilya Prigogine: It does. In some circumstances, animals, or even plants, can be in situations (corresponding to bifurcation points) in which deterministic descriptions must be replaced by probabilistic descriptions. In case of animals of sufficient sophistication, conscious free will may select the branch that is taken. However, since conscious free will is a physical process taking place in the brain, the process should be describable in some way in physical terms (though the complexity of the processes may possibly prevent descriptions at very detailed levels).

PVL: It is stated at different places in your work that pure states in quantum theory (and also superpositions of pure states), like individual, localized particles in classical physics, are theoretical constructs suited mainly for simple situations that can be easily realized in a labatory. In many natural circumstances, these concepts have to be replaced by irreducible probabilities. As a consequence, I think you would not suggest that the transition from superposition to pure state is related with consciousness (as is done by different contributors to this book).

Ilya Prigogine: Indeed, in our physical work based on irreducible ensembles, no reductions of wave-packets take place. For systems that are described by states not belonging to the Hilbert space, the differentiation between pure state and superposition becomes meaningless. Since complex systems tend have this type of state, it is not to be expected that the transition from a superposition to a pure state plays a role in the generation of consciousness.

PVL: Consciousness appears in systems of which irreversibility is a striking property, but also non-locality may appear in such systems. You have shown, together with your colleagues (Karpov, Ordonez et al. 2000), that Hegerfeldt's theorems (1994, 1998) do not lead to a violation of Einstein causality in the sense that apparent superluminal propagation (of probabilities) can be explained in terms of non-local wave-packets propagating with velocity c. However, is the very fact of the existence of non-local entities compatible with Einstein causality?

Ilya Prigogine: The extension of the Hilbert space leads to irreducible probabilities, which means that they cannot be expressed in terms of trajectories. As a consequence, this passage outside the Hilbert space entails that one cannot apply the concept of localization that is present in Newtonian trajectories. The non-locality in the sense of Hegerfeldt is certainly an unexpected concept. There is no violation of the Lorentz transformation. But indeed as shown in Karpov, Ordonez et al. (2000), an observer can perceive a phenomenon beyond the light cone. This is certainly a surprise in the frame of special relativity. We are still working on this problem.

PVL: In order to describe natural systems, a 'thermodynamic limit' (in the sense of a limit for an infinite number of degrees of freedom) has to be taken. Even in case of quantum systems, discrete quantum spectra are considered as typical for isolated laboratory systems, as opposed to natural systems of which the continuous nature is an essential property. Does this entail that nature is not computable in the sense that cannot be simulated on discrete, finite precision digital computers?

Ilya Prigogine: One can 'simulate' nature with computers. The behavior of a sufficiently large, finite system can help one to understand the behavior of large systems with continuous spectra. Obviously, one has to be careful and realize that a simulation becomes useless once a critical time has passed. In addition, the thermodynamic limit remains a fundamental one. Already in equilibrium thermodynamics, one has to go to the thermodynamic limit in order to define the transition points between different physical phases. But the study of systems with continuous spectra with help of finite systems is important because it helps one to understand what happens at this limit.

PVL: In the philosophical part of your works, you often refer to Bergson. As has been emphasized, for instance by Barrow and Tipler (1984), Bergson's work has a strong teleological dimension. They put this teleology in a perspective of, among others, the path integral formulation of quantum (field) theory, where the formalism constructs different possible futures and then selects the future obeying best an extremal principle. In your work, classical causality is not applicable to a wide range of systems because the concepts presupposed by this causality (like individual particles with well-defined trajectories) are not applicable. However, one general feature of causality remains unaffected: the principle that the past of a system only, and not its possible future, is required to specify its next state. Hence, in this respect, it appears that you would not follow Bergson.

Ilya Prigogine: I refer to Bergson because he insisted on creativity, but not for reasons of teleology. Classical physics or quantum theory can be based on an extremal principle, as is also the case for equilibrium thermodynamics (in terms of maximum of entropy). But in case of the description of irreducible phenomena, there is in general no extremal principle. Further, causality, in our theory, remains applicable to ensembles beyond the Hilbert space. Wether or not our theory has a formulation in terms of an extremal principle, it is always the past contributing to the formation of the future. There is a large difference between the behavior of inert systems, such as leading to dissipative structures, and the behavior in living systems. In living systems, even very simple ones, the behavior at a given time is partly determined by the memory and by the anticipation of the future. In this sense, the future contributes to the present. Still bifurcations and self-organization play an essential role at all levels of observation.

References

Barrow, J., Tipler, F. (1984) *The anthropic cosmological principle,* Oxford: Oxford University Press.

Driebe, D. (1997) *Fully Chaotic Maps and Broken Time Symmetry.* Kluwer Academic Publishers.

Hegerfeldt, G. (1994) Causality problems for Fermi's two-atom systems. *Physical Review Letters* 72: 596–599.

Hegerfeldt, G. (1998) Irreversibility and causality in quantum theory A. Bohm, H. Dobner, P. Kielanowski (eds.), *Semigroups and rigged Hilbert spaces.* Springer Lecture Notes in Physics, 504.

Karpov, E., Ordonez, G., Petrosky, G., Prigogine, I., Pronko, G. (2000) Causality, delocalization and positivity of energy, *Physical Review* (to appear).

Petrosky, T. and Prigogine I. (1997) The Liouville Space Extension of Quantum Mechanics. *Advances in Chemical Physics,* vol. XCIX, Wiley & Sons, 1997.

Petrosky, T. and Prigogine I. (1996) Extension of Classical Dynamics — The Case of Anharmonic Lattices. In *Gravity, Particles and Space–time,* Eds. Pronin and Sardanashvily, Ivanenko Memorial Volume, 1996.

Prigogine, I., Stengers, I. (1979) *La nouvelle alliance.* Paris: Gallimard.

Prigogine, I., Stengers, I. (1988) *Entre temps et éternité.* Paris: Gallimard.

Prigogine, I. (1993) *"Le Leggi del Caos", Lezioni Italiane.* Fondazione Sigma-Tau e Laterza, Bari, Italy (traduit en français: "Les Lois du Chaos", Collection "Nouvelle Bibliothèque Scientifique", Flammarion, Paris, France, 1994.).

Prigogine I. (1997) *La Fin des certitudes,* Odile Jacob, 1996 (traduit en anglais: "The End of Certainty", The Free Press, New York, 1997.

Matter, Mind and the quantum

A Topological Geometro-Dynamics perspective

Matti Pitkanen

Abstract

Topological Geometro-Dynamics (TGD) is a unified theory of fundamental interactions. TGD involves a quite far-reaching generalization of the space–time concept and, apart from the notion of quantum jump, reduces quantum theory to infinite-dimensional geometry. General coordinate invariance forces the identification of the quantum states as quantum histories rather than time-constant snapshots of a single quantum history: this solves the basic determinism/non-determinism paradox of quantum measurement theory. The identification of the quantum jump as a moment of consciousness defines the microscopic theory of consciousness. p-Adic numbers is one of the basic new mathematical concepts necessary for the formulation of quantum TGD. The notion of the self as a subsystem remaining p-adically unentangled under the action of the "time evolution" operator U (S-matrix) associated with the sequential quantum jumps $\Psi_i \rightarrow U\Psi_i \rightarrow \Psi_f$ is central for the macroscopic theory of consciousness. Vanishing p-adic entanglement means subcritical real entanglement so that the self can be regarded as a critical phenomenon. The moments of consciousness which occurred after the last "wake-up" bind temporally to a single experience and give rise to immediate subjective memory. Each self represents a self-organizing system approaching a stable self-organization pattern selected by dissipation. A self can have sub-selves and experiences sub-selves as mental images which are averages about mental images of sub-sub-selves. An infinite hierarchy of selves giving rise to an abstraction hierarchy is predicted. The notion of the many-sheeted spacetime and the classical non-determinism of the Kähler action defining configuration space geometry are crucial for understanding how psychological time and cognition emerge in the TGD-universe and a rather radical generalization of the views about the relationship of subjective and geometric time is forced.

1. Introduction

Topological Geometro-Dynamics (TGD) is a unified theory of fundamental interactions. TGD involves a quite far-reaching generalization of the spacetime concept and, apart from the notion of quantum jump, reduces quantum theory to infinite-dimensional geometry. Quantum TGD requires introduction of several new mathematical tools and concepts, in particular p-adic numbers. TGD-based theory of consciousness has developed gradually during the last thirteen years side by side with TGD-based quantum measurement theory. For an extended exposition of TGD, p-adic aspects of TGD and TGD inspired theory of consciousness see my online books "Topological Geometro-Dynamics" (Pitkänen 1995a), "TGD and p-Adic Numbers" (Pitkänen 1995b) and "TGD inspired theory of consciousness with applications to biosystems" (Pitkänen 1998). The basic concepts and ideas of TGD based theory of consciousnes can be summarized as follows.

Identification of quantum states as quantum histories

General coordinate invariance forces the identification of the quantum states as quantum histories rather than time-constant snapshots of a single quantum history. This identification has several important consequences.

a. The possibility to regard state function collapse as a quantum jump between quantum histories solves the basic paradox posed by the determinism of the Schrödinger equation contra the non-determinism of the state function collapse.[1]
b. A radical reconsideration of the concepts of psychological time and observer becomes necessary and forces a profound generalization of the standard views about time.
c. One must reformulate quantum measurement theory. Only quantum jumps which can be regarded as quantum measurements of the density matrix of some subsystem are allowed.

The Negentropy Maximization Principle (NMP) specifies which subsystems are subject to quantum measurement in a given quantum jump. NMP can be regarded as a basic law for the dynamics of quantum jumps. NMP also specifies which subsystems can have a moment of consciousness in a given quantum state.

Quantum notion of self

An important step in the development of the theory was the discovery of the quantum level definition of the concept of self. The self can be identified as a subsystem able to remain p-adically unentangled during unitary "time evolutions" *U* associated with sequential quantum jumps. A subsystem possessing a self behaves thus p-adically like its own independent sub-Universe. The quantum notion of self together with some natural assumptions about how the contents of consciousness are determined, leads to an understanding of the phenomenology of everyday consciousness and to some rather dramatic and often testable predictions.

Quantum criticality

The systems possessing a self correspond to macroscopic quantum phases. In standard physics context the existence of the required macroscopic quantum phases is not at all obvious whereas the new physics implied by TGD predicts their existence. The point is that the Universe according to TGD is a quantum critical system. Quantum criticality is mathematically very similar to thermodynamical criticality and implies long range quantum correlations in all length scales. This in turn implies the existence of macroscopic quantum phases.

TGD based space–time concept and the existence of macroscopic quantum phases

TGD implies a radical generalization of the space–time concept in all length and time scales. The concept of manysheeted space–time leads to fresh proposals for how biosystems manage to be macroscopic quantum systems. Examples of these mechanisms are so called wormhole superconductivity, electronic high T_c superconductivity, neutrino super-conductivity and a mechanism for generating coherent light and gravitons (see the chapter "Biosystems as macroscopic quantum systems" of Pitkänen (1998)).

p-Adic numbers and consciousness

p-Adic number fields R_p (one number field for each prime $p = 2, 3, 5, \ldots$) are analogous to real numbers but differ from them in that p-adic numbers are not well-ordered. p-Adic numbers play an essential role in the formulation of quantum TGD and of TGD inspired theory of consciousness. The mapping of the real geometric structures to their p-adic counterparts is a basic feature of quantum TGD and plays also a key role in TGD inspired theory of consciousness. The emergence of p-adic numbers is related to the fact that the TGD universe is a quantum spin glass. This has deep implications concerning our understanding of the functioning of living systems: for instance, the spin glass state provides a model of long term memory.

2. TGD inspired theory of consciousness

Before continuing some comments on the definition of the quantum history concept are in order. In TGD, quantum states corresponds to *Diff*^{4} invariant configuration space spinor fields defined in the space of 3-surfaces. By general coordinate invariance the value of the configuration space spinor field is the same for all 3-surfaces $X^3 \subset X^4(Y^3)$ related by diffomorphisms, especially by time translations of $X^4(Y^3)$. This means that the configuration space spinor field cannot be localized temporally unless $X^4(Y^3)$ has finite time duration and is therefore vacuum 4-surface. Hence it is natural to speak of quantum history. Note that 'quantum history' in this sense does not refer to Schrödinger time evolution (since the Schrödinger evolution operator is generalized by TGD) nor to evolution by quantum jumps (since, in TGD, these are jumps between entire quantum histories) but is quantum history with respect to the geometric time of $X^4(Y^3)$ and determined by the requirement of general coordinate invariance.

Quantum histories can be also regarded as superpositions of classical space–time surfaces since the definition of the configuration space geometry assigns to each 3-surface Y^3 a unique space–time surface $X^4(Y^3)$ and since configuration space spinor field is invariant under general coordinate transformations. As a consequence, classical TGD becomes an exact part of quantum TGD.

2.1 *Quantum jumps between quantum histories as moments of consciousness*

The individual quantum jump between quantum histories has the following anatomy. The quantum jump consists of the unitary, informational "time evolution"

$$\Psi_i \rightarrow U\Psi_i$$

of the initial quantum history Ψ_i described by the unitary operator U (essentially an S-matrix), followed by the quantum jump proper to the final quantum history Ψ_f:

$$U\Psi_i \rightarrow \Psi_f$$

It should be emphasized that the operator U, or the equivalent S-matrix, is only the formal counterpart of the Schrödinger evolution lasting an infinite time: there is no actual Schrödinger equation involved and U has nothing to do with geometric time development.[2] U codes all the statistical predictions of quantum TGD and is the counterpart of the S-matrix of quantum field theories.

Subjective time development understood as a sequence of quantum jumps occurs outside the realm of the geometric spacetime. It could be regarded as a non-deterministic hopping in the space of the configuration space spinor fields. The individual quantum jump is however fundamentally irreducible in the sense that one cannot model it by any dynamical time development. The identification of a quantum jump as a moment of consciousness defines what might be called a microscopic theory of consciousness. The subjective time development presumably obeys some variational principle consistent with the quantum measurement theory, in particular, with its nondeterminism.[3] This principle dictates which systems for given initial quantum history can perform quantum jumps and have moments of consciousness. This variational principle will be discussed in Section 2.2.2.

2.1.1 *The quantum jump as a measurement of the density matrix*

The need to generalize standard quantum measurement theory suggests that the allowed quantum jumps should allow interpretation as a quantum measurement for some subsystem. The only universal observable is the density matrix of the subsystem, which should be thus measured in the quantum jump. Hence the basic assumption is that any quantum jump corresponds to a quantum measurement for the density matrix of some subsystem (possibly decomposing to unentangled subsystems).

It is however far from obvious what the notion of quantum measurement means when quantum states are quantum histories. For instance, the precise definition of the subsystem concept involves nontrivial delicacies caused by the classical non-determinism of Kähler action. They can be overcome only by allowing association sequences and cognitive space–time sheets (see Section 2.3.2). These delicacies are crucial from the point of view of consciousness theory since cognition is made possible by the classical non-determinism of the Kähler action.

2.1.2 *The quantum jump as quantum computation*

The Universe according to TGD is a quantum computer in an extremely general sense of the word. Every quantum jump involves unitary informational "time development" U (quantum computation) and the "quantum jump proper" involving a localization in the zero modes (halting of the computation). It is neither possible nor necessary to associate a Schrödinger equation with U. U is however completely analogous to the time evolution operator U(−t, t), t→∞, defining the S-matrix in quantum field theories. It is important to notice that also in quantum field theories one is interested only in the S-matrix so that the new interpretation brings in nothing new at practical level.

There are thus three time developments in TGD:

a. The geometric time development of the space–time surface determined by the absolute minimization of the Kähler action, which also via general coordinate invariance defines in what sense quantum histories are histories;
b. the informational "time development" U analogous to quantum computation (hence the attribute 'informational') represented by an S-matrix;
c. the subjective time development by quantum jumps taking outside the realm of the space–time.

These three notions of time development fuse to single "holy trinity" of geometric, informational and subjective time evolutions. This "holy trinity" of time evolutions corresponds to the "holy trinity" of

a. matter in the sense of res extensa identified as 3-surfaces,
b. ideas/objective realities (logos–cosmos) identified as quantum histories (physics–mathematics)[4]
c. the world of subjective experiences defined by the quantum jump sequences for selves (for instance, mathematicians exist subjectively in the quantum jumps between mathematical ideas)

It should be emphasized that in this framework the standard physics identification of the time parameter of the Schrödinger equation with geometric time is wrong. We will discuss in Section 2.3.3 how the value of the geometric time associated with the contents of a conscious experience is determined.

2.1.3 *How can the world of conscious experience look classical?*

If quantum histories (/states) are quantum superpositions over a huge number of classical space–time surfaces, it is very difficult to understand how the world of conscious experience manages to look classical. The solution of the problem comes out from the requirement that quantum jumps in a well-defined sense reduce to quantum measurements performed in a space–time with a fixed macroscopic geometry as in quantum field theory. The macroscopic aspects of the space–time surface are determined completely by the zero modes of the configuration space characterizing the induced Kähler field and the geometric size and shape of the four-surface totally. Thus, if each quantum measurement involves localization in zero modes, then the classicality of the universe of subjective experience is achieved automatically.

2.1.4 *Information gain and conscious experience*

One can claim that it is impossible to write any formula for the contents of the conscious experience in terms of, say, the final quantum history Ψ_f: qualities are not in the world but in the no-where-land between the initial and final worlds of the quantum jump. This might indeed be the case at least when the component of the conscious experience is not about quantities as sensory experiences might be. Despite this it is possible to assign well-defined information measures for the contents of conscious experience associated with a single quantum jump. The idea is simple: interpret conscious systems as "information eaters"[5] in the sense that the information gain ΔI in a conscious experience is the difference for the information measures for the initial and final states Ψ_i and Ψ_f respectively:

$$\Delta I = I(U\Psi_i) - I(\Psi_f)$$

Since one can write a formula for a quantum history (quantities are in the world), it is possible to assign well-defined information measures to them.

In real context these information measures would be typically infinite by the mere reason that the universe is infinite. A crucial role is played by the unique pinary cutoff associated with any mapping of a real geometric object to its p-adic counterpart and by the fact that the real counterpart of integer n regarded as p-adic integer is finite even in the case that n is infinite as ordinary integer. p-Adicization and pinary cutoff suggest a universal manner to characterize the finiteness of the mental capacity of a particular self caused by its finite size (information gains are bounded by $p \times \log(p)$).

The assumption that information measures are local with respect to configuration space together with the fact that configuration space spinors are analogous to ordinary single particle Schrödinger amplitudes, makes it possible to assign a unique measure to a given type of information. These kind of measures are not possible in quantum field theory. A more detailed discussion of the information measures of conscious experience can be found in the chapter "Information and consciousness" of Pitkänen (1998).

One can question the claim that a formula for the contents of conscious experience is not possible. In particular, one could claim that sensory experiences are exceptional since they represent basically quantities. Indeed, a working hypothesis worth of studying is that the values of the zero modes (which are same for all the macroscopically equivalent space–time surfaces present in the final quantum history) determine the contents of the sensory experience. If this is the case, then the p-adic information measures $I(\Psi_f)$ for the final state of the quantum jump provide measures for the information contents of the sensory experience. Pinary cutoff would automatically take care of the finite resolution of the sensory experience caused by the finite size of the experiencer.

2.2 *Quantum self*

In the following the notion of self is introduced. To avoid confusions it must be emphasized that the notion of self is completely general and by no means restricted to the brain. Brain consciousness is in this framework only a special form of consciousness.

2.2.1 *The notions of self and subjective memory*

The simplest hypothesis is that the contents of consciousness are determined by a single quantum jump. There are two objections to this view:

a. The idea about the self as a continuous stream of consciousness is very attractive and it seems difficult to believe that our consciousness could be actually a sequence of moments of consciousness with gaps between.
b. Furthermore, if the contents of consciousness are determined completely by the initial and final states of a single quantum jump, we cannot have any memories about our previous conscious experiences. Subjective memories would be only pseudo-memories perhaps resulting from the simulations of the subjective past.

It took quite a long time to realize the real strength of these objections and to discover that a proper quantum definition of the concept of self provides a manner to overcome these obstacles.

a. Entanglement is one of the basic non-classical notions of quantum theory. An unentangled subsystem, as opposed to an entangled one, behaves as its own sub-universe and can be regarded as a pure quantum state. The natural guess is that a self should be identified as a subsystem able to remain unentangled. This kind of definition looks intuitively very satisfactory since the me-external world separation is a basic characteristic of consciousness. The problem is that in standard quantum mechanics even the slightest interaction generates entanglement and kills the self. The only self would be the entire universe.

b. p-Adics come however in rescue. The self can be defined as a subsystem able to remain p-adically unentangled during informational time evolutions U associated with the sequential quantum jumps. Or putting it differently: the self is a subsystem behaving p-adically like its own sub-Universe (with respect to

NMP, see 2.2.2). This concept of self makes sense in the quantum TGD framework since the mapping of the real system to its p-adic counterpart is characterized by a unique pinary cutoff and maps subcritical real entanglement to a vanishing p-adic entanglement. The vanishing of p-adic entanglement means vanishing of the pinary cutoffs of all but one entanglement coefficient. The real entanglement coefficients differ from zero only by an amount determined by the pinary cutoff. This means that the self exists in real context only when entanglement is subcritical: the self is a critical phenomenon.

c. The hypothesis that the experiences of the self associated with the quantum jumps which occurred after the "wake-up" (the quantum jump during which U made the subsystem p-adically unentangled) sum up to a single experience, implies that the self can have memories about earlier moments of consciousness (see 2.2.3). Therefore the self becomes an extended object with respect to the subjective time and has a well-defined "personal history". Subjective memory has a natural identification as a short-term memory with a duration of the order of a second.

d. If the temporal binding of experiences involves some kind of averaging, that is, if quantum statistical determinism generalizes to the level of the subjective experience, then the total experience defined by the heap of the experiences associated with individual quantum jumps is reliable.

e. A self can have sub-selves: this corresponds geometrically to a space–time sheet having smaller space–time sheets glued to it. An irreducible self is defined as a self having no subselves. Reducible and irreducible selves give rise to two modes of consciousness identifiable as ordinary and "whole-body" consciousness.

f. A subsystem can wake-up (become a conscious self) in two manners. In every quantum jump of an existing self two new sub-self candidates are created. These candidates are the subsystem whose entanglement entropy was largest before the quantum jump and its complement (see 2.2.2). If the subsequent action of U leaves the p-adic entanglement vanishing, the two subsystems indeed wake-up. The second possibility is that some subsystem and its complement become spontaneously p-adically unentangled during the action of U and thus also become sub-selves. Long-lived selves should have weak quantum interaction (characterized by U) with the surrounding world. Sufficiently intelligent selves can apply two strategies to wake-up their sub-selves or other selves (this is what we do routinely).

2.2.2 *Negentropy Maximization Principle*

The requirement that allowed quantum jumps are quantum measurements of the density matrix of some subsystem leaves completely open which subsystem makes the quantum jump. This would mean panpsychism. There should exist some law telling which subsystems for a given initial quantum history $U\Psi_i$ aresubject to the quantum measurement. The Negentropy Maximization Principle generalizes the quantum measurement theory and provides this law (see the chapter "Negentropy Maximization principle" of Pitkänen (1998)).

a. NMP applies to each irreducible self (a self without sub-selves) separately and is therefore in a well-defined sense a local principle. Every self in $U\Psi_i$ participates in the quantum jump $U\Psi_i \rightarrow \Psi_f$, which means that some subsystem of the self is quantum measured.

b. A quantum jump for a given irreducible self X corresponds to a measurement of the density matrix for some subsystem Y of X. In this measurement subsystem Y goes to an eigenstate of the density matrix and Y becomes unentangled. The same happens to the complement of Y inside X. The amount of entanglement is measured by entanglement entropy S and S vanishes for the final state of the quantum jump. Thus S can be regarded as a negentropy gain having interpretation as some kind of conscious information. The conscious experience must be assigned with the self X. One cannot associate it with the measured subsystem or its complement inside the self: they are in a completely symmetric position since the diagonalized density matrices are identical. Hence there is no manner to tell which is the measured system and which the measuring subsystem. Thus one must define the quantum measurement as creating an unentangled subsystem-complement pair inside a self and identify the self as the conscious measurer.

c. NMP states that the entanglement entropy reduction associated with the conscious experience of an irreducible self X is maximal. Interpreting entanglement negentropy gain as conscious information, one can say that we live in the best possible world. Only the quantum jumps giving rise to maximum information content of conscious experience occur. This requirement fixes the quantum measured subsystem Y of a given self uniquely unless there are several subsystems giving rise to same maximum negentropy gain: in this case any of the quantum jumps occurs with the same probability.

The precise formulation of NMP involves delicate issues. In the real context NMP does not make sense since in the generic case the entire universe is the only self in question and entanglement entropies for candidate subsystems are infinite. In the p-adic context an elegant formulation of NMP with sensical predictions is possible since the universe decomposes to subselves possessing finite p-adic entanglement entropies (even at the limit of infinite subsystems!). In p-adic context NMP reduces to a local principle applying separately to each irreducible self. Pinary cutoff is crucial for this to occur: in real context this decomposition does not happen in the generic case. In p-adic context entanglement negentropy gain is defined as the real counterpart of the p-adic negentropy gain with p-adic prime p characterizing the subsystem in question. The definition of the negentropy concept in p-adic framework involves quite interesting delicacies. For instance, entanglement with a vanishing entanglement entropy is possible (see the chapters "Self and binding" and "Time and consciousness" of Pitkänen 1998). One must also define the concept of subsystem very carefully since quantum states are identified as quantum histories in a TGD framework.

2.2.3 *Summation hypothesis and binding of experiences*

Every subsystem X possessing a self behaves essentially as a separate sub-Universe with respect to NMP. Also the sub-selves X_i of X have their own experiences. The question is: how are the experience of X and the experiences of X_i related? The following basic hypothesis provides a possible answer to this question.

a. X experiences the sub-selves X_i as separate mental images superposed to the pure self experience of X: this is natural since sub-selves are unentangled and hence behave like separate sub-Universes.

b. The experiences of the self X about the experiences of its sub-selves X_i are abstractions. The sub-self X_i experiences its sub-selves X_{ij} as separate mental images. X however experiences them as a single mental image representing what it is to be a sub-self of X_i, that is the average $\langle X_{ij} \rangle$ of the mental images X_{ij}. Thus the mental images of sub-sub-...selves of X are smoothed out to an average mental image and become effectively unconcious to X. The averaging hypothesis generalizes quantum statistical determinism to the level of subjective experience and is analogous to the hypothesis about averaging related to temporal binding.

Temporal binding with averaging implies that the experiences of the individual selves are reliable and abstraction brings in the possibility of quantum statistical determinism at the level of ensembles. The inability to perceive the flickering of light when the frequency of the flickering is larger than about one Hz is consistent with the hypothesis that subjective sensory memory a has duration of the order 0.1 seconds and that temporal averaging indeed occurs. The summation hypothesis and temporal binding imply a hierarchy of conscious experiences with increasingly richer contents and at the top of the hierarchy is the entire universe, God, enjoying eternal self-consciousness since it cannot entangle with any larger system. Also we are mental images of some higher level self. This hierarchy obviously has far-reaching consequences.

The binding of experiencers is also possible. The binding of selves by quantum entanglement however means that they lose their consciousness. This process naturally corresponds to the formation of wholes from their parts at the level of conscious experiences. The formation of a mental image (sub-self) representing a word from the mental images representing letters is an example of this process. The entanglement mechanism provides also a possible mechanism for "enlightment" experiences involving the extension of the self (see the chapter "Self and binding" and "Time and consciousness" of Pitkänen 1998).

2.2.4 *How to understand evolution and self-organization?*

One could argue that, since a quantum jump is random (this should be qualified, since the selection occurs between the eigenstates of the density matrix), the identification of quantum jumps with moments of consciousness cannot explain evolution. In standard physics it is difficult to circumvent this objection. Even worse, heat death seems to be the ultimate fate of the universe according to standard physics. However, it can be shown that time evolution by quantum jumps corresponds to a sequence of p-adic primes increasing in a statistical sense (Pitkänen 1998). This means that the concept of nearness defining the effective topology becomes gradually more refined, that the complexity of the universe increases, and that the maximal information contents of conscious experiences increase in the long run (like $p \times \log(p)$ or at least as $\log(p)$ as a function of the p-adic prime characterizing the system). This is nothing but evolution. NMP, which states that entanglement negentropy gain is maximal for allowed quantum jumps, enhances this tendency.

Quantum jumps between quantum histories make also possible genuine quantum self-organization. The concept of self-organization gets quite new additional meaning in the TGD framework. Self-organization means also evolution of self-hierarchies. Self-organization by quantum jumps can be regarded as a hopping in the zero modes characterizing the macroscopic aspects of the space–time surface. Each self is a dissipative system which ends up in some asymptotic self-organization pattern in the presence of the external energy feed (or even without it). Dissipation is the ultimate Darwinian selector picking up the winning selves as favored self-organization patterns. Since sub-selves correspond to mental images, the immediate implication is that also memes are subject to a similar selection. For instance, the formation of long term memories and habits could be understood as a formation of surviving sub-selves.

The proposed realization of the quantum criticality, besides making macroscopic quantum systems possible, in a well-defined sense maximizes the intelligence and complexity of the universe (see the chapter "Information and consciousness" of Pitkänen 1998). The TGD universe is a quantum spin glass and this adds an additional aspect to the self-organization process. For instance, the energy landscape of the spin glass is a fractal-like structure containing valleys inside valleys and provides an ideal dynamical memory mechanism.

2.2.5 *How to understand morally responsible free will?*

One could argue that the randomness of the quantum jump means that moral choices are impossible. Volition can however be associated with the selections between different degenerate branches of the space–time surface having the same value of Kähler action but possibly different decomposition to regions obeying effective p-adic topology.

P-adic evolution defines the fundamental value of the quantum ethics. The selections which tend to increase the value of the p-adic prime represent good deeds since they mean evolution. The values of this ethics are not in the physical world but in the quantum jumps defining the subjective reality. Selves can make plans since they have geometric memory (conscious experience contains information from a (four-dimensional) space–time region, rather than only from a time-constant snapshot, and gives rise to a "prophecy", a prediction for the future and past on condition that the world were completely classical). Selves can make decisions and select between various classical macroscopic time developments. Selves are able to remember their choices since they have subjective memories about the previous quantum jumps. Thus selves are genuine moral agents if they can experience directly that increase of p is good and decrease of p is bad.

2.3 *Cognition and space–time geometry*

The notion of the manysheeted space–time and the classical non-determinism of the Kähler action making possible experiences with temporally localized information contents, are the key elements of the TGD based model of cognition. The notions 'cognitive space–time sheet' and 'association sequence' are the geometric correlates for the notions of self and thought (or rather, 'geometric' memory). These notions, not possible in the standard physics framework, are very general and by no means restricted to brain consciousness.

2.3.1 *What do space–time surfaces look like?*

The notion of space–time surface deserves some explanation. A mathematician's notion of the space–time surface is more general than the intuitive notion. For instance, a space–time surface can be the union of disjoint surfaces. The term 'space–time sheet' is more near to what one intuitively would understand with a space–time surface. The TGD notion of space–time surface is roughly the following:

a. One obtains a piece of Minkowski space as a 4-surface defined by putting CP_2 coordinates constant: this is the simplest kind of vacuum extremal. By suitably deforming one obtains infinitely much vacuum extremals. Vacuum extremals can have finite time duration: in this case they correspond to cognitive space–time sheets (see below).

b. Allowing several values for CP_2 coordinates one obtains several 'parallel' pieces of Minkowski space which can be deformed to more general vacuum extremals. These sheets can be glued together by wormhole contacts and deformed so that they are not vacua anymore.

c. By gluing together extremely small surfaces representing elementary particles to this complex one obtains a rough view about what a TGD space–time surface looks like.

A two-dimensional visualization might also help. Put z-coordinate constant in 3-space and allow several values of z-coordinate: you get several parallel pieces of plane. Deform them and glue them together by wormhole contacts. Then, glue elementary particle like surfaces, represented by, say, extremely tiny spheres and tori.

2.3.2 *Association sequences and cognitive space–time sheets*

The concepts of cognitive space–time sheet and association sequence are crucial for the TGD based quantum model of intelligent systems (see the chapter "TGD inspired theory of intelligent systems" of Pitkänen (1998)). Cognitive space–time sheets are geometric correlates of selves. They are made possible by the huge vacuum degeneracy of the Kähler action, which sharply differentiates between TGD and more standard theories of physics. By gluing vacuum extremals to non-vacuum space–time surfaces and suitably deforming, one obtains new degenerate absolute minima. One manner to see cognitive space–time sheets is as the classical counterparts of the virtual particles of quantum field theories (in TGD particles are 3-surfaces!) created from vacuum and returning to it. By definition material space–time sheets have infinite temporal extension whereas cognitive space–time sheets have *finite* temporal extension. Finite temporal extension is possible since classically conserved quantities like energy can flow to a cognitive space–time sheet and flow back to a material space–time sheet when the cognitive space–time sheet ends. The finite temporal extension implies that the information contents of the conscious experiences for selves associated with the cognitive space–time sheets are temporally localized. Thus the notion of psychological time emerges.

Association sequences provide a model for thought understood as a simulation of the classical time development.

a. The origin of the association sequence concept is the vacuum degeneracy of the Kähler action. This degeneracy implies classical non-determinism in the sense that the absolute minimum $X^4(Y^3)$ of the Kähler action associated with a given space-like 3-surface Y^3 on the lightcone boundary $\delta M_4^+ \times CP_2$ is not unique in general. In order to get rid of this non-determinism one must generalize the concept of 3-surface. "Association sequences", defined as 3-surfaces consisting of unions of some minimal number of disjoint 3-surfaces with time-like(!) separations, must be allowed in order to fix uniquely which degenerate absolute minimum is in question.

b. An association sequence provides a simulation of the classical time evolution and gives rise to what might be called "geometric memory" involved with the intentional aspects of consciousness (planning, expectations, desires, ...). Geometric memory can be regarded as a "prophecy" for what will happen and what must have happened earlier provided the world were classical (which means that there are no quantum jumps replacing the macroscopic classical space–time with a new one). Each quantum jump involves naturally a comparison of the expected time development provided by the "geometric memory" and the actual subjective time development stored in the subjective memory.

c. Association sequences of ... of association sequences (thoughts about thoughts about...) are also possible and the average spatial and temporal distances ΔL and ΔT between fundamental building blocks of the association sequence give measures for the temporal and spatial resolutions of the cognitive representation provided by the association sequence.

2.3.3 *How to understand psychological time and its arrow?*

If quantum states are entire quantum histories, then it is not at all obvious how the contents of our everyday consciousness can be concentrated around a definite moment of the geometric time. One must show that the theory predicts the emergence of selves with the property that the information contents of their conscious experiences are concentrated around a definite value of the geometric time or possibly several of them. One must also understand why the value of this time parameter increases in a statistical sense.

The classical non-determinism of the Kähler action gives excellent hopes that the time localization for the information contents of the conscious experience takes place. Cognitive space–time sheets are the geometric correlates of selves and psychological time can be identified as the average center of mass time coordinate for the cognitive space–time sheet, which has finite time duration.

This coordinate is naturally a zero mode and therefore has the same value for all space–time surfaces appearing in the superposition of the macroscopically equivalent space–time surfaces defined by the final quantum history Ψ_f. Since there is much more room in the future of a given point of the future lightcone than in its past, and since the presence of the lightcone boundary is felt in each quantum jump (the magnitude for the increase of the psychological time can be arbitrarily large whereas the magnitude for the decrease is bounded by the presence of the lightcone boundary) the average increase of the psychological time in a quantum jump is non-negative. Thus the evolution by evolution by quantum jumps is analogous to diffusion in the presence of a future directed drift force and leads to a drift of the cognitive space–time sheet in the direction of future. Therefore a local arrow of psychological time results.

The simplest guess is that the average increment of the psychological time in a single quantum jump does not depend on the properties of the self and is of the order of CP_2 time about 10^4 Planck times. This means that consciousness in biological length scales is in a well-defined sense a macroscopic phenomenon and that the single quantum jump corresponds to a microscopic building block of the self. A natural assumption is that the self-hierarchy starts already from selves having duration of few quantum jumps (which may be the level of elementary particles).

The new concept of the psychological time means a dramatic generalization of the standard view about subjective existence. Cognitive space–time sheets are distributed everywhere around material space–time sheets of infinite time duration and all of them can participate in a given quantum jump. Therefore one can say that the entire space–time is a conscious, living being. Civilizations of the geometric past and future exist simultaneously with us. We are members of a four-dimensional society in the sense that our actions affect the life of selves of both geometric past and future since each quantum jump performed by us changes the macroscopic space–time in both past and future. It is quite possible that there are new versions of me in the geometric past represented by cognitive space–time sheets drifting in future time direction along the material space–time sheet describing “material me”. Therefore this particular life of mine is only one among very many ones. P-adic evolution implies that in the statistical sense the quality of these lives tends to get better. We in our youth now experience in a slightly deeper manner and live in a society having slightly higher level of moral.

2.3.4 *Estimate for the “wake-up time” of the self from the p-adic length scale hypothesis*

The p-adic length scale hypothesis suggests that the typical duration of a self characterized by p-adic prime p is given by the p-adic time scale $T_p = L_p/c$, where $L_p \approx 10^4 p^{(1/2)}$ Planck lengths is the p-adic length scale (Pitkänen 1998). The duration of our immediate memory of about .1 second would correspond to a p–adic length scale of the order of the circumference of the Earth! Either the estimate is wrong or our picture about brain as a seat of consciousness is quite not correct! TGD predicts an entire self-hierarchy so that it is not at all obvious which option is correct.

The time scale of .1 seconds corresponds to the time scale of an EEG. The currents generating an EEG certainly create weak electromagnetic radiation fields which in TGD framework correspond to topological field quanta of Earth size. It is known that EEG frequencies are in the same frequency range as so called Schumann frequencies (Sentman 1985) associated with the resonances of the electromagnetic fields in the 80 km thick wave cavity between Earth surface and ionosphere. Magnetic perturbations near Schumann frequencies are known to have profound effects on human brain inducing altered states of consciousness and neural instabilities (Persinger 1995). Furthermore, the estimate for the thickness of the magnetic flux tubes of the Earth's magnetic field based on the quantization of the magnetic flux is about cell size. These observations raise the question whether our "physical" body is only a dip of an iceberg and formed by the topological condensation of the biomatter around electromagnetic topological field quanta serving as templates for the biostructures as suggested in the chapter "Biosystems as macroscopic quantum systems" of Pitkänen (1998).

2.3.5 *Time delays of consciousness and other anomalies*

The TGD based concept of time has rather dramatic implications and it is important to show that the new time concept indeed solves the conceptual problems and anomalies of standard physics.

a. Dissipation is the black sheep in the family of theoretical physics and the quantum jump between quantum histories concept explains dissipation in an elegant manner. The ad hoc addition of various parameters characterizing dissipation to the reversible fundamental equations of classical physics can be understood as a phenomenological model for the subjective time evolution as a sequence of macroscopic space–times defined by the final states of the quantum jumps. Dissipative space–time is a kind of envelope for a sequence of non-dissipative space–times. Dissipation is a signature of quantum jumps which, by the basic assumptions related to the formulation of NMP, correspond to a sequence of quantum measurements and can occur only inside selves. Hence dissipation gives direct evidence for consciousness. TGD predicts the possibility of whole-body consciousness with anomalously low dissipation and this spectacular effect provides a test of the TGD approach (see the chapter "Self and Binding" of Pitkänen 1998).

b. The quantum jumps between quantum histories concept, together with the notion of self, explains also the peculiar time delays of consciousness revealed in the experiments described in (Deeke, Grötchinger et al. (1976) and Libet et al. (1979) relating to the active and passive roles of consciousness and described by Penrose (1989). The basic observation is that a quantum jump replaces a macroscopic space–time with a new one and that both the geometric past and future change. For instance, the EEG activity preceding the conscious decision to raise the index finger in experiments of Libet can be interpreted as classical electromagnetic fields present in the geometric past of the new macroscopic space–time generated by the decision to raise the finger.

c. It is also possible to explain the causal anomalies revealed by the experiments of Radin and Bierman (Bierman & Radin 1997, 1998; Radin 1997). In these experiences pictures with emotionally provocative content generated galvanic skin responses already before they were seen. A natural looking assumption about the contents of conscious experience is that the change of the geometric past is larger for emotional than for non-emotional quantum jumps (e-motion!): this is also consistent with the important role of emotion as a motivator and with the fact that neural transmitters involved with the emotion induce long term synaptic changes. With this assumption the change of the past recordings about galvanic skin response is predicted to be larger for the emotional pictures than for the non-emotional ones. TGD predicts "tribar effect" as a general signature for the quantum jump between quantum histories concept. For material about this topic see the chapter "Time and consciousness" of Pitkänen (1998).

2.4 *Biosystems as macroscopic quantum systems*

Quite generally, selves are identified as subsystems able to remain p-adically unentangled.[6] Or equivalently, the real entanglement generated by U remains below the critical entanglement repeatedly. Critical entanglement is defined by the unique pinary cutoff associated with the mapping of the real geometric structures to their p-adic counterparts. For macroscopic quantum systems there is typically a gap between ground state and excited states and under favorable conditions U could repeatedly generate sub-critical real entanglement for these systems.

In the standard physics context there are not many candidates for the macroscopic quantum systems required. In the TGD-framework the situation is different since quantum criticality predicts long range quantum correlations in all length scales.

a. Coherent photons and coherent gravitons created by vacuum electromagnetic currents and vacuum energy density are a phenomenon characteristic for TGD and might be crucial for the functioning of bio-systems as macroscopic quantum systems (see the chapter "Microtubules as quantum antennae" of Pitkänen (1998)).
b. Wormhole contacts feeding gauge fluxes between space–time sheets behave like bosons and form BE condensates. The quantum model of EEG and nerve pulses based on wormholes is described in the chapter "TGD inspired model of EEG and nerve pulse" of Pitkänen (1998)).
c. Neutrino super conductivity, made possible by the presence of the classical long range Z^0 fields, might provide the realization of thinking systems as magnetized defects in type I super conductors near criticality. The geometric form of the cellular and endoplasma membranes and chiral selection support this picture.
d. A new form of electronic super conductivity is made possible by the manysheeted space–time concept. The new form of electron superconductivity is a good candidate for the mechanism behind high T_c super conductivity (see the chapter "Biosystems as superconductors" of Pitkänen (1998)).

3. Various types of conscious experiences

In the following some general properties and types of conscious experience are discussed. Most predictions are brain independent. Assuming that the zero modes of the configuration space, characterizing the geometry of macroscopic classical space–time, determine the contents of conscious experience, and identifying macroscopic quantum phases as quantum correlates of various sensory modalities, one can make rather far reaching predictions about basic aspects of, say, the sensory experience of any experiencer, be it human brain or some strange life form in distant galaxy (see Pitkänen 1998 for a technical exposition).

3.1 *Whole-body consciousness and ordinary consciousness*

TGD predicts two basic modes of consciousness.

a. Reducible self is the state in which sub-selves are "falling asleep" and "waking up" all the time. This state corresponds to the ordinary state of consciousness. Sub-selves represent mental images which pop out and disappear all the time.

b. In case of irreducible self quantum jumps do not lead to the generation of sub-selves. This is achieved if sub-self candidates generated in a given quantum jump generate in informational "time evolution" U associated with the next quantum jump nonvanishing p-adic (overcritial real) quantum entanglement so that they do not wake-up. This state is presumably accompanied by the experience of "oneness" and could therefore be called a state of "whole-body consciousness". The absence of the sub-selves means the absence of mental images so that the identification as a state of pure self-awareness without any contents is natural. A less ideal situation is that sub-selves are generated but are very short-lived and represent short flashes against background awareness. "Whole-body-consciousness" presumably means abnormally low metabolism since dissipation inside sub-selves is not present.

3.2 *Active and passive aspects of conscious experience*

Conscious experience involves two fundamental contributions.

a. The "non-classical" contribution from the quantum measurement reducing quantum entanglement associated with the fermionic degrees of freedom and with the quantum fluctuating configuration space degrees of freedom (as opposed to zero modes).
b. The "classical" contribution determined by the localization in zero modes and by the selection between different degenerate absolute minimum space–time surfaces having different decompositions into p-adic regions.

The natural guess is that the experienced free will corresponds to the non-determinism of the quantum jump. The standard objection to this hypothesis is that the non-determinism of the quantum measurement gives rise to randomness rather than volition. Further, quantum numbers relate to the microscopic aspects of the quantum jump and the average quantum numbers measured in quantum jumps probably sum up to zero in the presence of energy feed and external perturbations. Indeed, if the temporal binding of the experiences of the self involves averaging, then this component of experience does not need to give rise to an experience of volition, since it is expected to average out for large numbers of quantum jumps (10^{40} per second by the argument for the arrow of psychological time). Therefore the time averaging involved with the temporal binding smooths out this non-determinism.

Here the special features of TGD however come in rescue.

a. The first candidate for the quantum correlate of volition is the localization in zero modes. This localization corresponds to the spontaneous symmetry breaking of quantum field theories and it selects one classical configuration among many degenerate ones. Spontaneous symmetry breaking has been suggested to be a basic aspect of the quantum jump also by Joel Henkel (Henkel 1998). The asymptotic localization in zero modes seems however to be determined statistically by the self-organization process taking the system to the bottom of some valley of the spin glass energy landscape. Hence volition is probably not in question.

b. The second candidate for volition is classical non-determinism of Kähler action (which gives rise to the geometric model of thought as "association sequence"). The selection between the different degenerate alternative classical time evolutions, that is different degenerate absolute minima $X^4(Y^3)$ going through a given 3-surface Y^3, is an excellent candidate for the volitional act. The reason is that absolute minima differ macroscopically so that the choice between degenerate minima dramatically affects the entire geometric future.

An interesting possibility is that the zero modes characterizing the macroscopic features of the macroscopically equivalent space–time surfaces present in the *final* quantum state of quantum jump determine the contents of at least sensory experiences. This would be in accord with the idea that pure sensory experiences represent quantities which indeed 'are in the world', the world being identified as the macroscopic space–time associated with the final quantum history of the quantum jump. Localization in zero modes involves the fixing of the parameters characterizing the shape and size of the 3-surface X^3 as well as the Kähler field of $X^4(X^3)$. The spatio-temporal patterns of the induced Kähler field should correlate strongly with the contents of the conscious experience.

3.3 *The function of nerve pulses*

The identification of the sensory qualia in terms of the macroscopic quantum phases is in conflict with the general belief that neuronal activity determines the contents of the sensory experiences. In a TGD-framework one can understand the role of the nerve pulse activity differently. The brain is quantum spin glass and the evolution of sub-selves/mental images is a dissipative self-organization process leading to some asymptotic self-organization patterns which correspond to the valleys of the spin glass energy landscape. The contents of the sensory experiences are determined by the zero modes which in turn determine the ground state patterns of the order parameters of various macroscopic quantum phases.

The crucial element of the self-organization is external energy feed making possible interesting self-organization patterns. One role of the nerve pulses is to provide this metabolic energy feed. This suggests that the axons are seats of the self-organization patterns coding at least part of the neuronal experience. Myelin sheets guarantee that external perturbations do not affect the self-organization patterns.

In a TGD framework, nerve pulse patterns as such do not give rise to the sensory experience. This suggests that also primary sensory organs participate in the sensory experience. Various examples (hallucinations, experiences generated by the stimulation of the sensory pathways, the phantom leg phenomenon, dreams) suggest that the entire sensory pathway or at least the sub-cortical part of the sensory pathway is the seat of the primary sensory experience. It is quite possible and even plausible that the part of the sensory pathway giving rise to the sensory experience is dynamical since various parts of the sensory pathway can combine to sub-selves of a larger self or entangle to an irreducible self. If part of the sensory pathway is the primary experiencer, then conscious experience can precede the neural activity in the cortex as observed by Libet in his classical experiments concerning the timing of the sensory experiencing (Libet et al. 1979).

3.4 *Directed attention*

Directed attention is one of the basic cognitive processes occurring continually. Directed attention seems to involve free choice but focusing of attention could also occur spontaneously. The simplest model for the focusing of attention is as a wake-up of the sub-self and keeping it in wake-up state and hence in short-term memory. This could occur at the expense of the other sub-selves, which would be in a wake-up state for only short times. If selection is involved it would seem that the self is somehow able to induce a generation of strong entanglement for the potential subsystem so that it wakes up by a quantum jump. If the sub-selves in the complement of the selected sub-selves inside the self are entangled, they form kind of a background for a figure represented by the object of attention. If this picture is correct then the interpretation of quantum entanglement as a measure for unconscious attentiveness is sensical. The 7±2 rule of cognitive science suggests that the maximum number of our cognitive sub-selves which can be awake simultaneously is rather limited. The rule might be based on the metabolic limitations: sub-selves self-organize to interesting patters only in the presence of external energy feed and metabolism must provide the needed energy feed.

The self directs automatically its attention only to subsystems immediately below it in the hierarchy. It seems however possible to direct attention to lower levels of the self-hierarchy. For instance, I can direct my attention to the entire sentence that I am writing here, or to some word of this sentence, or to individual letters of this word. The phenomenon of bio-feedback demonstrates that it is possible to learn to direct the attention to even single neurons. This suggests that selves are able to modify the hierarchy of selves by raising some sub...sub-self to the role of sub-self temporarily and thus experience the former sub...sub-self as a direct mental image. The formation of a join along boundary bonds between cognitive space–time sheets at various levels of the self-hierarchy provides a general geometric mechanism making possible temporary changes of the structure of the self-hierarchy.

3.5 *Memories*

There are two times in TGD: subjective and geometric. In accordance with this there are also two kinds of memories: subjective and geometric.[7]

a. The temporal binding of the experiences associated with quantum jumps which occurred after the last "wake-up" of the self gives rise to subjective memory defined as a memory about earlier conscious experiences and is identifiable as conscious memory, presumably of a duration of a fraction of a second in case of sensory experiences. There is an infinite hierarchy of subjective memories and if long term memories are genuine subjective memories (this needs not be the case), they could correspond to conscious short term memories of higher level selves somehow communicated to the lower level.

b. Geometric memories are like a classical physics based model for the universe. They are memories with respect to geometric rather than subjective time and predict what must have happened in the geometric past and what will happen in the geometric future assuming that world is classical (no quantum jumps). The temporal extension of the cognitive space–time sheets and the notion of the association sequence (3-surfaces consisting of a sequence of space-like 3-surfaces with time-like separations providing a simulation of classical history) make possible geometric memories. A natural hypothesis is that the macroscopic space–time associated with the final state of the quantum jump represents the geometric memory. Of course, only part of it becomes conscious and temporal binding implies that the self experiences a kind of temporal average of the geometric memories associated with the quantum jumps.

An attractive possibility is that our long-term memories, which have narrative character and are unreliable, correspond to geometric memories. Learning by repetition would in this framework replicate given memory and would make more probable that it is re-experienced in multi-time experience. This means that a cognitive space–time sheet is generated with much greater probability in that part of the material space–time sheet which corresponds to the repeated events giving rise to the long term memory.

Intentionality manifests itself in many ways: as expectations of the future, planning, goals, desires, fears, imagination, intuition et cetera. It seems natural, and this is the only possibility given the fact that it is not possible to know anything about future quantum jumps, to identify all aspects of intentionality with the predictions of the expected geometric future provided by the cognitive space–time sheet. Geometry as such contains nothing intentional. Rather, the intentional aspects of the conscious experience reflect the attitudes towards the expectations provided by the geometric memory.

3.6 *Emotions*

The basic element of mentality is the comparison between the expectations of the future and what actually occurs. In the TGD framework this tension between potential and actual can be understood. Subjective and geometric memories make it possible to compare the expectations with what really occurred during the time interval since the subjective memory is a kind of heap of predictions for the future arranged with respect to the value of the psychological time. Many higher emotions such as happiness, feeling of relief, fear, envy, etc... clearly involve a comparison of expectations and reality. This could perhaps mean that these emotions are created by the comparison of the predicted or desired geometric time history and subjective time history (what really happened). This would mean that at least higher emotions differ from the sensory qualia, which seem to be determined solely by the localization into zero modes representing the non-quantum fluctuating aspects of space–time geometry.

It is difficult to assign any comparison to an emotion like deep love since it involves a complete acceptance of the object of love and is free of desires. Perhaps the claim of mystics that deep experience of love means that subject and object of love cease to exist as separate objects, makes sense. Lovers quantum entangle and die as separate selves (for some fraction of time only, of course!) and the higher self consisting of lovers experiences whole-body consciousness. Perhaps more mundane love means that my sub-selves representing me and the loved one entangle to form a sub-self experiencing whole-body consciousness. Perhaps also feelings like empathy belong to this class of emotions.

4. Solutions to some paradoxes

The TGD inspired theory of consciousness provides a solution to many paradoxes related to basic quantum physics and to the philosophy of conscious mind. The solution of these paradoxes is basically due to the replacement of the dualistic and monistic world views by the tripartistic world view of TGD.

4.1 *Paradoxes related to quantum physics*

The basic paradox is the conflict between the non-determinism of the state function reduction and the determinism of the Schrödinger equation. At a more general level this paradox is the conflict between the subjectively experienced actuality of the free will and the determinism of the objective world. The resolution of this paradox is simple in the TGD context. One must give up the idea of a single objective reality and replace it with a deterministic quantum history, which changes in each quantum jump, which is a genuine act of free will occurring outside the realm of the geometric space–time. Thus the objective reality, in the sense of a physical theory, is indeed deterministic, apart from the non-determinism related to the special properties of the Kähler action. In fact, a determinism of the Kähler action is achieved by replacing the ordinary concept of the 3-space with the concept of an association sequence and this naturally leads to a model for thinking systems. Volition seems to correspond to the selection between various degenerate absolute minima of the Kähler action and has thus a direct classical counterpart.

In the context of the deterministic physics, the theoretician encounters a rather unpleasant paradox. The determinism implies that the unique objective reality corresponds to a single solution of the field equations. The question is "What determines the initial conditions, say at the moment of the big bang?" The attempt to answer this question leads necessarily outside the physical theory: one possibility is to postulate an antrophic principle. In TGD, objective reality changes at each quantum jump and NMP implies a genuine evolution: therefore the recent objective reality is an outcome of conscious selections.

The famous Einstein-Bohr debate was related with the question whether God plays dice or not. In TGD context both were correct in their own ways. Quantum histories are indeed deterministic but God can replace the old quantum history with a new one: perhaps one should not however call this act dice playing but simply an act of free will. Einstein was also an advocate of local realism: this led to the Einstein-Podolski-Rosen paradox created by the possibility of quantum entanglement between distant systems. In a TGD framework local realism holds true at the level of the infinite-dimensional configuration space but not at the level of space–time since point like particles are replaced with 3-surfaces.

The Schrödinger cat paradox has also an elegant solution in TGD context. The point is that conscious experience is associated with a quantum jump leading to a final state in which the cat is either dead or alive. There is no conscious experience about the situation in which the cat is both dead and alive giving answer to the question "Dead or alive?". More generally, this feature of consciousness also could explain why the world of our conscious experience looks classical: it simply cannot look but classical since the very moment of consciousness makes it classical. In fact, the world is predicted to be genuinely classical to the extent that mutual quantum entanglement between different p–adic sub-Universes seems impossible for purely mathematical reasons. The localization into zero modes occurring in quantum jumps strengthens this conclusion considerably since it implies that the final states of quantum jumps are superpositions of macroscopically equivalent space–time surfaces: the world of conscious experience is genuinely classical.

The phenomenon of dissipation is paradoxal from the point of view of standard physics. It is generally accepted that the fundamental laws of classical physics are reversible whereas everyday reality is manifestly irreversible. Thus the situation is rather schizophrenic. Two worlds, the reversible and beautiful world of the fundamental physics and the irreversible and mathematically rather ugly "real" world, seem to exist simultaneously. The quantum jumps between quantum histories concept solves the paradox and one can understand the dissipative world as an effective description forming an 'almost'-envelope for the sequence of reversible worlds (time developments).

4.2 *Paradoxes related to the theories of consciousness*

Chalmers describes in his book 'Conscious Mind' (Chalmers 1996) several paradoxes related to the materialistic and dualistic theories of mind. A common denominator for these problems is the assumption that consciousness is a property of a physical state: hence these paradoxes disappear in TGD context. These paradoxes are encountered also in the quantum theories of consciousness identifying consciousness as a property of a macroscopic quantum state, say Bose Einstein condensate.

In the materialistic theories of mind, postulating a unique objective reality, consciousness is an epiphenomenon and free will is necessarily a peculiar illusion. One can always ask why consciousness is needed at all: nothing changes in physical reality if consciousness is dropped away. It is also very difficult to understand how the contents of consciousness are determined by the state of the material world.

In the dualistic theories postulating a unique objective reality (say the theory of Chalmers (1996)), the problems are related to the coupling between matter and mind. The basic problem of the dualistic theories is what Chalmers calls the 'hard problem': how do the physical processes in the brain give rise to conscious experience? If the laws of physics determine the behavior of the system completely then one ends up immediately either with a complete separation of mind and matter so that our conscious experience tells nothing about the material world or with materialism and epiphenomenalism. One can also consider a nontrivial coupling between matter and "mind like" fields, but assuming a deterministic physics one ends up with a situation in which the mind fields are effectively just additional physical fields and consciousness is again redundant.

An exotic example of this kind of paradox is the following one described in Chalmers (1996). In the dualistic theories in which the physical laws determine the objective reality, all psychological (third person) aspects of the mind are in principle purely physical. The book written by Chalmers about consciousness is obviously an example of a completely physical phenomenon. Therefore the contents of the book need not have anything to do with Chalmers's ideas about consciousness! More generally, the reports about the states of consciousness need not have anything to do with the states of consciousness in the dualistic theories of this kind. The only manner to save the day (and the uniqueness of the objective reality) is to accept materialism and epiphenomenalism.

In TGD framework, which could be called tripartistic, the hard problem and other problems of the dualistic theories disappear since there is no need to assign consciousness to quantum history. The moment of consciousness as quantum jump between quantum histories hypothesis allows even to define measures for the information contents of the conscious experience despite the fact that one cannot write explicit formulas for the contents of conscious experience.

Acknowledgments

I am grateful for John Henderson for very valuable help during the editing of the text and for enjoyable discussions and continual encouragement. During preparation of the text I had also very fruitful and inspiring discussions with Gene Johnson concerning the realization of the long-term memories and for Philip Loocke for very useful criticism and comments.

Notes

1. The notion of quantum jump is more general than the notion of state function collapse which suggests localization of the wavepacket.
2. From the TGD point of view the identification of the geometric time and the time coordinate appearing in the general Schrödinger equation of quantum field theories quantized using the Hamiltonian formalism is wrong. A Schrödinger equation is not even needed. The identification of the time coordinate of the Dirac equation as a geometric time however makes sense from TGD point of view.
3. This means that the variational principle in question must be more akin to the second law of thermodynamics rather than to the ordinary variational principles of physics.
4. Quantum histories can be regarded as superpositions of Boolean statements represented by many-fermion Fock states (fermion number $=1 \rightarrow$ true, fermion number $=-1 \rightarrow$ false), hence the logos–cosmos identification.
5. Information gain can be also negative.
6. Brain consciousness is predicted to be only a special type of consciousness.
7. The attribute 'subjective', as it is used in TGD context, does not have quite the same meaning as it usually has as something non-objective and unreliable: 'subjective' derives its meaning from 'subjective time' as consciously experienced time as opposed to the geometric time of physics.

References

Bierman, D., Radin, D. (1997) Anamalous anticipatory response on randomized future conditions. *Perceptual and motor skills,* 84, 689–690.

Bierman, D., Radin, D. (1998) Anamalous unconscious emotional repsonses: evidence for a reversal of the arrow of time, http: //wsww-psy.uva.nl/resedu/pn/PUBS/ BIERMAN/1998/tucson/tucson3/html.

Chalmers, D. (1996) *The conscious mind: in search of a fundamental theory,* New York: Oxford University Press.

Deeke, L., Goetzinger, B., Kornhuber, H., Voluntary finger movements in man: cerebral potentials and theory, *Biological Cybernetics,* 23, 99.

Hameroff, S., Penrose, R. (1996) Orchestrated reduction of quantum coherence in brain microtubules: a model for consciousness, in: *Toward a science of consciousness — the first Tucson Discussions and Debates,* in S. Hameroff, A. Kazniak and A. Scott (Eds.), MIT Press, Cambridge, pp. 507–540.

Henkel, J. (1998) How life learns: an epistemological basis for consciousness, http: //www.tiac.net/users/knowweb/lifern2.html.

Libet B., Wright, E., Feinstein, B., Pearl, D. (1979) Subjective referral of the timing for a conscious sensory experience, *Brain* 102: 193–224.

Penrose, R. (1989) *The emperor's new mind.* Oxford: Oxford University press.

Pitkänen, M. (1995a) Topological geometrodynamics, Internal report HU-TFT-IR-95-4 (helsinki University), http: //blues.helsinki.fi/~matpitka.

Pitkänen, M. (1995b) Topological Geometrodynamics and p-Adic numbers, Internal report HU-TFT-IR-95-5 (Helsinki University). Report on application of p-adic numbers in attempts to understand quantum field theory limit of TGD, http://blues.helsinki.fi/~matpitka.

Pitkänen, M. (1998) TGD inspired theory of consciousness with applications to biosystems, http: //blues.helsinki.fi/~matpitka/cbook.html.

Radin, D. (1997) Unconscious perception of future emotions: an experiment in presentiment. *Journal of Scientific Exploration,* 11(2): 163–180.

Sentman, D. (1985) Schumann resonances, in: H. Volland (ed.), *CRC Handbook of atmospheric electrodynamics.* Boca Raton, CRC Press. http: //sprite.gi.alaska.edu/schuchar.html.

What is it not Like to be a Brain?

Colin Mc Ginn

Abstract

The standard objection to materialism is inverted. It is argued that materialism fails to do justice to the nature of *matter*; it omits or distorts the distinctive character of physical phenomena. The symmetry of identity plays a crucial role in the argument.

1. Introduction

Materialism is the thesis that facts about the mind are entirely reducible to facts about the brain. To be in pain, say, is to have one's C-fibres firing or for this brain state to realize a physically defined functional role. The usual objection to materialism, expressed in many different forms, is that it fails to do justice to the nature of the mind; it omits or distorts the distinctive character of mental phenomena. In this paper I shall *not* be pressing this objection to materialism. Instead, I shall invert the standard objection and argue that materialism fails to do justice to the nature of *matter*; it omits or distorts the distinctive character of physical phenomena. The symmetry of identity will play a crucial role in this argument.

2. The mental and the physical

Let me begin by listing a familiar set of characteristics commonly ascribed to mental phenomena which are held to set the mind apart from the physical world. (My 'mental phenomena' I shall primarily mean conscious states and processes.) The list is eclectic and not uncontroversial; my intention is not to supply a full defence of it, but only to provide a foil for my own argument. The mind is held to be:

1. Unobservable — in the sense that mental states are not perceptible by means of the senses.
2. Asymmetrically accessible — in the sense that the owner of a mental state has a kind of immediate access to it that other people do not.
3. Subjective — in the sense that its nature is knowable only from a single "point of view" (Nagel 1979, 1986).
4. Nonspatial — in the sense that mental states do not take up a well-defined region of space.[1]
5. Subject-dependent — in the sense that mental states only exist for a subject of awareness.[2]

The usual claim, then, is that physical phenomena, such as brain states, do not exhibit these features, and hence cannot satisfactorily reduce mental states. Suppose the materialist maintains that pain is identical to C-fibre firing, so that there is nothing more to the state of being in pain than having one's C-fibres fire. The firing of C-fibres has the following characteristics: it is observable by means of the sense organs; it is accessible to oneself and others in the same way; it is objective in that it can be grasped from any point of view, not necessarily that of a pain-feeler; it is spatially defined; it could in principle exist without being experienced by a subject. The objection, accordingly, is that C-fibres are just the wrong kind of thing to identify with pain. If there were really nothing more to pain talk than C-fibres firing, then there would be no pain after all, since pain is defined by the opposite set of characteristics. The putative reduction would amount to a form of elimination. Of course, this line of argument would be disputed by a materialist at various points, but prima facie it would seem that the anti-reductionist at least has a case that needs to be answered. The distinctive character of the mental certainly appears to be lost under such a reduction. It needs to be explained why it is that the reduction does not omit or distort the intrinsic nature of the mental. Let me summarise this objection by saying that materialism makes the subjective too objective. I shall take it that this is a familiar story, in one or another version.

3. The symmetry of identity

The logical properties of identity statements have played a significant role in the defence and criticism of materialism. Thus the epistemic contingency and metaphysical necessity of identity statements such as 'pain = C-fibre firing' have figured heavily in these debates.[3] I want to draw attention to the least controversial property of the identity relation: its symmetry. This property allows us to say that if pain = C-fibre firing, then C-fibre firing = pain. And just as the truth of such an identity statement licenses us to say that there is nothing more to pain than C-fibre firing, so it licenses us to say that there is nothing more to C-fibre firing than pain. For C-fibre firing simply *is* pain, neither more nor less. If A = B, then there is nothing more to A than B *and* vice versa. C-fibre firing is not anything over and above pain. It has no properties not possessed by pain. It reduces to pain, collapses into it. It consists of pain. It has no reality beyond that of pain. C-fibre firing is constituted by pain. Pain is what C-fibre firing turns out to *be*. The *essence* of C-fibre firing is pain.

But surely this sounds wrong: one wants to say that such an identification fails to do justice to the objectivity of C-fibre firing. If C-fibre firing were really nothing but pain, then it would not be observable, symmetrically accessible, conceivable from many points of view, spatial and subject-independent. The identification makes the objective too subjective. It has the flavour of an elimination, not a reality-preserving reduction. If the reduction were correct, then C-fibre firing would not be an objective property of the world after all, contrary to the appearances. The case is quite unlike, say, the identification of molecular motion with heat: here there is no strain in saying that molecular motion amounts to nothing but heat, since heat is not itself a subjective phenomenon. The objectivity of molecular motion is preserved in this reduction, whereas in the case of identifying C-fibre firing with pain we have an attempt to characterize an objective property in subjective terms.

Thus the inversion permitted by the symmetry of identity results in an implausible reduction of the objective to the subjective — a loss of objectivity in the property we started out with. It might be thought that this argument works only on condition that the reductionism takes the form of an identity claim. What if the reduction is formulated in terms of composition?[4]

Suppose we say that water is composed of H_2O molecules; we cannot then symmetrically say that H_2O molecules are composed of water — yet such a claim permits a thesis of reduction of water to H_2O molecules. Thus we might analogously maintain that pain is (wholly) composed of the firings of C-fibres without committing ourselves to the converse claim. This certainly avoids the simple move from symmetry that I made against the identity formulation of reductionism, but I think that parallel problems beset the composition formulation too. First, if water is composed of H_2O molecules, then H_2O molecules are constituents or parts of water; equally C-fibre firings must be constituents or parts of pain if they compose pain. But how could something be literally a *part* of pain without being itself subjective? Consider a more familiar part-whole relation in respect of pain: I experience a complex pain resulting from banging my elbow against something hot. We might say that the resulting pain has both a collision component and a burn component; but these parts of my complex pain are clearly themselves subjective. If anything is a part of a subjective state, and not merely part of the neural correlate of that state, then it has to be subjective too. The claim is that pain is composed of nothing but C-fibre firings, but then C-fibre firings have to be the very elements that constitute pain, and hence must share its subjectivity. Just as a part of something objective must be objective, so a part of something subjective must be subjective. We would never allow that a putatively objective property might be wholly constituted by subjective elements, so why dispense a comparable leniency in the other direction?

Secondly, we can always derive an identity statement from a claim of composition. If X is composed of Fs, then there is some Y that is an aggregation of Fs such that Y = X. If water is composed of H_2O molecules, then there an aggregation of those molecules such that that aggregation is identical to water. Water is not merely composed of H_2O molecules singly considered; it also *is* a collection of such molecules: it is identical to the aggregate of the elements that compose it. But then pain must be identical to the aggregate of the C-fibre firings that compose it, which is to say that that aggregate is identical to pain. This implies that (suitable) aggregates of C-fibre firings are as subjective as pains. When you put the C-fibre firings together you get something that is nothing over and above a pain. But surely an aggregate of objective elements should itself be an objective entity. Composition is not symmetrical, but it generates a symmetrical relation via the operation of aggregation. Again, the objective is collapsing into the subjective. So composition does not help the reductionist escape the argument. From now on, then, I shall persist with the simpler identity formulation.

4. Mentalism and reduction

A good way to get a feel for what I am arguing is to consider an imaginary school of philosophers who adopt a wholesale reduction of the objective to the subjective. These philosophers, call them 'mentalists', are troubled by the notion of objectivity; they find it hard to understand how there can be irreducible objective physical facts. Perhaps they think that the idea of such facts require an 'absolute conception' that abstracts totally aware from their specific sensory point of view, and they cannot see how we could acquire such transcendent concepts.[5]

Objectivity requires a "view from nowhere", and they cannot conceive of such a detached view of the world. In any case, they find the idea of objective facts problematic, for whatever reason. Yet they are not eliminativist, at least not officially: they agree that there really are objects that are square and electrically charged and made of neurons. They agree too that such facts can obtain whether or not they are being perceived by us (or by God); the mentalists are not idealists. What they insist is that every such fact is identical to a subjective fact. When an object is square, for example, they hold that this consists in the object's having a certain conscious state: there is something it is like to be square *for* the object. So-called objective properties are reducible to subjective properties, by way of suitable identity statements. They may not always know *which* subjective property a given objective property reduces to, but they are confident that there always is one. Every physical property is identical to a *quale* of some sort, known or unknown. This mentalistic metaphysics is different from panpsychism: panpsychism says that every object has some mental property, in addition to its physical properties; mentalism says that every physical property of every object is itself mental. There is no fact there is not something it is like to have.

What should we say about this startling mentalist doctrine? The obvious objection to it is that it is a reduction that signally fails to do justice to the objective physical world as we ordinarily understand it. If such a reduction were correct, then physical properties like being square or electrically charged would turn out to be unobservable, asymmetrically accessible, subjective, nonspatial and subject-dependent — given that mental states have these defining characteristics. Such properties would turn out to have all the proprietary features of the mental: they would be unobservable inner states of a subject of consciousness, not the publically accessible objective properties we naively take them to be. And that is objectionably eliminativist, no matter what the official line of the mentalists may be. (One can imagine all the fancy footwork they would have to do in order to fend off the objection that we can *see* that being square is not an unobservable mental state just be looking at a square object. Compare the objection that we can see that a pain isn't C-fibre firing just by introspecting our pains.)

But if global mentalism of this kind is guilty of denying the objectivity of the physical, then surely local mentalism is too, albeit more narrowly. It is just as implausible to suggest that *some* physical properties are really mental as that all are. The global mentalists in effect treat physical terms as if they are natural kind terms for properties that will turn out to have a subjective essence — analogously to the way materialists take mental terms to be natural kind terms for properties that will turn out to have an objective essence. But local mentalists are really no better off: they take some physical terms — those for (some) brain states — to be natural kind terms for properties that will turn out to have a subjective essence. But this involves an implausibly subjectivist interpretation of an objective property, sacrificing all the objective features we naively ascribe to such properties. The subjectivist sin is not any less because it is localized. (Compare: some moral 'oughts' are reducible to naturalistic facts and some are not.) But local mentalism is the *same doctrine* as materialism, by the symmetry of identity, since materialists precisely hold that some physical properties can be identified with subjective properties. They hold, for example, that C-fibre firing in the brain is identical to a sensation of pain felt by a conscious subject, and has no characteristics beyond those of pain. They hold that a physical property consists in a property defined by what it is like for its owner.

The trouble with materialism, ironically enough, is that it is not materialist enough about matter. It makes some pockets of matter too subjective in nature. It has essentially the same fault as global mentalism — a failure to respect the intrinsic objectivity of physical properties.

5. A problem for localized materialism

Let me incidentally note how odd the localized character of materialism is when seen for what it is. Offhand one might have thought that all physical properties are on a par, none having a fundamentally different essence from the others. But according to materialism some physical properties have a subjective essence while some do not. And it is not merely that physical states of the kidneys don't have a subjective essence while states of the brain do; some states of the brain itself have a subjective essence while some do not — despite the fact that all brain states consist of neurons and their firings. Not every brain state has a "correlated" mental state. Whence this strange violation of the uniformity of nature? Induction would suggest that all neural states have a purely objective essence, since so many do; but when we come to a particular subset of them we allegedly find that they have a subjective essence. It is like discovering that some molecular motion is heat and some is not, despite the uniformity of the molecules and their motions. That would seem arbitrary and miraculous. But materialism finds itself coutenancing something equally arbitrary and miraculous — the fact that some physical states but not others reduce to mental states. At the very least we need to be told what it is about this remarkable subset of physical states that makes them alone reducible to subjective states. Once we permit a robust notion of subjectivity this must seem a pressing question.

6. Parallels with arguments surrounding materialist reduction

I now want to briefly consider some instructive parallels with the usual arguments surrounding materialist reduction.

1. *What it is like*. Thomas Nagel argued that there is something it is like to undergo conscious experience, and that this something is accessible only to those beings who enjoy similar experiences (Nagel 1979, 1986). He then argued that brain states are not defined in such terms; they are accessible from a variety of experiential standpoints. Hence the claim of reduction is flawed: we cannot find a place for the subjective in our objective conception of the world, including the brain. Inverting this, I insist that it is part of the very definition of a physical state of the brain that it is objective, in the sense that it is knowable by beings with the right intelligence irrespective of the particular types of experience they enjoy, so that we cannot reduce such states to states bearing the marks of subjectivity. Just as it is important that there is something it is like to be a bat, so it is important that there is nothing it is like to have a bat's brain: that is, it is important that bat brain states are objective properties of the world. We do not want to collapse bat brain states into purely inner processes. Indeed, if we did we would not know what properties the bat's brain has, since we do not know what kinds of experience it has — which is absurd. If facts about bat brains are identical to facts about what it is like to be a bat, then such facts are not knowable without sharing the subjectivity of a bat — i.e. they are subjective facts. But they are not subjective facts, since the neurophysiology of bats is knowable by beings other than bats. Thus the objectivity of a bat's brain is just as inconsistent with materialist reduction as the subjectivity of its experience is. Either we deny the subjectivity of the experience in order to sustain the reduction to brain states, or we deny the objectivity of the brain in order to conform to the subjectivity of experience. If Nagel is right about the inherent subjectivity of experience, as I think he is, then materialism results in a denial of the objectivity of matter. The B-fibres that are identified with the bat's subjective experience will turn out to have all the subjectivity of those experiences, and nothing more.

2. *The knowledge argument*. Frank Jackson's Mary is said to know all the physical facts without being thereby apprised of all the facts about the mind; she cannot deduce subjective facts from her comprehensive knowledge of objective facts (Jackson 1982, 1986). When Mary emerges from her black-and-white room armed with complete knowledge of neurophysiology she learns something new when she first enjoys an experience of red. So what she learns was not prefigured in what she already knew. Hence materialism is not a complete theory of the mind. Now consider Maisie: she knows all the phenomenal facts — all the

facts about her own mental states and their interrelations. She spends the early years of her life floating in a vat enjoying her own phenomenology, thinking about her experiences, classifying them, revelling in them. There is little outside distraction from her inner world; specifically, she is taught no physics, including neurophysiology. One day she is removed from her phenomenological vat and forced to learn physics. In the course of her studies, at which she proves remarkably adept, she learns all about her brain, including the correlates of the phenomenal states she knows so well. Does she thereby learn anything new? She used only to know what experiences of red were like; now she also knows all about the R-fibres that underlie these experiences. Well, it certainly seems like she learns a new fact — that she has R-fibres that correlate with her familiar old experience of red. Moreover, she learns a fact of a new kind — an objective fact, as distinct from a subjective phenomenal fact. Therefore R-fibres cannot be identical with experiences of red. Just as subjective facts cannot be deduced from objective facts, this creating a knowledge gap, so objective facts cannot be deduced from subjective facts, this also creating a knowledge gap. The gap is as large whichever direction you approach it from. Maisie is as ignorant as Mary before both their life-styles change. (Of course, there are replies to the knowledge argument, which I will not go into here,[6] and replies to these replies, but my point is just that the argument cuts both ways.)

3. *What God had to do*. Saul Kripke maintains that when God created pain he had to do more than create C-fibre firing — whereas to create heat it sufficed to create molecular motion (Kripke 1980). At least that is our strong intuition. If the intuition is correct, then the mind is not necessarily supervenient on the brain. Pain must be something over above C-fibre firing. Accordingly, zombies are conceivable: beings in some possible world who share our physical properties but differ from us in having no mental states at all.[7] There is a modal and ontological gap between C-fibres and pain, marked by the tasks God had to perform to make a world like ours. But it is no less intuitive to make the opposite point: in order to create C-fibres it was not enough for God to create pain — he had some additional work to do in order to bring C-fibres into the world. Accordingly, mental states do not logically determine physical states: there is a lack of supervenience here, and disembodiment seems logically conceivable. That is, after having created pain it was up to God (i) *what* physical state to correlate with it and (ii) whether to correlate *any* physical state with it. There is thus a modal and ontological gap between pain and C-fibres, marked by the extra effort involved in producing the latter after producing the former. The arguments are exactly parallel.

Now it is not that I myself subscribe to either of these arguments: I actually believe that the connexions here are necessary despite our modal intuitions to the contrary.[8] What I am saying is that the arguments are exactly parallel, so that anyone who accepts them one way round has to ask whether to accept them the other way round. In particular, those who believe in the possibility of zombies need to ask whether they also believe in the possibility of disembodied minds.

4. *The epistemic interpretation.* A standard reply to the above anti-reductionist arguments is that they confuse ontology with epistemology.[9] Our *concepts* of pain and C-fibre firing may indeed be distinct, but it does not follow that they denote distinct *properties*; and mental properties may be reducible to physical properties without the concepts that denote them being reducible to physical concepts. The idea is that 'subjective' and 'objective' are predicates that apply to properties or facts only under certain descriptions or concepts. A property P might be subjective under the description 'pain' and objective under the description 'C-fibre firing'. The ontological gap that seems to separate the subjective from the objective is really just an epistemic gap between the *concept* of pain and the *concept* of C-fibre firing, not a gap between the properties themselves.

Now a lot can be said about this form of reply, but I want to make only one point relevant to the argument of this paper.[10] The epistemic reply to the claim that materialist reduction fails to do justice to the nature of the subjective is that pain is only subjective as so described; it is subjective *de dicto* but not *de re*. When we redescribe pain as C-fibre firing we can see that it is really an objective property in itself (*de re*). The characteristics I listed at the beginning as distinctive of the mind belong to it only under a mental description — they apply to pain only *de dicto*. In effect, they all generate opaque contexts. But if this is true of the subjective it must also be true of the objective: properties are only objective under certain descriptions, and never *de re*.

When I redescribe C-fibre firing as pain it ceases to be objective, save relative to that physical description. C-fibre firing is only objective under a description and not in itself. And similarly for any other apparently objective property: we cannot say that having an electrical charge is objective *de re* but only that it is objective *de dicto*, since the notion of objectivity is being interpreted merely epistemically. If I think of an electrical charge under the description 'that which causes pain in humans', then I consign it to the class of subjective facts. According to this view, it makes no sense to attribute objectivity (or subjectivity) to states of affairs in themselves. We cannot even say that a universe in which there are no minds contains purely objective facts, unless reference is made to our current concepts. This seems very odd. Surely it is an inherent intrinsic *de re* fact that physical states in general are objective states, in the sense I spelled out at the beginning. It is not that they *become* objective only when we decide to describe them in a certain way. It is absurd to suggest, say, that physical objects are only spatial under a description and not in themselves. It is in the very nature of physical facts that they are objective.

The point I am making is that materialists implicitly adopt an invidious attitude towards the subjective and the objective: they are only too happy to assert that properties are subjective only under a certain description, but the parallel move for objectivity looks distinctly unappealing once its implications are appreciated. Yet it is this move that is necessary if we are going to object to my argument by saying that C-fibres can be objective under that description but not under the description 'pain'. That is no way to protect the robust objectivity of physical facts. The plain truth is that if pain is allowed to be robustly subjective, in the *de re* sense, then identifying C-fibre firing with pain results in divesting this physical process of its vaunted objectivity. This objectivity cannot be plausibly restored by retreating to the thesis that C-fibre firing is objective only *de dicto* — on pain of making all objective facts similarly weakly objective. So the epistemic interpretation fails to deliver a robust notion of objectivity, just as it fails to provide a robust sense of subjectivity. The latter is tolerable to a materialist, given his ontological biases; but the former is surely highly unpalatable to the materialist.

There are three options here: (i) the characteristic marks of subjectivity or objectivity are not possessed at all, so that we end up with eliminativism either about the subjective or the objective; (ii) these characteristics are possessed only in the *de dicto* sense, so that we end up denying that anything can be subjective *or* objective in itself; (iii) we allow that properties can be subjective or objective *de re*, so that we end up either distorting the nature of the subjective *or* (the plaint of this paper) distorting the nature of objectivity. Assuming that we want to avoid eliminativism, we have the result that you cannot be an identity theorist who respects the robustness of subjectivity *and* respects the robustness of objectivity. If you identify a physical property with a genuinely mental property, then you cannot avoid an unacceptable subjectivization of the objective. The trouble with materialism is that it does not take the objectivity of matter seriously enough, despite its overt intentions.

7. Conclusion

What should we conclude from this discussion? I think we can conclude that classic type-identity materialism is false, either the central state version or physicalistic functionalism (and behaviourism). But I do not think we can conclude either that mental states are irreducible or that there are merely contingent connexions between mental states and brain states. Maybe mental states are reducible to something that does not have the marks of full-blown objectivity, unlike C-fibre firing and its kin. Maybe new properties could be discovered that both reduce mental states and are not themselves objective; and even if they could not be discovered they might nevertheless exist.[11]

And there may be necessary connexions between pain and C-fibre firing even though it is not possible to *identify* the two; these may be distinct properties that are noncontingently connected. The nature of the necessary links might be hidden and not be inferable from our current concepts, but they might exist anyway (McGinn 1991, 1997). So nothing I have said entails a rejection of supervenience or an acceptance of irreducibly mental properties. The correct view of the mind-body relation is left open by what I have argued. All I have contended is that the usual kinds of materialistic identity theory are committed to an unacceptably subjective conception of the physical world. As Kripke remarked after presenting his own modal argument against the identity theory, the mind-body problem is 'wide open and extremely confusing'.[12]

Notes

1. I discuss the nonspatiality of the mind in McGinn (1995)
2. John Searle (1992) expresses this point by saying that conscious states have "first-person ontology"
3. On the epistemic contingency of psychophysical identity statements see J. J. C. Smart (1959). On the metaphysical necessity of identity statements see Saul Kripke (1980)
4. Thomas Nagel suggested that I consider this line of defence.
5. On the availability of the "absolute conception" see: Bernard Williams (1978), Nagel (1986) and Mc Ginn (1982).
6. I make a few remarks about one standard reply below. For a much fuller discussion see my 'How not to Solve the Mind-Body Problem', forthcoming in a collection on physicalism edited by Barry Loewer (Cambridge University Press: 2000).
7. See David Chalmers (1996), in which the alleged conceivability of zombies plays a pivotal role.
8. On the idea of hidden necessary connexions see my *The Problem of Consciousness* (1991), esp. pp. 19–21, and my review of Chalmers in my *Minds and Bodies* (1997).
9. For example, Paul Churchland (1998). For a different version of this line see Brian Loar (1998)
10. The obvious question is what *makes* concepts different if not the properties they express: see my 'How not to Solve the Mind-Body Problem' (2000) for more on this.
11. I believe, for reasons not entered into in this paper, that the most likely hypothesis is that the properties that are needed to solve the mind-body problem are in principle inaccessible to the

human mind; my present point is just that a reduction *might* exist that we shall never discover. See my *The Problem of Consciousness* (1991) for a discussion of the insolubility thesis.

12. Kripke, (1980), p. 155, note 77.

References

Chalmers, D. (1996) *The Conscious Mind,* Oxford University Press.

Churchland, P. (1998) 'Knowing Qualia: A Reply to Jackson', reprinted in P.M Churchland and P. S. Churchland, *On the Contrary.* Cambridge, MIT Press.

Jackson, F. (1982) Epiphenomenalism and Qualia. *Philosophical Quarterly,* 1982, XXXII: 127–136.

Jackson, F. (1986) What Mary Didn't Know. *Journal of Philosophy* LXXXIII, 291–295.

Kripke, S. (1980) *Naming and Necessity.* Cambridge, Harvard University Press.

Loar, B. (1998) 'Phenomenal States.' In N. Block, O. Flanagan and G. Guzeldere (eds.) *The Nature of Consciousness.* Cambridge, MIT Press.

McGinn, C. (1982) *The Subjective View.* Oxford University Press.

McGinn, C. (1991) *The problem of consciousness.* Oxford, Basil Blackwell.

McGinn, C. (1995) Consciousness and Space. In Metzinger, T. (ed.) *Conscious Experience.* Imprint Academic.

McGinn, C. (1997) *Minds and bodies.* New York: Oxford University Press.

McGinn, C. (1999) How not to Solve the Mind-Body Problem. In Loewer, B. (ed.) *Physicalism.* Cambridge University Press: 2000 (to appear).

Nagel, T. (1979) What is it Like to be a Bat?, reprinted in *Mortal Questions.* Cambridge University Press.

Nagel, T. (1986) *The View From Nowhere.* Oxford University Press.

Smart, J. (1959) Sensations and Brain Processes, *Philosophical Review* LXVII, 141–156.

Searle, J. (1992) *The Rediscovery of the Mind.* Cambridge, MIT Press.

Williams, B. (1978) Descartes: *The Project of Pure Enquiry.* Harmondsworth, Penguin Books.

On the nature of anamalous phenomena

Another reality between the world of subjective consciousness and the objective world of physics?

Dick J. Bierman

Abstract

Cumulating evidence suggests that anomalous correlations occur between mental (conscious and non-conscious) states and apparently unrelated physical or mental phenomena at a distance in space and time. In spite of the fact that the evidence is very strong, these correlations are difficult to replicate. Several examples are given of 'failures' to empirically replicate[1] original anomalies. It is speculated that this failure to replicate, rather than indicating that the original findings are due to statistical flukes or errors, suggests that when consciousness interacts with matter, an underlying reality arises. This reality is somewhere in between the purely objective shareable reality and the purely subjective reality of one's individual consciousness. Efforts to 'push' anomalous phenomena observed in this intermediate reality into the objective one apparently destroy the phenomena. Possible explanations within a physical and within a system theoretical model are discussed. The physical model is based upon an analysis of the role of consciousness in the so-called 'Measurement Problem' in Quantum Physics. Based upon these discussions a new systematic experimental approach for the study of anomalous phenomena is suggested.

1. Introduction

History is replete with accounts of so-called psychic phenomena like telepathy or precognition. The use of oracles during Greek civilization is just one example to illustrate that belief in the reality of these phenomena was widespread for millennia. However with the advent of modern western science and especially with the success of physics and derived disciplines in explaining and controlling natural phenomena, belief in, and serious study of such 'unexplainable' phenomena has generally been viewed as superstitious or even as anti-scientific behaviour.

The findings of experimental psychology seem to support this view. Human memory is extremely fallible as has been demonstrated by research on the false-memory syndrome (Loftus 1997). As suggested long ago by William James by his statement: ... *whilst part of what we perceive comes through our senses from the object before us, another part (and maybe the larger part) always comes out of our head* (William James 1890), perception is now generally seen as a constructive process and perceptual experience only partly reflects objective reality (Gordon 1996). Thus human accounts of spontaneous or natural events are not acceptable as objective scientific evidence.

Nevertheless, during the last 100 years, a limited number of scholars have persisted in serious study of the alleged paranormal. Confronted with the shortcomings of personal accounts and the fact that deception and fraud were unavoidable outside of a well-controlled environment, most serious work was done within experimental laboratories.

It is fair to say that not many scientists share Dennett's opinion that consciousness 'has been explained' already. The growth of interest in what arguably is the most complex scientific topic has brought about a renewed interest in paranormal (psi) phenomena that, if real, would pose strong constraints on any comprehensive theory of mind. To illustrate this point, Dennett's Multiple Drafts model (Dennett 1991) is not capable of explaining precognition because precognition is a violation of temporal causal principles while Dennett's model is purely causal.

Dennett's confidence nonwithstanding, decades of cumulating laboratory evidence strongly suggests that real correlations exist between mental states and randomized events that are distant in space and time, some even in the future. The laboratory findings are generally weaker than those reported from the field and because of the experimental paradigms used, they are basically statistical in nature. In other words large number of trials is needed to reach statistical significance. What is worse is that it is difficult to replicate the phenomena even when allowing for their intrinsic statistical character. Because of the claimed transcendental nature of the phenomena, the experimenter is an intrinsic part of the experiment and therefore replication from one experimenter to another is not expected to be easily accomplished. Replication by independent scientists is of course the requirement for a phenomenon to be considered objective and real. Therefore the controversy about the reality of these phenomena continues in spite of the cumulating evidence. In this chapter we will try to formulate a theoretical position which assimilates both points of view.

2. The database of experimental parapsychology

In a review article in *Statistical Science*, Utts argued that for four different parapsychological paradigms there is overwhelming meta-analytic evidence for the occurrence of anomalous correlations between either mental states of separated people, or mental states and some objective material state (Utts 1991).

The first paradigm concerns the so-called Ganzfeld telepathy experiments. In these double blind experiments one participant (*the Receiver*) is brought to a slightly altered state of consciousness (hypnagogic state) and reports his/her experiences while at a remote location another participant (*the Sender*) is looking at a picture or video-clip (the target) randomly picked out of a pool of many such pictures or clips. After half an hour *the Receiver* is shown a copy of the actual target along with three decoys, in random order, and is requested to pick the actual target. The probability for the participant picking the actual target is thus 1/4. Utts reports two meta-analysis with mean effect sizes of 0.28 (experiments from 1970–1985) and 0.20 (for the 11 automated series performed between 1983–1990). These effect sizes are quite unlikely to occur by chance as can be seen in the column 'associated p value' of Table 1.

The second paradigm that Utts reviews concerns card guessing experiments. A meta-analysis of all precognitive card-guessing experiments from 1935–1987 shows a mean effect size of 0.033. Although this effect size is much smaller than the ones reported for the Ganzfeld paradigm the statistical significance is impressive due to the large number of trials involved. The third and fourth paradigm for which meta-analyses were done are of the so-called mind-over-matter kind. Participants are asked to 'influence' the behavior of electronic Random Number Generators (based on quantum mechanical noise). The mean effect size in the 597 studies reviewed was only 0.00032 but the total result was still quite significant. Finally 148 studies designed to test whether or not a conscious intention to influence the outcome of tossing dice, biases the outcome distribution of dice throwing were reviewed. Here the over-all effectsize was 0.0122. A review of her findings is presented in the first 5 rows of table 1.

An omission in Utts' review of 'convincing' parapsychological meta-analyses concerns a research program by the Mind-Science laboratory that lasted from the late seventies to the early nineties (Braud & Schlitz 1991). The major research effort was concentrated on the effect of distant attention on remote biological

Table 1. *A review of important meta-analytic results used to argue the reality of psi-phenomena*

Paradigm	*Mean effect size*	*Associated p-value*	*Original publication*
Mind over Matter Dice	0.0122	$\sim 10^{-14}$ (z=7.617)	Radin & Ferrari (1991)
Ganzfeld telepathy (1972–1985)	0.28	3.37×10^{-11}	Rosenthal (1986)
Ganzfeld telepathy automatic (~1990)	0.20	5×10^{-5}	Bem & Honorton (1994)
Card Guessing (precognition)	0.033	6.3×10^{-25}	Honorton & Ferrari (1989)
Mind over Matter RNG's	0.00032	$\sim 5 \times 10^{-5}$ (z=4.1)	Radin & Nelson (1989)
Mind over Matter Biological systems	0.33	2.85×10^{-14}	Braud & Schlitz (1991)

systems and the over-all results were again highly significant (see last row Table 1).

It should be stressed that, according to Utts, normal 'explanations' for these significant findings like selective publication or methodological errors were ruled out. Thus, from these findings, the case for the reality of so-called psi phenomena looks very strong. However a closer look at the data reveals an intriguing sequential structure known as the 'decline effect' (see figure 8).

3. The decline effect

Originally the label 'decline effect' was used to describe decreasing performance of subjects when doing a sequence of trials. Actually the decline in performance was generally followed by a rebound in performance when the end of the run of trials approached. Rhine used the position effects that were established *post hoc* as an argument for the reality of the psi effect (Rhine 1969). The position effects then were attributed to intervening psychological variables like motivation and boredom. However it soon became clear that apart from sequential effects within a run of trials it was quite difficult to exactly 'replicate' (see footnote 1) the results of original studies: a sequence of similar studies tended to show a decline of effect size from study to study.

3.1 *Dice throwing studies*

As a first example we consider the meta-analytical results of Radin & Ferrari (Radin & Ferrari 1991) concerning dice-throwing experiments. These experiments started in the thirties based upon anecdotal evidence that some people were consistently more lucky when throwing dice than others. Using dice throwing devices Rhine and other researchers tried to test the idea that these individual differences were due to difference in psychokinetic abilities. A regression plot of the normalized (z) score of each of these studies versus year reveals a steady decline with a regression coefficient of −0.053 ($p = 0.0020$).[2]

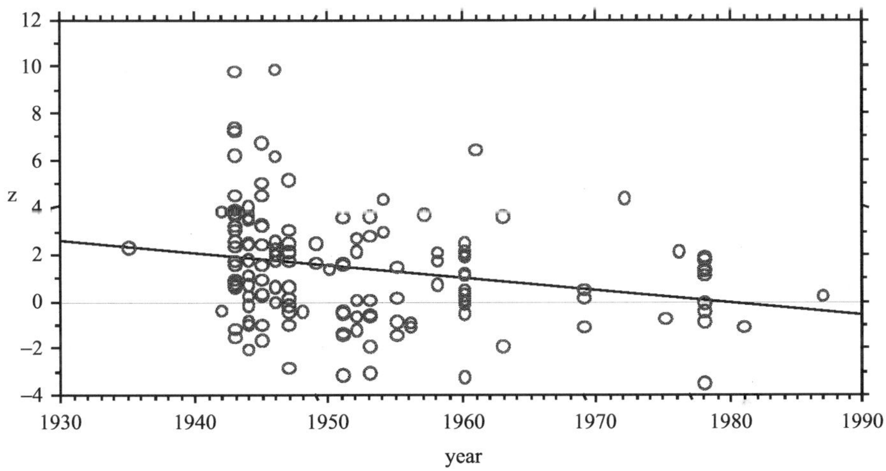

Figure 1. *Regression plot of normalized scores versus year of all dice throwing studies*

3.2 *Ganzfeld studies*

The first Ganzfeld ESP studies were done in the early seventies and continue to date. These experiments were used for the first meta-analysis ever done on psi experiments (Honorton 1985). This meta-analysis eventually resulted in a joint report of a well-known sceptic of the paranormal and a major psi researcher in the field of ganzfeld studies (Hyman & Honorton 1986). In the report both authors concluded that the over-all results differed from chance expectation, but there remained a difference of opinion about the interpretation of this difference. Some recommendations were made to standardize procedures and eliminate potential methodological weaknesses. In 1994 a second review was published in a main stream journal concerning a series of studies that had followed closely the prescriptions described in the joint report (Bem & Honorton 1994). Although these results did globally confirm the earlier meta-analysis, a closer inspection yielded some findings that put the claimed replicability into question. The earlier 1985 meta-analysis concerned ganzfeld experiments with static targets having a mean scoring rate of about 33%. However the 1994 data were a mixture of static and dynamic targets also yielding a mean scoring rate of about 33%. When using the results for static targets alone the scoring rate in the 1994 analyses dropped to a non significant 28% level. Thus there was an indication of a decline in scoring rate when the analyses were restricted to comparable experiments.

Also the 1994 analysis was performed on the results of only one research-group although many more experiments had been done by other researchers in the period from 1985. A regression plot (Figure 2) of ALL studies from the early 1970's to 1994 revealed a steady and significant decline in effectsize with a regression coefficient of −0.027 ($p=0.022$) (see Bierman 1995).[3]

Not only was there a steady decline in scoring rate but also the variance in the experimental outcomes declined considerably. There is strong difference in variance between the pre-1985 studies and the post-1985 studies ($F=4.903$, $df1=27$, $df2=14$, $p=0.018$). Adding the recent data from 1994 to 1997 decreases the regression coefficient to −0.017 but increases the statistical significance of this decline considerably ($p=0.0013$).

A rather spectacular example of the decline in effectsize in ganzfeld experiments happened when in 1995 two independent groups, one from Durham NC, the other from Amsterdam, published the data of the first part of their respective ganzfeld series (Broughton & Alexander 1995; Bierman 1995). The over-all hit rates were: 33% (N=100) and 38.2% (N=76). One year later the series were finished with the following astonishing figures for the second part: Durham 13.7% (N=51) and Amsterdam: 15.6% (N=32) (Broughton & Alexander 1996; Wezelman & Bierman 1997). Thus results of the first and second part of both series differed significantly between the years while within the same year the groups replicated each other as if some outside factor in 1996 had influenced both groups to go from hitting into missing (Figure 3).

Recently a new meta-analysis on Ganzfeld experiments up to 1998 was

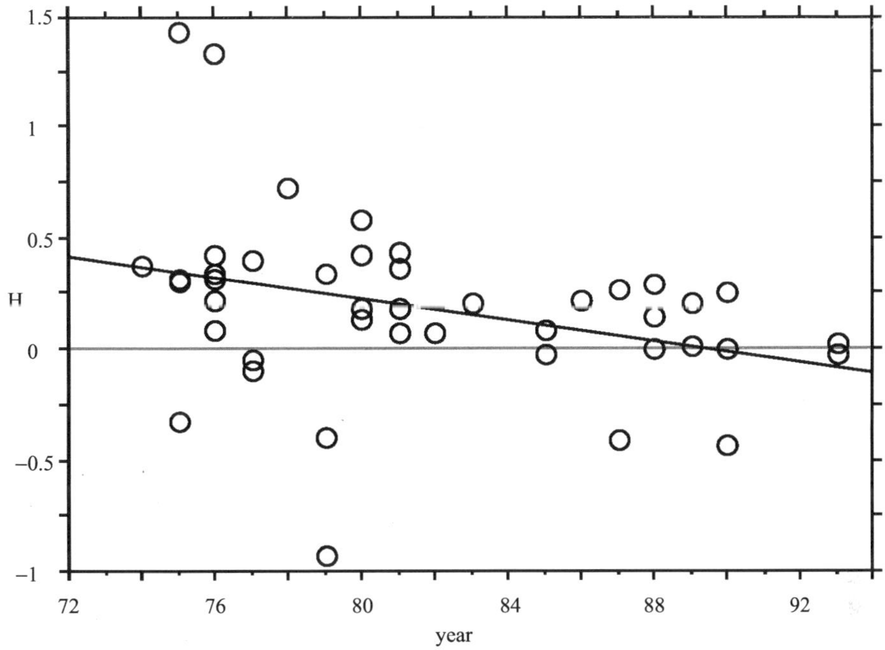

Figure 2. *Regression plot of the effectsizes versus year of all Ganzfeld experiments in the period 1974–1994*

reported concluding that the post 1985 data do not show any effect (Milton & Wiseman 1999). Although this conclusion is quite dependent on the choice of criteria to include studies in the meta-analysis there is no doubt that when adding the data from 1994 to 1998 the decline effect still is present. When including the more recent and significant data that were omitted in the Milton & Wiseman analysis the decline is dampened considerably. One could even interpret these data to represent a recovery from the decline effect.

3.3 *PK effects on RNG's*

Experiments where true Random Number Generators have been used as a target in psychokinesis experiments are very interesting because this paradigm is generally completely automated and therefore:

1. the experimenter is less involved in doing the experiment, very often participants are doing the experiments on their own. And

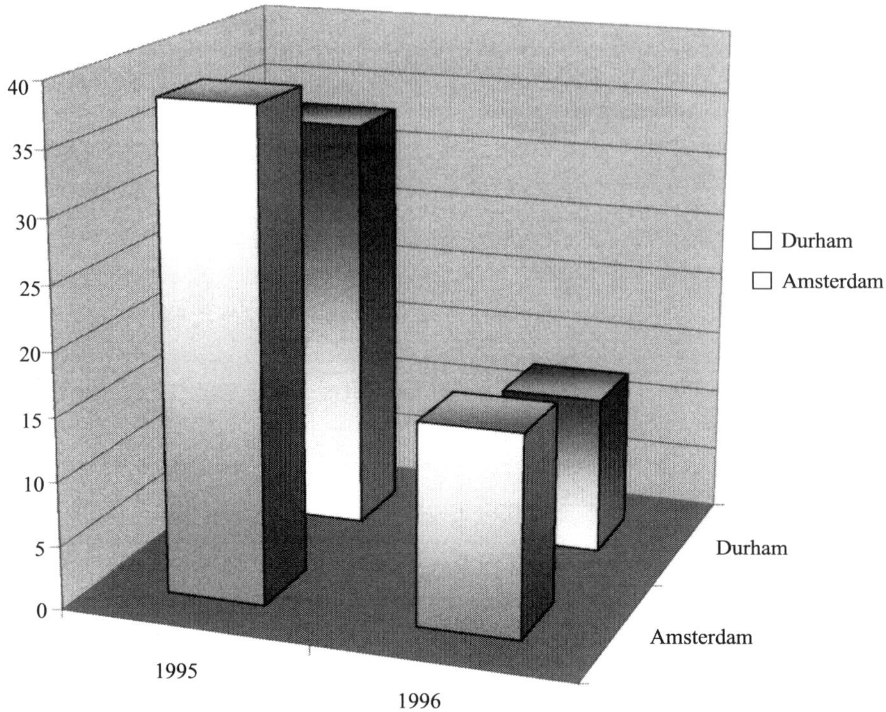

Figure 3. *Decline in scoring rate in Ganzfeld ESP experiments in two independent laboratories in two consecutive years*

2. the quality of the studies is more stable than for any other paradigm.

A regression plot for the database of about 600 studies reported by Radin and Nelson (Radin & Nelson 1989) doesn't show a clear decline. However this database is a mixture of data, the majority contributed by the PEAR group and by a single experimenter (Helmut Schmidt) using different procedures than the other groups. In the Princeton data and for a part in the Schmidt data, we have three possible target directions namely high aim, low aim and no-aim. The other researchers, although also using the methodologically sound target counterbalancing procedure, do not split the results in this way. If we exclude the data obtained with the first procedure we are left with 264 studies. Plotting these reveals a sequential effect that differs from the straight decline effects reported above (Figure 4).

Rather than just declining, the effect size seems to recover after a period of

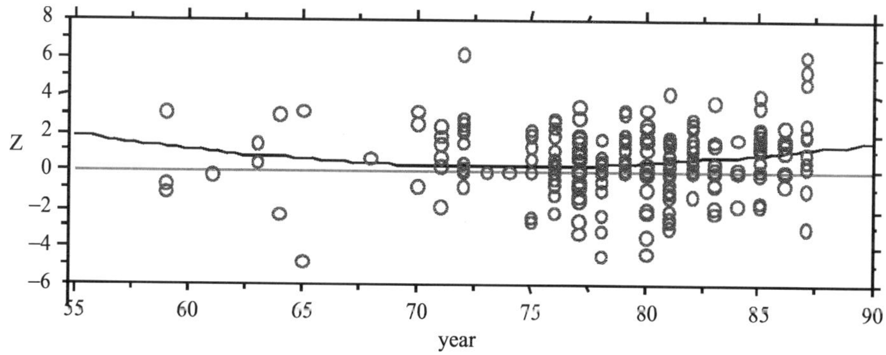

Figure 4. *Polynomial regression plot of all RNG-PK study results under exclusion of PEAR and Schmidt data*

about 15 years. Both polynomial regression coefficients are significant ($p < 0.03$). What we might see here is the onset of a kind of oscillatory behaviour which fits well with the models we will discuss in the theoretical section. Note by the way that in spite of a period of about 10 years where no effects were found, the total residual database provides strong support for the existence of a true anomaly (mean z-score is 0.541, N = 264, t = 5.34, $p < 0.00001$).

When we analyze the data for the high aim and low aim separately we find regression coefficients indicating an incline with time for the low aim and decline in time for the high aim in the RNG experiments of Helmut Schmidt and in the PK-RNG data of the PEAR group. However none of these values are significant.

Recent major attempts though to replicate the findings of the PEAR RNG-PK work in two independent laboratories as well as by the PEAR group themselves, resulted in a failure. Detailed data are not yet public so it remains to be seen if this is another example of the 'decline effect' (personal communication).

3.4 *PK effects on biological systems*

In the research program of the Mind Science foundation many biological target systems were used (Braud & Schlitz 1991). We will restrict ourselves here to a series of identical studies that was replicated often enough to check for a potential decline. In these studies a remote 'influencer' tried to increase or decease the arousal of an 'influencee' during randomly assigned periods. The dependent variable was the electro-dermal response of the 'influencee'. Of course the 'influencee' was blind with respect to the influencing periods. A regression plot of the results of these studies versus their sequence number (the experimental years were not available in the publication) shows again a steady decline with a regression coefficient of −0.034 ($p=0.043$).

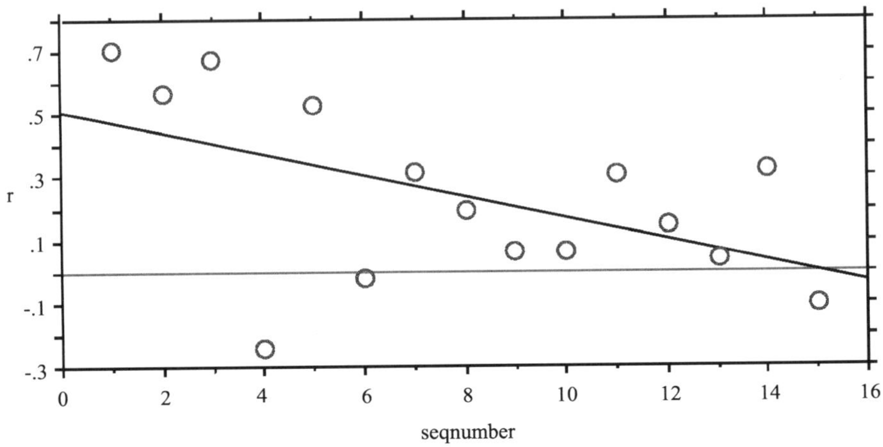

Figure 5. *A regression plot of the effect sizes found in all studies on the effect of distant attention on arousal*

Also the effects in experiments with other biological target systems (like orientation of fish, blood pressure and human ideomotor activity) with the exception of the mamal locomotion experiments show a tendency to decline over time though the number of experiments is too small to do a proper statistical evaluation.

3.5 *Process oriented findings: Psi correlations*

In Utt's review article it is claimed that not only the evidence for the existence of psi is overwhelming but also that some intrinsic correlations of psi scores with external independent variables have been replicated. As an example the correlation of performance in a psi task with the personality variable 'extraversion' is mentioned. This weak correlation of about 0.20 was originally established by examining the relevant free-response studies between 1945 and 1983 (Honorton, Ferrari & Bem 1992) and was later 'confirmed' in the Auto Ganzfeld database where a slightly smaller correlation between extraversion and psi-score of 0.18

was found. However in the replication attempts of the Utrecht, Durham and Edinburgh group in the mid nineties the correlations declined even further from r = 0.15 in the Utrecht replication via virtually nothing in the Durham replication to even a negative relationship in the Edinburgh replication (Van Kampen et al. 1994; Broughton & Alexander 1996; Morris et al. 1995).

One of the most cited correlations in the parapsychological literature is the correlation of performance in a psi task with the score on the Defense Mechanism Test (DMT). A close inspection of all the experiments which tried to assess this correlation reveals again a strong decline in the correlation coefficient (see Figure 6, database from Haraldsson & Houtkooper 1995). The regression coefficient is −0.034 ($p = 0.0002$).

3.6 *Card guessing*

So far we have discussed all databases from table I except the precognitive card-guessing database. Table I is generally taken by parapsychologists as the best evidence for the existence of genuine anomalies. However, besides the undeniable cumulative evidence for anomalies, we have also established in all cases significant sequential effects. Thus it seems that original effect sizes can not be replicated in the weak sense explained in footnote 1. In spite of my many efforts to trace the card-guessing database it appears that it has disappeared and it is just too large of a job to reconstruct the database from scratch. But, based on observations in the other databases, we would expect that this database too would exhibit decline effects. It appears that these sequential effects are the rule in the study of psi phenomena. However, some exceptions have been claimed by individual researchers.

3.7 *Paradigms with 'stable' effect sizes: Remote viewing*

It has been claimed by May and others that remote viewing (clairvoyance) experiments do not exhibit a decline (Utts 1996). However this is only true for the remote viewing experiments that were run in or just outside of the framework of the (US government formerly) classified "Stargate" program. By contrast, the effect sizes in the remote viewing database of the Princeton PEAR group declined over years with a regression of −0.085 ($p = 0.0006$; Spottiswoode 1993). It may be that the difference in decline effects for the same paradigm, but between the two research labs, points us into the direction of an explanation.

4. Possible explanations of decline effects

This section starts with two possible explanations that deny that there is any real anomaly to be accounted for. I don't share this opinion but leave it to the reader to decide.

4.1 *Statistical artefact, selective publication*

Regression to the mean has been proposed as an explanation for decline effects. Thus the first experiment is published because it found some significant effect by chance. Further replications will of course converge the result toward the true null-effect value. However, this explanation doesn't fit the data because the mean of the 'unselected' study 2 and further on, should show a mean null effect size. In almost all the examples given in the previous chapter, this is not the case. The analysis of across-investigator PK-RNG studies shows an incline after about 15–20 years of decline. This of course does not fit with a 'regression to the mean' hypothesis.

In one experimental parapsychological journal the official publication policy is that the research plan and design have to be submitted before the experiment starts, and that acceptance is on the basis of this design rather than on the basis of the results. Thus selective reporting is prohibited. However it is uncertain how often this official policy is actually applied.

Starting around 1970, all parapsychological journals began to accept articles with null-results while before that date only significant studies tended to be published. If we look at the subset of the dice throwing studies that were done after 1970, for instance, we find that there is no over-all effect left. Thus, it could be argued that the change in publication policy artificially induced a decline. However, if we just focus on the dice experiments from 1970 to the present, we find that the regression coefficient is even higher (−0.219 for this subset of 17 studies while it was −0.053 for the whole data set; interestingly, when we take the subset before 1970 the regression coefficient is −0.097 ($p = 0.0045$).) This suggests that a break-down in the two subsets reveals different declines, the first one less strong, possibly due to selective effects of the publication policy in that period.

4.2 *Increasing study quality*

Another explanation of decline, like the previous one mostly put forward by sceptics, is that the earlier studies are of lower quality, resulting in artificially large effects. Later, with increasing quality the spurious effects would disappear. Several authors have argued (for instance Kennedy 1938) that an increase in the experimental rigor of ESP research had resulted in a corresponding decline in ESP results, suggesting that extra chance ESP scores were due solely to loose experimental conditions.

This explanation, which indeed could apply to early card-guessing & dice experiments, does not apply to the automated psychokinesis experiments with RNG's as targets. The decline effects reported above for PK-RNG experiments are the weakest. Thus the quality hypothesis seems to fit the data at first sight. However, as already mentioned, recent replication attempts of the PEAR PK-RNG-studies using the same methods and hence the same quality as in the original PEAR studies, failed. Furthermore the remaining PK-RNG database after 1965 shows an incline rather than a decline.

Utts argued that in most meta-analyses no dependence of effect size versus study quality could be established. However, rather than supporting the idea that no correlation exists, it can also be argued that some relation might exist because the study quality score is determined using the written report rather than an assessment of quality based on a close inspection of the actual experiments. In low effect size studies the authors generally limit their report in such a way that a later meta-analyzer rates the quality lower than it actually was (e.g. authors tend not to report extensive randomness tests or safety measures when the outcome of the study was nonsignificant). Thus, the quality scores for low effect size studies may be higher than the figures used in the analyses cited by Utts. It can be seen that if one corrects for this potential reporting artifact, that this would result in a negative correlation between study quality and effect size.

4.3 *From proof-oriented to process-oriented research*

One of the 'explanations' put forward to account for declines is that during the last 20 years the focus on proof-oriented research has shifted toward process-oriented research. In the latter type of research one tries to derive underlying processes by either correlational analyses or manipulations of experimental variables. The latter could include manipulations deliberately introduced to obtain smaller effects. Thus the over-all effect size would be smaller. However, in practice most studies are either of the type using secondary correlational analyses or they involve manipulations intended to increase effect-size, not to decrease effect size. Actually this explanation cannot account easily for ANY of the declines described above, with the possible exception of some of the recent

Ganzfeld experiments where in order to study the effect of the emotional content of target clips some extremely boring target-clips were used.

4.4 *Psychological 'explanations'*

Human performance in many types of tasks decline with time. Generally these declines can be attributed to a gradual change in physical or psychological variables that are relevant for the performance under study. Physically the body might become tired throughout a session; mentally, the subject might become bored with the task.

Thus within session/subject decline effects in psi tasks could easily be 'explained' by assuming that the subjects became bored with the task. However declines have also been reported in psi-tasks with fish (Braud 1976). It may be doubted that mental fatigue is a good explanation for the decline from day 1 to day 2 of experiments involving fish, although similar declines had been found in conventional behavioral research using the same fish (Baenninger 1966). Nevertheless, the explanation that within-session decline effects are due to fatigue seems the most natural one.

However between-experiment declines of effect sizes cannot be explained by fatigue on the part of the participating subjects because generally the subjects are different from experiment to experiment. If the replication attempts are conducted by the same experimenter it still seems possible to 'explain' them by assuming that the experimenter is getting bored and 'communicating' this non-verbally to the subjects. In the parapsychological literature experimenter effects have been reported extensively. Not only of the subjects-influencing kind described by Rosenthal (Rosenthal 1969) but also of a more subtle experimenter psi-influencing kind (Kennedy & Taddonio 1976). Thus the attribution of between-experiment decline to the experimenters becoming more and more bored with the experiments is not as far-fetched as it seems. Note though, that for the classified remote viewing series that used the same experimenters and subjects over a period of more than 15 years there seems to be no decline. If ever boredom should have struck then it should have been within these series.

The third kind of declines, declines between-experiments and between-experimenters (between-labs), is most difficult to 'explain' by some gradually changing psychological variable. Of course the excitement of trying out something completely new is lost upon a replication, but the replicating experimenters are often novices with regard to the experiment that they try to replicate and their psychological set therefore does not differ much from the experimenter that did the original study.

4.5 *Physical explanations*

The striking finding by Spottiswoode of a correlation between cosmological time (LST) and performance in (free response) psi tasks has renewed interest in the possibility of some physical background variables playing a role in the psi process. Earlier, weak correlations with geomagnetic activity had been reported (Persinger & Krippner 1989) but the LST-psi effect showed a dramatic 380% increase of the effect when the galaxy disappears behind the horizon (Spottiswoode 1997).

Thus declines could possibly be 'explained' by some gradually changing physical variable. One argument against this explanation is that most physical (including cosmological, like sunspot frequency) variables have cyclic components with a period smaller than the period that parapsychological experimentation has been going on. Most of our databases do show a more or less steady decline but the PK-RNG database suggests that a cyclic component of about 30 years might be present providing some support for the influence of a cyclic background variable. If different psi phenomena are affected in the same (or in opposite) ways by the (cosmological) background variables one should be able to see some correlation between the long term sequential effects in different databases. The databases do not overlap enough to see if this is the case.

4.6 *Von Lucadou's system theoretical 'explanation'*

In a provocative paper von Lucadou (1990) claims that for all complex information processing systems, including human consciousness, a quantum-*like* description is required. I.e. the formalism to describe these systems has basically the same structure as Quantum Physics. As a direct consequence these systems should, under specific conditions, also show some of the remarkable aspects of quantum systems. Most notably parts of the systems might show EPR-like correlations. Within the framework of quantum physics it has been shown that these 'non-local' correlations cannot be used to transfer bits of information. If the experiment is prepared in such a way that it is possible to do a measurement which could give information about specific parts of the system these non-local correlations will not occur. The actual potentiality of a measurement of classical information transfer using non-local correlations will destroy the 'carrier' of this information. So, according to von Lucadou, there is no way to construct a public experiment in which apparent psi information can be *used*. On the other hand by using a triple blind set up it must be possible to show that more correlations arise in the system than can arise by chance. However, specific correlations tend to decline and other correlations unexpectedly will pop up in the system. Thus the system theoretical framework of von Lucadou's offers a natural explanation of the rather elusive character of laboratory experiments while simultaneously not prohibiting strong anomalous correlations to occur spontaneously in the field.

4.7 *Walker's observational 'explanation'*

In the early seventies Walker (1975) extended Wigner's interpretation of the measurement problem. According to Wigner, the idea that physical measurement had a special status and therefore was responsible for the transition of a quantum system from its superposed state into a singular observed state (a.k.a. the collapse), was false (Wigner 1967). He therefore speculated that it was the interaction with consciousness, that was responsible for the collapse of the state-vector. At that time, the measurement problem had become more popular due to the formulation of Bell's theorem a few years before and the growing body of evidence that physical hidden variables did not exist. In other words, it became a more popular idea that the collapse of the physical system was a real physical transition and not just a gain in knowledge.

Walker assumed that the observational process (i.e. the interaction of the physical system with consciousness) was not a unidirectional one but that in the process information could flow from the observer into the observed system. This information then could bias the distributions predicted by quantum physical calculations and hence anomalous correlations could arise between the observed system and the mental (intentional) state of the observer. The theory predicted that it wouldn't matter if in psychokinesis experiments the data were first stored before the subject tried to influence those into a later specified target direction (so called PK on prerecorded targets). This rather contra-intuitive prediction was then confirmed. The theory also unified all psi phenomena by including the random processes in the subject's brain as a possible target for 'retro-active' PK. Upon feedback (or observation) brain states could retro-actively be biased so that they would 'correlate' to observed feedback. A fundamental problem in the theory was how to describe the process of multiple observation. Several flavors of the Observational theories have been developed that deal with that problem (Houtkooper 1977, 1983; Schmidt 1975, 1978). In a number of those, further observation of the data still has an 'influence' on the observed outcome. Thus, it was not only the subjects in an experiment who were relevant for the outcome but also experimenters, people who later analyzed or checked the data and even readers of the final article. The so-called "checker effect" had already been experimentally established (Weiner & Zingrone 1989), but remained a mystery within the already mysterious world of the paranormal until Walker's formulation of the observational theory.

The fact that uncontrolled multiple and future observers of an experimental outcome might have an effect on the outcome could also 'explain' the difficulty to replicate these effects because it is obvious that after an initial success the number of potential future observers for a second experiment increases dramatically.

One even could argue that such an effect would be strongest after a meta-analysis or another widely cited publication. Houtkooper (Houtkooper 1983) argued that there is ample evidence for such a special strong effect after publications of meta-analyses. He labeled this the MAD (Meta-analysis Destruction) effect.

The fact that the Durham and Amsterdam Ganzfeld series declined so strongly between 1995 and 1996 might also be interpreted in this light. The 1995 outcomes of the experiments were used by Utts in 1996 in a widely published paper dealing with the evaluation of the 'until then' classified StarGate psi research program. It should be noted however that if one would like to interpret this decline in this way one should adhere to the so-called potential observer theory (Hartwell 1977; Millar & Hartwell 1978) in which not the actual observers of data are tied to the outcome but the potentiality of becoming an observer is the important factor.

In an article specifically dealing with the (non) replicability issue, Walker (1983) wrote:

> … The time has passed when we may reasonably expect to accidentally discover some simple psychological test that will separate out individuals who can assure repeatability, or when we may, without understanding of the underlying physical principles, prescribe experimental procedures to circumvent the current difficulties …

He then continues to give a formal treatment of models that include the effect of 'other observers' but assumes a constant experimental success rate rather than one in which the success rate is dependent on a factor related to the number of (potential) observers of the outcome and their world view. If one corrects his equations accordingly the solution shows an oscillatory behaviour for the success rate. We have found one clear indication for such a cyclic behaviour in the PK-RNG data (see Figure 4). The only database that covers a similarly long period is the PK-Dice database. Visual inspection of Figure 1 suggests that maybe in that database we have a full cycle of decline, incline followed by the start of another decline. If we leave out the few data points after 1965 which might be related to the start of the next decline phase the resulting datapoints show a sequential effect quite comparable to the PK-RNG sequential effect.

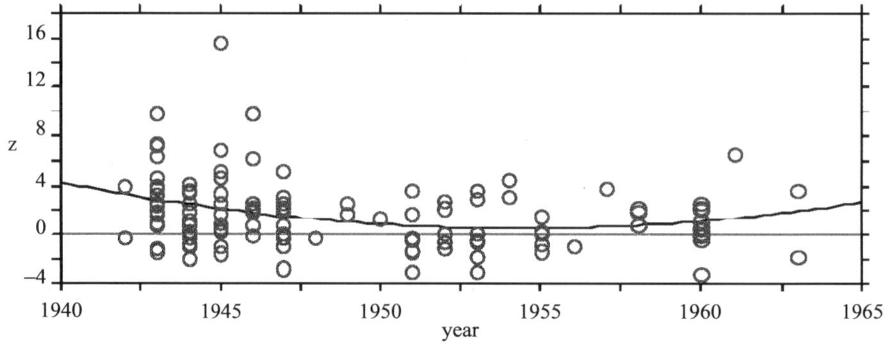

Figure 7. *The Dice throwing experiments analyzed for a non-linear effect between 1940 and 1965*

Both regression coefficients are significant at the $p < 0.025$ level (figure 7).

A similar analysis for the Ganzfeld data including the more recent studies and excluding 2 Ganzfeld studies that were completely atypical because auditory targets rather than visual targets were used, results in a similar plot, suggestive of a recovery from the decline after a period of about 17 years (Figure 8).

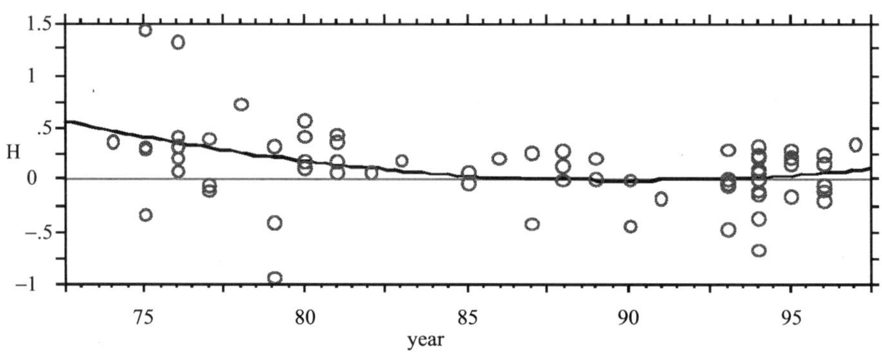

Figure 8. *The Ganzfeld experiments analyzed for a non-linear effect between 1972 and present*

Both regression coefficients are marginally significant.

4.8 *A new position about reality*

Anomalous phenomena like telepathy, psychokinesis and precognition have long been seen as 'just an extension' of people's normal sensory capabilities. Hence labels like Extra Sensory Perception (ESP) and more recently 'anomalous cognition'. In this view the phenomena are discussed in terms of information transfer, bandwidth and signal to noise ratio. The low signal to noise ratio is then seen as the culprit of the difficulties to replicate and the research can be characterized as a kind of engineering approach to the properties of the information transfer channel. Such an approach does not (at first sight) require a fundamental change of world view. Even the apparent retrocausal aspects of some (if not all) of the phenomena are not necessarily incompatible with a mechanistic world view, as Newtonian physics is basically time-symmetric.

However, while explanations like those mentioned above cannot be ruled out, I speculate that the difficulty to replicate is not just due to a low signal-to-noise ratio but has a deeper reason, a reason that suggested by the theoretical approaches by von Lucadou and Walker. Both theoretical frameworks account for psi phenomena by either using directly or metaphorically non-local EPR-like correlations.

Von Lucadou argues that no signal can be transferred using these correlations and any situation where such a signal *could* be encoded in the psi-induced correlations would tend to destroy the correlations itself. This logically explains why in exploratory situations these correlations seem to appear easily while in confirmatory replication attempts (where in principle given the knowledge from the first experiment one could use some scheme to encode a signal) it is difficult to replicate. That some correlations are still found in some of the later replication attempts could be explained by the fact that in order for a parapsychological experiment to be valid the information that supposedly is going to be 'transferred' has to be randomized. Thus the experimenter generally is not 'free' to select this information so that we cannot really speak of intended information transfer but merely of correlations between target information and behavior of the percipient. In von Lucadou's terms there is only a signal if meaningful information is transferred, i.e. a signal that can result in some meaningful action. If a system is closed in such a way that these actions have no effect upon the outside world then it still would be possible to have anomalous correlations within the system. Von Lucadou used the concept of organizational closure from the domain of self-organizing systems to characterize systems that have this property of having no meaningful action on the outside world.

Thus, according to both von Lucadou and Walker, some closed-system correlations between mental states and other mental or physical states which are EPR-like could be real. However, when one tries to move these phenomena into the realm of the purely objective, i.e. make them sharable by everybody, they disappear, the local reality disappears.

I have called this local reality 'tribal' reality (Bierman 1999), because it nicely accounts for the disappearance of the power of the shamans. Originally, mental states of the shaman could indeed correlate in an EPR like way with mental or bodily states of clients. However when the tribe was broken open by *Coca Cola* and *MacDonald's* the 'powers' of the shaman got lost and objective science was unable to establish any reality to the stories from the past. The parapsychological research community can also be seen as a kind of a tribe in this respect.

5. Conclusion

The account given here for the difficulty to replicate paranormal phenomena requires a radical change in world view. We cannot expect science, or society, to change a time-honored (at least in the West) world view on the basis of data that appear to be extremely difficult to replicate. Is there a way out of this vicious circle?

According to Walker, a slowly changing world view would lead to gradually easier replications so that psi phenomena in the end would become part of the objective world (Walker 1983).

However there might be another option which has been overlooked. If the replication problems are due to the fact that any situation in which signals could be deduced from them prohibit the correlations from occurring, then we should realize that we are talking about *classical* bits of information. There is no restriction on the transfer of quantum bits. Thus one could try to set up experimental systems that are a macroscopic analogy of quantum teleportation systems.

How should we conceptualize what constitutes a macroscopic analogy of a quantum bit? According to Hameroff & Penrose (1996) non-conscious states are superposed (non-collapsed) states and therefore 'contain' quantum bits. This suggests that correlations between non-conscious states of two subjects at a distance in time and space might become EPR-like correlated, especially if there has been a strong interaction between the two subjects in the past. This would argue for experiments with twins. Of course measurement of non-conscious states is difficult but it could be done using psychophysiological variables or brain imaging techniques. In fact some experiments have been reported in the parapsychological literature that come close to the experimental approach suggested here, and they were extremely successful, but not part of a theoretically driven research program and hence they had no follow up (Grinberg-Zylberbaum et al. 1992). It remains to be seen if these correlations could be used (i.e. result in some meaningful action) or if the correlations will disappear if one tries to "use" the system in some way.

A quote from the star subject in the US Governmental StarGate program, Joseph W. McMoneagle:

> ...I've observed that elusiveness more times than I care to count. I agree that it would seem to be an element itself that requires study. There is always a tendency to search for order in the stream, when it may be a function of disorder being observed. Or perhaps a relaxation in the expectation for order...

Notes

1. We use the term 'failure to replicate' here loosely. I.e. if an original effectsize shows a significant regression to zero we call this a failure to replicate the original finding although the elements of the database might not differ in a statistically significant way.
2. One outlier was removed. This does not affect the regression statistics at all.
3. The analysis is not sensitive for the removal of three outliers. In fact the analysis is conservative because part of the data produced by PRL using dynamic targets (which runs counter to the decline effect) is included twice in the database because it is unclear which auto-ganzfeld data from the final publication (Honorton et al. 1990) had been reported before.

References

Baenninger, R. (1966) Waning of Aggressive motivation in Betta Splendens. *Psychonomic Science* 5: 207–208.

Bem, D. J. and Honorton, C. (1994) Does psi exist? Replicable evidence for an anomalous process of information transfer. *Psychological Bulletin* 115: 4–18.

Bierman, D. J. (1995) The Amsterdam Ganzfeld series III & IV: Target Clip emotionality, effect sizes and openess. *Proceedings of the 38th Annual P. A. Convention*, 27–37.

Bierman, D. J. (1999) Is non-replication a fundamental characteristic of psi? *Proceedings of the 42nd Annual P. A. Convention*, 417.

Braud, W. G. (1976) Psychokinesis in aggressive and non aggressive fish with mirror presentation feedback for hits: Some preliminary experiments. *Journal of Parapsychology* 40(4): 296–307.

Braud, W. G. and Schlitz, M. J. (1991) Consciousness Interactions with Remote Biological Systems: Anomalous Intentionality Effects. *Subtle Energies* 2(1): 1–46.

Broughton, R. and Alexander, C. (1995) AutoGanzfeld II: the first 100 sessions. *Proceedings of the 38th Annual P. A. Convention*, 53–61.

Broughton, R. and Alexander, C. (1996) AutoGanzfeld II: An attempted replication of the PRL Ganzfeld research. *Proceedings of the 39th Annual P. A. Convention*, 45–56.

Dennett, D. C. (1991) *Consciousness Explained.* Penquin Books, London. ISBN 0–7139–9037–6.

Gordon, I. E. (1996) Empiricism: perception as a constructive process. In: *Theories of Visual Perception*, 154–179. John Wiley & Sons, Chisester.

Grinberg-Zylberbaum, J.; Delaflor, M., Sanchez Arellano, M. E., Guevara, M. A. and Perez, M. (1992) Human Communication and the Electrophysiological Activity of the Brain. *Subtle Energies* 3(3): 25–43.

Hameroff, S. R., and Penrose, R. (1996) Conscious events as orchestrated spacetime selections. *Journal of Consciousness Studies* 3(1): 36–53.

Haraldsson, E. and Houtkooper, J. M. (1995) Meta-analysis of Ten Experiments on Perceptual Defensiveness and ESP: ESP Scoring Patterns, Experimenter and Decline Effects. *Journal of Parapsychology* 59: 251–271.

Hartwell, J. W. (1977) A bound for the observational theories of psi. *European Journal of Parapsychology* 2(1): 19–28.

Honorton, C. (1985) Meta-analysis of psi ganzfeld research: A response to Hyman. *Journal of Parapsychology* 49: 51–91.

Honorton, C., Ferrari, D. C. and Bem, D. J. (1992) Extraversion and ESP performance: Meta-analysis and a new confirmation. In L. A. Henkel and G. R. Schmeidler (Eds.), *Research in parapsychology 1990* (pp. 35–38). Metuchen, NJ: Scarecrow Press.

Houtkooper, J. M. (1977) A comment on Schmidt's mathematical model of psi. *European Journal of Parapsychology* 2(1): 15–18.

Houtkooper, J. M. (1983) Observational Theory: A research programme for Paranormal phenomena. Thesis University Utrecht, dec. 1983, 57–64.

Hyman, R. and Honorton, C. (1986) Joint communiqué: the psi ganzfeld controversy. *Journal of Parapsychology* 50: 351–364.

James, W. (1890). cit. Gordon, 1996.

Van Kampen, D., Bierman, D. J. and Wezelman, R. (1994) 'Personality and psi: Unravelling relations between extraversion, agreeableness and openness to experience with Ganzfeld performance.' In D. J. Bierman (Ed.) *Proceedings of the 37th PA Convention*, University of Amsterdam, 175–181.

Kennedy, J. L. (1938) The visual cues from the backs of ESP cards, *Journal of Psychology* 6: 149–153.

Kennedy, J. E. and Taddonio, J. L. (1976) Experimenter effects in parapsychological research. *Journal of Parapsychology* 40: 1–33.

Loftus, E. F. (1997) 'Creating False memories.' *Scientific American*, September 1997, 277(3): 70–75.

Millar, B. and Hartwell, J. (1978) Dealing with divergence. In W. C. Roll (Ed.), *Research in parapsychology, 1978*. Metuchen, NJ.: Scarecrow Press, 1979.

Milton, J. and Wiseman, R. (1999) Does psi exist? Lack of replication of an anomalous process of information transfer. *Psychological Bulletin* 125: 387–391.

Morris, R. L., Dalton, K., Delanoy, D. L. and Watt, C. (1996) Comparison of sender/no sender condition in the Ganzfeld. *Proceedings of the 38th Annual P. A. Convention*, 244–259.

Persinger, M. A. amd Krippner, S. (1989) Dream ESP experiments and geomagnetic activity. *Journal of the American SPR* 83: 101–116.

Radin, D. I. and Ferrari, D. C. (1991) Evidence of consciousness on the fall of dice: a meta-analysis. *Journal of Scientific Exploration* 5: 61–83.

Radin, D. I. and Nelson, R. D. (1989) Evidence for consciousness-related anomalies in random physical systems. *Foundations of Physics* 19: 1499–1514.

Rhine, B. (1969) Position Effects in Psi Test Results, *Journal of Parapsychology* 33: 136–157.

Rosenthal, R. (1969) Interpersonal Expectancies: The effects of the experimenter's hypothesis. In: R. Rosenthal and R. Rosnow (Eds.) *Artifacts in Behavioral Research*, Academic Press, New York.

Schmidt, H. (1975) Toward a mathematical theory of psi. *Journal of the American Society for Psychical Research* 69: 301–319.

Schmidt, H. (1978) A remark on the "divergence problem". *European Journal of Parapsychology* 2: 163–166.

Spottiswoode, S. J. P. (1993) Personal communication on (SMTP/TCP) e-mail (message_id's: <9304160128.AA19945@jsasoc.com> of april 16 1993 and <9304132041.AA16375 @jsasoc.com> of april 13 1993).

Spottiswoode, J. (1997) Geomagnetic fluctuations and Free Response Anomalous Cognition: A new Understanding. *Journal of Parapsychology* 61(1): 3–12.

Utts, J. (1991) Replication and Meta-Analysis in Parapsychology. *Statistical Science* 6(4): 363–403.

Utts, J. (1996) An assessment of the evidence for psychic functioning, *Journal of Scientific Exploration* 10(1): 3–30.

von Lucadou, W. (1990) Some remarks on the problem of repeatabilty of experiments dealing with complex systems, *NATO Advanced Study Institute, Information Dynamics*, Irsee, FRG, June 15–26, 1990.

Walker, E. H. (1975) Foundations of paraphysical and parapsychological phenomena. In Laura Oteri (Ed.), *Quantum physics and parapsychology*. New York: Parapsychology Foundation.

Walker, E. H. (1983) The repeatability problem in Parapsychology. In: Betty Shapin adn Lisette Cly (Eds), *Procs. Of an International Conference held in San Antonio*, Texas, oct. 28–29, Parapsychology Foundation, New York, N. Y., 98–143.

Weiner, D. H. and Zingrone, N. L. (1989) In the eye of the beholder: further research on the "checker effect". *Journal of Parapsychology* 53: 203–233.

Wigner, E. P. (1967) Symmetries and Reflections. Bloomington: Indiana University Press.

Wezelman, R. and Bierman, D. J. (1997) Process Oriented Ganzfeld Research in Amsterdam: Series IVb, emotionality of target material, series V and series VI: judging procedure & altered states of consciousness, *Proceedings of the 40th P. A. Convention*, 477–491.

The philosophy of consciousness, 'deep' teleology and objective selection

Philip Van Loocke

Abstract

We consider systems in which forces and selection (or 'reduction') procedures cooperate to determine present states. Forces work on the immediate past of a system and determine a set of possible states. Selection works in the immediate future and selects one of these states as the actual state of the system. Selection can be constrained in terms of a criterion not reducible to the forces operating on the system. It is shown that the performance of different types of procedures increases when this type of teleology is inserted. This is illustrated with an example from the cognitive domain and with examples that belong to the context of generative art. More fundamentally, it is conjectured that, given the complexity of our universe, selection can operate systematically without leading to replicable violation of physical laws. The relation between selection and the philosophy of consciousness is discussed.

1. Introduction: Matter, phase transitions and consciousness

In this introductory section, the view on consciousness that will be put forward is situated relative to a number of familiar views. These views on the nature of consciousness are briefly discussed. The first view to be considered is the most widespread functionalist version of the materialist attitude towards consciousness:

> (p1) Consciousness becomes a property of particular configurations of classically describable matter when these configurations realize the appropriate functional schema

This proposition is often explained with the life-metaphor. If one analyzes a living entity in terms of its parts, one observes that it is composed of molecules.

The interactions between these molecules are fairly complex, but there is no special 'life-substance' that mixes up with the latter. Similarly, the appearance of consciousness does not require that something non-material enters the molecules of the brain. 'Life' is a property of particular assemblies of molecules, and so is 'consciousness' (Churchland 1995). Further, since the ordinary evolutionary processes of mutation and selection gave advantage to configurations of matter of which consciousness is a property, the historical appearance of consciousness in the material world is not a fundamental problem. Future science will fill in the details about the neural configurations of which consciousness is a property, but the materialist world view will not be shaken by the details to come. This stance is not only popular in several philosophy faculties, but appears to be widespread in biology and neurology courses, even if it is not always formulated explicitly.

Nevertheless, there are some deep problems associated with this view. I mention three of them.

a. The first problem may be called a problem of demarcation. The functionalist aspect of (p1) entails that consciousness is a property of matter as soon as it realizes a particular functional schema C. The total number of possible functional schemas forms an extremely large space S. A tiny part of them is realized in our universe in the form of airplanes, brains, stars, computers, and so on. The question then is why the structural schema that is realized by a brain is the schema that delivers consciousness. The demarcation of one schema as giving raise to consciousness is usually made implicitly on anthropomorphic (or at best biomorphic) grounds: the flow chart realized in the brain demarcates the point C in S that automatically leads to the additional property of consciousness. An argument for the selection of this point (and possibly its small neighborhood) is lacking in functionalist materialism.

Further, functionalist materialism claims that no demarcation has to be made in terms of the substrate that realizes C: it does not take a special physical substrate to generate consciousness. It can be generated by the wetware of a brain, but a hardware-only realization of the same functional schema would generate the same consciousness. If — even for a single moment — a set of molecules in a star behaves in such a way that their mutual interactions satisfy the functional schema, the set of molecules is conscious. Functionalists typically object that the brain is the most complex object in the universe, and that other realizations of this complexity are not present in non-brain systems (Churchland 1981). But the more we know about the zoo of astrophysical objects in our cosmos, the harder it seems to put the brain a priori at the number one place of the complexity hierarchy. And since there are a lot of such objects, momentary realizations of parts of the functional schema seem less improbable. This is especially so if the region around C is taken in a broader, less anthropomorphically constrained way. In other terms, a consequent functionalist materialist attitude can lead to types of panpsychism which most adherents of this view want to avoid.

b. The second problem for functionalist materialism is the epiphenomenalist charge. According to the functionalist version of (p1), the fact that phenomenal consciousness supervenes on a functional schema does not affect the schema itself (Popper & Eccles 1976; Eccles 1994). Matter does not change its causal behavior when it is configured in a way that gives raise to phenomenal consciousness; it remains governed by the same physical forces. It follows that this view on consciousness is at variance with the adaptation view on evolution. On the one hand, phenomenal consciousness is a pretty remarkable phenomenon that has emerged in the course of evolution. On the other hand, it does not modify the functional relations of the configurations of matter on which it supervenes. Consequently, it can have no adaptive value for these configurations of matter. Hence, consciousness is a remarkable phenomenon that appeared in the course of evolution, but without adaptive value. This is at odds with evolution theory. We notice that life and consciousness have a profoundly different relation to this theory. Evolution theory explains life and its various forms; that is its reason of existence. But it has no explanation for the fact that matter that takes part in life obtains the additional property of consciousness.

c. Third, there is the so-called 'hard problem' of consciousness. Once one has a demarcation of the schemas leading to consciousness, it remains to be explained why or how these schemas always lead to something additional when they are materially realized. The 'hardness' of this philosophical problem has recently been emphasized (Chalmers 1995). Its difficulty has been cast in a variety of terms. Fodor (1992: 5) puts this as follows: 'Nobody has the slightest idea how anything material could be conscious. Nobody even knows what it would be like to have the slightest idea about how anything material could be conscious. So much for the philosophy of consciousness'. Some philosophers suggest that this problem may remain with us for a very long time. Human thinking may be 'cognitively closed', and it may not be able to solve the hard problem of consciousness (McGinn 1993; Pinker 1997). At this moment, (p1) still has many adherents, but it is certainly not a generally adopted view anymore.

The following proposition is sometimes added as a comment on (p1):

> (p2) The appearance of consciousness in matter can be clarified with the phase transition metaphor

If matter goes from a liquid phase to a solid phase, it obtains properties that it did not have before. It has hardness, its surface has friction, in some cases band spectra for electrons flowing through the matter appear, and so on. Likewise, a brain in which consciousness appears can be described with help of properties that are irrelevant for other phases of matter. Here, these properties refer to phenomenal qualities. But just like friction, hardness, et cetera, have an explanation in terms of this underlying molecular structure, so the additional properties of a conscious brain can be reduced to the interactions between the material constituents of the brain.

One can give different interpretations to (p2). For instance, one may utter that (p2) is only a loose metaphor. In that case, it does not add much specificity to the functionalist view on consciousness. But suppose that the phase-transition metaphor is taken serious. Then, matter has an ordinary phase and a special phase that is consciousness-sympathetic, and a new physical sub-discipline should be attempted. Like solid state physics and plasma physics describe matter in a particular phase, consciousness physics should describe matter in the consciousness phase. This extension of physics would require a substantial change of the matter concept, a change probably not intended by (p1) — materialists using the (p2) metaphor. It can be remarked that all detailed physical descriptions of phase transitions require quantum mechanics (this holds especially for transitions of matter from a less ordered to a more ordered phase, for instance when a liquid freezes to a solid). Hence, a consequent version of (p2) suggests that quantum theory is required for a quantitative description of consciousness. Such a position is rejected by most advocates of the functionalist version of (p1).

A version of (p2) which makes recourse to quantum theory leads to several conceptual changes. The addition of new terms, and the inclusion of those terms in laws, is fairly familiar in quantum theory, especially in quantum field theory. For instance, in order to describe the excitation of a piece of solid matter, quantum theory applies a Fourrier transform on the wave function. This way, the spatial variable is 'transformed away', and boson 'particles', like the fonon, appear. The dynamics of the system can be described in terms of new operators (like ladder operators) working on these new terms. Similarly, it has been suggested that the application of quantum mechanics to the brain leads to new concepts like 'psychons' (Eccles 1994), and that consciousness may be described in terms of the dynamics of psychons.

Such an approach may have an answer for objection a) that was raised against functionalist materialism. It can demarcate the systems in which consciousness is present. Since consciousness is associated with specific physical processes instead of with abstract structures, a demarcation problem at the level of abstract structures does not appear. Further, as far as the demarcation singles out processes with evolutionary advantage, also objection b) can be answered. This, however, is true to the extent that b) is treated while omitting questions referring to c), since part of the hard problem remains. Suppose that matter, in a particular phase described by quantum theory, would require new concepts like 'psychons' for its description, and suppose that these psychons could be regarded as atoms of consciousness. Then, matter in this special phase would have a quantum physical description, and some terms of the description would have a physical interpretation as well as an interpretation in terms of phenomenal consciousness. This means that, every time a particular material quantum phenomenon takes place, two types of events correlate: a phenomenal event and a material event. This, however, remains a theory on the level of correlation, and it does not give the deeper reasons why the phenomenal event is there as well. In the other sciences, the identification of correlations between variables is not regarded as a satisfying, final theory; rather, one wants a model that explains why the correlations are there. There is no a priori reason why a science of consciousness should be less ambitious (Gray 1974).

One would have a psycho-physical theory that is satisfactory in this sense if one could formulate laws in which variables appear with a physical interpretation only, as well as variables with a phenomenal interpretation only. Then, the question why two different types of events always correlate would disappear, since the theory would undo their systematic correlation. Such a theory could take a form, for instance, in which phenomenal consciousness is a field that influences material processes (Libet 1995). This hypothesis corresponds to a phase transition that is stronger than the one that is met in ordinary physics. It would entail that, with the appearance of consciousness, matter enters a phase in which it starts to interact with non-material, phenomenal entities. We will call this stance hypothesis (p3):

> (p3). Matter enters a phase in which it interacts with non-material entities when consciousness appears

According to this view, consciousness and matter both are irreducible ontological entities. The problem why matter generates a subjective correlate in particular conditions disappears, since the correlate is not assumed to be generated by matter, but considered to be equally fundamental. Stance (p3) is pretty remote from present orthodox science. In fact, there are other positions that can be taken if one does not accept that consciousness is associated with classically interacting matter (some important instances of these positions are described in the other chapters of this book). One of these starts with the observation that, in a materialistic context, two epistemologically and ontologically distinct concepts are present: matter and the forces between pieces of matter. The forces between pieces of matter are never seen directly. They are hidden 'behind' the matter, and are manifested only as changes in the state of motion of matter. Matter is localized; forces acting between distant pieces of matter have no strict localization. Quantum field theory may seem to treat matter and force more on equal footing, since it quantizises force fields and gives particle-like names to the elementary quantities that result. But the boson fields resulting from the quantization remain fundamentally different from the fermion particles between which they mediate interaction.

Consciousness may be in a situation comparable to the one of force. It is not visible when one looks at a brain, like one does not see gravitation when looking at the solar system. But one sees its effects, by its influence on brain states. Suppose that the analogy between force and consciousness is made in a consequent way. Then, we would have three types of ontological entities: matter, interactions of the classical/material-type, and interactions of the consciousness-type. In the context of quantum approaches to consciousness, it has been emphasized that the nature of the latter interaction may be different from the former. Material forces may determine a set of possible present states of a system in accordance with quantum theory. Then, consciousness may select one of them in accordance with a criterion that cannot be reformulated in terms of an additional force field. This approach has its own variation of the hard problem: in principle, it is conceivable that the selection mechanism would work as a physical mechanism only, without giving raise to consciousness. The question why consciousness joins a physical principle reappears. The present chapter will comment on the selection procedure, but it leaves part of the hard question partially unanswered. The fact that some processes have two aspects still has something mysterious, even if these processes are clearly differentiable from ordinary matter-interaction.

2. On selection and its observable effects

Consider an indeterministic system that is subject to a set of forces, and suppose that these forces determine a set of possible present states. Suppose that a function F is provided that takes particular physical variables of the system as its arguments, and suppose that a selection criterion X stipulates that the possible present state that maximizes F is chosen as the actual present state. Such a selection criterion may have effects that differ profoundly from the effects of an additional force. The effect of an additional force depends on its magnitude in comparison with the other forces. If the latter are large, it will have little effect, and vice versa. The determining factor for the strength of the effect of a selection criterion is the difference between the possible present states. If these are resembling one another very closely, then the presence of the criterion does not matter very much. If they are strongly divergent, the presence of the criterion will lead to a clear distinction in comparison with a random choice condition. A selection criterion may have strong or little effect in case of small, but also in case of large forces. It does not require a 'coupling strength' that determines a constant relative weight to the forces.

A selection criterion can be deterministic or indeterministic. Especially in case of a deterministic selection, one may expect that selection rules lead to significant, easily detectable differences when compared with systems for which a random choice determines a present state. This, in fact, is less trivial than it seems. A detection of deviations from statistical laws presumes that the system at issue allows for replications. Only if enough replications can be made, reliable statistics can be produced. In case of relatively simple physical systems, this possibility is straightforwardly present. However, for very complex systems, it may be impossible to create two times the same initial conditions for the system, and very slightly different initial conditions may lead to profoundly different behavior. We know that nature works at finite resolution. For example, it makes no physical sense to add hundreds of decimals to spatial variables. Every additional decimal reduces the scale referred to with an order of magnitude, and beyond a particular decimal place, the scale is reached where space itself becomes unstable and is subject to fluctuation.

Hence, even a classical physics description of a system has to attribute a volume in phase space to it that is strictly larger than zero. We know from Liouville's theorem that the volume is conserved, but we know as well from complex systems science that it may be scattered very rapidly over different parts of phase space. Now suppose that a selection criterion singles out one point from this scattered volume, and that this point defines the next state of the system. Then, nothing would happen that is forbidden by classical physics, since the selected point belongs to the set of possible points (Van Loocke 2000a).

Of course, if replication would be possible, a deviation from classical physics would be detectable, since the latter predicts that the different parts of the scattered phase space volume are effectively taken by the system when it is run sufficiently often. But in case of very complex systems, replication can be impossible. Consider a chaotic system. By its nature, such a system has high sensitivity to initial conditions, and the replication of the behavior of the system requires very precise control of its initial conditions. The difficulty to control the initial conditions (and also the precision with which this control has to be realized) increases when the system has large amounts of degrees of freedom, and when the system is not isolated. In the latter case, replication presumes that also the part of the environment that influences the behavior of the system is given the same initial conditions.

Consider a brain. It can be conjectured on basis of observational data that a brain has chaotic dynamics. The number of degrees of freedom in a brain is enormous (exceeding the number of neural units, which is of the order of 10^{11}), and a brain interacts with an environment that may be more complicated than itself (for instance when the environment contains several other brains). The capacity to put a brain state in the same small volume in phase space for the sake of replication is very far beyond present technology. This fact is strengthened when the combined system of a brain and its environment is considered. Hence, replications which would show a deviation from the prediction of classical physics, and which would reveal a selection procedure are practically impossible. This practical impossibility may be of a more principled nature. Replication would assume that complicated measurement devices are used. Hence, the environment of the brain would be changed, so that also the system brain/environment would change if replication would be attempted. Hence, physical theory leaves room for selection processes not described by the familiar forces of nature if the matter of the brain is described by classical physics. The same argument can be repeated for quantum brains (if one replaces 'phase space' by 'Hilbert space'; see Van Loocke 2000b).

3. Selection and teleology

Forces and the differential equations in which they occur determine possible present states on basis of the immediate past. In this sense, forces connect the immediate past with the present. The selection criteria considered in this chapter make the complementary temporal move, and connect the immediate (or further) future with the present. More specifically, the selection is based on possible states of the system taken a few time steps ahead of the present time step. We illustrate in the next section (and in Section 5) how this leads to systems of higher performance in cognitive and in aesthetic contexts. In more concise terms, we mean the following if we say that selection can work on basis of future states.

Suppose that a system is provided of a non-deterministic rule that allows one to specify a set of possible present states $S_i(t)$ $(i=1, \ldots, n)$ given the state $S(t-1)$ of the system at $t-1$. If this rule is applied $k+1$ times, then $n \cdot (k+1)$ possible states $S_j(t+k)$ $(j=1, \ldots, n \cdot (k+1))$ are defined at time step $t+k$. Suppose that a selection criterion C is given that selects one of these states $S_C(t+k)$. C may be a deterministic or an indeterministic criterion that selects a state that maximizes a particular function F. Then, we differentiate between two types of teleological dynamics:

> (Ta) The state taken by the system after it was in $S(t-1)$ is the state $S_C(t)$ at t that eventually would lead to $S_C(t+k)$ at $t+k$

The second type of dynamics is a computational simplification of (Ta):

> (Tb) In order to determine the state taken by the system after it was in $S(t-1)$, the possible states at t are considered. Then, the 2 states $S_i(t)$ $(i=1, 2)$ at t that best satisfy C are selected. For both states, the possible future states at $t+1$ are considered. The possible state at t that leads to the possible state $S_C(t+1)$ at $t+1$ that best satisfies C is the effective state taken by the system at t.

This type of process is an instance of (Ta) for $k=1$ and for which the selection criterion selects two states at t, and subsequently decides between these states by taking into account the immediate future of the system. In simulations, (Tb) usually is computationally significantly less demanding than (Ta), since the latter may require a computer to calculate a high number of possible futures. Further, (Tb) can be made more complex if the criterion that selects two states from the entire set of possible states is made different from the criterion that selects between the two selected states. This will be made more concrete in the example of Section 2.

4. Comparison of a teleological cellular system with its non-teleological counterpart

This section describes the method for which a teleological variation will be examined. It concerns a new approach to function approximation and classification problems that has recently been described at different places in literature (Van Loocke 1999b, 2000b, c, d). The method is implemented by a system of artificial cells that carry out very simple operations. Like a backpropagation connectionist system, the present type of system can approximate any arbitrary continuous function between R^n and R^m (Leshno, Ya Lin et al. 1993). In effect, the same error function as in case of connectionism is minimized in a step-wise way. However, there are five main differences with standard connectionism:

i. Suppose that an n-dimensional input space is mapped on an m-dimensional output space. Then, the input given to every cellular unit is an n-dimensional vector instead of a scalar. Every unit receives the same vector as input vector. Every cell generates an m-dimensional output.
ii. Not only individual cells, but also every set S of cells has an output associated with it. This (vector-) output is proportional to the sum of the (vector-) outputs of the cells that belong to it.
iii. The system has no connections. In every unit, n+m parameters are defined which are called 'fields'. They determine the details of the computation carried out by a unit.
iv. The array of cells involved in the solution of a task is not fixed but grows until the problem at hand is solved.
v. If the fields in the cells are given appropriate structure, then the 'black box' nature of a neural network is undone. Instead of giving a complicated connection matrix without visualization, this method solves problems with two-dimensional fractals (often of a pretty aesthetic nature, see Van Loocke 1999b, 2000b). Such a pattern can easily be stored in an automaton in a connectionist way. Then, one obtains a network in which the stored patterns correspond to meta-patterns (i.e. mappings between input and output patterns) instead of to ordinary patterns. This fact can be exploited when information with inner structure, or when meta-patterns and higher order meta-patterns have to be represented (Van Loocke 2000c, d).

The type of cells used by this method can be specified as follows. For every input vector $(a_1, \ldots, a_n)$, a cell of the automaton generates an output o in accordance with the expression $o = \mathrm{sgn}(f^1 a_1 + \ldots + f^n a_n)$, where $f^1, \ldots, f^n$ are numbers between -1 and $+1$, and sgn is the signum function. The numbers $f^1, \ldots, f^n$ are called 'fields'. In the expression for the output value of a cell, they play the role of the connection strengths of classical connectionism. The problem considered here has a single output dimension, so that no phase fields differentiating between different output values have to be introduced. The output o_S associated with a set S of cells is given by $o_S = \varepsilon \times \Sigma_{C in S} \times o_C$.

Consider an array with linearly indexed sites. At every site of the array, four cells with randomly determined fields are located. Suppose that a function approximation (or a classification) task is approached as follows. The initialization of the system happens by selection of the best cell at the site with index 1 (the best cell is the cell that produces the lowest value for the error function for the training set with which the system is confronted). Then, the site with index 2 is considered, and for each of the four cells at this site, the outputs associated with the set consisting of this cell and the cell that was selected at site one are compared to the target values. The cell at site 2 that leads to the set with best performance is effectively included, and so on. At every site, the best cell is included, even if this means that the error associated with the set of selected cells temporarily increases.

The teleological variation of this algorithm (in accordance with (Tb) of Section 3) works as follows. At every site i, the four cells are examined. The two best cells are selected. For both cells, all possible additions of four cells at site i + 1 are evaluated. The teleological algorithm then selects the cell at site i that leads to the set with the best outputs at site i + 1. Subsequently, the cell at i + 1 is selected that leads to the best set at site i + 2, and so on. This way, the best choice at a present time step may be replaced by the second best choice if the latter entails that, in view of the future best choices, a better future system would result.

The following table gives the values of the error function (defined as the sum of the squared errors) and the number of correctly classified input vectors after different numbers of time steps for an 8-parity problem and for a run of the non-teleological as well as for a run of the teleological algorithm. A parity problem is a typical benchmark problem in connectionism (Rumelhart & Mc Clelland 1986). It maps a binary vector on +1 if it has an odd number of components equal to +1; else, it maps the vector on −1. More examples of the presently illustrated fact are described in (Van Loocke 1999a, 2000a, e).

We notice that the non-teleological condition does not lead to a solution of the problem, whereas the teleological condition does. Hence, the difference in performance with the non-teleological algorithm from which it is derived is not only a quantitative one, but even a qualitative one.

5. Generative art and selection in terms of coherence of the future

The second application of the teleological algorithm concerns again a cellular system, but this time it is not related to connectionism, but to generative art instead. A linear indexing of sites[1] arranged in a two-dimensional array defines time evolution. Like in the example of Section 4, the teleological algorithm selects the two best cells (from a set of s cells) in every site, and the future of the system is used to differentiate between these alternatives. For the illustrations that follow, s = 6. The method uses a number of pictures that is equal to s. The

Table 1. *Evolution of the error function for a run of the non-teleological and for a run of the teleological algorithm*

Time step	Error teleo.	Error non-tel.	Corr. items tel.	Corr. It. n-tel.
2500	52.2	72.2	190	134
5000	42.7	69.0	211	138
7500	34.4	71.9	240	133
10000	27.0	71.0	241	134
12500	19.6	71.9	252	141
15000	14.3	71.4	254	140
17500	10.3	72.6	256	141

The first column shows the number of time steps. The second and the third columns show the evolution of the error function for the teleological and the non-teleological algorithm. The two last columns contain the numbers of correctly classified input vectors for both algorithms. The value of ε was put to 0.01.

size of the pictures is normalized in such a way that they cover the entire cellular automaton. The j-th cell ($j = 1, \ldots, s$) in a site corresponds to the pixel with the same coordinates in the j-th picture (which means that the red-, then green- and the blue-value of the color of the latter pixel are used to define rgb-values in the cell at issue).

In the present application, the measure that selects the two best cells is different from the measure that differentiates between the two best choices. The former measure combines a color homogeneity measure H with a measure S that expresses similarity to an additional picture (say the s + 1-th picture). Consider a cell C_j at a site i ($j = 1, \ldots, s$), and consider its square neighborhood. Suppose that, in the sites $h_1, \ldots, h_q$ of this neighborhood, the algorithm has already selected a cell. Then, one can take the differences between the red, the green and the blue-values of C_j and the cells selected at $h_1, \ldots, h_q$. The sum of the squares of these differences determines the measure H. One can also take the differences between the red, the green and the blue-values of C_j and the pixel at the same place in the s + 1-th picture. The summed squares of these differences determine the similarity measure S. The (weighted) sum of the measures $H + \alpha S$ is used to select the two best cells in a site (since homogeneity and similarity increase when H and S decrease, the two cells with lowest values for $H + \alpha S$ are chosen). Then, another measure Z is used to select one of these cells. For each of both cells, Z counts the number of selected cells in the neighboring sites $h_1, \ldots h_q$ that stem from the same picture (Z measures local coherence in the sense that it takes higher value when the same picture can be recognized locally in the image that is being generated). For the non-teleological algorithm, the cell with highest Z-value is effectively selected and included in the pattern that is grown over the automaton; for the teleological algorithm, the cell leading to the highest Z-value at the next time step is included. This process is continued until the entire automaton is covered.

The simulations that follow are made for an automaton of 1000 × 1000 cells (the sites of the automaton are indexed from left to right and from top to bottom). The six pictures used for the homogeneity measure, as well as the seventh picture that was used for the simulation leading to Figure 2, are shown in Figure 1 (as shown, the former six figures are obtained by tiling the automaton with reductions — some of which in complementary color — of the seventh one). Similarly processed versions of the pictures in Figure 3a and 3b lead to the results in Figures 4 and 5 (Figure 5 is in color on the cover of the book — it generally takes color to appreciate the aesthetic effects of this type of algorithm). All these figures have been obtained for the teleological condition. The average Z-values for the teleological condition for Figures 2, 4 and 5 are 3.05, 2.94 and 3.06, respectively. For the non-teleological condition, these values decrease to 2.95, 2.82 and 2.97.

The teleological algorithm systematically leads to better results for the average value of the measure on which the final selection is based. For the present algorithm, and for the present type of picture sets, this means that the reduced parts of a figure (in original as well as in complementary color) are more recognizable in the image that is generated. This enhances the aesthetic quality of the forms that result (similar facts have been illustrated in Van Loocke 2000e for different measures and for different types of picture sets, leading to other types of artwork).

6. Discussion

We studied some instances of selection mechanisms. As was noticed in Section 2, selection can operate in addition to physical forces without replicable violation of physical laws if a system and its environment are sufficiently complex. This condition can be fulfilled for a classical world as well as for a quantum world. We concentrated ourselves on selection mechanisms of a teleological nature. This way, a temporal asymmetry results: forces determine possible present states based on the immediate past of the system, and selection operates by evaluation of the possible futures of the system.

We described two examples of teleological selection. The first example was based on a new cellular method for function approximation and for the represen-

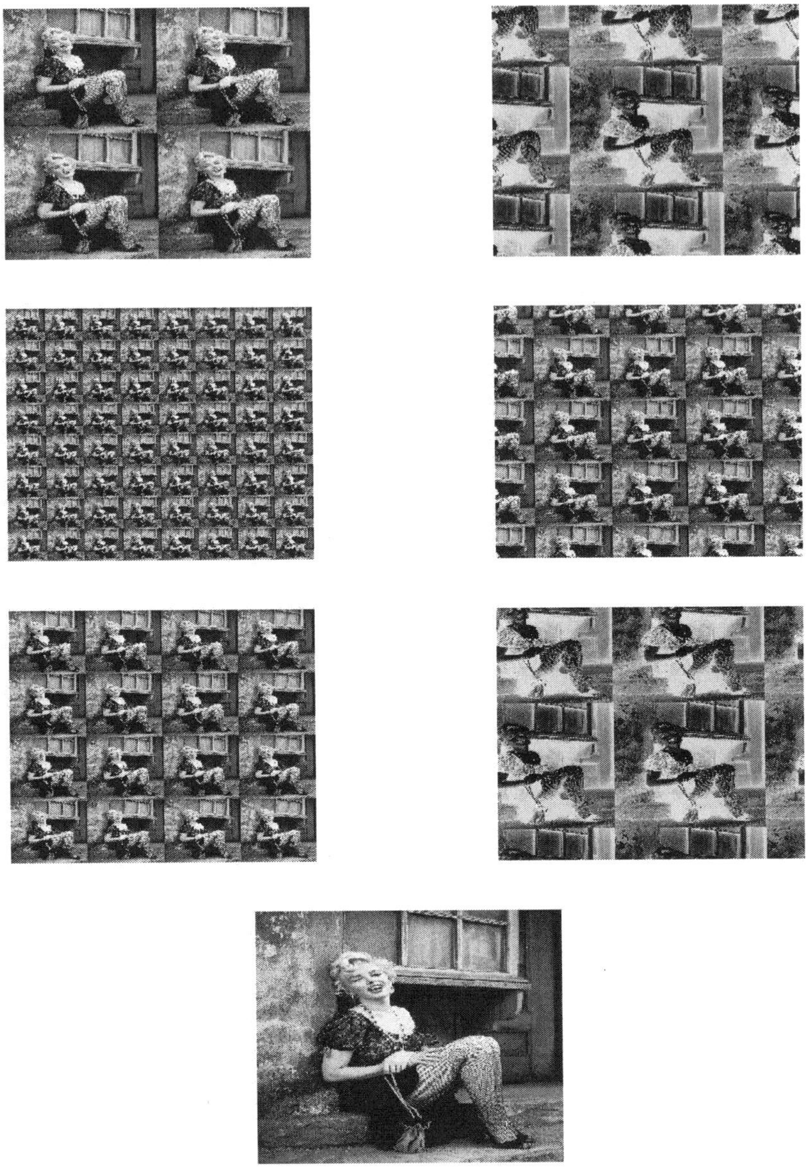

Figure 1. *Figures used in the simulation leading to Figure 2*

Figure 2. *Form generated by the teleological algorithm and for Figures 1a–1g*

tation of structural information. We have seen that the addition of teleology can be a decisive advantage for such systems. This way, an approach has been followed that is complementary to most of the theories described in the present volume. Selection mechanisms must be tied to the biological brain if they are to be taken serious as candidates for the correlate of consciousness. But one can also wonder about their relation to familiar methods in cognitive science, such as connectionism. It has been described at different places that also 'classical' connectionism is enhanced if teleological selection is included in its basic dynamics (Van Loocke 1999a, 2000a). There is a conceptual relation between the present type of selection and objective reduction in the Penrose-Hameroff model. Selection in the present approach is not random, but happens in accordance with an 'objective' criterion that is independent of the forces operating on a system. One of the differences is that the present type of selection, although it happens

Figure 3. *Figures used in the simulations leading to Figures 4–5*

in the future, can still be simulated on computers — as far as the future is computable.

Teleology is familiar in studies of consciousness (Baars 1988). Humans often evaluate possible futures consciously. Similarly, plans for future actions are generated often by conscious thought. Much of our daydreaming can be interpreted in terms of anticipation of possible futures, and so on. The type of teleology studied in the present chapter is of a different nature. It has been termed 'deep teleology'. It is at the level of cells instead of at the much higher level of concepts. In principle, there are two ways in which it may be implemented in brains. First, possible futures may be simulated. At a deep level, neural units may simulate possible future states of other units, and these may co-determine the actual state of the latter. Second, neural structures might get information from the future in some way or other. Some of the authors who are defending the role of quantum theory for consciousness make explicitly reference to teleological theories (e.g. Penrose 1994: 389). Also on a psychological level, teleological hypothesises have been formulated (Radin 1997), though the evidence in support of them is not universally accepted. (We notice that, in view of our considerations in Section 2, the fact that it appears hard to replicate such evidence is what we should expect if the evidence is related to the present type of selection). Hence, at the moment, we prefer to take a prudent position.

We can identify at least part of the evolutionary survival value of the present type of teleological selection, since it makes connectionist mechanisms more efficient. Such a view, therefore, does not suffer from epiphenomenalism. But it does not explain why selection based on future states would be conscious,

Figure 4. *Form obtained for 7 processed versions of Figure 3a*

and why processes involving only forces would not be conscious. Similarly, it does not tell if the selection procedure could operate — in principle — without giving rise to consciousness. Part of the mysteries of consciousness remain with us — maybe for a long time.

Notes

1. In the simulations that follow, a linearly increasing index is used to number sites from left to right and from top to bottom (which means that the number q appearing later in this section (for non-boundary sites) is equal to 4).

Figure 5. *Form obtained for 7 processed versions of Figure 3b*

References

Baars, B. (1988) *A cognitive theory of consciousness.* Cambridge: Cambridge University Press.

Chalmers, D. (1995) Facing up the problem of consciousness. *Journal of Consciousness Studies* 2: 200–219.

Churchland, P. M., Churchland, P. S. (1981) Functionalism, qualia and intentionality. *Philosophical Topics,* 12(1): 121–145.

Churchland, P. (1995) *The engine of reason, the seat of the soul.* Cambridge: MIT Press.

Eccles, J. (1994) *How the self controls its brain.* Berlin/New York: Springer.

Gray, W. (1974) The mind-brain identity theory as a scientific hypothesis, *Philosophical Quarterly* 21: 247–252.

Leshno, M., Ya Lin, V., Minkus, A., Schocken, S. (1993). Multi layer feedforward networks with a non-polynomial activation function can approximate any function. *Neural Networks,* 6: 861–871.

Mc Ginn, C. (1993) *Problems in philosophy: The limits of inquiry.* Cambridge: Blackwell.

Popper, K., Eccles, J. (1976) *The self and its brain.* Berlin/New York: Springer Verlag.

Radin, D. (1997) *The conscious universe.* San Francisco: Harper Collins.

Rumelhart, D., Mc Clelland, J. (eds), *Parallel Distributed Processing,* 2 Volumes. Cambridge: MIT Press.

Van Loocke, Ph. (1999a) Properties of conscious systems and teleology: a cellular automaton perspective. *Journal of Intelligent Systems* 9: 1–29.

Van Loocke, Ph. (1999b) The art of growth and the solution of cognitive problems. In Soddu, C. *Proceedings of the second international generative art congress.* Milan UP.

Van Loocke, Ph. (2000a) A general teleological principle for dynamical systems. *International Journal of General Systems* (accepted).

Van Loocke, Ph. (2000b) Fractals as solutions for cognitive processes. *Fractals,* 8. 7–14.

Van Loocke, Ph. (2000c) Meta-patterns and higher-order meta-patterns in cellular automata. *Artificial Intelligence Review* (accepted).

Van Loocke, Ph. (2000d) Variations of phase fields in cellular automata and aesthetic solutions for cognitive problems, in Dubois, D. (ed.), *Proceedings of the Third Congress on Computing Anticipatory Systems.* New York. American Institute of Physics Press.

Van Loocke, Ph. (2000e) Deep teleology in artificial systems. *Minds and Machines* (accepted).

Name index

Subject index